Withdrawal from Multilateral Treaties

Theory and Practice of Public International Law

Series Editor

Vincent Chetail

VOLUME 4

The titles published in this series are listed at *brill.com/tppi*

Withdrawal from Multilateral Treaties

By

Antonio Morelli

BRILL
NIJHOFF

LEIDEN | BOSTON

Library of Congress Cataloging-in-Publication Data

Names: Morelli, Antonio (Writer on law) author.
Title: Withdrawal from multilateral treaties / by Antonio Morelli.
Description: Leiden ; Boston : Brill Nijhoff, [2022] | Series: Theory and practice of public international law, 2405-6847 ; volume 4 | Based on author's thesis (doctoral - American University Washington College of Law, 2019) issued under title: High-profile withdrawal from international treaties : risk management in international negotiations and states' commitment to multilateralism. | Includes bibliographical references and index. | Summary: This is the first comprehensive and systematic monograph on withdrawal from multilateral treaties, which explains the evolution of the concept of withdrawal and examines its increasing use over time. International scholars and policy makers have long addressed treaty making and treaty maintenance in light of the binary choice between compliance and breach, while leaving unregulated or at least under-regulated the actual act of withdrawal. In the age of global retrenchment, is there still room for international law to regulate the rules of the game, or will unilateral decisions overturn the current architecture of a multilateral global order?
Identifiers: LCCN 2021031658 (print) | LCCN 2021031659 (ebook) | ISBN 9789004467613 (hardback) | ISBN 9789004467644 (ebook)
Subjects: LCSH: Treaties–Termination. | International relations.
Classification: LCC KZ1303.4 .M67 2021 (print) | LCC KZ1303.4 (ebook) | DDC 341.3/7–dc23
LC record available at https://lccn.loc.gov/2021031658
LC ebook record available at https://lccn.loc.gov/2021031659

Typeface for the Latin, Greek, and Cyrillic scripts: "Brill". See and download: brill.com/brill-typeface.

ISSN 2405-6847
ISBN 978-90-04-46761-3 (hardback)
ISBN 978-90-04-46764-4 (e-book)

This book is printed on acid-free paper and produced in a sustainable manner.

To my grandmother Liliana.

Contents

Foreword

The book *Withdrawal from Multilateral Treaties* by Antonio Morelli fills an important existing vacuum. As the author states, "international scholars and policy makers have long addressed treaty making and treaty maintenance in light of the binary choice between compliance and breach, while leaving unregulated or at least under-regulated the act of pulling out."

This choice acquires a special significance in a political environment where the criticism of a rule-based approach to international relations has gained traction, promoted by phenomena such as chauvinism and populism. In such a context, often fueled by concepts that prioritize the exercise of raw power, treaty breach, rather than being a singular exceptional act, threatens to become a way to reject international law as a whole or, at a minimum, to reduce radically its significance.

Morelli's book, through a well-researched and rigorous analysis, focuses on withdrawal, seeking to enrich the toolkit of available possibilities for policy makers. Withdrawal, as a valid legal option, includes all the advantages of legal, orderly action. This option contributes on the one hand to broaden the political space for states that are not simply constrained to the stark need to react against violations of international law and, on the other hand, creates incentives for states to choose withdrawal in accordance with international law rather than simply resort to the breach of their legal obligations. Withdrawal is, needless to say, neither a breach nor a breach with a different name, but an orderly path that allows for reflection, assessment of alternatives, and in some circumstances adaptations and negotiations.

To analyze withdrawal, the author places the topic in a political and legal framework relevant to treaty making and the continuity of legal obligations, namely the Law of Treaties as codified in the VCLT.

Of special value is the taxonomy that the author presents, identifying the denunciations of treaty obligations that have occurred through time and their evolution—including the current worrisome trend of denunciation of multilateral treaties. Morelli analyses as well the justifications that motivate different types of states' behavior, which constitute politically reactive or protective steps in the conduct of foreign policy. He explains the evolution of withdrawal in international relations and formulates recommendations to policy makers designed to strengthen orderly withdrawal. The author places the topic in the broader context of international law, stressing the significance of defining "the rules of the game in the international legal order."

The book can be seen as an attempt to formulate necessary accommodations to keep international law relevant while adapting to the conditions of the current political environment. Nevertheless, this understanding does not fully capture the value of *Withdrawal from Multilateral Treaties*. Through a serious and systematic analysis, Morelli's recommendations present withdrawal as a valuable mechanism that not only adapts but also promotes the rule of law.

Claudio Grossman
Professor of Law & Dean Emeritus
American University Washington College of Law
Member International Law Commission UN

Preface

International scholars and policy makers have long addressed treaty making and treaty maintenance in light of the binary choice between compliance and breach, while leaving unregulated or at least under-regulated the act of pulling out. As governments change on the edge of a nationalist wave, there is an overturning of the status quo that is expressed through withdrawal. As a result, parties to international agreements are facing not a dilemma but rather a trilemma, with three options in interstate cooperation: compliance, breach, and withdrawal.

This monograph is the first comprehensive and systematic legal analysis of withdrawal in the context of the international law of treaties. It examines the political and legal framework around treaty making and treaty maintenance to explain how withdrawal evolved over time and suggests solutions for addressing and improving conditions for orderly withdrawal.

By defining the legal framework for withdrawal, this book reviews applicable principles under general international law and focuses on the approach used in the Vienna Convention on the Law of the Treaties of 1969. Additionally, it conceptualizes withdrawal through the lens of commitment to and compliance with multilateral agreements. The existing literature has not explored the concept of commitment as much as compliance in the context of terminating treaties. Just as withdrawal is the opposite of commitment, breach is the opposite of compliance. The analysis demonstrates that there is a direct relationship between politicizing commitment and noncooperation, as evidenced by the behavior of states resulting in a trend of withdrawal, especially in the context of global retrenchment.

A comprehensive taxonomy on the subject of withdrawal from international agreements categorizes instances of denunciation and the rationales for states' practices, showing that withdrawal can represent either a reactive or proactive step in foreign policy. Moreover, a quantitative study shows that a significant number of multilateral treaties have been objects of denunciation, especially in the last decade, and reveals the progressive evolution of withdrawal from a cooperative act de jure to a noncooperative act de facto.

In the light of withdrawal, we can measure the level of stability achieved by multilateralism despite unilateral trends. This book questions what role lawmaking still plays in defining the rules of the game in the international legal order. In a system that lacks centralized enforcement, it is of paramount importance to regularize conditions ex ante to enhance orderly withdrawal ex post. With this goal, the book prescribes some recommendations for consideration by policy makers, international lawyers, diplomats, and, more generally, treaty negotiators.

Acknowledgments

I am sincerely grateful to the American University Washington College of Law for believing in my doctoral research project, in which this book is rooted.

I am particularly indebted to Prof. David Hunter for his mentorship and guidance throughout my doctoral studies. Our work together at the International Legal Studies Program of American University Washington College of Law and our many valuable discussions provided the most important intellectual stimulus for this manuscript.

Dean Emeritus Claudio Grossman's continuous support of my academic pursuits has been invaluable. Assisting him at the International Law Commission was a particularly significant opportunity in my career that allowed me to grow in my academic field and to gain knowledge and inspiration in the development of my research.

I must also acknowledge Prof. Padideh Ala'i, Prof. Fernanda Nicola, Prof. Juan Mendez, Prof. Robert Goldman, and Prof. Diane Orentlicher of American University Washington College of Law for their extraordinary guidance and unfailing encouragement of my doctoral studies and academic activities.

Several people have provided technical help with my work. In this regard, I would like to thank the faculty and staff of the SJD Program of American University Washington College of Law, including Prof. Heather Hughes and Prof. Amanda Frost for their distinguished leadership and Prof. Elizabeth Cavanagh and Prof. Amy Tenney for their unending support. Thanks are also due to Prof. Nehal Bhuta for his supervision during my visiting fellowship at the European University Institute of Florence.

During my research for this book, numerous international scholars and professional colleagues have discussed with me many of the issues that I cover in this manuscript. I am particularly grateful to Prof. Laurence Helfer, Prof. Sean Murphy, Prof. Fausto Pocar, and Prof. Vincent-Joël Proulx for giving me excellent professional assistance that has improved the quality of my manuscript.

I am also forever indebted to my family and friends for inspiring and encouraging me throughout these years, as they always have.

I began my doctoral studies with the idea that writing a book is like drawing a map, as they both entail the projection of a particular segment of the world on the plane surface of a page. This is a perfect synthesis of liberty and rigor. In this regard, I would, finally, like to express my deepest appreciation of and gratitude to Ambassador Francesco Olivieri for teaching me the importance of liberty in international negotiations, and Dr. Maurizio Ragazzi for teaching me rigor in international law.

Antonio Morelli

Abbreviations

ABA	American Bar Association
ABM	Antiballistic Missile
ACHR	American Convention on Human Rights
AJIL	American Journal of International Law
AJIL Supp.	American Journal of International Law Supplement
ARSIWA	Articles on Responsibility of States for International Wrongful Acts
ATT	Arms Trade Treaty
Aust. YBIL	Australian Yearbook of International law
BIT	Bilateral Investment Treaty
BYIL	British Yearbook of International Law
COP	Conference of Parties
ECHR	European Court of Human Rights
ECT	Energy Charter Treaty
EJIL	European Journal of International Law
EPIL	Encyclopedia of Public International Law
ERPL	European Review of Public Law
EU	European Union
EYIEL	European Yearbook of International Economic Law
HRC	Human Rights Council
IACmHR	Inter-American Commission on Human Rights
IACtHR	Inter-American Court on Human Rights
IAEA	International Atomic Energy Agency
IBRD	International Bank for Reconstruction and Development
ICC	International Criminal Court
ICCPR	International Covenant on Civil and Political Rights
ICJ	International Court of Justice
ICLQ	International and Comparative Law Quarterly
ICSID	International Centre for Settlement of Investment Disputes
ICTY	International Criminal Tribunal for the Former Yugoslavia
IDB	Inter-American Development Bank
IDI	Institut de Droit International
IFIS	International Financial Institutions
IJHR	International Journal of Human Rights
ILC	International Law Commission
ILM	International Legal Materials
ILO	International Labour Organization
ILQ	International Law Quarterly
ILR	International Law Reports

INF	Intermediate-Range Nuclear Force
JCPOA	Joint Comprehensive Plan of Action
MPEPIL	Max Planck Encyclopedia of Public International Law
NPT	Nuclear Non-Proliferation Treaty
OAS	Organization of the American States
OECD	Organization for Economic Cooperation and Development
PCIJ	Permanent Court of International Justice
RDI	Revue de Droit International, de Sciences Diplomatiques et Politiques
SCC	Stockholm Chamber of Commerce
TEU	Treaty on European Union
UN	United Nations
UNCLOS	United Nations Convention on the Law of the Sea
UNFCCC	United Nations Framework Convention on Climate Change
UNESCO	United Nations Educational Scientific and Cultural Organization
UNICEF	United Nations Children's Fund
UNTS	United Nations Treaty Series
UNYB	Yearbook of the United Nations
UNYBILC	Yearbook of the International Law Commission
UST	United States Treaties and Other International Agreements
VCCR	Vienna Convention on Consular Relations
VCDR	Vienna Convention on Diplomatic Relations
VCLT	Vienna Convention on the Law of Treaties
WBG	World Bank Group
WHO	World Health Organization
WTO	World Trade Organization
YIEL	Yearbook of International Environmental Law

Table of Documents

I. International Agreements

African Charter on Human and Peoples' Rights, Jun. 27, 1981 1520 U.N.T.S. 217.
Agreement Establishing the African Development Bank, Aug. 4, 1963 510 U.N.T.S. 3.
Agreement Establishing the Asian Development Bank, Aug. 22, 1966 571 U.N.T.S. 123.
Agreement Establishing the Inter-American Development Bank, Dec. 30, 1959 69 U.N.T.S. 389.
American Convention on Human Rights (Pact of San Jose, Costa Rica), Nov. 22, 1969, 1144 U.N.T.S.123.
American Treaty on Pacific Settlement (Pact of Bogotá), Apr. 30, 1948, 17 O.A.S.T.S. 61.
Arms Trade Treaty, C.N. 266. 2013. Treaties-XXVI.8 (Apr. 2, 2013).
Articles of Agreement of the International Monetary Fund (Bretton Woods Agreement), Dec. 27, 1945 2 U.N.T.S. 39.
Basel Convention on the Control of Transboundary Movements of Hazardous Wastes and Their Disposal, Mar. 22, 1989 1673 U.N.T.S. 125.
Cartagena Protocol on Biosafety to the Convention on Biological Diversity, Jan. 29, 2000 2226 U.N.T.S. 208.
Charter of the Organization of American States, Apr. 30, 1948 119 U.N.T.S. 3.
Charter of the United Nations and Statute of the International Court of Justice (ICJ).
Comprehensive Economic and Trade Agreement (CETA) between Canada, of the one part, and the European Union and its Member States, of the other part, Jan 14, 2017, L. 11/23.
Comprehensive Nuclear Test-Ban Treaty, Sept. 10, 1996 35 I.L.M. 1439.
Conference of the Parties, Adoption of the Paris Agreement, Dec. 12, 2015 U.N. Doc. FCCC/CP/2015/L.9/Rev/1 (Dec. 12, 2015).
Conference on Security and Cooperation in Europe (Helsinki Final Act), Aug. 1, 1975, 14 I.L.M. 1292 (1975).
Constitution of the Food and Agriculture Organization (FAO), Oct. 16, 1945 CTS 1945/32.
Constitution of the International Labour Organization (ILO), May 10, 1944 15 U.N.T.S. 40.
Constitution of the United Nations Educational, Scientific and Cultural Organization (UNESCO), Nov. 16, 1945 4 U.N.T.S. 275.
Constitution of the World Health Organization (WHO), Jul. 22, 1946 14 U.N.T.S. 185.

Convention for the Amelioration of the Condition of Wounded, Sick and Shipwrecked Members of Armed Forces at Sea, Aug. 12, 1949 75 U.N.T.S. 85.
Convention for the Prevention of Marine Pollution from Land-Based Sources, June 4, 1974 1546 U.N.T.S. 119.
Convention of the World Meteorological Organization, Oct. 11, 1947 77 U.N.T.S. 143.
Convention on Biological Diversity, June 5, 1992 1760 U.N.T.S. 79.
Convention on International Trade in Endangered Species of Wild Fauna and Flora, Mar. 3, 1973 993 U.N.T.S. 243.
Convention on Nuclear Safety, June 17, 1994 1963 U.N.T.S. 293.
Convention on the Elimination of All Forms of Discrimination against Women, Dec. 18, 1979 1249 U.N.T.S. 13.
Convention on the Organisation for Economic Co-operation and Development, Dec. 14 1960 888 U.N.T.S. 174.
Convention on the Prevention and Punishment of the Crime of Genocide, Dec. 9, 1948 78 U.N.T.S. 277.
Convention on the Prohibition of the Development, Production, Stockpiling and Use of Chemical Weapons and on their Destructions, September 3, 1992, 1975 U.N.T.S. 45.
Convention on the Prohibition of the Use, Stockpiling, Production and Transfer of Anti-Personnel Mines and their Destruction, Sept. 18, 1997, Oslo, 18 September 1997, 2056 U.N.T.S. 211.
Convention on the Reduction of Cases of Multiple Nationality and on Military Obligations in Cases of Multiple Nationality, E.T.S. 043 (1963).
Convention on the Settlement of Investment Disputes between States and Nationals of Other States, Mar. 18, 1965 575 U.N.T.S. 159.
Draft Treaty Establishing the European Union [Spinelli Report], Feb. 14, 1984, O.J. (C 77) 33 1.
Energy Charter Treaty, Dec. 17, 1994 2080 U.N.T.S. 95.
Final Act Embodying the Results of the Uruguay Round of Multilateral Trade Negotiations, Apr. 15, 1994 1867 U.N.T.S. 14.
General Agreement on Tariffs and Trade, Oct. 30, 1947 55 U.N.T.S. 194.
General Agreement on Tariffs and Trade, 1994, Apr. 15, 1994 Marrakesh Agreement Establishing the World Trade Organization, Annex 1A, 1867 U.N.T.S. 187.
General Agreement on Trade in Services, Apr. 15, 1994 Marrakesh Agreement Establishing the World Trade Organization, Annex 1B, 1869 U.N.T.S. 183.
Geneva Convention Relative to the Protection of Civilian Persons in Time of War, Aug. 12, 1949, 75 U.N.T.S. 287.
Geneva Convention Relative to the Treatment of Prisoners of War, Aug. 12, 1949 75 U.N.T.S. 135.

International Bank for Reconstruction and Development Articles of Agreement, Dec. 27, 1945 2 U.N.T.S. 13.

International Convention for the Prevention of Pollution from Ships, Nov. 2, 1973 1340 U.N.T.S. 61.

International Convention for the Regulation of Whaling, Dec. 2, 1946 161 U.N.T.S. 72.

International Convention on the Elimination of All Forms of Racial Discrimination, Dec. 21, 1965 660 U.N.T.S. 195.

International Covenant on Civil and Political Rights, Dec. 16, 1966 999 U.N.T.S. 171.

International Covenant on Economic, Social and Cultural Rights, Dec. 16, 1966, 993 U.N.T.S. 3.

International Development Association Articles of Agreement, 24 January 1960, 439 U.N.T.S. 249.

Japan-EU Economic Partnership Agreement (JEEPA), Apr. 18, 2018, COM/2018/192 final, 2018/0091 (NLE).

Kyoto Protocol to the United Nations Framework Convention on Climate Change, Dec. 10, 1997 2303 U.N.T.S. 148.

Limitation of Anti-Ballistic Missile Systems, May 26, 1972, U.S.-U.S.S.R., 23 U.S.T. 3435.

Amendment to Montreal Protocol on Substances that Deplete the Ozone Layer (London Amendment), Aug. 27, 1991 1958 U.N.T.S. 469.

Marrakesh Agreement Establishing the World Trade Organization, Apr. 15, 1994 1867 U.N.T.S. 154.

Montreal Protocol on Substances that Deplete the Ozone Layer, Sep. 16, 1987 1522 U.N.T.S. 3.

North American Free Trade Agreement, Can.-Mex.-U.S., Dec. 17, 1992, 32 I.L.M. 289 (1993).

North Atlantic Treaty, Apr. 4, 1949 34 U.N.T.S. 243.

Optional Protocol concerning the Compulsory Settlement of Disputes, Apr. 24, 1963 596 U.N.T.S. 487.

Optional Protocol to the International Covenant on Civil and Political Rights, Dec. 16, 1966 999 U.N.T.S. 171.

Protocol on Environmental Protection to the Antarctic Treaty, Oct. 4, 1991 30 I.L.M. 1455 (1991).

Protocol to the 1979 Convention on Long-Range Transboundary Air Pollution on the Reduction of Sulphur Emissions or their Transboundary Fluxes by at least 30 per cent, Jul. 8, 1985, U.N.T.S 1480, 215.

Rio Declaration on Environment and Development, Report of the United Nations Conference on Environment and Development, U.N. Doc. A/CONF.151/26(Vol I). (Aug. 12, 1992).

Rome Statute of the International Criminal Court, July 17, 1998 2187 U.N.T.S. 90.

II. United Nations Materials

Draft Articles on Responsibility of States for Internationally Wrongful Acts, with commentaries, Supp. No. 10, at ch. IV.E.1., U.N. Doc. A/56/10 (Nov. 2001).

Draft Articles on the Law of Treaties with Commentaries, Adopted by the International Law Commission at its Eighteenth Session, *in U.N. Conference on the Law of Treaties, 1st & 2nd Sess., Vienna, 26 March–24 May 1968 and 9 April–22 May 1969*, U.N. Doc. A/CONF.39/11/Add.2 (1971).

G.A. Res. 2166 (XXI) U.N. Doc. A/6516 (1966), U.N. International Conference of Plenipotentiaries on the Law of Treaties.

G.A. Res. 217A (III) A, at 71 U.N. Doc. A/810, at 71 (1948), Universal Declaration of Human Rights.

G.A. Res. 2287 (XXII) U.N. Doc. A/Conf. 39/6 (1967), U.N. Conference on the Law of Treaties.

G.A. Res. 94 (I) (Dec. 11, 1946).

G.A. Res. 174 (II) (Nov. 21, 1947).

Guiding Principles on Business and Human Rights: Implementing the United Nations 'Protect, Respect and Remedy' Framework, Report of the Special Representative of the Secretary-General on the Issue of Human Rights and Transnational Corporations and Other Business Enterprises, UN Doc. A/HRC/17/31 (Mar. 21, 2011).

Int'l Law Comm'n, Rep. of the Study Group, U.N. Doc. A/CN4/L.682 (Apr. 13, 2006).

Int'l Law Comm'n, Rep. on the Work of Its Eighteenth Session, U.N. Doc. A/6309/Rev.1, at 266 (1966).

Int'l Law Comm'n, Rep. on the Work of Its Sixth Session, U.N. Doc. A/2693, at 140 (1954).

Int'l Law Comm'n, Rep. on the Work of Its Sixty-Fourth Session, U.N. Doc. A/67/10, at 46–51 (2012).

Int'l Law Comm'n, Rep. on the Work of Its Twentieth Session, U.N. Doc. A/7209/Rev.1, at 192 (1968).

Kennedy v. Trinidad & Tobago, Communication No. 845/1999, *reprinted in Rep. of the Hum. Rts. Comm.*, U.N. Doc A/55/40 [Vol. II] (Dec. 31, 1999).

S.C. Res. 1718 (Oct. 14, 2006).

S.C. Res. 1874 (June 12, 2009).

S.C. Res. 2087 (Jan. 22, 2013).

S.C. Res. 2094 (Mar. 7, 2013).

S.C. Res. 2231 (July 20, 2015).

S.C. Res. 2255 (Nov. 30, 2016).

S.C. Res. 2270 (Mar. 2, 2016).

S.C. Res. 2371 (Aug. 5, 2017).

S.C. Res. 2375 (Sept. 11, 2017).

U.N. Conference on International Organization, 27th mtg. Committee I/2 at 1–6, U.N. Doc. 1086, I/2/77 (June 17, 1945), *reprinted in* 7 Documents of the U.N. Conference on International Organization 261–67.

U.N. Conference on the Law of Treaties Res. 2287 (XXII) (Dec. 6, 1967).

U.N. Depositary Notification from the UN Secretary-General, UN Doc. C.N.314.2019.Treaties-XXVI.8 (Jul. 19, 2019).

U.N. Division of Immunities and Registration of Treaties, Legal Dep't, *Handbook of Final Clauses*, U.N. Doc. ST/LEG/1 (1951).

U.N. Treaty Section, Office of Legal Affairs, Final Clauses of Multilateral Treaties Handbook, U.N. Sales No. E.04.V.3 (2003).

U.N. Treaty Section, Office of Legal Affairs, Handbook of Final Clauses, U.N. Doc. ST/LEG/6 (1957).

U.N. Treaty Section, Office of Legal Affairs, Treaty Handbook, U.N. Sales No. E.12.V.1 (2012).

Yasseen v. Guyana, Communication No. 676/1998, *reprinted in* Rep. of the Hum. Rts. Comm., at 151, U.N. Doc. A/53/40 [Vol. II] (1998).

III. Domestic Statutes and Constitutions

Al Nizam AlAsasi lil Hukm [Basic Law of Government of Saudi Arabia] Mar. 1, 1992.

American Sovereignty Restoration Act of 2017, H.R. 204, 116th Cong. (1st Sess. 2019).

Constitución Española [Constitution of Spain], Dec. 27, 1987.

Constituţia Republicii Moldova [Constitution of Moldova], Aug. 27, 1994.

Constitution de la République Française [Constitution of the French Republic], Oct. 4, 1958.

Costituzione della Repubblica Italiana [Constitution of the Italian Republic], Dec. 27, 1947.

Eesti Vabariigi Põhiseadus [Constitution of Estonia], Jun. 26, 1992.

Federal Tort Claims Act, 28 U.S.C. 2401 (1988).

Foreign Sovereign Immunity Act, 28 U.S.C. 1602 *et seq.* (1976).

Grondwet Van Die Republiek Van Suid-Afrika [Constitution of the Republic of South Africa] Dec. 18, 1996.

International Organizations Immunity Act, 22 U.S.C. 288 (1945).

Kanstytucyja Respubliki Bielaruś [Constitution of the Republic of Belarus], Mar. 15, 1994.

MASS. CONST. of 1780, *reprinted in* 10 SOURCES AND DOCUMENTS OF UNITED STATES CONSTITUTIONS 96 (W. S. Windler ed., 1979).

U.S. CONSTITUTION.

USTAVA CESKÉ REPUBLIKY [CONSTITUTION OF THE CZECH REPUBLIC], Dec. 16, 1992.

VA. CONST. of 1776, *reprinted in* 10 SOURCES AND DOCUMENTS OF UNITED STATES CONSTITUTIONS 52 (W. S. Windler ed., 1979).

Table of Cases

I. International Court of Justice and Permanent Court of International Justice

Alleged Violations of Sovereign Rights and Maritime Spaces in the Caribbean Sea (Nicaragua v. Colombia), Counter-Claims Order, 2017 I.C.J. 289 (Nov. 15).
Appeal Relating to the Jurisdiction of the ICAO Council (India v. Pakistan), Judgment, 1972 I.C.J. 46 (Aug. 18).
Application for Review of Judgment No. 158 of the United Nations Administrative Tribunal, Advisory Opinion, 1973 I.C.J. 166 (Jul. 12).
Application of the Convention on the Prevention and Punishment of the Crime of Genocide (Croatia v. Yugoslavia), Order, 2000 I.C.J. 118 (Jun. 27).
Armed Activities on the Territory of Congo (Democratic Republic of Congo v. Uganda), Judgment, 2006 I.C.J. Reports 6 (Feb. 3).
Barcelona Traction, Light and Power Company, Limited (Belgium v. Spain), Order, 1961 I.C.J. 9 (Apr. 10).
Barcelona Traction, Light and Power Company, Limited (New Application: 1962) (Belgium v. Spain), Judgment, 1970 I.C.J. 3 (Feb. 5).
Case Concerning Military and Paramilitary Activities in and against Nicaragua (Nicaragua v. United States of America), Judgment, 1984 I.C.J. 14 (Nov., 26).
Case Concerning Rights of Nationals of the United States of America in Morocco (France v. United States of America), Judgment, 1952 I.C.J. 176 (Aug., 27).
Case Concerning the Arrest Warrant of 11 April 2000 (Democratic Republic of the Congo v. Belgium), Judgment, 2002 I.C.J. 3 (Feb.14).
Certain Expenses of the United Nations, Advisory Opinion, 1962 I.C.J. 151 (Jul. 20).
Competence of the General Assembly for the Admission of a State to the United Nations, Advisory Opinion, 1950 I.C.J. 4 (Mar. 3).
Conditions of Admission of a State to a Membership in the United Nations (Article 4 of Charter), Advisory Opinion, 1947–48 I.C.J. 57 (May 28).
East Timor (Portugal v. Australia), Judgment, 1995 I.C.J. 90 (June 30).
Fisheries Jurisdiction (Spain v. Canada), Order, 1996 I.C.J. 58 (May 8).
Fisheries Jurisdiction (United Kingdom v. Iceland), Judgment, 1974 I.C.J. 19 (July 25).
Gabčíkovo-Nagymaros Project (Hungary v. Slovakia), Judgment, 1997 I.C.J. 7 (Sept. 25).
Gabcikovo-Nagymaros Project (Hungary/Slovakia), Order, 1997 I.C.J. 3 (Feb. 5).
Interpretation of the Agreement of 25 March 1951 between the WHO and Egypt, Advisory Opinion, 1980 I.C.J. 73 (Dec. 20).

Judgments of the Administrative Tribunal of the ILO upon Complaints Made against Unesco, Advisory Opinion, 1956 I.C.J. 77 (Oct. 23).
Jurisdiction of the European Commission of the Danube between Galatz and Braila, Advisory Opinion, 1927, P.C.I.J. (ser. B) No. 14 (Dec. 8, 1927).
LaGrand (Germany v. United States of America), Judgment, 2001 I.C.J. 466 (Jun. 27).
Land and Maritime Boundary (Cameroon v. Nigeria), Judgment, 1998 I.C.J. 301 (Jun. 11).
Legal Consequences for States of the Continued Presence of South Africa in Namibia (South West Africa) notwithstanding Security Council Resolution 276 (1970), Advisory Opinion, 1971 I.C.J. 16 (Jun. 21).
Legal Consequences of the Construction of a Wall in the Occupied Palestinian Territory, Advisory Opinion, 2004 I.C.J. 136 (Jul. 9).
Legality of the Treat or Use of Nuclear Weapons, Advisory Opinion, 1996 I.C.J. 226 (Jul. 8).
Legality of the Use by a State of Nuclear Weapons in Armed Conflict, Advisory Opinion, 1996 I.C.J. 66 (Jul. 8).
Legality of Use of Force (Yugoslavia v. Italy), Provisional Measures Order, 1999 I.C.J. 481 (Jun. 2).
Maritime Delimitation and Territorial Questions Between Qatar and Bahrain (Qatar v. Bahrain), Judgment, 2001 I.C.J. 40 (Mar. 16).
Maritime Delimitation between Nicaragua and Honduras in the Caribbean Sea (Nicaragua v. Honduras), Order, 2000 I.C.J. 659 (Mar. 21).
Mavrommatis Palestine Concessions (Greece v. Great Britain), 1924 P.C.I.J. Series A, No. 2 (Aug. 1924).
Nationality Decrees Issued in Tunis and Morocco, Advisory Opinion, 1923 P.C.I.J. (Ser. B) No. 4 (Feb. 7).
Nottebohm (Liechtenstein v. Guatemala), 2nd Phase Judgment, 1955 I.C.J. 4 (Apr. 6).
Nottebohm (Liechtenstein v. Guatemala), Preliminary Objection Judgment, 1953 I.C.J. 111 (Nov. 18).
Questions of Interpretation and Application of the 1971 Montreal Convention Arising from the Aerial Incident at Lockerbie (Libyan Arab Jamahiriya v. United Kingdom), Preliminary Objections Judgment, 1998 I.C.J. 9 (Feb. 27).
Reparations for Injuries Suffered in the Service of the United Nations, Advisory Opinion, 1949 I.C.J. Rep. 174 (Apr. 11).
Request for an Examination of the Situation in Accordance with Paragraph 63 of the Court's Judgment of 20 December 1974 in the Nuclear Tests (New Zealand v. France) Case, Order, 1995 I.C.J. 288 (Sept. 22).
Reservations to the Convention on the Prevention and Punishment of the Crime of Genocide, Advisory Opinion, 1951 I.C.J. 15 (May 28).

S.S. Lotus (France v. Turkey), Judgment, 1927 P.C.I.J. (ser. A) No. 10 (Sept. 7, 1927).
S.S. Wimbledon (Great Britain v. Germany), Judgment, 1923 P.C.I.J. (ser. A) No. 1 (Aug. 17, 1923).
Temple of Preah Vihear (Cambodia v. Thailand), Judgment, 1962 I.C.J. 6, 43 (June 15).
United States Diplomatic and Consular Staff in Tehran (United States of America v. Iran), Judgment, 1980 I.C.J. 3 (May 24).
Vienna Convention on Consular Relations (Paraguay v. United States of America), Provisional Measures Order, 1998 I.C.J. 248 (Apr. 9).
Western Sahara, Advisory Opinion, 1975 I.C.J. 12 (Oct. 16).

II. Other Courts

Alejandre v. Republic of Cuba, 996 F. Supp. 1239 (S.D. Fla. 1997).
A. Racke GmbH & Co v. Hauptzollamt Mainz, 1998 Judgment of the Court of Justice of the European Communities, C-162/96, Jun. 16, 1998, E.C.R. I-03655.
Baruch Ivcher Bronstein v. Peru, Jurisdiction, Judgment, Inter-Am. Ct. H.R. (ser. C) No. 54, ¶ 37 (Sept. 24, 1999).
Beacon Products Corp. v. Reagan, 633 F. Supp. 1191 (D. Mass. 1986).
Democratic Alliance v. Minister of International Relations and Cooperation [2017] (3) SA 212 (S. Afr.).
Goldwater v. Carter, 444 U.S. 996 (1979).
Goldwater v. Carter, 481 F. Supp. 949 (D.D.C. 1979).
Goldwater v. Carter, 617 F.2d 697 (D.C. Cir. 1979).
Interpretation of the American Declaration of the Rights and Duties of Man Within the Framework of Article 64 of the American Convention on Human Rights (Art. 64 American Convention on Human Rights), Advisory Opinion OC-10/89, Inter-Am. Ct. H.R. (Ser. A) No. 10, ¶ 35–45 (Jul. 14, 1989).
Ireland v. United Kingdom, 25 Eur. Ct. H.R. (Ser. A) (1978).
Kucinich v. Bush, 236 F. Supp. 2d 1 (D.D.C. 2002).
Loayza Tamayo Case, Preliminary Objections, Judgment, Inter-Am. Ct. H.R. (ser. C) No. 25, ¶ 40 (Jan. 31, 1996).
Loizidou v. Turkey, 310 Eur. Ct. H.R. 19 (1995).
McCann and Others v. United Kingdom, 324 Eur. Ct. H.R. (Ser. A) (1995).
Miller (and other Respondents) v. Secretary of State for Exiting the European Union (Appellant), UKSC 2016/0196 R, Judgment (Jan. 24, 2017).
Panel Report, United States – Standards for Reformulated and Conventional Gasoline ("US – Gasoline"), W.T.O. Doc., WT/DS2/AB/R, 16 (adopted May 20, 1996).

Prosecutor v. Omar Hassan Ahmad Al-Bashir, Judgment ICC-02/05–01/09 (July 6, 2017).
R. v. Secretary of State for Transport, ex parte Factotrame Ltd. (No. 2) [1990] 3 WLR 818.
Roodal v. Trinidad and Tobago, Case 12.342, Inter-Am. Comm'n H.R. Report No. 89, OEA/ser L/V/II.114, doc. 5 rev. (2001).
Siderman de Blake v. Republic of Argentina, 965 F.2d 699, 714–17 (9th Cir. 1992).
Slovak Republic v. Achmea B.V., C-284/16, 2018 E.C.R. I-158.
The Word "Laws" in Article 30 of the American Convention of Human Rights (Art. 30 American Convention of Human Rights), Advisory Opinion OC-6/86, Inter-Am. Ct. H.R. (Ser. A) No. 65, ¶ 29 (May 9, 1986).
United States v. Curtiss-Wright Export Corp., 299 U.S. 304 (1936).
Velasquez Rodriguez case, Judgment, Inter-Am. Ct. H.R. (ser. C) No. 4, ¶ 167 (Jul. 29, 1986).
Youngstown Sheet & Tube Co. v. Sawyer, 343 U.S. 579 (1952).

III. Arbitral Tribunals

Belenergia S.A. v. Italian Republic, ICSID Case No. ARB/15/40 (registered Sept. 22, 2015).
Blusun S.A., Jean-Pierre Lecorcier and Michael Stein v. Italian Republic, ICSID Case No. ARB/14/3 (registered Feb. 21, 2014).
CEF Energia BV v. Italian Republic, SCC Case No. 158/2015 (registered Nov. 20, 2015).
Eskosol S.p.A. in Liquidazione v. Italian Republic, ICSID Case No. ARB/15/50 (registered Dec. 22, 2015).
ESPF Beteiligungs, GmbH ESPF Nr. 2 Austria Beteiligungs GmbH, and Infra Class Energie 5 GmbH & Co. KG v. Italian Republic, ICSID Case No. ARB/16/5 (registered Mar. 8, 2016).
Greentech Energy Systems and Novenergia v. Italian Republic, Stockholm Chamber of Commerce (SCC) Case No. 095/2015 (registered Jul. 7, 2015).
Pinson v. United Mexican States, 5 R.I.A.A. 327 (France-Mexico Claims Commission, 1928).

Figures

CHAPTER 1

The Legal Framework of Withdrawal from Multilateral Treaties

"Everything begins with an interruption."
PAUL VALERY

Introduction

Based on the principle of *pacta sunt servanda*, treaty adherence is narrowly construed as fostering interstate cooperation while discouraging unilateral deviations.[1] However, since treaties do not operate in a static environment, withdrawal allows legal termination of treaty-based cooperation that no longer matches national interests, providing flexibility to states' commitments.[2]

This chapter defines withdrawal, outlining the progressive codification of this instrument. Scholarly discussion among international lawyers and international relations theorists has largely ignored the practice of exiting treaties.[3] Historically, policy makers—hearing the echoes of one of the most dramatic moments in history, the collapse of the League of Nations—have been particularly cautious in addressing the issue of withdrawal. The codification of withdrawal clauses arrived, significantly, only years later as an outcome of the dynamics of the Cold War, which led to disengagement from multilateral institutions. From a functionalist perspective, contracting parties preferred to regulate ex ante the conditions and procedures of withdrawal to be applied ex post in the event of denunciation.

1 *See* IAN SINCLAIR, THE VIENNA CONVENTION ON THE LAW OF THE TREATIES, 188–90 (1984).

2 *See* Laurence R. Helfer, *Exiting Treaties*, 91 VA. L. REV. 1579, 1595 (2005); *see also* Laurence R. Helfer, *Terminating Treaties*, *in* THE OXFORD GUIDE TO TREATIES 624, 626 (Duncan B. Hollis ed., 2020).

3 *See* Barbara Koremenos & Allison Nau, *Exit, No Exit*, 81 DUKE J. COMP. & INT'L. L. 81, 84 (2010) (addressing the gap in the literature between international law and international relations theory).

 | DOI: 10.1163/9789004467644_002

After describing the evolution of withdrawal in the context of the law of treaties, this chapter seeks to understand how this instrument operates, defining its legal framework under general rules of international law, the Vienna Convention on the Law of the Treaties of 1969 (VCLT),[4] and domestic legal systems. First, it analyzes withdrawal in the light of the principle of *rebus sic stantibus*, explaining the lasting need for flexibility as times and conditions change.[5] Second, it identifies the most salient aspects of withdrawal both substantively and procedurally, reviewing the VCLT preparatory work,[6] which was much more focused on entering treaties than exiting them, and explaining why VCLT regulation on withdrawal clauses has been largely neglected in states' practices. Third, it examines domestic regulatory approaches to withdrawal and their evolution in modern constitutionalism and scholarly debate. Finally, it defines a conceptual framework of analysis that will inspire the following chapters.

I. Understanding Withdrawal

The scope of this book is limited to the analysis of multilateral sources of the law of treaties. This choice mirrors the intrinsic goal of the book, which is to understand the enduring tension between engagement with and disengagement from multilateralism from an international legal perspective. Article 2 of the VCLT defines a "treaty" as

> an international agreement between sovereign States in written form and governed by international law, whether embodied in a single instrument or in two or more instruments and whatever its particular designation.

Focusing on the whole spectrum of international treaties, including bilateral ones, would have expanded the scope of the analysis too much. Even though termination of bilateral treaties—especially bilateral investment treaties—is also on the rise, the book does not consider bilateral treaties for methodological reasons. A combined analysis of multilateral and bilateral agreements would have entailed the risk of undermining the collection of sources and classification and processing of the information to test the hypothesis and to provide a

4 Vienna Convention on the Law of Treaties, May 23, 1969, 1155 U.N.T.S. 331, 8 I.L.M. 679 (1969).

5 *See* Athanassios Vamvoukos, Termination of Treaties in International Law: The Doctrines of Rebus Sic Stantibus and Desuetude 302 (1985).

6 *See* Mark E. Villiger, Commentary on the 1969 Vienna Convention on the Law of Treaties 3699 (2009).

clear picture of the topic. In other words, the whole spectrum of international treaties would have been too broad to be workable and too heterogeneous to be synthetized.[7] Limiting the analysis to multilateral agreements fosters an understanding of the field and the factors underlying multilateral cooperation, which is treated as an ad hoc category for the law of treaties.

From both a legal and political perspective, withdrawal, or even the threat of withdrawal, is a drastic step that represents a unilateral act to end obligations or interstate cooperation in relation to the subject matter covered by the denounced treaty.[8] If we assume that a treaty can be compared to a marriage between contracting parties, it is possible to conceive of withdrawal as a divorce. In other words, it can be understood as a last-resort tool used as *extrema ratio* and indicating that a member state has been unable to adequately meet its needs within the treaty framework it negotiated.[9] This section defines withdrawal and describes the process of its codification in the law of treaties. Moreover, it maps the evolution of this phenomenon in international relations, examining it as an expression of states' voluntarism.

A. *Definition of Withdrawal*

Exiting international treaties occurs pursuant to a specific legal mechanism, often a treaty clause, that allows for the unilateral termination of treaty obligations or the end of membership in international organizations. Therefore, using the marriage metaphor, just as divorce is part of the marriage contract, withdrawal is regulated by the law of the denounced treaty itself. Since the international law of treaties is voluntary in nature, treaty entry and exit are inevitably results of the will of the parties.

Withdrawal is a formal, public act that consents the withdrawing state to inform its counterparts about its voluntary decision to end cooperation under the treaty framework.[10] This is a lawful act that permits a party to an international treaty or international organization to behave in a publicly compliant way rather than breach its commitment.[11]

---

7 Some limited examples of withdrawal from bilateral treaties are used in the text, whenever they are relevant examples of disengagement from international cooperation, especially in the arms control field.

8 *See generally* Helfer, *Terminating Treaties*, *supra* note 2, at 626.

9 *See* Jochen Herbst, *Observations on the Right to Withdrawal from the EU: Who Are the Masters of Treaties*, 6 GERMAN L.J. 1755 (2005).

10 *See* Helfer, *Terminating Treaties*, *supra* note 2, at 625 (providing a definition of withdrawal in international law).

11 *See* Andrew T. Guzman, *The Cost of Credibility: Explaining Resistance to Interstate Dispute Resolution Mechanisms*, 31 J. LEGAL STUD. 303, 325 (2002).

In international legal argot, even though "withdrawal" and "denunciation" are generally used interchangeably,[12] some scholars contend that the term "withdrawal" relates better to the multilateral context, not only due to the possibly misleading meaning of "denunciation" but, mainly, due to its implications about the continuity of the treaty itself.[13] Denouncing a bilateral treaty inevitably implies its termination because—just like in the field of contract law—there must be at least two parties for the deal to be valid. However, the withdrawal of a party to a multilateral treaty does not imply its termination because it can remain in force for the remaining contracting parties. In practice, "withdrawal" and "denunciation" are generally used interchangeably in treaty language in both bilateral and multilateral contexts.[14] Nonetheless, this book prefers the term "withdrawal" with respect to the act of terminating membership in a multilateral treaty since it describes the legal concept more precisely.

B. *The Progressive Codification of Withdrawal*

Scholarly discussion among international lawyers and international relations theorists has largely ignored the practice of exiting treaties. Historically, in the aftermath of World War II, policy makers were particularly cautious to address the issue of withdrawal during the process of treaty making. They had not forgotten one of the most dramatic moments in history, the collapse of the League of Nations. In October 1933, Germany's departure from that international organization, followed by its massive rearmament, meant the end of legality in international relations.[15] That legal act unleashed an unstoppable crescendo of violations of international law. Combined with the denunciation of the Locarno Treaties[16] in 1936, Germany's withdrawal from the League of

---

12 UN Treaty Section, Office of Legal Affairs, *Final Clauses of Multilateral Treaties Handbook*, UN Sales No. E04V3 109 (2003) (affirming that the terms "denunciation" and "withdrawal" express the same legal concept).

13 *See* Anthony Aust, Handbook of International Law, 93 (2010); *see also* Anthony Aust, *Treaties, Termination, in* MPEPIL (2006), https://opil.ouplaw.com/view/10.1093/law:epil/9780199231690/law-9780199231690-e1491; Helfer, *Terminating Treaties*, *supra* note 2, at 635.

14 The UN's Final Clauses of Multilateral Treaties Handbook generally refers to "withdrawal" and "denunciation" interchangeably. *See supra,* note 12. By contrast, the VCLT maintains a distinction between these two terms.

15 Nine months after Adolf Hitler's appointment as chancellor of Germany, in 1933, the German foreign minister, Konstantin Freiherr Von Neurath, informed the League of Nations Secretary-General, Joseph Avenol, of Germany's withdrawal.

16 The Locarno Treaties were seven agreements negotiated at Locarno, Switzerland, in 1925 between the Western European Allied powers and the new states of Central and Eastern

Nations allowed the Nazi government a free hand in foreign policy. Once Germany abandoned diplomatic channels, the absence of legality brought to military solutions.[17]

The treaty-making process that emerged from the aftermath of World War II was largely oriented to excluding withdrawal clauses from the range of treaty provisions, in order to seek perpetuity or, at least, continuity of international agreements. This was the case with the Charter of the United Nations (UN Charter),[18] which was meant to be a permanent instrument in international law. The League of Nations having revealed its limitations as parties repudiated the system, the drafters of the UN Charter followed a different strategy during preliminary steps in Dumbarton Oaks[19] and then at the 1945 San Francisco Conference.[20] The UN Charter, aiming to prevent political pressures and preserve treaty maintenance over time, intentionally did not contemplate withdrawal by state parties.[21]

Europe. They grounded peace and collective security on good will, conciliation, and arbitration as they aimed at securing the postwar territorial settlement while normalizing relations with defeated Germany. Hitler decided to withdraw unilaterally from the Treaty of Locarno when France promised its intervention to the Soviet Union in the event of a German attack. In his view, this was a non-allowed exception to the Treaties that irremediably hindered the non-aggression agreement between France and Germany. The member parties of the Locarno Treaties vainly proposed to bring the case before the Permanent Court of International Justice. The Nazi regime had already begun operations to invade the Rhineland, prioritizing force over justice. As a result of this behavior, Francois-Poncet, the French Foreign Minister, defined Hitler as a pirate who would not accept any ground for peaceful negotiation. *See, e.g.*, JEAN BAPTISTE DUROSELLE, HISTOIRE DIPLOMATIQUE DE 1919 À NOS JOURS (11th ed., 1994).

17 First Germany realized the Austrian Anschluss, in 1938, and the annexation of the Czechoslovak provinces of Bohemia and Moravia, in 1939, to unify German people under one state. The absence of legality culminated in the German attack on Poland of September 1, 1939, and the outbreak of World War II. *See generally* HENRY KISSINGER, DIPLOMACY, 288 et seq. (1994) (analyzing the destruction of Versailles and the end of an illusion); *see also* DUROSELLE, *supra* note 16, at 221 et seq. (analyzing foreign policy under totalitarianism).

18 U.N. Charter.

19 The Washington Conversation on International Peace and Security Organization, commonly known as the Dumbarton Oaks Conference, was an international conference held at Dumbarton Oaks, Washington, D.C., from August 21, 1944, to October 7, 1944, to define the future architecture of the United Nations.

20 The United Nations Conference on International Organization (UNCIO), commonly known as the San Francisco Conference, was a convention of delegates of fifty Allied nations that took place from April 25, 1945, to June 26, 1945, in San Francisco, California. The delegates reviewed and amended the Dumbarton Oaks agreements, aiming at the creation of the UN Charter, which was opened for signature on the last day of the conference.

21 The original approach undertaken in Dumbarton Oaks entailed no provision either to allow withdrawal or to veto it. Similarly, during the San Francisco Conference, the with-

Originally, with regard to the UN Charter, the debate on pulling out was about secessionism because policy makers were trying to apply multilaterally the traditional instruments of international law. Nonetheless, the term "secessionism" was eventually avoided because of its negative historical connotations related to colonialism and the category was eventually labeled as "withdrawal."[22]

During the *travaux preparatoires* of the UN Charter,[23] it was expressed that whenever a member felt compelled to withdraw due to exceptional circumstances, the organization could not coerce that member otherwise. Rather, it should embrace the maintenance of international peace and security without the withdrawing party.[24] This was the argument upheld by the U.S. delegation. Because the organization lacked the compulsive power to force membership, it was left to the international community to judge whether withdrawal was justifiable or not.[25]

As sovereign states could voluntarily join the organization, they could voluntarily leave it. The UN Charter did not imply to push member States into a new governmental experience, but to set forth a joint venture.[26] In particular, from the U.S. perspective, this entailed a general right to withdrawal that could be implicitly deduced, even in the silence of the agreement.[27]

The absence of an ad hoc clause in the UN Charter would eventually give the agreement an aspirational character that would bind the states of the entire international community together. Based on that experience,

---

drawal of a state was neither expressly nor impliedly prohibited. *See* Thomas M. Franck, *Is the U.N. Charter a Constitution?*, in NEGOTIATING FOR PEACE 95, 96 (Jochen Abr. Frowein et al., eds., 2003); *see also* LELAND GOODRICH & EDVARD HAMBRO, CHARTER OF THE UNITED NATIONS – COMMENTARY AND DOCUMENTS 144 (1946).

22 Three U.S. representatives before the United States Senate Committee on Foreign Relations—namely John Foster Dulles, one of the chief advisors of the U.S. delegation to the San Francisco Conference; Green H. Hackworth, legal advisor of the Department of State; and Leo Pasvolsky, a representative of the Department of State—analyzed the use of the wording "secession" vis-à-vis "withdrawal."

23 U.N. Charter.

24 The Report of Committed I/2 approved by Commission I and the Conference in plenary session contains the debate on withdrawal. United Nation Conference on International Organizations (U.N.C.I.O) Summary Report of Twenty-Eight Meeting of Committee I/2, June 17, 1945, Doc. 1086, I/2/77 (Documents VII, 262–267) [hereinafter UNCIO Summary Report].

25 Howard Newcombe Morse, *The New Secession, A Study of the Legal Right of the United States to Withdraw from the United Nations*, 57 DICK. L. REV. 134 (1952).

26 *See* id.

27 UNCIO Summary Report, *supra* note 24.

subsequent international treaty making was framed with that aim, through agreements with no exit procedures, to secure perpetuity and continuity in treaty maintenance.[28]

Withdrawal clauses progressively emerged in practice and codification as a risk management tool in international cooperation and final norms in the international law of treaties. In the absence of express provisions, in the beginning they were framed as "reservations" to the agreement. In other words, a contracting party would join an international treaty or organization conditioned on reserving its right to withdraw. For instance, this was the case with the United States' conditional acceptance of the World Health Organization (WHO) Constitution[29] in 1947. In that case, the United States was implicitly acquiring a right that other members would not.[30] The Indian representative before the WHO proposed to the World Health Assembly—the WHO governing body—including in the agency's constitution the right of a member to withdraw as a principle of general application. However, the Indian proposal found no success—it was opposed by the other fifty-two delegations in the Assembly. As a result, as noted by Nathan Feinberg, in its embryonic state, withdrawal appeared as a specific reservation to the general principle of perpetuity of international agreements.[31]

Later, as the Cold War broke out, withdrawal emerged more significantly and became an expression of dissatisfaction of one bloc with another. Even without withdrawal clauses, states began disengaging from international organizations to pursue a geopolitical strategy rather than a multilateral one.[32] From 1949, the U.S.S.R., along with the other socialist bloc countries, began

---

28 The goal of the parties in Dumbarton Oaks revealed positive outcomes for the resiliency of the UN Charter, since, as of the date of this writing, only Indonesia has expressed its intention to withdraw, though without succeeding. Indeed, changes in the domestic political system during the time of the execution of the withdrawal procedure frustrated the original intention to pull out. *See* Egon Schwelb, *Withdrawal from the United Nations: The Indonesian Intermezzo*, 61 AJIL 661, 666–71 (1967).

29 World Health Organization [WHO], Constitution, 14 U.N.T.S. 185 (July 22, 1946).

30 The United States Congress had attached the condition to withdraw to acceptance of the WHO Constitution. Section 4 of the United States Joint Resolution of 7 July 1947 upheld that, in the absence of any withdrawal provision, the United States reserved its right to withdraw, based on a one-year notice period. By accepting unanimously the validity of the United States reservation, the World Health Assembly granted the United States a right that was not granted to other parties, through its Resolution of 2 July 1948.

31 *See* Nathan Feinberg, *Unilateral Withdrawal from an International Organization*, 39 BYIL 189, 202–05 (1963).

32 *See infra*, Chapter 2, Part III.A.i (conceptualizing withdrawal as a tool for geopolitical strategy during the Cold War period).

denouncing constituency agreements establishing international organizations. The first case concerned the collective withdrawal of socialist countries from the World Health Organization (WHO)[33] between 1949 and 1950; this included the U.S.S.R., Bulgaria, Romania, Albania, Czechoslovakia, Hungary, Poland, and China.[34] Later, between 1952 and 1953, some countries of the Eastern Soviet bloc, including Poland, Hungary, and Czechoslovakia, withdrew from the United Nations Educational, Scientific and Cultural Organization (UNESCO), notwithstanding the lack of a withdrawal clause.[35]

The executive boards of WHO and UNESCO, seeking to limit the effects of the Soviet disengagement, approached the denunciations cautiously. After repeated appeals that they reconsider, the Soviet bloc eventually rejoined both organizations, returning to active membership. The executive boards of both organizations refused to consider the Soviet action as a real denunciation, and tried to facilitate their return to active collaboration, based on the principle of universality of membership. Indeed, as the Soviet withdrawal represented just a temporal parenthesis in the life of the organization, it was never considered institutionally as a termination of membership, but rather "inactive membership" of the parties.[36]

After the Soviet impasse, international lawyers and diplomats began questioning the possibility of including withdrawal clauses in multilateral agreements. Even if parties could eventually restore cooperation within the treaty framework of each organization, something was inevitably broken with regard to states' perception of multilateral perpetuity. Therefore, at the General Conference of UNESCO in 1954, contracting parties decided to amend UNESCO's constitution to include a specific withdrawal provision.[37]

---

33 Since the WHO Constitution had no withdrawal clause, the WHO Director General, along with the Executive Board, did not accept the notice of denunciation. Eventually, even though they had to accept the factual condition of membership termination, they still encouraged participation. *WHO Official Records*, No. 17, Report of the Executive Council, 3rd Session 52 (Geneva, 1949).

34 *See* WORLD HEALTH ORGANIZATION [WHO], THE FIRST TEN YEARS OF THE WORLD HEALTH ORGANIZATION 80 (1958), https://apps.who.int/iris/handle/10665/37089.

35 *See infra*, Chapter 4, Part II.B (analyzing the cases of withdrawal from UN agencies).

36 It is debatable whether "inactive membership" represents a real category of membership or a mere administrative convenience used by the organization to overcome a political impasse. Because "inactive membership" describes a factual situation of temporary suspension of participation in the organization's work, which is not reflected in the Constitution, it may be concluded that the latter is true. Nathan Feinberg, *Unilateral Withdrawal from an International Organization*, 39 BYIL 189, 202–05 (1963).

37 UNESCO's Constitution was amended through Article II, para. 6, including an explicit provision for withdrawal regulation.

Even though withdrawal began to be included in international agreements, it was not yet fully accepted among scholars and policy makers due to its potential for encouraging noncooperation. A clear example of this trend can be found in the preparatory work of the VCLT, which began in 1949.[38] The working sessions of the International Law Commission (ILC),[39] preliminary to the adoption of the draft articles on the law of treaties with commentaries, in 1966, sparked critics and oppositions within its members, since the proposed rule was perceived as dangerous to the stability and security of treaties.[40] The ILC debate on the original draft provision on withdrawal mirrored the skepticism within the UN Conference on the Law of Treaties[41] during approval of the text, when only thirteen member governments—around 13% of the participants—commented positively. Eventually, the final draft tailored withdrawal to the intentions of the parties in what would become Article 54 and Article 56 of the VCLT.[42] Thus, in 1969, it was possible to reach unanimous acceptance of the provisions, first among ILC members and later among governments.[43]

Due to an emerging states' practice, withdrawal clauses began appearing with more frequency in treaty-making processes as *lex specialis ad recedendum*

38 During its first session, in 1949, the ILC chose, among its priorities, the "law of treaties" as a topic for codification and, with that aim, appointed as first special rapporteur J.L. Brierly (1949–1951), who was followed by Hersch Lauterpacht (1952–1954), Gerald Fitzmaurice (1955–1960), and Humphrey Waldock (1961–1966). *See* MARK E. VILLIGER, COMMENTARY ON THE 1969 VIENNA CONVENTION ON THE LAW OF TREATIES 3699 (2009).

39 With Resolution 94 of December 11, 1946, the International Law Commission (ILC) was created, its mandate being to make recommendations to the UN Secretary-General on the way the General Assembly should approach international law. UN General Assembly, *Progressive Development of International Law and Codification*, UN GA Resolution 94, (Dec. 11, 1946), https://documents-dds-ny.un.org/doc/resolution/gen/nr0/033/45/img/nr003345.pdf.

40 ILC members Castren, Tsurouka, De Luna, Amado, and Verdross were radically opposed to the withdrawal provision. *See* Humphrey Waldock, *Special Rapporteur on the Law of the Treaties, Second Report on the Law of the Treaties*, 2 UNYBILC 64 (1963).

41 In submitting the final report to the UN General Assembly, the ILC recommended convening an ad hoc conference of plenipotentiaries to study the draft articles on the law of treaties and to conclude a convention on the subject. The General Assembly, by resolution 2166 (XXI) of December 5, 1966, did so and, the following year, on the recommendation of the Sixth Committee, by resolution 2287 (XXII) of December 6, 1967, the first session of the UN Conference on the Law of Treaties was convened in Vienna in March 1968. The second session was held in Vienna from April to May 1969 and it led to the adoption of the VCLT on May 22, 1969. *See* U.N. International Conference of Plenipotentiaries on the Law of Treaties, U.N. Doc. A/6516, G.A. Res. 2166 (XXI) (Dec. 5, 1966); U.N. Conference on the Law of Treaties, U.N. Doc. A/CONF. 39/6, G.A. Res. 2287 (XXII) (Dec. 6, 1967).

42 *See infra*, Chapter 1, Part II.B (reviewing withdrawal under the lens of the VCLT's provisions).

43 Six states, however, abstained, expressing concern about the stability of the law of treaties in international law. *See* Waldock, *supra* note 40, at 25.

that contravened the general aspiration for perpetuity in the international law of treaties. Indeed, withdrawal began to be seen as a risk management tool that would allow contracting parties to protect national supreme interests when cooperation through the agreement was no longer viable.[44] As the international treaty-making process evolved, policy makers began including withdrawal clauses from a functionalist perspective, as they preferred to regulate ex ante the conditions and procedures of withdrawal to be applied ex post, in the event of denunciation.

Today, withdrawal clauses have been affirmed as an international legal instrument because, by allowing cooperation under the treaty framework to end, they make it possible for a state to adapt to changed circumstances.[45] They are a specific category of final clauses, which include those provisions regulating the bringing into force of a treaty, the scope of its operations, its temporal duration, and other relevant aspects of its existence.[46] Based on a 2010 study of the United Nations Treaty Series (UNTS), approximately 60% of multilateral treaties contain a withdrawal clause.[47] The relative prevalence of withdrawal clauses varies depending on the field covered by the treaty. On one hand, in reciprocal agreements, as in the fields of security and economics, withdrawal clauses have been relatively uncommon, with only some agreements incorporating them. On the other hand, in nonreciprocal agreements, such as in the fields of human rights and environmental law, where more delicate political matters are at stake, withdrawal clauses have been usually incorporated.[48]

C. *Withdrawal as an Expression of States' Voluntarism*

Withdrawal clauses are a regularized component of modern treaty practice, while they represent a key element in international governance. Some scholars have questioned the codification of something that was already enabled by

---

44 *See infra*, Chapter 2, Part II (analyzing withdrawal through the lens of risk management).

45 *See* Kal Raustiala, *Form & Substance in International Agreements*, 90 AJIL 581, 614 (2005).

46 United Nations Office of Legal Affairs, *Final Clauses of Multilateral Treaties Handbook*, U.N. Sales No. E.04.V.3 109 (2003).

47 *See* Barbara Koremenos & Allison Nau, *Exit, No Exit*, 81 Duke J. Comp. & Int'l. L. 81, 106 (2010); *but see* Kevin Widdows, *The Unilateral Denunciation of Treaties Containing No Denunciation Clause*, 53 BYIL 83 (1982) (finding that nearly 90% of bilateral and multilateral agreements registered between 1967 and 1971 contained withdrawal clauses).

48 In a random sample of 142 agreements, Koremenos and Nau found that (a) in the security field, 11 agreements included withdrawal clauses, while 14 did not; (b) in the economic field, 39 agreements included withdrawal clauses, while 30 did not; (c) in the environmental field, 16 agreements included withdrawal agreements, while 9 did not; and (d) in the human rights field, 20 agreements included withdrawal clauses, while 3 did not. *See* Koremenos & Nau, *supra* note 47, at 106.

the anarchic nature of the international legal system.[49] Lacking a centralized enforcement model in international law, withdrawal clauses serve as a way to harness the ability of states to unilaterally defect from what they previously committed to. According to the doctrine of treaty dissolution, as Laurence Helfer pointed out, withdrawal can be defined as the unilateral act that a member state to a treaty performs to end its treaty participation or its membership in international organizations. The foundational principle of state consent that governs the design and operations of international agreements inspires the law of the treaties up to the moment of termination.[50]

Since states are the masters of treaty rules, sovereign voluntarism grounds the whole architecture of the international legal system.[51] No state can be compelled to join or to stay in an international agreement or organization in opposition to its sovereign will. Once states ratify or accede to an international agreement, they accept the conditions they negotiated ex ante, during the implementation phase, to guide their behavior ex post.

Withdrawal clauses can be seen as a tool for risk management in international cooperation because they provide flexibility to states' commitments—with practical, theoretical, and normative implications.[52] They are a rational response to the uncertain framework in which states negotiate commitments with imperfect information; in other words, they are insurance that encourages states to join an agreement.[53] They mirror states' need for flexibility, allowing contracting parties to enter agreements they would otherwise avoid joining. Whenever a state believes that an international agreement hampers national interests, it is unlikely that it will continue to act in accordance with the conventional provisions. Withdrawal clauses offer member States a way out.[54]

Governments pay close attention to the conditions and contours of exit, both when they negotiate international agreements and when they evaluate the

---

49 *See* id. at 83–84; *see also* Barbara Koremenos, *Loosening the Ties that Bind: A Learning Model of Agreement Flexibility*, 55 INT'L ORG. 289 (2001) (framing a rational design for international law in an anarchic system).

50 *See* Helfer, *Terminating Treaties*, *supra* note 2, at 626.

51 *See* Jochen Herbst, *Observations on the Right to Withdrawal from the EU: Who Are the Masters of Treaties*, 6 GERMAN L.J. 1755 (2005).

52 *See infra*, Chapter 2, Part II (conceptualizing withdrawal as a tool for risk management in interstate cooperation).

53 *See* Kal Raustiala, *Form & Substance in International Agreements*, 90 AJIL 581, 613 (2005) (agreeing with the argument that states will join an agreement only if the anticipated benefits will outweigh the expected costs).

54 *See* HANS BLIX & JIRINA H. EMERSON, THE TREATY MAKER'S HANDBOOK 104–15 (1973) (analyzing typical provisions on termination and suspension of the operations of treaties).

costs and benefits of continuing to comply with those agreements over time.[55] Withdrawal clauses are not blank checks. They set prerequisites to guide states' action, limiting their free discretion and creating deterrents to exiting.[56]

Treaty adherence is narrowly construed as a way to promote cooperation between contracting parties while discouraging their unilateral deviations.[57] However, treaties don't operate in a static environment, and changes in the life of a state can influence its desire to remain in a treaty framework it joined. International law requires states to either obey international rules and accept sanctions for noncompliance or cooperate to revise or abrogate the rules.[58] In this light, withdrawal clauses represent a safe escape—or, as previously described, an insurance policy—that allows for ending treaty-based cooperation in the event of a negative outcome.

As withdrawal clauses regulate circumstances under which states can effectively pull out of an international agreement, they allow the withdrawing state to remain in compliance with their international obligations. Therefore, states are not only masters of treaty commitments but also masters of treaty exit rules.[59]

II. Withdrawal in International and Domestic Law

To understand how withdrawal operates, defining its legal framework under the international law of treaties and domestic legal systems is of paramount importance. The language of the treaty, general rules of international law, and the VCLT[60] set the main international legal framework of reference, while domestic constitutions mainly regulate withdrawal in domestic law. The principle of *pacta sunt servanda* inspires the whole architecture of the treaty-making process in international law and, therefore, should guide our approach to withdrawal. First, this section defines the general rules of international law concerning withdrawal. Second, it analyzes the VCLT to identify the most salient aspects of exit regulation from both a substantive and procedural perspectives.

---

55 *See* Helfer, *Terminating Treaties*, *supra* note 2, at 626.

56 *See* Barbara Koremenos, Charles Lipson & Duncan Snidal, *The Rational Design of International Institutions*, 55 INT'L ORG. 761 (2001) (analyzing under rational theories how to design a sound legal framework for international agreements).

57 *See* IAN SINCLAIR, THE VIENNA CONVENTION ON THE LAW OF THE TREATIES, 188–90 (1984).

58 *See* Laurence R. Helfer, *Exiting Treaties*, 91 VA. L. REV. 1579, 1581 (2005).

59 *See* Helfer, *Terminating Treaties*, *supra* note 2, at 630 (stating that member states to a treaty are the only ones entitled to define treaty exit rules).

60 Vienna Convention on the Law of Treaties, 1155 U.N.T.S. 331, 8 I.L.M. 679 (1969).

Third, it describes the domestic approach to treaty-making to shed light on constitutional procedures for entering and exiting international agreements. Finally, it provides a conceptual framework for approaching the subject matter at hand that will inspire the following chapters.

A. *Withdrawal in General International Law*

The whole architecture of international law is grounded on the aspiration of perpetuity.[61] As international law aims at preserving the integrity of international treaties and treaty provisions, it limits the possibility for termination, withdrawal, or suspension. This is an idea that can be traced back to one of the cardinal principles in international law, *pacta sunt servanda*.[62] Article 26 of the VCLT[63] codifies this principle as follows: "Every treaty in force is binding upon the parties to it and must be performed by them in good faith."

Despite this principle, it is possible for a state to unburden itself of its treaty commitments: the *rebus sic stantibus* exception allows this when there is a change in fundamental circumstances. This exception can be seen as a stepping-stone to withdrawal, inasmuch as whenever a substantial unforeseen change in circumstances occurs in the life of a treaty, it may be terminated.[64] The *rebus sic stantibus* is a long-standing legal doctrine that can be traced back to the *Corpus Juris Civilis* of Justinian. In international law, it is diametrically opposed to the general principle *pacta sunt servanda*; they stand at the two opposite poles of continuity and discontinuity of treaty obligations.

The *rebus sic stantibus* doctrine has evolved over time. Originally, it was considered an implied term of a treaty;[65] now, it represents an objective rule existing independently of the wills of the parties.[66] This doctrine was codified in Article 62(1) of the VCLT,[67] which allows termination or withdrawal in the event of a fundamental change of circumstances:

---

61 *See generally* John Fischer Williams, *The Permanence of Treaties*, 22 AJIL 89, 89–104 (1928); *see also* Theodore P. Ion, *Sanctity of Treaties*, 20 Yale L.J. 268, 268–91 (1911).

62 *See infra,* Chapter 2, Part III (analyzing withdrawal through the lens of the principle "*pacta sunt servanda*").

63 VCLT art. 26 ("*Pacta sunt servanda*").

64 *See* ATHANASSIOS VAMVOUKOS, TERMINATION OF TREATIES IN INTERNATIONAL LAW: THE DOCTRINES OF REBUS SIC STANTIBUS AND DESUETUDE 302 (1985).

65 Customarily, the doctrine is considered to be "tacitly annexed to every covenant." *See* James W. Garner, *The Doctrine of Rebus Sic Stantibus and the Termination of Treaties*, 21 AJIL 509, 509 (1927).

66 *See* VAMVOUKOS, *supra* note 64, at 328.

67 VCLT art. 62 ("Fundamental change of circumstances").

> A fundamental change of circumstances which has occurred with regard to those existing at the time of the conclusion of a treaty, and which was not foreseen by the parties, may not be invoked as a ground for terminating or withdrawing from the treaty unless:
> a. the existence of those circumstances constituted an essential basis of the consent of the parties to be bound by the treaty; and
> b. the effect of the change is radically to transform the extent of obligations still to be performed under the treaty.

The negative wording of Article 62(1) of the VCLT reflects the exceptional nature of the doctrine, which has objective and subjective elements. First, the fundamental circumstances already existing at the time the treaty was concluded must be such that, were they to change, would radically transform the obligations still to be performed. Second, these circumstances must not have been foreseen by the parties and must have been essential to the state's consent to the treaty.[68]

States' practice, in general international law, based on the doctrine of *rebus sic stantibus*, explains how mutated circumstances have served over time as a bulwark against the risk of perpetuity of treaties. Important changes at the economic and political level that have taken place in the life of many states have been invoked to further revision or termination of international agreements.[69] The invocation of the *rebus sic stantibus* doctrine as a tool for disengaging from international agreements was particularly relevant at the beginning of the twentieth century and, later, during postcolonialism. Some examples related to China and Austria-Hungary, along with denunciation of the agreements related to the League of Nations and colonialism, demonstrate how withdrawal can serve as an act for terminating the status quo ante in foreign relations.

The decision of the Chinese government in the 1920s to terminate the so-called unequal treaties[70] subjugating China to Western powers, in force

---

68 *See* Julian Kulaga, *A Renaissance of the Doctrine Rebus Sic Stantibus*, 69 INT'L & COMP. L. QUART., 477, 478 (2020) (identifying the essential elements underlying the *rebus sic stantibus* doctrine).

69 *See* James W. Garner, *The Doctrine of Rebus Sic Stantibus and the Termination of Treaties*, 21 AJIL 509, 509–10 (1927).

70 The expression "unequal treaties" refers to those treaties signed by the Qing dynasty with foreign powers after military attacks or military threats. In the 1920s, the rise of Chinese nationalism, led by the Kuomintang and Communist Party, developed these concepts in an anti-imperialist key to characterize the Chinese experience with loss of sovereignty between the mid-nineteenth century and mid-twentieth century—the so-called "century of humiliation."

since the nineteenth century, was based on the *rebus sic stantibus* clause.[71] Chinese scholarship of that time interpreted the governmental notification of termination as a change in fundamental circumstances of the facts.[72] Similarly, the principle was also invoked around the same time, in 1908, when the Austro-Hungarian Empire denounced the Treaty of Berlin of 1878,[73] and the Convention of Constantinople of 1881.[74] As those instruments regulated the conditions of the administration and occupation of Bosnia and Herzegovina, the Austro-Hungarian government denounced them to annex those territories.[75]

Later, two peaks of disengagement from international commitments arose: in the aftermath of the collapse of the League of Nations and in the postcolonial period between colonized countries and colonial powers. A fundamental change in circumstances pushed several states to seek withdrawal to adapt the juridical status of their foreign relations to different political and diplomatic conditions.[76]

The exceptional, restrictive nature of the doctrine has been emphasized in the international jurisprudence. In the *Fisheries Jurisdiction* case,[77] the International Court of Justice (ICJ) adopted a strict approach to *rebus sic stantibus*, limiting the principle to situations in which radical and fundamental changes would imperil the existence or vital development of one of the parties. Similarly, in the *Gabčikovo-Nagymaros Project* case,[78] the ICJ ruled that the changed

71 *See* Garner, *supra* note 69, at 509–10.

72 *See* Yang Kwang-Sheng, *China Abrogating Unfair Treaties with Powers*, 25 CURRENT HIST. 697, 698 (1927).

73 Treaty Between Austria-Hungary, France, Germany, Great Britain and Ireland, Italy, Russia, and the Ottoman Empire for the Settlement of Affairs in the East, July 13, 1878, 153 C.T.S. 171.

74 The Convention of Constantinople was signed between the Ottoman Empire and the Kingdom of Greece for the rectification of their common borderlines, on July 2, 1881.

75 *See* Jacques Blociszewski, *L'Annexion de la Bosnie et de l'Herzegovine*, 17 REV. GÉN DE DR. INT. PUB. 417, 441 (1910).

76 *See infra*, Chapter 3, Part II.B.ii (analyzing the evolution of withdrawal over time and explaining how it changed from the postwar period to the postcolonial period).

77 One of the main cases grounded on the *rebus sic stantibus* principle is the *Fisheries Jurisdiction* case, in which the ICJ ruled on a dispute between the United Kingdom and Iceland. The latter sought to extend its fisheries jurisdiction from 12 to 50 miles, notwithstanding a previous settlement with its counterpart on this matter, due to a change in circumstances. The Court based its test on whether the change in circumstance had increased the burden of the obligation so much as to be considered essentially different from what was originally undertaken. Fisheries Jurisdiction (United Kingdom v. Iceland), Merits, Judgment, I.C.J. Rep. 1974, p. 3, at 19, https://www.icj-cij.org/public/files/case-related/55/055-19740725-JUD-01-00 EN.pdf.

78 In the *Gabčikovo Nagymaros Project* case, the ICJ referred to the *rebus sic stantibus* doctrine in determining whether profound changes of a political and economic nature could justify the termination of a bilateral treaty between Czechoslovakia and Hungary, signed

circumstances should radically transform the extent of the obligations still to be performed to allow parties to legitimately terminate a treaty. The narrowly construed framework has been reiterated at the European Union level since the opinion of the Advocate General at the Court of Justice of the European Communities.[79] A change of circumstances, especially those that constituted an essential basis for concluding the treaty, would radically alter the extent of the obligations still to be fulfilled under the treaty. Therefore, the application of this principle remains an exception to the traditional notion of *pacta sunt servanda* that imposes on states an obligation to honor treaties they committed to in good faith.[80]

B. *Withdrawal in the Vienna Convention on the Law of Treaties*

The main principles of withdrawal in the international law of treaties are defined in the VCLT. The VCLT regulates withdrawal from international agreements in its Part V, "Invalidity, Termination and Suspension of the Operation of Treaties." The VCLT is drafted in such a way that the power to terminate treaties belongs to states as much as the power to enter into treaties does. Therefore, withdrawal was framed in a way symmetrical to treaty entrance.[81]

Below, the VCLT's provisions regarding withdrawal are explored. First, the analysis focuses on the process of withdrawal codified in the VCLT, shedding light on the debates in the working sessions of the ILC that would lead, in 1966,

---

in 1977, for a joint project for the production of energy, the control of floods, and the improvement of navigation on the Danube River. The Court held that the political and economic conditions in the former Socialist states were not so strictly linked to the object and purpose of the agreement as to constitute an essential basis for consent of the parties. In the Court's view, given the exceptionality of Article 62, the changed circumstances were not of such nature, either individually or collectively, to transform the extent of the obligations still to be performed in order to terminate the project. Although the Court found that both parties failed to comply with their obligations, this reciprocal wrongful conduct did not bring the treaty to and end nor justified its termination. Gabčíkovo-Nagymaros Project (Hungary v. Slovakia), Judgment, 1997 I.C.J. 7 (Sept. 25) (n.3) 64 [104].

79 Opinion of Mr. Advocate General Francis Jacobs delivered on Dec. 4, 1997, *A. Racke GmbH & Co. v Hauptzollamt Mainz*, Case C-162/96, E.C.R. I-03655 (1998).

80 *See* Sylvanus A. Tiewul, *The Fisheries Jurisdiction Cases (1973) and the Ghost of Rebus Sic Stantibus,* 6 N.Y.U. J. INT'L L. & POL. 455, 463–64 (1973); *see also* Donald A. Joung, *Contributions to International Law and World Order by the World Court's Adjudication of the Icelandic Fisheries Controversy*, 1 B.C. INT'L & COMP. L. REV. 175, 188 (1977); Stephen R. Katz, *Issues Arising in the Icelandic Fisheries Case*, 22 INT'L & COMP. L.Q. 83, 103 (1973).

81 Sir Humphrey Waldock, the ILC Special Rapporteur on the law of treaties, during the ILC working sessions that led to the approval of the draft articles on the law of treaties, envisioned treaty exit as a moment symmetrical to entrance, depending on the principle of states' voluntarism. *See* Waldock, *supra* note 40, at 85.

to the adoption and submission to the UN General Assembly of draft articles, with commentaries, on the law of treaties. Second, it addresses the absence of withdrawal clauses in regard to various doctrinal interpretations and states' practices. Third, it examines the procedural framework for the invocation of withdrawal defined in the VCLT.

i. Codifying Withdrawal

With the aim of reconstructing the architecture for withdrawal, first of all, it is worth analyzing possibilities for states to exit an international treaty, and the limitations thereon, pursuant to the VCLT.

Under Article 42 of VCLT,[82] a state can withdraw from an international treaty only as a result of the application of a treaty provision or, if that is not possible, in compliance with VCLT provisions. Under Article 45 of the VCLT,[83] a state may lose its right to withdraw from a treaty if it has expressly agreed on its validity or continuation into force or when its behavior acquiesces to the treaty.[84]

Section 3 of Part V of the VCLT provides a detailed framework for withdrawal. Pursuant to Article 54 of the VCLT,[85] withdrawal can occur only on a voluntary basis:

> The termination of a treaty or the withdrawal of a party may take place:
> a. in conformity with the provisions of the treaty;
> b. at any time by consent of all the parties after consultation with the other contracting States.

From a procedural standpoint, VCLT regulates withdrawal in a negative form, in that it limits the ways in which States may withdraw. Specifically, under Article 56 of the VCLT,[86] withdrawal is not allowed unless contracting parties intended to allow it. Withdrawal must be authorized either by the provisions of the treaty or a different ancillary agreement. Therefore, the law of the treaty or the agreement that was subsidiarily negotiated regulates the circumstances in which withdrawal is permitted and the ways to realize it. Just as the

82 VCLT art. 42 ("Validity and continuance in force of treaties").

83 VCLT art. 45 ("Loss of a right to invoke a ground for invalidating, terminating, withdrawing from or suspending the operation of a treaty").

84 *See* BARRY E. CARTER & ALLEN S. WEINER, INTERNATIONAL LAW 86 (Wolters Kluwer, 6th ed. 2011).

85 VCLT art. 54 ("Termination of or withdrawal from a treaty under its provisions or by consent of the parties").

86 VCLT art. 46 ("Denunciation of or withdrawal from a treaty containing no provision regarding termination, denunciation or withdrawal").

international law of treaties is grounded in states' voluntarism, so does withdrawal follow the will of the contracting parties.

ii. The Absence of a Withdrawal Clause

In current state practice, most international agreements include final clauses regarding terminating, denouncing, or withdrawing from them. However, there are treaties with no withdrawal clause, including the UN Charter,[87] the 1958 Geneva Law of the Sea Convention, the 1961 and the 1963 Conventions on Consular and Diplomatic Relations, and even the Vienna Convention on the Law of Treaties.

Absent a withdrawal clause, parties should express whether the possibility of withdrawing is implicit in the treaty's language or nature. The lack of a withdrawal clause could imply that some treaties could be meant to be *ad libitum* and, therefore, last indefinitely. In that event, supplementary means of interpretation may be helpful in reconstructing the will of the parties to the treaty-making process through a study of the *travaux preparatoires* or the circumstances of its conclusion.[88]

Article 56(1) of the VCLT addressed the lack of withdrawal clauses in international treaties as follows:

> A treaty which contains no provision regarding its termination and which does not provide for denunciation or withdrawal is not subject to denunciation or withdrawal unless:
> a. It is established that the parties intended to admit the possibility of denunciation or withdrawal; or
> b. A right of denunciation or withdrawal may be implied by the nature of the treaty.

The provision set out in the final text of the VCLT was the result of an uneasy compromise among members of the ILC during its working sessions. In his 1957 report to the ILC, the special rapporteur in the law of treaties, Gerald Fitzmaurice, interpreted the lack of a withdrawal provision in a treaty as a presumption against exit.[89] The following special rapporteur for the topic,

---

87 *See supra*, Chapter 1, Part I.B (analyzing the reasons behind the absence of a withdrawal clause in the UN Charter).

88 Article 32 of the Vienna Convention on the Law of the Treaties regulates the "Supplementary means of interpretation" to clarify the meaning of a provision of a treaty when it remains ambiguous or obscure.

89 *See* Gerald Fitzmaurice, *Special Rapporteur on the Law of the Treaties, Second Report on the Law of the Treaties*, 2 UNYBILC 16, ¶ 22 (1957).

Humphrey Waldock, however, in his 1963 report to the ILC, identified a twofold trend in states' practice.[90] First, there are treaties that allow withdrawal. This catalogue includes commercial and trading treaties; treaties of alliance or of military cooperation; treaties for technical cooperation in economic, cultural, scientific, and communication-related matters; treaties of arbitration, conciliation or judicial settlement; and treaties establishing international organizations.[91] Second, there are treaties that continue to be in force indefinitely, such as treaties establishing boundaries or regarding the cession of territory; treaties establishing a special regime in a particular area, territory, waterway or airspace; treaties of peace and disarmament; treaties establishing a final settlement of an international dispute; and treaties for codification or progressive development in international law.[92]

The alternatives in Article 56(1) of the VCLT are difficult to prove. However, they give the parties to a treaty a path for legal withdrawal.[93] Though it is doubtful whether the final version of Article 56 of the VCLT reflected customary international law at the time it was adopted, some scholars have written that it generated a new rule of customary law, furthering progressive development on this matter. [94]

iii. Procedural Framework for Withdrawal

Procedural provisions for withdrawal aim at setting minimum standards and harnessing unfettered unilateralism. With this purpose, the VCLT provided states with an ad hoc instrument, codified in Article 65,[95] that, however, remained a dead letter:[96]

> Procedure to be followed with respect to invalidity, termination, withdrawal from or suspension of the operation of a treaty:
>
> 1. A party which, under the provisions of the present Convention, invokes either a defect in its consent to be bound by a treaty or a ground for impeaching the validity of a treaty, terminating it, withdrawing from it

---

90 *See* Waldock, *supra* note 40, at 36 (draft Article 17).

91 *See* id. (draft Article 17(3)(a)(b)).

92 *See* id. (draft Article 17 (3)(c)).

93 *See* Kevin Widdows, *The Unilateral Denunciation of Treaties Containing No Denunciation Clause*, 53 BYIL 83 (1982).

94 VILLIGER, *supra* note 38, at 689; *see also* Helfer, *Terminating Treaties*, *supra* note 2, at 627–28.

95 VCLT art. 65 ("Procedure to be Followed with Respect to Invalidity, Termination, Withdrawal from or Suspension of the Operation of a Treaty").

96 *See* JAN KLABBERS, INTERNATIONAL LAW 70 (2017).

or suspending its operation, must notify the other parties of its claim. The notification shall indicate the measure proposed to be taken with respect to the treaty and the reasons therefor.

2. If, after the expiry of a period which, except in cases of special urgency, shall not be less than three months after the receipt of the notification, no party has raised any objection, the party making the notification may carry out in the manner provided in article 67 the measure which it has proposed.
3. If, however, objection has been raised by any other party, the parties shall seek a solution through the means indicated in Article 33 of the Charter of the United Nations.
4. Nothing in the foregoing paragraphs shall affect the rights or obligations of the parties under any provisions in force binding the parties with regard to the settlement of disputes.
5. Without prejudice to article 45, the fact that a State has not previously made the notification prescribed in paragraph 1 shall not prevent it from making such notification in answer to another party claiming performance of the treaty or alleging its violation.

The procedural mechanism of Article 65 of the VCLT[97] imposes a duty on the withdrawing state to communicate with its counterparts. If no objection is raised, the withdrawal can be completed within three months from the notification (unless extreme urgency requires a shorter time period). If objections are raised, parties have a duty to settle their dispute peacefully, in line with Article 33 of the UN Charter.[98] Whenever parties are not able to reach a settlement within one year from an objection to withdrawal, Article 66(b) of the VCLT provides for a conciliation procedure—regulated under the Annex to the Convention—that can be activated unilaterally by one of the contracting parties through the submission of a request to the UN Secretary-General.[99]

97 VCLT art. 65 ("Procedure to be followed with respect to invalidity, termination, withdrawal from or suspension of the operation of a treaty").

98 Article 33 of the UN Charter provides: "1. The parties to any dispute, the continuance of which is likely to endanger the maintenance of international peace and security, shall, first of all, seek a solution by negotiation, enquiry, mediation, conciliation, arbitration, judicial settlement, resort to regional agencies or arrangements, or other peaceful means of their own choice. 2. The Security Council shall, when it deems necessary, call upon the parties to settle their dispute by such means."

99 VCLT art. 66 ("Procedures for judicial settlement, arbitration and conciliation") provides: "If, under paragraph 3 of article 65, no solution has been reached within a period of 12 months following the date on which the objection was raised, the following procedures

During the U.N. Conference on the Law of Treaties, in 1968, member states debated whether to give binding force to the conciliation procedure. A diplomatic impasse on this issue generated a standstill in the VCLT negotiations, which was eventually resolved through a difficult compromise.[100] It was agreed that arbitral and judicial solutions would be permitted for disputes over conflicts of *jus cogens* norms under Article 66(a), while other disputes would be subject to a nonbinding default procedure under Article 66(b). Thus, the VCLT leaves open the risk of a persistent dispute between contracting parties.[101]

Procedural norms embedded in the VCLT have not so far been activated in states' practice. They were not meant to reflect customary legal practice with regard to withdrawal, as they sought to promote the progressive development of international law on the subject. This fact has been discussed both in international jurisprudence and scholarly debate.

In *Armed Activities on the Territory of Congo*, the ICJ wrote that Article 66 of the VCLT was not customarily followed.[102] Similarly, in Europe, in *Racke v. Hauptzollamt Mainz*, the Court of Justice of the European Communities noted that the procedural requirements laid down in Article 65 of the VCLT were not part of customary law.[103] In *Gabčikovo-Nagymaros*, the ICJ affirmed that the VCLT articles on procedural aspects of withdrawal did not codify existing customary law, though they involved procedural principles in international law grounded on the obligation of good faith in the execution of international

---

shall be followed: (a) any one of the parties to a dispute concerning the application or the interpretation of article 53 or 64 may, by a written application, submit it to the International Court of Justice for a decision unless the parties by common consent agree to submit the dispute to arbitration; (b) any one of the parties to a dispute concerning the application or the interpretation of any of the other articles in part V of the present Convention may set in motion the procedure specified in the Annex to the Convention by submitting a request to that effect to the Secretary-General of the United Nations."

100 *See* Shabtai Rosenne, *The Settlement of Treaty Disputes Under the Vienna Convention of 1969*, 31 HEIDELBERG J. INT'L L. 61 (1979).

101 *See* Annalisa Ciampi, *Invalidity and Termination of Treaties and Rules of Procedures*, *in* THE LAW OF TREATIES BEYOND THE VIENNA CONVENTION 362 (Enzo Cannizzaro ed., 2011).

102 *Armed Activities on the Territory of Congo* involved a procedural issue with regard to the ICJ's jurisdiction to settle disputes arising from the violation of *jus cogens* norms based on Article 66 of the VCLT. The Court eventually found that this provision could not provide a basis for jurisdiction. Armed Activities on the Territory of Congo (Democratic Republic of Congo v. Uganda), 2006 Judgment I.C.J. Reports 6, Feb. 3, 2006, p. 52, para. 125.

103 In *Racke v. Hauptzollamt Mainz*, the European Court of Justice assessed whether it was possible to suspend a cooperation agreement between parties with no notification or waiting period. A. Racke GmbH & Co v. Hauptzollamt Mainz, 1998 Judgment of the Court of Justice of the European Communities, C-162/96, Jun. 16, 1998, E.C.R. I-03655, p. 293, para. 59.

treaties.[104] In its decision, the Court recalled the reasoning in the *Advisory Opinion on the Interpretation of the Agreement of 25 March 1951 between the WHO and Egypt*, wherein it found:[105]

> Precisely what periods of time may be involved in the observance of the duties to consult and negotiate, and what period of notice of termination should be given, are matters which necessarily vary according to the requirements of the particular case. In principle, therefore, it is for the parties in each case to determine the length of those periods by consultation and negotiation in good faith.

Two scholarly views addressed the reasons for ignoring the VCLT procedures for settlement of treaty disputes. Robert Kolb wrote that states have preferred ad hoc negotiations and special arrangements on a case-by-case basis rather than the complex framework of the VCLT.[106] Mark Villiger believed that the VCLT created a deterrent effect that has discouraged states' diverging postures from evolving into legal disputes.[107] It is notable that withdrawal decisions have been rarely been objected to on legal grounds; more frequently, they have been objected to out of political opportunism.[108] In this regard, treaty secretariats play a crucial role in establishing a political dialogue among parties with the aim of resolving potential diplomatic *differendo*.[109] All this having been

---

104 In the *Gabčikovo Nagymaros Project* case, the ICJ addressed whether Hungary's notification of termination of its 1977 bilateral treaty with Czechoslovakia was premature because it was dated May 19, 1992, and was to take effect six days later on May 25, 1992. Gabčíkovo-Nagymaros Project (Hungary v. Slovakia), 1997 Judgment I.C.J. Reports 7, Sept. 25, 1997, p. 66, para. 109.

105 In the *Advisory Opinion on the Interpretation of the Agreement of 25 March 1951 Between the WHO and Egypt*, the Court addressed the issue of a possible transfer of the seat of a regional office of the World Health Organization (WHO), based in Alexandria, stating that the organization and Egypt were under a mutual obligation to consult and fulfill their obligations in good faith. *Interpretation of the Agreement of 25 March 1951 Between the WHO and Egypt*, 1980 Advisory Opinion 1. C. J. Reports, May 28, 1980, p. 96, para. 49.

106 *See* ROBERT KOLB, THE LAW OF TREATIES: AN INTRODUCTION 254–55 (2016) (testing how political solutions have continually overcome the VCLT procedure in disputes concerning withdrawal).

107 *See* MARK E. VILLIGER, COMMENTARY ON THE 1969 VIENNA CONVENTION ON THE LAW OF TREATIES 815 (2009).

108 In withdrawing from multilateral treaties, states have generally preferred to leave their hands untied rather than to follow the VCLT Article 65 procedure. *See* KLABBERS, *supra* note 96, at 70.

109 *See* Antonio Morelli, *Commentary to Article 42 of the Energy Charter Treaty*, *in* COMMENTARY ON THE ENERGY CHARTER TREATY (Raphael Leal-Arcas ed., 2018) (analyzing the role

said, inasmuch as Article 65 was framed to pave the way for progressive development of international law, the increasing invocation of withdrawal in states' practice could trigger a revival of its procedures.[110]

C. *Withdrawal in Domestic Law*

The rationales for international and domestic rules governing treaty-making are fundamentally different. Therefore, whether one analyzes withdrawal from an international or domestic legal perspective determines its features. In international law, withdrawal clauses aim to prescribe clear and objective rules to define the parties to a treaty on a particular date. In domestic law, withdrawal has a more political significance, since it concerns a matter of distribution of power among domestic political branches.[111]

Joining and leaving a treaty can be seen as two faces of the same coin. The *Second Report on the Law of Treaties* by Sir Humphrey Waldock[112] clarified that "the power to annul, terminate, withdraw from or suspend treaties, no less than the power to conclude treaties, forms part of the treaty-making power of the State." Since the VCLT uses a holistic approach in the definition of treaty making—one that takes into account both the expression and the revocation of states' consent—it tends to apply to withdrawal the same rules that govern the formation of an international agreement.[113]

In defining a procedural framework for withdrawal, the VCLT touches the matter of states' domestic competences but leaves unregulated most of their aspects, which can be dealt with through an analogical application of the rules regarding conclusion and entry into force of treaties.[114] Article 67 of the VCLT requires the executive, through the head of state or head of government, to provide written notification of withdrawal to the treaty depository.[115] However,

---

of the treaty secretariat established by the Energy Charter Treaty in providing administrative support and granting the necessary assistance to the contracting parties).

110 *See infra,* Chapter 6, Part I.A.iv. (analyzing the opportunity to use the procedural framework of VCLT Article 65, especially with regard to considering a notice period in withdrawal clauses).

111 *See* Laurence R. Helfer, *Treaty Exit and Intra-Branch Conflict at the Interface of International and Domestic Law, in* THE OXFORD HANDBOOK OF COMPARATIVE FOREIGN RELATIONS LAW (C.A. Bradley ed., 2019).

112 Waldock, *supra* note 40, at 85.

113 *See infra,* Chapter 6, Part II.A (exploring separation of powers as a way to enhance orderly withdrawal from international agreements).

114 The VCLT regulates in its Part III conclusion and entry into force of international treaties.

115 Article 67(1) of the VCLT ("Instruments for declaring invalid, terminating, withdrawing from or suspending the operation of a treaty") provides: "The notification provided for under article 65, paragraph 1, must be made in writing."

the VCLT is silent regarding internal authority to make a decision to withdraw from an international agreement, which is left to domestic law.

The debate within the ILC during the working sessions that led, in 1966, to the adoption and submission to the UN General Assembly of the draft articles on the law of treaties with commentaries, mainly covered legitimacy in treaty making with regard to joining international agreements; exiting them was overlooked. The 1963 *Second Report on the Law of Treaties* by Humphrey Waldock addressed, under draft Article 23, this topic. Grounded on the *acte contraire* principle,[116] it defined the treaty-terminating power as the opposite of the power to conclude. This approach was eventually embedded in the 1966 commentary to the draft articles on the law of treaties, which furthered a symmetrical procedure.[117] Therefore, based on the ILC's rulings, the rules for the authority to denounce should mirror those regarding the expression of states' consent.[118]

States' competences with respect to withdrawal have been addressed through two different doctrinal approaches. Some scholars recognize the sole authority of the executive to pull out of international agreements.[119] This view is that there is an overarching governmental power, the so-called *ius representationis omnimodae* typical of nineteenth-century diplomacy, which used to delegate foreign policy decisions exclusively to the executive power, as a legacy of monarchical practice in international relations.[120] Under this view,

116 The *acte contraire* principle is borrowed from French administrative law, which creates a symmetrical procedural that allows an act to be modified or abrogated only by following the same procedure used for its approval. *Mutatis mutandis*, this principle can be applied to international legal procedures for treaty entry and treaty exit.

117 The International Law Commission, in its commentary to Draft Article 63, recognizes that "the rule concerning evidence of authority to denounce, terminate, etc., should be analogous to that governing 'full powers' to express the consent of a State to be bound by a treaty." Draft Articles on the Law of Treaties with Commentaries, Adopted by the International Law Commission at its Eighteenth Session, *in U.N. Conference on the Law of Treaties, 1st & 2nd Sess., Vienna, 26 March–24 May 1968 and 9 April–22 May 1969*, at 83, U.N. Doc. A/CONF.39/11/Add.2 (1971).

118 *See* Waldock, *supra* note 40, at 85.

119 In the U.S. legal system, this doctrinal view is grounded on Article II, section 1 of the U.S. Constitution, which defines presidential prerogatives. *See* John C. Yoo, *Rejoinder: Treaties and Public Lawmaking: A Textual and Structural Defense of Non-Self-Execution*, 99 COLUM. L. REV. 2218, 2218 (1999); MICHAEL D. RAMSEY, THE CONSTITUTION'S TEXT IN FOREIGN AFFAIRS 158 (2007); Curtis A. Bradley, *Treaty Termination and Historical Gloss*, 92 TEX. L. REV. 773, 782 (2014). Judicially, this doctrine refers to a decision of the U.S. Supreme Court, *United States v. Curtis-Wright Export Corp.*, 299 U.S. 304 (1936).

120 *Jus representationis omnimodae* represents the general and potentially indefinite power in the hands of the head of state or government with regard to decision making in foreign policy.

the power to withdraw from international agreements is in only one hand and entails the unilateral decision of one political branch. This approach has been criticized because, if the executive of a global power decided to withdraw from most of the international commitments it is a party to, it might transform the entire post-World War II international order.[121] Indeed, based on a different scholarly approach, it would be more desirable to bolster the democratic legitimacy of maintaining or leaving international commitments by involving the legislative branch. Shared authority among domestic branches may facilitate more balanced decisions in foreign policy. If the same domestic powers involved in the formation of commitment through negotiation and ratification of international agreements were the ones determining the end of commitment, a symmetric process in treaty making would be created. This view advocates for a domestic opening of states' powers to foreign policy to reflect the modern globalized context in which countries operate.[122]

A comparative analysis of constitutional systems worldwide shows that most constitutions create an asymmetrical system for joining and leaving international agreements.[123] According to the findings of the Comparative Constitutions Project, more than 80% of the constitutions worldwide do not provide a legal framework for withdrawal.[124] Absent a domestic law otherwise, the executive has generally carried out this function. Some scholars and commentators found that withdrawal is considered a governmental power in most jurisdictions.[125] For instance, the US legal system is silent regarding withdrawal

---

121 *See* Harold H. Koh, The Trump Administration and International Law 49 (2018) (analyzing cases of unilateral presidential withdrawal of the United States from multilateral agreements); *see also* David Wolff, *Reasserting Its Constitutional Role: Congress' Power to Independently Terminate a Treaty*, 46 U. S.F. L. Rev. 953 (2012).

122 More symmetrical rules within a constitutional system may ultimately enhance democratization of the domestic approach to foreign policy. *See* Helfer, *supra* note 111.

123 *See infra*, Chapter 6, Part II.A.ii. (analyzing the role that the separation of powers in foreign policy can play in furthering orderly withdrawal from international agreements).

124 The Comparative Constitutions Project found that 43 of 190 constitutions currently in force worldwide contain provisions regulating treaty exit. The Comparative Constitutions Project is a leading comparative academic project that analyzes and quantifies information regarding domestic constitutions of every country since 1789. According to this study, 43 of the 190 constitutions currently in force provide for withdrawal, denunciation, or termination of international agreements. The information is available at http://comparativeconstitutionsproject.org/.

125 Pierre-Hugues Verdier and Mila Versteeg explored domestic regulation and practices related to withdrawal in 101 countries in the period between 1818 and 2013 and found that it was mostly an executive prerogative in every jurisdiction. *See* Pierre-Hugues Verdier & Mila Versteeg, *Separation of Powers, Treaty-Making, and Treaty Withdrawal: A Global Survey*, *in* The Oxford Handbook, *supra* note 111.

procedures, which are left to domestic practice. While the executive is entitled to make treaties, Article II, section 2 of the U.S. Constitution[126]—the so-called treaty clause—provides that Senate advice and consent is required to ratify international treaties.[127] Absent a constitutional provision on withdrawal, some commentators have upheld the executive power to withdraw due to the president's preeminent position in carrying out foreign affairs.[128] Others have affirmed that a president's power to withdraw from international agreements cannot be in conflict with the legislative branch.[129] In U.S. practice, originally, withdrawal occurred with legislative participation, either before or after a denunciation notification. However, since the Franklin D. Roosevelt administration, the practice of unilateral presidential withdrawal has increased significantly.[130]

The trend of constitutional silence related to withdrawal from international agreements has slightly declined since the 1970s.[131] Modern constitutionalism has paid increasing attention to foreign policy as it has become more and more relevant domestically. Some constitutions have included provisions that regulate domestic procedures for withdrawal that reflect the progressive inclusion of withdrawal clauses in modern treaty making[132] in line with Article 42 of the VCLT.[133]

---

126 U.S. CONST. art. II, § 2, cl. 2.

127 In the U.S. system, entering into an international treaty follows a constitutionally regulated procedure under which it must be approved by a two-thirds majority of the Senate and subsequently ratified by the president. This procedure is applicable only to international treaties, not to other categories of agreements such as executive agreements and political commitments. With regard to the latter, the executive power is broader and not subject to congressional approval. *See* RESTATEMENT (FOURTH) OF THE FOREIGN RELATIONS LAW OF THE UNITED STATES § 301 (1) (Am. Law Inst. 2018). The Restatement is a persuasive, though not binding, source. *See* Jean Galbraith, *Rejoining Treaties,* 106 VA. L. REV. 73, 81 (2020); *see also* ANTHONY S. WINER, MARY ANN E. ARCHER & LYONETTE LOUIS-JACQUES, INTERNATIONAL LAW LEGAL RESEARCH 242–43 (2013).

128 For an analysis of case law, see *United States v. Curtiss-Wright Export Corp.*, 299 U.S. 304 (1936). For doctrinal analysis, see John C. Yoo, *Rejoinder: Treaties and Public Lawmaking: A Textual and Structural Defense of Non-Self-Execution*, 99 COLUM. L. REV. 2218, 2242 (1999).

129 *See* Barry M. Goldwater, *Treaty Termination Is a Shared Power*, 65 ABA J. 198 (1978); *see also* James J. Moriarty, *Congressional Claims for Treaty Termination Powers in the Age of the Diminished Presidency*, 14 CONN. J. INT'L L. 123, 132 (1999).

130 *See infra,* Chapter 2, Part I.B.ii (focusing on the politicization of international commitments in the United States and its impact on the U.S. withdrawal trend).

131 The proportion of unilateral governmental denunciations, compared to the other political branches, went down from 89%, in the 1970s, to the current level of 72%. *See* Verdier & Versteeg, *supra* note 125.

132 *See supra,* Chapter 1, Part I.B. (analyzing the progressive inclusion of withdrawal clauses into international agreements).

133 Article 42(2) of the VCLT ("Validity and continuance in force of treaties") affirms that "[t]he termination of a treaty, its denunciation or the withdrawal of a party, may take place

Today, though only about 20% of constitutions in force worldwide regulate withdrawal, those that do mostly include participation of the legislative branch.[134] Some countries, such as Moldova,[135] require parliamentary authorization for pulling out of all international agreements; others, such as Estonia[136] and Spain,[137] require it only for agreements pertaining to enumerated subjects; and still others, such as Belarus,[138] provide a programmatic framework for withdrawal that is further regulated through ad hoc statutes or administrative rules. Those examples indicate that there is an increasing trend of regulation of withdrawal procedures embedded in the last generation of constitutionalism, which defined competences of state's powers in treaty exit.[139] In this way, states' will in foreign policy is subject to procedures in domestic constitutions to regulate internal competences on withdrawal.

The illegitimacy of exit procedures that are contrary to domestic regulation has been largely overlooked in the scholarly debate. Nonetheless, an increasing states' practice in denouncing international treaties brought attention to this issue, which has been addressed in judicial decisions.[140] Based on Article 46 of the VCLT, states carry a heavy burden in invalidating their consent to be bound by an agreement, which can occur only in cases of manifest violation of

---

only as a result of the application of the provisions of the treaty or of the present Convention. The same rule applies to suspension of the operation of a treaty."

134 Among the 43 constitutions that regulate withdrawal, 39 provide that the authority to withdraw from an international agreement requires the participation of the legislative branch. The information is available at http://comparativeconstitutionsproject.org/.

135 CONSTITUŢIA REPUBLICII MOLDOVA [CONSTITUTION OF MOLDOVA], Aug. 27, 1994, tit. III, ch. IV, § 1(66).

136 EESTI VABARIIGI PÕHISEADUS [CONSTITUTION OF ESTONIA], Jun. 26, 1992, ch. IX, art. 121 (listing, among the subject matters of treaties that require parliamentary approval, treaties that alter state border; treaties that require the passage, amendment or repeal of domestic laws; related to membership into international organizations; related to military or proprietary obligations).

137 Articles 94(1) and 96(2) of the 1978 Spanish Constitution provide that withdrawal requires parliamentary approval in the case of treaties related to political or military matters, fundamental rights, financial duties, and legislative amendments. CONSTITUCIÓN ESPAÑOLA [CONSTITUTION OF SPAIN], Dec. 27, 1987.

138 KANSTYTUCYJA RESPUBLIKI BIELARUŚ [CONSTITUTION OF THE REPUBLIC OF BELARUS], Mar. 15, 1994, ch. 4, art. 97 (defining the powers of Parliament).

139 *See* Helfer, *supra* note 111 (analyzing domestic rules governing withdrawal from international agreements, based on the Comparative Constitutions project, and exploring which actors have the power to denounce them).

140 *See infra*, Chapter 6, Part II.A.i. (analyzing judicial decisions concerning separation of powers in withdrawal decisions).

a domestic rule of fundamental importance.[141] Though this provision applies only to the act of joining a treaty, its rationale can also be used with regard to withdrawal.[142] This could lead to a paradoxical legal situation in which a state may denounce a treaty, ending its status as a treaty party, in contravention of its domestic obligations. Therefore, even if withdrawal produces its intended effects internationally, it could have no effects domestically.[143]

D. *The Limits of Legal Formalism and the Way Forward*

The traditional methodology for approaching the international law of treaties, grounded on the application of the VCLT, reveals some gaps in treaty making and maintenance. To have an integrated approach to withdrawal, it is important to consider the conditions that lead countries to exit international treaties and also to identify the conditions necessary to maintain states' commitment. The methodological and practical concerns faced by international lawyers working to create a framework for withdrawal clauses entail not only legal but also political, economic, and sociological considerations.

The goal of the VCLT, at the time of its adoption, was to provide a simple, uniform set of international rules applicable to a broad range of international treaties. During its working sessions on the law of treaties, the ILC was primarily influenced by the positivist approach that had shaped international law since the mid-nineteenth century. Based on the analogy between treaties and contracts, the international legal system was conceived in a way similar to domestic contract law.[144] Since the rise of multilateralism, and especially

141 Article 46 of the VCLT ("Provisions of internal law regarding competence to conclude treaties") provides: "1. A State may not invoke the fact that its consent to be bound by a treaty has been expressed in violation of a provision of its internal law regarding competence to conclude treaties as invalidating its consent unless that violation was manifest and concerned a rule of its internal law of fundamental importance. 2. A violation is manifest if it would be objectively evident to any State conducting itself in the matter in accordance with normal practice and in good faith."

142 *See* Helfer, *supra* note 111; *see also* Hannah Woolaver, *State Engagement with Treaties: Interactions Between International and Domestic Law*, *in* The Oxford Handbook of Comparative Foreign Relations Law (C.A. Bradley ed., 2019).

143 Laurence Helfer proposed a categorization of conflicts that can arise due to differences in how international and domestic law regulate withdrawal. *See* Helfer, *supra* note 111.

144 The international law of treaties reflected the influence of the Romano-Germanic legal culture in the international legal system. *See* Hirsch Lauterpacht, Private Law Sources and Analogies of International Law, 155 (1927); *see also* Hersch Lauterpacht, The Function of Law in the International Community 423 (2011) (analyzing the rise and evolution of a legal power beyond states, from a purely contractual to an objective basis). *But see* Heinrich Triepel, International Law and National Law 26 (1899) (identifying a dichotomy between treaty-law and treaty-contract; in treaty-law the individual will

with the advent of new countries in the international community as a result of postcolonialism, a new paradigm became predominant in the treaty-making process, which rendered the previous domestic-based approach obsolete.[145] Beyond the contract-based approach, international treaties, being legal instruments to regulate the relationships of a global community, resulted from organizational and transactional needs.[146]

As its main goal was to produce a restatement based on existing international treaty law, the VCLT was not intended to encapsulate progressive developments in law that were already occurring. The formalism and uniformity fostered through the VCLT seem out of step with the plurality of instruments and practices in modern treaty law.[147] Even if the formalistic approach is still very pertinent when it comes to litigation, government officials, international bureaucrats, and diplomats found it too academic to be workable. Especially in modern times, in a context of extremely rapid changes, innovation and flexibility are core elements in dealing with international agreements.[148]

International lawyers face the challenge of finding appropriate solutions to the rapidly changing dynamics of negotiating and implementing international treaties.[149] With increasing diversity in each functional area, negotiations of international agreements have come to rely on approaches from various disciplines to respond to different problems. Even though topics and strategies from the different fields could be treated at "separate tables," international negotiations have taken an increasingly cross-cutting approach, and this comprehensive perspective is reflected in the structure of modern treaties and regimes.[150]

---

merges in the common will of the parties, whereas in treaty-contract the individual will remains separate).

145 *See* GUYORA BINDER, TREATY CONFLICT AND POLITICAL CONTRADICTION: THE DIALECTIC OF DUPLICITY 27 (1988); *see also* MARIO TOSCANO, THE HISTORY OF TREATIES AND INTERNATIONAL POLITICS 50 (1966).

146 *See* David Kennedy, *The Move to Institutions*, 8 CARDOZO L. REV. 841, 956 (1987).

147 *See* DOUGLAS M. JOHNSTON, CONSENT AND COMMITMENT IN THE WORLD COMMUNITY: THE CLASSIFICATION AND ANALYSIS OF INTERNATIONAL INSTRUMENTS 46–47 (1997).

148 *See* id. (analyzing the limits of the VCLT in addressing the complexity of the modern international law of treaties).

149 *See* id. at 50 (reconstructing a taxonomy in international law of treaties to provide a classification based on explanatory, predictive, and heuristic methods).

150 *See generally* GABRIEL A. ALMOND, A DISCIPLINE DIVIDED: SCHOOLS AND SECTS IN POLITICAL SCIENCE (1990) (discussing specialists in law and politics sitting at "different tables"); Keith E. Whittington et al., *Overview of Law and Politics: The Study of Law and Politics*, in THE OXFORD HANDBOOK OF POLITICAL SCIENCE 241 (Robert E. Godin ed., 2011) (discussing the scholarly community's engagement in different approaches in law and politics in various disciplines).

To develop an integrated theory in international law to understand how withdrawal operates, it is important to study the interconnections between different sources that have an impact on the international legal system—not only law, but also politics, economics and sociology—and examine the way they have been shaping international agreements.[151] Indeed, as noted by Phillip Allott, a combination of the two spheres of legal and extra-legal settings is possible, despite endemic contradictions.[152] Therefore, the combination of law with other sources determines new balances in the law of treaties. In other words, it may be preferable to envision these fields as overlapping spheres, instead of separate and contiguous subjects.[153]

The impact of international legal theory through the years shows that not only has international law served as an expression of political ideology, it has also functioned as a vehicle for shaping political outlooks.[154] Whether the international order is still a self-contained system is questionable, in light of the evolution of the international law of treaties through commitment and compliance theory, along with the increasing plurality of subjects involved. Only by understanding the forces behind the international law of treaties—commitment and compliance—is it possible to identify the rules of the game concerning withdrawal, which may serve sovereign interests better than a realist anarchy to improve treaty making and treaty maintenance.

151 *See* Martin M. Shapiro, *Law and Politics: The Problem of Boundaries*, in The Oxford Handbook of Law And Politics 767 (Gregory A. Caldeira, R. Daniel Kelemen & Keith Whittington eds., 2008) (on political scientists' approach to legal doctrine); *see generally* Martti Koskenniemi, *The Politics of International Law*, 1 EJIL 4, 12–13 (1990); *see also* Alasdair MacIntyre, *The Indispensability of Political Theory*, in The Nature of Political Theory 19–33 (David Miller & Larry Siedentop eds., 1983).

152 *See* Phillip Allott, *Language, Method and the Nature of International Law*, 45 BYIL 79, 123–25 (1971).

153 *See* Shapiro, *supra* note 151, at 767 (analyzing the "law and . . ." movements that have arisen in recent years).

154 *See* Whittington et al., *supra* note 150; *see also* David Trubek & Alvaro Santos, The New Law and Economic Development : A Critical Appraisal (2006).

CHAPTER 2

Conceptualizing Withdrawal

> "Unless commitment is made, there are only promises and hopes; but no plans."
>
> PETER F. DRUCKER

Introduction

This chapter conceptualizes withdrawal on the basis of three pillars: (a) commitment and compliance; (b) risk management; and (c) the principle of *pacta sunt servanda*. First, it problematizes the current gap in the literature on commitment and compliance, reconstructing endogenous issues in treaty-making and treaty-maintenance processes. International scholars and policy makers have mostly focused on molding states' behavior through compliance—a way of furthering conformity or identity between an actor's behavior and a given rule.[1] Nonetheless, they have overlooked the salience to international agreements of commitment, which secures engagement to cooperation with respect to a given functional area or a given obligation. The progressive recourse to nonbinding obligations diluted the salience of commitment, generating politicized decisions to enter and to exit international agreements.

This chapter also understands withdrawal under the lens of risk management. Every multilateral agreement is inherently risky because it strikes a balance between domestic needs and international prerogatives that is directly proportional to the degree of commitment being undertaken.[2] From this perspective, withdrawal clauses represent an *extrema ratio*—last resort—in risk management that are to be used when a contracting party is unwilling or unable to express its needs adequately within the framework of the treaty it joined.

---

1 *See generally* ABRAM CHAYES & ANTONIA HANDLER CHAYES, THE NEW SOVEREIGNTY: COMPLIANCE WITH INTERNATIONAL REGULATORY AGREEMENTS (1995); *see also* Abram Chayes et al., *Managing Compliance: A Comparative Perspective, in* ENGAGING COUNTRIES: STRENGTHENING COMPLIANCE WITH INTERNATIONAL ENVIRONMENTAL ACCORDS, 39, 43 (Edith Brown Weiss & Harold K. Jacobson eds., 2000); Kal Rustiala, Compliance and Effectiveness in International Regulatory Cooperation, 32 CASE W. RES. J. INT'L L. 387, 391 (2000); Lisa L. Martin, *Compliance or Effectiveness? Assessing the Reach (and Limits) of Treaty-Making, in* THE OXFORD GUIDE TO TREATIES 89 (Duncan B. Hollis ed., 2nd ed., 2020).

2 *See* RICHARD B. BILDER, MANAGING THE RISK OF INTERNATIONAL AGREEMENT (1981).

 | DOI: 10.1163/9789004467644_003

Eventually, this chapter analyzes the ways withdrawal may ultimately be a noncooperative process, notwithstanding its legality. Withdrawal clauses regulate circumstances under which states can effectively pull out of an international agreement while remaining in compliance with their international obligations.[3] Even though they authorize a lawful act *de jure*, they can trigger noncooperative outcomes de facto. Good-faith principles guide or at least should guide states' behavior in treaty making and treaty maintenance.[4] Such principles can be used as indicators to test the cooperativeness of a state's exercise of its right to withdraw. The lack of good faith in a withdrawal from an international agreement is directly proportional to the politicization of the decision to pull out. Whenever the driving force behind the decision to pull out is political opportunism, there may be an abuse of withdrawal. This was particularly relevant in the years of the Cold War, when withdrawal was used as an instrument for geopolitical strategies, as well as in modern times, when withdrawal responds to domestic politicization of international issues. States, as parties to international agreements, face, not a dilemma of choosing between cooperate or breach, but rather a "trilemma"—choosing between compliance, breach, and withdrawal. From this perspective, withdrawal may end up being a legitimate instrument for noncooperation in the international legal order, contrary to the principle of *pacta sunt servanda*.[5]

I. Analyzing Withdrawal through the Lens of Commitment and Compliance in International Treaties

This section seeks to conceptualize withdrawal from multilateral treaties through the lens of states' commitment and compliance. The result is a roadmap for scholars and policy makers defining the architecture of withdrawal and identifying the pillars that support commitment to international agreements. Historically, the literature has focused more on whether countries comply with international agreements than on examining the circumstances necessary to maintain states' commitment. Identifying that doctrinal gap and addressing it

---

3 *See* Herbert W. Briggs, *Unilateral Denunciation of Treaties: The Vienna Convention and the International Court of Justice*, 68 AJIL 51 (1974); *see also* Laurence R. Helfer, *Terminating Treaties*, in THE OXFORD GUIDE TO TREATIES, *supra* note 1, at 624.

4 *See* RONALD DWORKIN, TAKING RIGHTS SERIOUSLY 25 (1977); *see also* Robert Kolb, *Apercus sur la Bonne Foi en Droit International Public*, 54 RHDI 1, 7 (2001).

5 *See* Laurence R. Helfer, *Exiting Treaties*, 91 VA. L. REV. 1579, 1611 (2005); *see also* Barbara Koremenos & Allison Nau, *Exit, No Exit*, 81 DUKE J. COMP. & INT'L. L. 81, 100 (2010) (assessing the noncooperative features of withdrawal).

allows to understand the factors that give rise to long-term commitments and outline the way ahead for the treaty-making process and treaty maintenance.

When states enter an international agreement, they do not renounce their sovereignty but rather exercise it. This view has been enshrined in international jurisprudence since the *Wimbledon* case from the Permanent Court of International Justice (PCIJ),[6] which affirmed that only sovereign entities can accede to international agreements. However, from a state's perspective, entering an international agreement entails risk management considerations. When entering an international agreement, a state faces two major risks: the risk related to the endemic uncertainty of the treaty and the risk that other parties may not perform or may render a performance less valuable than promised. The first risk is related to the negotiation phases, when states cannot clearly see the real scope of the obligations to be undertaken or the risks that will be at stake during the life of the treaty.[7] The second risk is related to a lack of confidence that another nation will not indulge in noncooperative behavior, which often represents a major obstacle for reaching and maintaining an international agreement.[8]

A state entering into an international agreement can seek protection against these risks through two different strategies: first, it can reduce its own vulnerability related to future uncertainty; second, it can increase the probability that its counterparts will perform their treaty obligations.[9] States have addressed these goals with an approach based on commitment and compliance. The evolution of negotiating techniques led to recourse to more and more informal legal instruments to overcome particular states' complaints, facilitating the achievement of a global agreement while loosening the agreement's grip on commitment.

This part defines and analyzes the evolution of commitment and compliance as the two main forces underlying the law of the treaties. The most

---

6 *See generally* S. S. Wimbledon, 1923 P.C.I.J. (ser. A) No. 1 (Aug. 17). Nonetheless, transnational non-state actors have progressively influenced, directly or indirectly, the international treaty-making process. *See* Jose E. Alvarez, *The Return of the State*, 20 MINN. J. INT'L L. 223, 224–231 (2011).

7 The consequences of the implementation of the agreement ex post create a burden that was not necessarily foreseeable ex ante.

8 Risk of noncooperative behaviors is present in very different areas, including arms control, peace agreements and armistices, nuclear nonproliferation agreements, and climate change agreements. *See* BILDER, *supra* note 2, at 106–07.

9 *See* Philip B. Heymann, *The Problem of Coordination: Bargaining and Rules*, 86 HARV. L. REV. 797, 812 (1973) (analyzing approaches to control performance risk with regard to nonperformance).

recent trend in treaty making has been to neglect the importance of commitment, which has generated an imbalance between the two forces during the phase of treaty maintenance. This imbalance lies at the heart of the problem of withdrawal, which can be seen as a way for states to recant what they had committed to. Rethinking the interplay of commitment and compliance in international law can help fill the knowledge gap related to withdrawal and enhance the quality of policy making.

A. *Shifting Balances from Compliance to Commitment in Times of Withdrawal*

Modern techniques to deal with risk in international agreements have evolved through commitment and compliance strategies. This process relies on a plurality of different elements and exogenous forces that go beyond the traditional contract-based approach taken by the Vienna Convention on the Law of the Treaties (VCLT) of 1969.[10] Political and economic factors, along with diplomatic pressures and public opinion, have been shaping treaty-making and treaty-maintenance strategy in a way that enhances the effectiveness of international agreements. Effectiveness lies in the contribution of the treaty to solving the underlying problems that the treaty seeks to address.[11] Effectiveness is measured by compliance.[12] This is a critical tool to ensure the implementation of an agreement while harnessing the behavior of the contracting parties.

Commitment and compliance refer to a state of conformity between the behavior of an actor and a given obligation. They can be pictured as a fluid process that shifts from the international to the domestic level. At the international level, commitment and compliance are related to states' obligations embedded in the agreement. At the domestic level, they are related to the implementation of domestic norms and policies. Therefore, in order to understand how commitment and compliance have evolved over time, it is important to understand the form underlying the obligations that the deal requires; to identify the actors involved in the functional area of the deal and the process it triggers.[13] Political and scholarly debates have focused on compliance, overlooking obedience through commitment.

---

10 Vienna Convention on the Law of Treaties, May 23, 1969 1155 U.N.T.S. 331, 8 I.L.M. 679 (1969).

11 *See* Martin, *supra* note 1, at 89 (criticizing existing scholarship on the law of treaties for never focusing on effectiveness).

12 *See* id. (analyzing compliance with international treaties through the lens of effectiveness).

13 *See* Richard B. Bilder, *Beyond Compliance: Helping Nations Cooperate*, *in* COMMITMENT AND COMPLIANCE: THE ROLE OF NON-BINDING NORMS IN THE INTERNATIONAL LEGAL SYSTEM 65–73 (Dana Shelton ed., 2003) (analyzing the legal standards for compliance).

In the face of a trend toward withdrawal, it is possible to challenge the methodology that has focused on treaty making and treaty maintenance based on compliance and shift the focus to commitment. Commitment to international agreements generated a backlash against what they were trying to secure. As international issues became progressively more influential in domestic politic agenda, these topics inevitably became politicized despite their highly technical nature.

i. Commitment

Commitment represents the will to undertake a credible pledge to a particular policy stance. It mirrors the obligations embedded within the text of the treaty and the expected compliant behavior of each state. Commitment, increasingly more politicized, has evolved in such a way that its legal significance has been diluted. This evolution has exposed international treaties to withdrawal.

Commitment crystallizes a shared ground of obligations that aims to have all contracting parties on board with regard to the subject matter under negotiation. International legal scholarship has mainly focused on commitment with regard to the binary choice between legal and political commitments. Whereas the former gives rise to international agreements that impose legal obligations, the latter creates only a political pledge.[14]

Commitment can be described as contracting parties' "lowest common denominator," which allows the formation of a negotiated common legal ground.[15] Translating a political commitment into a legal commitment communicates to the international community the seriousness of the position of each country with regard to the functional area covered by the agreement.[16] This has a direct impact on the behavior of each state and consequences with regard to states' responsibilities.[17]

---

14 *See generally* Timothy Meyer, *Alternatives to Treaty-making: Informal Agreements, in* The Oxford Guide to Treaties, *supra* note 1, at 59; *see also* Wolfgang H. Reincke & Jan Martin Witte, *Challenges to the International Legal System Interdependence, Globalization, and Sovereignty: The Role of Non-binding International Legal Accords, in* Commitment and Compliance, *supra* note 13, at 75; Christine Chinkin, *Normative Development in the International Legal System, in* Commitment and Compliance, *supra* note 13, at 21.

15 *See* Bilder, *supra* note 2, at 64.

16 Commitment represents a crucial factor in determining States' policies in specific functional areas related to the subject matter of the agreement. *See* Beth A. Simmons, *International Law and State Behavior: Commitment and Compliance in International Monetary Affairs*, 94 Am. Pol. Sci. Rev. 4, 819–35 (2000).

17 *See* Robert Howse & Ruti Teitel, *Beyond Compliance: Rethinking Why International Law Really Matters*, in 1 Global Pol'y 2, 127, 133 (2010).

Treaties are instruments that embrace legal commitments, as they are designed to regulate states' pledges, encouraging adherence to them.[18] By choosing legal rather than political commitment, states signal a higher degree of credibility of their pledge. For instance, during the time of the Helsinki Accords[19] for security and cooperation in Europe during the Cold War, the Soviet Union's compliance with its commitments was minimal. Its noncompliance delegitimized the Soviet bloc's behavior because the Soviet bloc had committed to the human rights norms embedded in the Accords, so it could no longer dismiss them as a vehicle for capitalist ideology.[20]

With regard to politically sensitive topics, progressive codification of certain functional areas has furthered the achievement of greater commitments. For instance, in the human rights and environmental fields, political commitments, generally expressed through declarations, have evolved into legal agreements.[21] This process has helped contracting parties progressively embrace the content of norms. International regimes' systems crystallized this trend, creating an initial commitment to a general framework agreement while leaving detailed regulation to future protocols. Almost all countries have signed the Chemical Weapons Convention,[22] the Convention on Biological Diversity,[23] and the United Nations Framework Convention on Climate Change (UNFCCC).[24] If national engagement originally was a reaction to increasing international diplomatic and public pressure, over time, these instruments have deeply shaped states' behaviors.[25]

---

18 *See generally* Kenneth Abbott & Duncan Snidal, *Hard and Soft Law in International Governance*, 54 INT'L ORG. 3, 421–56 (2000).

19 The Helsinki Accords grew out of the final act of the Conference on Security and Cooperation in Europe to improve relations between the two blocs during the Cold War. *See* Conference on Security and Cooperation in Europe: Final Act, Aug. 1975, *reprinted in* 73 DEP'T STATE BULL. 323 (1975), *in* 14 INT'L L. MATERIALS 1292 (1975), and *in* 13 VAND. J. TRANSNAT'L L. 575 (1980).

20 *See* DANIEL C. THOMAS, THE HELSINKI EFFECT: INTERNATIONAL NORMS, HUMAN RIGHTS AND THE DEMISE OF COMMUNISM (2001).

21 *See* Douglass Cassell, *Inter-American Human Rights Law, Soft and Hard,* in COMMITMENT AND COMPLIANCE, *supra* note 13, at 393, 395 (analyzing the process of hardening political commitments into binding rules).

22 Convention on the Prohibition of the Development, Production, Stockpiling and Use of Chemical Weapons and on their Destructions, September 3, 1992, 1975 U.N.T.S. 45.

23 Convention on Biological Diversity, June 5, 1992 1760 U.N.T.S. 79.

24 United Nations Framework Convention on Climate Change, May 9, 1992 1771 U.N.T.S. 107.

25 This system fosters cooperation and enhances states' commitments. First, it fosters a learning process throughout governments and other all relevant actors. Second, it seeks to corroborate an environment for the implementation and maintenance of the agreement. *See* Abram Chayes, Antonia Handler Chayes & Ronald B. Mitchell, *Managing Compliance:*

Moreover, commitment ties each contracting party's interests to the interests of others. Potential costs may play a crucial role in reinforcing the value of commitment.[26] Once the agreement is made, it is costly for a government to renege on it because there are legal, economic and reputational consequences. Legal commitments are crucial to domestic policy choices, which allow sovereign states to establish or reestablish their credibility in specific functional areas. In the period after the adoption of the agreement, each member state follows the steps necessary for the implementation of the agreement. In many cases, this process entails building legal and bureaucratic capacity with respect to regime characteristics. In the human rights and environmental fields, it allows for the consolidation of a culture around sensitive topics. In the field of economics, especially in countries that are not yet fully stabilized and going through a liberalization process, commitment represents an important step toward achieving and maintaining a specific economic or financial line. For instance, countries joining the International Monetary Fund (IMF) Articles of Agreements[27] have given a clear message to the international community and to international markets that they are willing to maintain credibility with regard to liberalization.[28]

Negotiations for international deals reflect a continuous struggle to find proper forms for states' commitments. The legal form of international agreements is a core topic in the debate about international negotiations.[29] The evolution of the treaty-making process expanded the scope of negotiating to cope with global issues.[30] In practice, states' perceptions of risk have progressively diluted the salience of commitment in international agreements as

---

A Comparative Perspective, in ENGAGING COUNTRIES: STRENGTHENING COMPLIANCE WITH INTERNATIONAL ENVIRONMENTAL ACCORDS, 39, 42 (Edith Brown Weiss & Harold K. Jacobson eds., 2000); DAVID B. HUNTER, JAMES SALZMAN & DURWOOD ZAELKE, INTERNATIONAL ENVIRONMENTAL LAW AND POLICY 400 (2011).

26 The acceptance of treaty obligations defines a behavioral path for parties to an international agreement that becomes costly for governments to violate. *See* Lisa L. Martin, *Credibility, Costs, and Institutions: Cooperation on Economic Sanctions*, 45 WORLD POL. 3, 406–32 (1993).

27 Articles of Agreement of the International Monetary Fund (Bretton Woods Agreement), Dec. 27, 1945 2 U.N.T.S. 39.

28 *See* Beth A. Simmons, *International law and State Behavior: Commitment and Compliance in International Monetary Affairs*, 94 AM. POL. SCI. REV. 4, 819–35 (2000).

29 *See* BILDER, *supra* note 2, at 17–18 (pointing out sovereign strategies to deal with risk and securing necessary assurances in international negotiations); *see also* Justin Worland, *What to Know About the Historic 'Paris Agreement' on Climate Change*, TIME (Dec. 12, 2015), http://time.com/4146764/paris-agreement-climate-cop-21.

30 *See infra*, Chapter 3, Part I.B.iii (analyzing the evolution of treaty negotiations and their impact on treaty making and treaty maintenance).

states have shifted from binding to nonbinding, or political, obligations and set goals that entail only minimal change. The shift to nonbinding obligations has affected treaty-making techniques by diluting the salience of commitment with recourse to "squishy" legal forms. Setting goals requiring only minimal change results in states tending to join commitments more suitable to their risk perception or, possibly, that they are already in compliance with; either way, the impact on their conduct is limited.[31]

Historically, scholarly debate has focused on testing how international agreements can shape states' conduct. International scholars have observed whether and to what extent sovereign states can align their behavioral patterns to the international commitments to which they agreed.[32] From this perspective, commitment became an endogenous variable used to test expectations about future compliance and lost its original significance.[33] The unintended consequence of treaty models primarily grounded on diluted forms of commitment mirrors the emergence of withdrawal.

ii. Compliance

Compliance theories monitor and study how and to what extent actors bound by a rule actually follow it.[34] The conceptual and, more recently, empirical study of compliance has rapidly emerged as a subfield of international law, so much so that scholars believe it represents one of the core criteria grounding the general theory of international law.[35] The international literature has begun to define new methodological and epistemological tenets underpinning the maintenance of international multilateral agreements through compliance theory.[36]

---

31 *See infra,* Chapter 2, Part I.B.i (defining the salience of commitment in the treaty-making process).

32 *See* Harold Hongju Koh, *Why Do Nations Obey International Law?*, 106 YALE L.J. 2599, 2603 (1997) (affirming that, like most laws, international rules are rarely enforced but usually obeyed).

33 International scholars focused on the evidence that legal commitment has a systematic effect on states' behavior. *See* GEORGE DOWNS & DAVID M. ROCKE. OPTIMAL IMPERFECTION? DOMESTIC UNCERTAINTY AND INSTITUTIONS IN INTERNATIONAL RELATIONS (1995).

34 If the question of why, how, and to what extent actors comply with rules has been overlooked at the domestic level as scholars have focused on the behavioral effects of rules, international scholars have systematized theories on compliance, providing conceptual and empirical support to their theses. *See* Howse & Teitel, *supra* note 17, at 128–29.

35 *See* William C. Bradford, *International Legal Compliance: An Annotated Bibliography*, 30 N.C.J. INT'L L. & COM. REG. 379 (2004); *see also* Andrew T. Guzman, *A Compliance-based Theory of International Law*, 90 CAL. L. REV. 1823, 1826 (2002).

36 *See* Martti Koskenniemi, *The Politics of International Law – 20 Years Later*, 20 EJIL 7, 7–19 (2009).

Compliance is the way to test states' commitments. It is a reflection of rational incentives for legal change in domestic systems as a consequence of commitment to an international agreement. States have developed structures in international agreements tailored to ease compliance or, at least, to make it seem like the best available option. From this perspective, compliance entails the traditional methodological concern in international law with creating a framework to harness politics. Increasing the probability that the other party will perform is a technique to protect against the risk of noncompliance or inadequate compliance by other contracting parties.[37]

Compliance usually represents a necessary, but not sufficient, precondition for the effectiveness of an international treaty.[38] Indeed, a treaty can be legally effective without being truly effective in solving the problem it addresses. On the one hand, if a treaty has minimal commitment to substantive obligations, even if there is high compliance the impact on the underlying problem will not be substantial. On the other hand, a treaty may have such great commitment to substantive obligations that even if the parties to it comply only minimally, their impact on solutions to the problem will be exponentially greater.[39]

Forms of compliance have evolved in a way that seeks to ease treaty maintenance through a managerial approach. The managerial approach to compliance uses a cooperative problem-solving methodology tailored to eliminate or mitigate problems related to the functional areas of the agreement.[40] Abram Chayes wrote that such an approach is grounded in three factors: (a) as treaties are based on the consent of their contracting parties—thus embedding national interests—states will likely respect them; (b) with the support of organizational structures and procedures, it is possible to increase flexibility and political consensus; and (c) furthering an efficiency-based rationale for future compliance, states will more likely comply with the dynamics of a regime they belong to.[41]

---

37 Compliance with international law is conditional on parties' behavior. *See* Philip B. Heymann, *The Problem of Coordination: Bargaining and Rules*, 86 Harv. L. Rev. 797, 812 (1973) (analyzing approaches in managing risk of performance).

38 To understand how international treaties work, international scholars have focused on effectiveness while measuring their impact based on compliance. *See* Hunter, Salzman & Zaelke, *supra* note 25, at 362; *see also* Martin, *supra* note 1, at 89.

39 *See* Hunter, Salzman & Zaelke, *supra* note 25, at 362.

40 *See infra,* Chapter 3, Part i.B.iii (exploring the managerial approach in treaty making under the lens of international legal theory).

41 *See infra,* Chapter 2, Part i.B.i (analyzing compliance strategies in the context of international regimes); *see generally* Chayes & Chayes, *supra* note 1.

This approach is a way of securing, long-term, states' self-interests through a cyclical process grounded in raising awareness, promoting and monitoring implementation, providing assistance, and measuring and reporting performances.[42] It promotes trust amongst contracting parties while reducing risk. Based on the assumption that all treaty members are engaged in achieving a common aim, cooperation is grounded in a transparent system that allows monitoring parties' behaviors and pursuing long-term goals while promoting awareness in the international community.[43] A transparent system that provides information about the compliance rate of each member reassures all contracting parties. For instance, in the field of arms control, a system that guarantees that other parties have not deployed nuclear weapons is key to guaranteeing that each party is credibly following the rules. In turn, a transparent system promotes deterrence by exposing noncooperative behaviors to the judgment of public opinion and the negative reaction of the international community.[44]

As Abram Chayes pointed out, very rarely does noncompliance reflect calculated domestic decisions; rather, its causes are complex and varied. Deliberate treaty violations exceptions rather than the rule.[45] This observation echoes Louis Henkin's famous statement about compliance: "almost all nations observe almost all of their obligations almost all of the time."[46]

B. *Withdrawal and Commitment: Two Sides of the Same Coin*

Both international legal theory and international relations scholarship have looked at the international law of treaties in light of the dichotomy between cooperative and noncooperative behaviors or, in other words, between compliance and breach. Nonetheless, existing scholarship has failed to explain the inverse relationship between withdrawal and commitment. As withdrawal can be used in different ways, commitment defines the degree of cooperation of the denouncing state. The following subsections explore the significance of commitment in light of withdrawal, and portray its evolution through progressive politicization to understand the conditions that make states decide to pull out of an agreement it joined.

---

42 *See* Hunter, Salzman & Zaelke, *supra* note 25, at 388.

43 *See* Chayes, Chayes & Mitchell, *supra* note 25, at 49.

44 The compliance model embedded in most multilateral agreements is based on the assumption that a party that wants to comply needs reassurance. Therefore, every party will comply as long as others do. *See* Chayes, Chayes & Mitchell, *supra* note 25, at 44–45.

45 *See* id. at 41.

46 *See* Louis Henkin, How Nations Behave 47 (1979).

i. The Significance of Commitment

Throughout the evolution of treaty making, commitment has evolved in a way that embraces more and more members to international agreements over time. New forms of commitment have arisen in a search to achieve consensus about sensitive global topics rather than deadlocked negotiations.[47]

The most effective way to ensure that state parties to an agreement perform their obligations is to make sure the agreement is perceived as being in the interests of all parties so each of them will voluntarily abide by it.[48] International legal theory has focused on different strategies for building an analytical framework around states' behavior, debating whether compliance with international treaties is volitional or non-volitional. The dichotomies and interactions between different schools mirror legal drafting techniques, as each perspective has tried to secure different strategies and results.[49]

As long as we consider international agreements voluntary choices, commitment and compliance will be the result of willingness to embrace and adapt to behavioral patterns required by the outcome of treaty negotiations.[50] In the constructivist and liberal views, international agents are generally willing to comply with international agreements but sometimes are unable to do so.[51] There are influences on states' behavior that go beyond a rational assessment of costs and benefits. States may perceive the agreement as illegitimate or ambiguous or too complex. Commitment and compliance are mainly reliant on each actor's knowledge, institutions, and financial recourses. Promotion of and assistance with compliance is key in securing the effectiveness of the agreement.[52] Under the lens of liberal legal theories, the bottom-up approach is the strategy for compliance.[53] States, but also non-state actors, are law-abiding and tend to commit and comply with international and transnational agreements.[54]

---

47 *See infra,* Chapter 3, Part I.B.ii (exploring the risks of politicizing international commitments).

48 *See* BILDER, *supra* note 2, at 109.

49 *See* Barbara Delcourt, *Theory of Compliance, in* MPEPIL (2013) (analyzing and classifying the evolution of the international scholarly debate, coupled with the one of international relations' scholars, on the theory of compliance).

50 *See* Niels Petersen, *How Rational is International Law?*, 20 EJIL 1247–62 (2010).

51 *See supra,* Chapter 2, Part I.A.ii (assessing compliance under the constructivist and the liberal lens in the international legal theory). *See generally* CHAYES & CHAYES, *supra* note 1 (analyzing parties' willingness to comply).

52 *See* Anne-Marie Slaughter Burley, International Law and International Relations Theory: A Dual Agenda, 87 AJIL 205, 220 (1993).

53 *See infra,* Chapter 3, Part I.B.ii (analyzing the innovative approach of bottom up diplomacy in the treaty-making process).

54 *See* Timothy F. Malloy, *Regulation, Compliance and the Firm*, 76 TEMP. L. REV. 451, 454 (2003); *see also* Anne-Marie Slaughter Burley, International Law in a World of Liberal

Therefore, drafting techniques tend to secure voluntarism by creating a sense of moral commitment among states and the regulated communities.

Rationalist criticism labeled this approach as "shallow." Higher levels of compliance are merely related to weak legal prescriptions.[55] Based on "strategic theory,"[56] states' behavior is dictated by a calculation of advantages. Therefore, to make the agreement work, treaties should build on states' propensity to comply. The negotiation processes behind international agreements are key in enhancing the prospect of states' compliance. Especially with regard to arms control, compliance strategies need to be tailored to make the treaty consistent with national interests.[57]

Increasing the level of commitments in international agreements makes compliance more costly. As compliance costs increase, the need for enforcement also increases.[58] Despite the benefits of collaboration based on complementary interests, a lack of international enforcement leads parties to choose noncompliant behaviors. This is especially relevant in the environmental sector. Rationalists analyze noncompliance as a set of calculated governmental decisions that divert from treaty obligations.[59] They have called attention to grounding compliance theory on a rational model, states being rational, self-interested actors. In turn, nations will adopt risk-management techniques enforceable through deterrence.[60]

From a rationalist perspective, in the commitment phase, states tend to crystallize a de facto behavior so as to be already in compliance. Therefore, during treaty negotiations, each state promotes language that requires no behavioral change. Whenever the agreement requires new behavior, its language tends to be vague, so compliance will be only coincidental. In other words, the

---

States, 6 EJIL 503, 532 (1995).

55 *See* THOMAS M. FRANCK, THE POWER OF LEGITIMACY AMONG NATIONS (1990); *see also* THOMAS M. FRANCK, FAIRNESS IN INTERNATIONAL LAW AND INSTITUTIONS (1995) (analyzing compliance under the constructivist lens based on the legitimacy of the norms); Koh, *supra* note 32, at 2599–659 (criticizing the managerial approach of constructivism).

56 Strategic theory is a method of analysis that includes game theory, operations research, systems analysis, and related disciplines to analyze rational behaviors and their motivations. *See* Abram Chayes, *An Inquiry into the Workings of Arms Control Agreements*, 85 HARV. L. REV. 905, 905–06 (1972).

57 *See* id. at 934.

58 *See* Kal Raustiala, *Compliance & Effectiveness in International Regulatory Cooperation*, 32 CASE W. RES. J. INT'L L. 387, 409 (2000).

59 *See infra*, Chapter 3, Part I.B.ii (analyzing international treaty making under the light of the rationalist theory).

60 *See* Slaughter Burley, *supra* note 52, at 220; see also ROBERT O. KEOHANE, AFTER HEGEMONY: COOPERATION AND DISCORD IN THE WORLD POLITICAL ECONOMY 244–46 (1984).

state would have behaved as required by treaty obligations in any case.[61] For instance, in the field of arms control, many countries comply with the Nuclear Non-Proliferation Treaty (NPT)[62] because they have no nuclear capacity, not because of treaty obligations. In the field of climate change, the Montreal Protocol on Substances that Deplete the Ozone Layer[63] is a pertinent example. In early 1970s, the United States, Canada, and northern countries took significant steps in reducing chlorofluorocarbons (CFCs) emissions for ozone protection, so much so that even after the Montreal Protocol entered into force they maintained more rigorous CFCs reduction policies than the treaty required. Even though their compliance with the treaty was coincidental, these states harnessed the outcomes of the Montreal Protocol negotiations, pushing for stringent regulation so they would the bear the cost of CFCs reduction alone.[64]

During treaty implementation, states being rational actors, they tend to comply only if they believe that noncompliance will be publicly revealed and adequately sanctioned.[65] In that regard, Andrew Guzman pointed out that the reputational effect, matched with direct sanctions, provides a solid framework for compliance.[66] Not only do sanctions prevent noncompliance, they also modify the cost-benefit analysis of each party, which as a rational agent acts to pursue an identifiable set of interests.[67]

ii. The Politicization of Commitment

As a result of the evolution of commitment and compliance in international law, the treaty-making process has sought to further cooperation through new instruments that are political rather than legal.[68] Nonbinding formulas have

---

61 *See* Hunter, Salzman & Zaelke, *supra* note 25.

62 Treaty on the Non-Proliferation of Nuclear Weapons, July 1, 1968, 729 U.N.T.S. 161.

63 Montreal Protocol on Substances that Deplete the Ozone Layer, Sept. 16, 1987, 1522 U.N.T.S. 3.

64 During the Montreal Protocol negotiations, if other countries, especially competitors of the United States, had not curbed their own emissions, the risk of the United States pulling out of the agreement would have been high. Domestic industries would have exerted pressure on the U.S. government to abandon the agreement, as they could not have stood the CFCs reduction alone. *See* Ronald Mitchell, *Compliance Theory: An Overview, in* Improving Compliance with International Environmental Law 7 (James Cameron et al., eds., 1996).

65 *See* Durwood Zaelke, Donald Kaniaru & Eva Kruzikova, *Domestic Enforcement Strategies*, in 1 Making Law Work: Environmental Compliance and Sustainable Development 371 (Durwood Zaelke et al. eds., 2005).

66 *See* Guzman, *supra* note 35, at 1827.

67 *See* Mitchell, *supra* note 64.

68 *See* Slaughter Burley, supra note 54, at 516.

appeared, blurring the legal contours of international agreements, while producing a dual effect on commitment.[69] First, they allow expansion of the critical mass of contracting parties because more states are willing to join the agreement. Second, they obviate the need for legislative approval through domestic parliaments, leaving the authority to express commitment solely to executive branches.[70] Some scholarship has argued in favor of direct governmental authority in closing international commitments but has overlooked its downside effect.[71] If it is true that this model furthers cooperation at the international level, it may create a democratic deficit at home.

For instance, in the U.S. legal system, international agreements can take the form of treaties, executive agreements, and nonlegal agreements.[72] Under the Restatement Fourth of U.S. Foreign Relations Law,[73] only the first category of agreements follow the procedure in Article II, section 2 of the U.S. Constitution,[74] which provides for a power shared between the executive and legislative branches to make an international treaty:[75] "The President . . . shall have power, by and with the Advice and Consent of the Senate, to make Treaties, provided two thirds of the Senators present concur."

---

69 *See generally* Abbott & Snidal, *supra* note 18, at 421–56; *see also* Hans J. Morgenthau, Politics Among Nations: The Struggle for Power and Peace 4–5, 25–26 (4th ed., 1967); Hans J. Morgenthau, *Positivism, Functionalism, and International Law*, 34 AJIL 260 (1940).

70 *See* Harold Hongju Koh, *Triptych's End: A Better Framework to Evaluate 21st Century International Lawmaking*, 126 Yale L.J. F. 338, 359–61 (2017) (analyzing internalization of international commitment in domestic legal order under the lens of the U.S. Constitution).

71 *See* Jean Galbraith, *From Treaties to International Commitments: The Changing Landscape of Foreign Relations Law*, 84 U. Chi. L. Rev. 1675, 1712–13 (2017); *but see* Michael D. Ramsey, *Evading the Treaty Power?: The Constitutionality of Nonbinding Agreements*, 11 F.I.U. L. Rev. 371, 375–76 (2016) (analyzing the constitutional problems underlying the constraints of political commitments on the U.S. executive branch).

72 *See* Stephen P. Mulligan, Withdrawal from International Agreements: Legal Framework, the Paris Agreement, and the Iran Nuclear Agreement, 7 Congressional Rsch. Serv. (2018) (upholding a tripartite system based on treaties, executive agreements and non legal agreements).

73 Restatement (Fourth) of the Foreign Relations Law of the United States § 301 (1) (Am. Law Inst. 2018). Though this is not a binding instrument in the U.S. legal system, it has persuasive value in domestic courts.

74 U.S. Const., art. II, § 2, cl. 2.

75 In the U.S. legal system, the word "treaty" refers only to agreements under Article II, section 2 of the U.S. Constitution. Therefore, the word has a narrower scope in the United States than in international legal argot; Article 2.1(a) of the VCLT refers to "an international agreement concluded between States in written form and governed by international law, whether embodied in a single instrument or in two or more related instruments and whatever its particular designation[.]"

Therefore, under U.S. domestic law, the term "treaty" has a narrower application than in international law, as it refers only to those instruments that have undergone the senatorial advice and consent process embedded in the Constitution.[76] The other two categories, which represent the great majority of international agreements that the United States enters into, are solely the expression of presidential power.[77] Executive agreements are the result of a simplified ratification procedure, which is also present in civil law systems,[78] having the same legal force as treaties concluded under Article II, section 2, of the U.S. Constitution.[79] Political commitments are nonlegal agreements with moral and political suasion, though they are ipso facto not meant to be binding.[80] Increasing recourse to executive agreements and nonlegal agreements determined two different trends in U.S. domestic practice: centralization of

---

76 The comment to section 301 of the Fourth Restatement explains the semantic difference of the term "treaty" in U.S. domestic law compared to international law. While the former relies on the definition in Article II of the U.S. Constitution, the latter refers to Article 1(a) of the VCLT. *See* RESTATEMENT (FOURTH) OF THE FOREIGN RELATIONS LAW OF THE UNITED STATES § 301 (1) (AM. LAW INST. 2018).

77 Over 90% of the international agreements concluded by the United States have been concluded as executive agreements or nonlegal agreements, so they have not followed the "treaty clause" constitutional procedure. *See* Michael John Garcia, *International Law and Agreements: Their Effect upon U.S. Law*, CRS Report RL32528 (2018); *see also* Jean Galbraith, *Rejoining Treaties*, 106 VA. L. REV. 73, 85–86 (2020) (exploring the progressive desuetude of Article II, which was invoked only once between 2001 and 2010, for the ratification of international agreements).

78 For a comparative analysis of civil law systems focusing on Italian, French, and Belgian examples of international agreements concluded through a simplified procedure, *see generally* BENEDETTO CONFORTI, DIRITTO INTERNAZIONALE (XI ed., 2018); Manlio Udina, *Gli Accordi Internazionali in Forma Semplificata e la Costituzione Italiana*, 1 RIVISTA DI DIRITTO INTERNAZIONALE 212 (1961); Claude Chayet, *Les Accords en Forme Semplifiée*, 1 ANNUAIRE FRANÇAIS DE DROIT INTERNATIONAL 3 (1957); PAUL F. SMETS, LA CONCLUSION DES ACCORDS EN FORME SIMPLIFIÉE: ÉTUDE DE DROIT INTERNATIONAL ET DE DROIT CONSTITUTIONNEL BELGE ET COMPARÉ (1969).

79 Although executive agreements have the same legal force as treaties concluded under Article II, section 2, of the U.S. Constitution, they cannot contradict the U.S. Constitution or preexisting federal norms. *See* CONG. RSCH. SERV, TREATIES AND OTHER INTERNATIONAL AGREEMENTS: THE ROLE OF THE UNITED STATES SENATE, Study Prepared for the Committee on Foreign Relations of the United States Senate, S. Prt. 106–71 (2001).

80 *See* Duncan B. Hollis & Joshua J. Newcomer, *Political Commitments and the Constitution*, 49 VA. J. INT'L. L. 507 (2009) (analyzing political commitments under the U.S. constitutional lens); *see also* Jack L. Goldsmith, *The Contributions of the Obama Administration to the Practice and Theory of International Law*, 57 HARV. INT'L L.J. 1, 11 (2016) (analyzing the legal effects of political commitments); O. SCHACHTER, *The Twilight Existence of Nonbinding International Agreements*, 71 AJIL 296, 300 (1977).

treaty-making power in the hands of the executive and avoidance of the necessity of congressional approval in the ratification phase.[81]

In this regard, the Obama administration, to secure the ratification of international treaties concluded under its mandate, circumvented the political opposition in the Senate, extending an already existing practice.[82] However, though agreements that are entered into without congressional advice and consent can accelerate the ratification phase of treaty making, they are ultimately less solid in the treaty-maintenance phase. Indeed, as a result of this procedure, any subsequent administration can—and, especially if it has a different foreign policy orientation, often will—easily pull out of international agreements joined by its predecessor. The president's power to unilaterally withdraw from international agreements not regulated under Article II of the Constitution is generally considered collateral to the ratification phase: the president has the power to terminate agreements the country joined.[83] Therefore, securing commitments exclusively through executive engagement is a short pathway that facilitates the achievement of core policy interests but exposes commitment to politicization. Though this strategy eases commitment in the treaty-making phase, it may generate problems in the phase of treaty-maintenance.

Based on the perspective one is assuming, commitment takes different shapes, influencing the outcome of the treaty-making process. Law can guide or inspire behaviors but not be the cause of them. International law can provide communication and coordination facilities to ease cooperation without binding forms, but only whenever it coincides with states' political agenda.[84]

---

81 *See supra,* Chapter 1, Part II.C (examining legal authorities entitled to withdrawal in the US domestic legal system).

82 *See* Goldsmith, *supra* note 74, at 471.

83 Under section 339 of the *Third Restatement, Reporter's* note 2, the presidential unilateral power of terminating treaties can be considered a domestic practice. *See* C. A. BRADLEY, J. L. GOLDSMITH, *Presidential Control over International Law*, 131 HARV. L. REV. 1201, 1212 (2018); *see also* Galbraith, *supra* note 77, at 87; Harold Hongju Koh, *Presidential Power to Terminate International Agreements*, 128 YALE L.J.F. 432, 436 (2018) (analyzing the symmetrical presidential authority to enter and pull out of international agreements). With regard to international agreements concluded under the Article 2 procedure, the debate is ongoing. One of the main congressional attempts to inhibit the presidential power to withdraw from international agreements can be traced back to a 1978 initiative of Senator Barry Goldwater. The Supreme Court declined to consider the merits of the case because it involved a political rather than legal situation. Goldwater v. Carter, 481 F. Supp. 949, 996 (D.D.C. 1979).

84 *See* John G. Ruggie, *Epistemology, Ontology and the Study of International Regimes, in* CONSTRUCTING THE WORLD POLITY 85–101 (John G. Ruggie ed., 1998); *See* JACK L. GOLDSMITH & ERIC A. POSNER, THE LIMITS OF INTERNATIONAL LAW (2006) (analyzing the ultimate causes of states' behaviors as encompassed in states' self-interests).

Whenever commitment ends up being an expression of political parties, the stability of cooperation is at risk.

C. *Differences between Withdrawal and Breach*

International relations theorists and legal scholars have, for a long time, studied breach of international treaties as the main noncooperative behavior in interstate cooperation. This approach, grounded in the prisoners' dilemma model,[85] envisions a binary choice in treaty maintenance: comply or breach.[86] The theoretical approach between the two choices is reflected in the treaty-making process, as treaty negotiators primarily focus on mechanisms to address and further compliance while leaving unregulated or at least under-regulated the process of stepping back from commitments. This approach ignored a plurality of salient aspects, triggering various legal, political, and reputational consequences. Between pure cooperation and breach there is a third way defined through withdrawal. Notwithstanding the legal nature of withdrawal, it can entail noncooperative outcomes. Therefore, state parties to international agreements are faced not with a dilemma, but rather a "trilemma": three options, namely compliance, noncompliance, and withdrawal.

International scholarship has given little attention to the difference between breach and exit. Only Laurence Helfer sought to strike a distinctive line between the two to understand the institutional, legal, political, and reputational differences through the lens of compliance.[87] In addition to existing contributions, it is important to identify the consequences for treaty commitment of withdrawal from international treaties. Indeed, even if withdrawal is a cooperative instrument de jure, it may end up being a noncooperative instrument de facto. This section sheds light on the most salient aspects of withdrawal, as compared to breach, expanding and updating the scholarship on this subject matter.

The following table synthetizes the main differences between withdrawal and breach:

---

85 The prisoner's dilemma is a game discussed in game theory. It seeks to demonstrate why two rational individuals might not cooperate, notwithstanding it being in their best interests to do so. See A. Rapoport & A. M Chammah, Prisoner's Dilemma: A Study in Conflict and Cooperation (1966).

86 *See* John M. Orbell et al., *Do Cooperators Exit More Readily Than Defectors?*, 78 Am. Pol. Sci. Rev. 147, 147–48 (1984); *see also* Duncan Snidal, *Coordination Versus Prisoners' Dilemma: Implications for International Cooperation and Regimes*, 79 Am. Pol. Sci. Rev. 923, 927 (1985).

87 *See* Helfer, *supra* note 5, at 1613 (assessing conceptual confusions regarding treaty exit and breach).

TABLE 1 Differences between withdrawal and breach

Withdrawal	Breach
– **Legality:** Lawful act	– **Legality:** Wrongful act
– **Secondary norms:** No responsibility	– **Secondary norms:** Responsibility
– **Life of the treaty:** Remains in force	– **Life of the treaty:** Suspension or termination
– **Authority:** Executive	– **Authority:** Every state's organ
– **Intent:** Deliberate	– **Intent:** Deliberate or accidental
– **Financial duties:** Exemption	– **Financial duties:** No exemption
– **Reputation:** Depends on good faith	– **Reputation:** Detrimental
– **Rule of Law:** Clean sheet	– **Rule of Law:** Undermined
– **Duration:** Permanent	– **Duration:** Temporary or permanent
– **Nature:** Cooperative?	– **Nature:** Noncooperative

First, while breach is a wrongful act, withdrawal is lawful. Based on Article 60(3) of the VCLT,[88] breach can consist of an illegitimate repudiation of the treaty or a violation of a treaty provision essential to its object and purpose. Withdrawal is, instead, done pursuant toa legitimate ground for terminating a treaty under Article 42 of the VCLT.[89] For this reason, negotiators have secured a sanctioning system only against noncompliance, envisioning withdrawal clauses as a risk-management tool of the agreement despite their effect on commitment.[90]

Second, because breach entails an international wrongful act, it triggers secondary norms concerning states' responsibility. Article 1 of the Draft Articles on the Responsibility of States for Internationally Wrongful Acts[91] provides that "[e]very internationally wrongful act of a State entails the international

88 VCLT, Article 60(3) ("Termination or suspension of the operation of a treaty as a consequence of its breach") defines breach as "(a) a repudiation of the treaty not sanctioned by the present Convention; or; (b) the violation of a provision essential to the accomplishment of the object or purpose of the treaty."

89 VCLT, Article 42(2) ("Validity and continuance in force of treaties") affirms that "[t]he termination of a treaty, its denunciation or the withdrawal of a party, may take place only as a result of the application of the provisions of the treaty or of the present Convention. The same rule applies to suspension of the operation of a treaty."

90 *See* Helfer, *supra* note 5, at1611.

91 U.N. Draft Articles on Responsibility of States for Internationally Wrongful Acts (ARSIWA), with commentaries, Supp. No. 10, at ch. IV.E.1., U.N. Doc. A/56/10 (Nov. 2001).

responsibility of that State." Depending on the magnitude of the breach, an array of responses is available to adversely affected states. Unlike breach, withdrawal does not impose any responsibility on the denouncing state as long as it is in compliance with withdrawal procedures. Contracting parties have an interest in avoiding the sanctioning of withdrawal because it is a risk management tool that can be exerted in the future. If a state decides to sanction withdrawal through retaliation or penalties, it may be in direct violation of treaty obligations, possibly resulting in a cascade effect on the sanctioning state.[92]

Third, breach can entail different consequences for the life of the treaty. Violations of treaty obligations can lead to the suspension or termination of the treaty in whole or in part. Termination does not affect any right, obligation, or legal situation regulated under the agreement, nor does it prejudice states' duties to fulfill its obligations. Article 60(1) of the VCLT regulates this matter, defining the suspension of treaty operation or termination *tout court* with regard to the affected party and the defaulting state or, in the most serious cases, all parties.[93] On the other hand, withdrawal from multilateral treaties, even if the number of contracting parties goes below the minimum threshold for its entry into force, leaves the treaty in force. Article 55 of the VCLT[94] embeds this principle, aiming to provide a clear framework for international lawyers since multilateral treaties often fail to cover this point.

Fourth, different authorities are connected with the two acts. Noncompliance derives from a plurality of actors in the legislative, executive, and/or judicial branch that are unable or, sometimes, unwilling to comply. Withdrawal represents, instead, an internal decision among the political branches. The VCLT is silent about states' domestic competences related to withdrawal, but Article 67 provides that the executive, through the head of state or the head of government, is entitled to notify the treaty depository.[95]

Fifth, the intention underlying withdrawal and breach can be different. Withdrawal always represents a voluntary decision by a state's political

92 *See* Helfer, *supra* note 5, at 1617.

93 Article 60(1) of the VCLT ("Termination or suspension of the operation of a treaty as a consequence of its breach") provides: "A material breach of a bilateral treaty by one of the parties entitles the other to invoke the breach as a ground for terminating the treaty or suspending its operation in whole or in part."

94 Article 55 of the VCLT ("Reduction of the parties to a multilateral treaty below the, number necessary for its entry into force"), states: "Unless the treaty otherwise provides, a multilateral treaty does not terminate by reason only of the fact that the number of the parties falls below the number necessary for its entry into force."

95 Article 67(1) of the VCLT ("Instruments for declaring invalid, terminating, withdrawing from or suspending the operation of a treaty") provides: "The notification provided for under article 65, paragraph 1, must be made in writing."

authority.[96] The 1966 Draft Articles on the Law of Treaties with Commentaries conceptualized exiting a treaty as symmetrical to joining it.[97] Therefore, withdrawal can be understood as the result of a rational decision by a political branch, just as is the expression of consent. Breach, on the other hand, can occur accidentally or be the result of an inability to comply.

Sixth, only in the case of denunciation is the withdrawing state exempted from financial duties. This circumstance is particularly relevant with regard to treaties establishing international organizations. If a state later rejoins the organization, it will be compelled to bring its payments up to date retroactively. On the one hand, this can be seen as a sort of ex post penalty for exit; on the other, it reflects the renewed willingness of the state to reengage with treaty obligations.[98]

Seventh, from a reputational point of view, withdrawal and breach can trigger similar consequences. Whenever a state hinders international cooperation, other states will likely be more reluctant to engage in future negotiations and enter into new agreements, or they will at least ask for more stringent assurances.[99] If withdrawal is a consequence of changed circumstances, the reputational impact will likely be limited or nil. In the implementation phase, a withdrawal clause may allow states facing a shifting situation at home to maintain lawful international standing by withdrawing from rather than breaching a treaty.[100]

Eighth, withdrawal and breach have different effects on the rule of law. Breach has a direct impact on the rule of law with regard to both abiding by rules and accountability. Therefore, a noncompliant state, as a consequence of its breach, will negatively affect the rule of law. In contrast, withdrawal has no negative effect on the rule of law; it gives the withdrawing state a clean slate. Nonetheless, opportunistic withdrawals, contrary to good faith,[101] may be just

96 *See supra,* Chapter 1, Part I.C (exploring states' competence in denouncing treaties in domestic legal systems).

97 Draft Articles on the Law of Treaties with Commentaries, Adopted by the International Law Commission at its Eighteenth Session, *in U.N. Conference on the Law of Treaties, 1st & 2nd Sess., Vienna, 26 March–24 May 1968 and 9 April–22 May 1969,* at 83, U.N. Doc. A/CONF.39/11/Add.2 (1971).

98 *See* Michael Akehust, *Withdrawal from International Organizations*, 32 Current Legal Probs. 143, 146–49 (1979).

99 *See* Guzman, *supra* note 35, at 1849.

100 *See* Helfer, *supra* note 5, at 1591.

101 *See infra,* Chapter 2, Part III.A (analyzing withdrawal under the lens of the principle of good faith in the execution of international agreements).

a way to overcome international commitments or obligations, creating, as a practical consequence, a negative outcome.[102]

Ninth, compared to breach, the act of withdrawal entails a decisive and permanent decision. Indeed, breach can lead only to termination and suspension of treaty operations in whole or in part. Pursuant to Article 60(2),[103] this is the consequence that arises out of a unanimous decision by all the parties to a treaty. Withdrawal represents a unilateral decision that need not be shared or accepted unanimously, and it automatically triggers a permanent consequence—termination of the withdrawing state's relationship with the treaty. From this perspective, withdrawal represents a greater and more consequential rejection than breach.

Tenth, the two instruments may or may not be differentiated by their cooperative nature. While breach, by definition, is a noncooperative act, withdrawal is defined as a legal tool; it might be seen as noncooperative, or it might not.

In conclusion, withdrawal can be understood as the opposite of commitment: the latter entails entering into treaty-based cooperation; the former, pulling out of it. The analysis just presented demonstrates that there is a direct relationship between politicizing commitment and noncooperation, as evidenced by states' behaviors, which has resulted in the trend of withdrawal. Because withdrawal can be a noncooperative act, it is important to understand how it differs from breach. Just as withdrawal is the opposite of commitment, breach is the opposite of compliance. The relationship between these two concepts can be expressed by the following formula, which allows understanding when there are oppositions and contradictions or consonance and congruity:

Withdrawal : Commitment = Breach : Compliance

Returning to the metaphor of an international agreement being like a marriage, the difference between withdrawal and breach can be generally understood as the difference between divorce and cheating. Notwithstanding its legality, can divorce always be seen as being cooperative?

---

102 Good faith should inspire states' behaviors in international relation, even in the moment of withdrawal from an international agreement. In the *Gabčikovo-Nagymaros Project* case, the ICJ attested that the VCLT procedural articles on termination of international treaties, regulated in its Part V, are grounded on this principle. Gabčíkovo-Nagymaros Project (Hungary v. Slovakia), 1997 Judgment I.C.J. Reports 7, Sept. 25, 1997, p. 66, para. 109.

103 Article 60(2) of the VCLT provides: "2. A material breach of a multilateral treaty by one of the parties entitles: (a) the other parties by unanimous agreement to suspend the operation of the treaty in whole or in part or to terminate it either: (i) in the relations between themselves and the defaulting State; or (ii) as between all the parties.

II. Analyzing Withdrawal through the Lens of Risk Management

Focusing on risk management in international treaties is key to understanding the functioning of commitment and compliance. Diplomatic and legal instruments and techniques in the treaty-making process serve as a way to cope with risk and preserve national interests multilaterally. As countries face long-term challenges with international commitments due to changing circumstances during the life of a treaty, risk serves as a thermometer for domestic uncertainty at the time of joining or leaving an international agreement.[104] Whenever a state cannot further its domestic interests multilaterally through an international agreement, it has the option of legally pulling out of it. From this perspective, withdrawal can be understood as insurance against the endemic risk in international relations.

The following sections explore the use of risk management in international agreements as a way to protect national interests in foreign policy. First, the concept of risk management is defined, and then the techniques that states adopt to secure their domestic interests during treaty making and treaty maintenance are described.

A. *Risk Management in International Treaties*

States tend to deal with uncertainty in international relations through risk management. Scholarly debate has used this concept to define key elements in interstate cooperation and, in turn, understand the reasons that push states to withdraw from agreements they joined. Diplomatic techniques and legal instruments serve as a tool for dealing with risk, preserving national interests at the international level.[105] A contribution on risk management primarily concerning withdrawal from international agreements sheds light on the two major forces underlying the law of treaties, namely commitment and compliance.[106] It entails a behavioral study of states' policies to understand how treaty maintenance can be enhanced over time. As the treaty-making process evolved through compliance strategies, commitment was largely overlooked and increasingly politicized. The imbalance that resulted from this generated problems during the phase of treaty maintenance, and the phenomenon of eventual withdrawal represents the tip of the iceberg.

---

104 *See* Bilder, *supra* note 2.

105 *See infra,* Chapter 3, Part I.B (analyzing international legal theory and the international relations' theory behind treaty making and their impact on the evolution of treaty maintenance).

106 For an extensive analysis of states' commitment and compliance to multilateral agreements, *see supra,* Chapter 2, Part I.A.

As a result of the endemic tension between the national and international sphere, different perceptions of risk arise at the domestic level. Through the lens of risk management, the dichotomy between multilateralism and unilateralism in foreign policy ultimately depends on whether a country, or a government, is more risk-prone or risk-adverse with respect to multilateral commitments.

i. Why Risk Matters

In order to understand the salience of risk management to the mechanism of withdrawal, it is important to understand risk and the way states cope with it. If one assumes that every international agreement involves risk, then it is possible to envision risk management as a way of securing solid legal structures to overcome obstacles to interstate cooperation stemming from politics, economics, technology, and many other fields in the orbit of the subject matter of the agreement.[107] Analyzing why risk matters focuses on the ways governments have to cope with risk in entering and maintaining international commitments. This is a cost-benefit analysis that aims at establishing whether the pros of participation overcome exposure to loss. Richard Bilder thoroughly analyzed risk in international agreements, influencing scholarship on the international law of treaties in this sphere by classifying and analyzing various degrees of risk management and compliance-enhancing devices for cooperation among nations.[108]

Whether international treaties are a form of a "meeting of the minds" entailing a quid pro quo exchange between the parties[109] or a "disagreement reduced to writing,"[110] they all imply a certain amount of risk because states cannot foresee ex ante, in the moment of signature, what they will have to face ex post, in the moment of implementation. International scholars have posed the question of risk in terms of the risk of entering into an international

---

107 *See supra,* Chapter 1, Part 1.B. (discussing how contracting parties to international agreements have progressively codified withdrawal clauses as a way to address risk in international relations).

108 *See generally* Bilder, *supra* note 2 (envisioning withdrawal clauses as flexibility mechanisms and risk management tools). Bilder's theory on risk management was later echoed by international legal scholars and international relations theorists. *See* Helfer, *supra* note 5, at 1586 (assessing the influential contribution of Bilder's scholarship).

109 *See* Jan Klabbers, International Law 70 (2017), questioning the quintessence of international treaties.

110 *See* Phillip Allott, *The Concept of International Law,* 10 EJIL 31, 43 (1999) (expressing how parties to a treaty enter into negotiations with different ideas and are pushed to a compromise based on things they didn't originally want but can accept).

agreement. However, risk considerations are also deeply present during the life of a treaty up to the moment of pulling out.[111]

Risk, inherent in international relations, can be defined as the possibility of facing harm or loss, which can be scaled depending on a state's vulnerability and the uncertainty of its choices.[112] Whether a state is more risk-prone or risk-adverse will have a direct effect on the probability of its entering or leaving an international agreement.[113] Traditionally, different nations have different perceptions of risk, depending on both internal and external factors.

Internal factors are related to states' vulnerability, which reflects internal stability or volatile conditions based on their political, economic and social conditions. Among them, security, historical and social considerations, and the political stripe of the party leading the government are the key elements to take into account, along with the role a state plays in the subject matter of the agreement. External factors relate to the degree of uncertainty implied in the treaty a state seeks to join. The perception of risk depends on the subject matter of the agreement, its parties, its impact on domestic politics, public opinion, *et alia.*

Risk implies consequences, whether the deal is reached or not. For instance, in the arms control field, the United States' refusal to ratify the SALT II[114] agreement during the Cold War resulted in an arms race with a risk of nuclear disaster not only for the United States but also for the international community *tout court.*[115] Similarly, in the climate change field, the failure of COP 15[116] negoti-

---

111 Withdrawal as a risk management tool in treaty making can be understood as a flexibility device to help states cope with future uncertainty. *See* Barbara Koremenos et al., *The Rational Design of International Institutions*, 55 INT'L ORG. 761, 762 (2001).

112 *See* Bilder, *supra* note 2, at 11 (defining the concepts of "risk" and "risk management" in the international legal context).

113 Vulnerability and uncertainty are necessary but not sufficient conditions for risk. Some international agreements can trigger uncertainty not necessarily related to risk. Particularly, this is the case with human rights agreements protecting fundamental rights already embedded in domestic constitutions or, more broadly, in domestic law. *See* id. at 13.

114 Treaty Between the United States of America and the Union of Soviet Socialist Republics on the Limitation of Strategic Offensive Arms (SALT II), June 18, 1979. The treaty never entered into force and was superseded by the START I Treaty in 1991.

115 *See* BILDER, *supra* note 2, at 15 (analyzing risks and opportunities related to non-agreement scenarios; international agreements can produce direct effects on the signatory parties but also indirect effects on third nations or, more generally, the whole international system).

116 The Copenhagen Climate Change Conference, representing the 15th session of the Conference of the Parties to the UNFCCC, took place in Copenhagen and was hosted by the government of Denmark in December 2009. *COP 15*, UNITED NATIONS FRAMEWORK CONVENTION ON CLIMATE CHANGE, https://unfccc.int/process-and-meetings/conferences/past-conferences/copenhagen-climate-change-conference-december-2009/cop-15 (last visited Jun. 20, 20219).

ations in Copenhagen, in 2009, stalled the development of a climate regime, endangering the global effort to curb global warming. These examples show the impact of domestic risk management at the international level. Even if the agreement is not reached or does not entirely fulfill the expected outcomes, there is still a given amount of risk that every state must take into account. To create an adequate balance between cooperation and noncooperation, the international community has developed different techniques that mirror the ways states cope with risks in multilateral contexts.

ii. Risk Management in a Multilateral Context

Multilateral agreements trigger several challenges because of the plurality of actors that participate. Whenever global interests of the international community are at stake, the objective of the agreement is more likely to be met if many sovereign states join the negotiations. In such circumstances, the effectiveness of the agreement is linked to the number and identities of the contracting parties.[117]

As the number of parties in treaty negotiations grows, finding appropriate solutions becomes more complicated because different states have different interests. This is particularly relevant if we consider states with a significant stance on the subject matter regulated by the agreement. A state may face a competitive disadvantage in joining a multilateral agreement and be ready to step in only if its competitors will also join.[118] For instance, that was the case with the US-China Joint Announcement on climate change on November 12, 2014, which secured an initial commitment between these two countries, both major global polluters, in advance of the Paris Agreement on climate change signed April 22, 2016.[119]

Multilateral agreements—more unpredictable than bilateral agreements—entail a greater risk of noncompliant behavior or, at least, they generate a greater perception of such a risk. Statistically, a larger number of contracting parties indicates a greater likelihood of noncompliance. Procedurally, the agreement can get stuck at the domestic level, during the signature or ratification phase, before it starts. For instance, in the trade sphere, the

117 *See* Bilder, *supra* note 2, at 64 (analyzing risk with a focus on the multilateral context).

118 *See* id. at 73.

119 With the U.S.–China Joint Announcement on climate change, the U.S. president, Barack Obama, and the Chinese president, Xi Jinping, stood together in Beijing to affirm their political commitment to the achievement of a climate agreement in Paris to reduce the global temperature to below 2 degrees Celsius. *See* Joanna Lewis, *The U.S.-China Climate and Energy Relationship*, Ctr. for Strategic & Int'l Stud. (Sept. 22, 2017), https://www.csis.org/us-china-climate-and-energy-relationship.

Comprehensive and Economic Trade Agreement (CETA)[120] between the EU and Canada could not complete the signature procedure at the EU level initially, as it was blocked domestically in one of the EU member states, namely, Belgium, where the Walloon regional Parliament voted against it, on October 14, 2016.[121] Similarly, an agreement can be rejected or delayed by national parliaments during ratification. In the climate change field, this was the case with the Kyoto Protocol,[122] which was signed on December 11, 1997, and did not enter into force until eight years later, on February 15, 2005, because delays during the ratification process.[123]

B. *Risk in Treaty Making and Treaty Maintenance*

Analyzing the risk factors underlying the phases of treaty making and treaty maintenance is critical to understanding what drives the evolution of the treaty-making process. The risk related to withdrawal is two-sided, and it needs to be analyzed from both perspectives to understand the magnitude of loss that is possible: it entails an exogenous element related to the risk that another party will withdraw from the agreement, and it entails an endogenous element relating to each state's own risk. The former may hinder the general commitment of contracting parties during the negotiation phase. The latter implies that a possible decline in utility of a state staying in the agreement may redefine the cost-benefit calculation.

The subsections below elaborate on risk in treaty making and treaty maintenance. With regard to treaty making, the analysis considers the causes of deadlock in international negotiations; with regard to treaty maintenance, it elaborates on methods that allow states to adjust to volatile conditions and to technicalities underlying the functional areas of the deal.

---

120 Comprehensive Economic and Trade Agreement (CETA) between Canada on one side and the European Union and its member states on the other, Jan. 14, 2017, L 11/23.

121 The Walloon Parliament approved the EU–Canada deal only two weeks after its first rejection, on October 28, 2016, allowing the EU to sign the deal. The agreement has been under provisional application since 2017. Press Release IP/17/3121, European Commission, EU-Canada Trade Agreement Enters into Force (Sept. 20, 2017). For an analysis of the CETA political *iter* before the Walloon Parliament, see Maia De La Baume, *Walloon Parliament Rejects CETA Deal*, POLITICO (Oct. 14, 2016), https://www.politico.eu/article/walloon-parliament-rejects-ceta-deal/; *see also* Robert-Jan Bartunek, *EU and Canada to Sign Trade Pact after Belgians Strike Key Deal*, REUTERS (Oct. 29, 2016), https://www.reuters.com/article/us-eu-canada-trade-id.

122 Kyoto Protocol to the United Nations Framework Convention on Climate Change, Dec. 10, 1997 2303 U.N.T.S. 148.

123 *See infra*, Chapter 4, Part III.C (assessing the impact of withdrawal on climate change agreements).

i. Risk in Treaty Making

The formation of multilateral deals tends to involve endemic hardship that is directly proportional to the complexity of the matter at stake and that can lead to the negotiations deadlocking. Not only the high stakes, but also the competing interests of the parties involved in negotiations, can hinder the closing of a deal. A deadlocking of negotiations reflects their complexity, especially when they are related to the common good of the international community. Even if the goals are clear, parties cannot clearly assess the scope of the obligations to be undertaken or the risks at stake, while the lack of clear procedural rules contributes to multilateral negotiations being particularly complex and long.[124]

With regard to deadlocks or prolonged negotiations, scholars usually point to long-lasting, and generally fruitless, attempts to achieve an international legally binding treaty. This is a process that tends to run aground during either of two different phases of the treaty-making process: the obtaining of signatures and the ratification of the agreement.[125] During the treaty-making process, sovereign states participate in the completion of international agreements in two phases. First is the formation of the agreement, with each state negotiating and accepting the text of the agreement and presenting comments and reservations. Second is the implementation of it, when each state transposes the provisions

---

124 *See* Christian Downie, The Politics of Climate Change Negotiations: Strategies and Variables in Prolonged International Negotiations 5 (2014) (describing how consultation rounds of Conference of the Parties presidents on a clear regulatory framework almost caused a halt without providing effective solutions to the problem); see also Robert Falkner, Hannes Stephan & John Vogler, International Climate Policy After Copenhagen: Towards a 'Building Blocks' Approach, 1 Glob. Pol'y 252 (2010) (expressing, with regard to the Kyoto Protocol, how difficult it was to establish a climate regime; there was a prolonged struggle to muster the established threshold for ratification); Elisabeth Corell & Michele M. Betsill, *Analytical Framework: Assessing the Influence of NGO Diplomats, in* NGO Diplomacy: The Influence of Nongovernmental Organizations in International Environmental Negotiations 19–42 (Elisabeth Corell & Michele M. Betsill eds., 2008).

125 *See generally* Stefan Persson, Deadlocks in International Negotiations, Cooperation and Conflict 29, 3, 211 (1994); see also Christian Downie, supra note 124, at 5; Christian Downie, *Prolonged International Environmental Negotiations: the Roles and Strategies of Non-State Actors in the EU*, 16 Int'l Env't Agreements: Pol., L. & Econ. 739–55 (2016); Carsten Daugberg & Alan Swinbank, Ideas, Institutions, and Trade: The WTO & The Curious Role of EU Farm Policy in Trade Liberalization (2009); Larry Crump & William Zartman, Multilateral Negotiation and the Management of Complexity, 8 Int'l Negot. 1 (2003); Pamela Chasek, A Comparative Analysis of Multilateral Environmental Negotiations, 6 Grp. Decision & Negot. 437 (1997); Pamela Chasek, Earth Negotiations: Analyzing Thirty Years of Environmental Diplomacy (2001); William Zartman & Maureen Berman, The Practical Negotiator (1982).

of the agreement into its domestic system.[126] It is quite difficult to foresee the precise long-term impact of each variable relevant to the multiplicity of issues underlying international agreements because scientific data and economic values may generate uncertainty. There is a constant trade-off between long-term gains and short-term costs that complicates negotiations politically.[127]

Even during the treaty-making phase, withdrawal is possible. After a state signs an agreement but before it implements it, signatory withdrawal can apply: a contracting party can decide to "undo" its signature.[128] For instance, this occurred when the United States denounced the Rome Statute establishing the jurisdiction of the International Criminal Court (ICC) and when it denounced the Kyoto Protocol on climate change.[129]

ii. Risk in Treaty Maintenance

Maintaining treaties over time represents a growing challenge, as treaties need to adapt to changing circumstances. In a globalized system, in which greater volatility is inherent, such a risk becomes particularly relevant because the long-term goals of international agreements must adjust to the reality of short-term domestic political agendas.

Traditionally, contracting parties have coped with changing circumstances through the interpretation process or, in a more sophisticated way, through different levels of adjustment mechanisms that allow the treaty to evolve without the need to negotiate a new agreement. These techniques have been used especially in the environmental, financial, and military fields.[130]

First, a treaty can evolve, through a mere interpretation process, under the aegis of an ad hoc organ established by the treaty. For instance, the IMF Articles of Agreement[131] delegates such interpretational power to the Governing Board, which may adjust the meaning of the treaty over time while maintaining the text unchanged.

---

126 *See generally* Barry E. Carter & Allen S. Weiner, International Law 85–95 (6th ed., 2011) (reviewing the process of creation of international norms; with regard to international treaties, under Article 18 of the Vienna Convention on the Law of Treaties, it is important to each signatory state not to defeat their object and purpose before their entry into force).

127 *See* Nicholas Stern, *The Economics of Climate Change*, The Stern Review 92 et seq. (2007) (mentioned in Christian Downie, *supra* note 124, at 7).

128 *See infra,* Chapter 4, Part IV (analyzing the category of signatory withdrawal).

129 *See* id. (exploring U.S. practice regarding signature withdrawal).

130 *See* Abram Chayes & Antonia Handler Chayes, *Nonproliferation Regimes in the Aftermath of the Gulf War, in* After the Storm: Lessons from the Gulf War 49–80 (Joseph S. Nye & Roger K. Smith eds., 1992).

131 Articles of Agreement of the International Monetary Fund (Bretton Woods Agreement), Dec. 27, 1945, 60 Stat. 1401; 2 U.N.T.S. 39.

Second, treaties can include mechanisms to adopt technical provisions, negotiated separately from the main agreement, which are approved upon parties' consent.[132] The Convention on International Trade in Endangered Species of Wild Fauna and Flora (CITES)[133] and the International Convention for the Regulation of Whaling[134] resort to such appendices whenever technical changes in the agreement are required. Similarly, some agreements relegate technical matters to regulation according to annexes. This was the case with the 1987 Montreal Protocol on Substances that Deplete the Ozone Layer[135] and the 1990 London Amendments to the Montreal Protocol.[136]

Third, treaties can contain adjustment mechanisms that allow to adjusting the goals of the contracting parties to the performance of the treaty. The need for and the degree of adjustment rely on evaluation of the level of compliance to date. If parties have demonstrated high rates of compliance to their agreements, the treaty can be amended in order to pursue higher goals. On the other hand, if compliance has been low, new rules and procedures are necessary to address underlying problems.[137]

Fourth, some treaties have evolved through the framework convention and protocol approach.[138] This involves parties coming to a general agreement—the framework convention—and leaving detailed regulation to a later instrument—the protocol—which defines technical and specific aspects. The framework defines the goals to be pursued through the establishment of broad commitments and enforcing a system of governance. Rules and targets are set over time through periodic meetings in which parties negotiate operational protocols.[139] In the environmental field, the most pertinent example is the UN Framework Convention on Climate Change (UNFCCC),[140] which was

132 *See* Chayes, Chayes & Mitchell, *supra* note 25, at 57.

133 Convention on International Trade in Endangered Species of Wild Fauna and Flora, Mar. 3, 1973, 27 U.S.T. 1087; 993 U.N.T.S. 243; 12 I.L.M. 1085 (1973).

134 International Convention for the Regulation of Whaling, Dec. 2, 1946, 62 Stat. 1716; 161 U.N.T.S. 72.

135 Montreal Protocol on Substances that Deplete the Ozone Layer art. 2(9), Sept. 16, 1987, U.N.T.S. 1522, 3 (1989).

136 London Amendments to Montreal Protocol, Aug. 27, 1991, C.N.133.1991.

137 *See* Chayes, Chayes & Mitchell, *supra* note 25, at 58.

138 *See* id. at 56.

139 Under international law, protocols follow the same ratification process as the original treaty. In order to overcome problems surrounding negotiations and entry into force, international agreements have developed different methods to adapt. *See* Nele Matz-Luck, *Framework Conventions as Regulatory Tools*, 3 GOETTINGEN J. INT'L L. 439, 452–58 (2009).

140 The UNFCCC today is composed of 197 parties, including the major contributors to climate change, and represents a global framework for the whole international community.

created as a framework convention under the UN umbrella to provide diplomatic solutions to the contracting parties' needs. Since its founding in 1992,[141] the UNFCCC has developed detailed protocols and agreements, especially at the annual Conference of Parties (COPs), setting ad hoc principles for international climate deals, such as the Kyoto Protocol and the Paris Agreement.[142]

In case contracting parties can no longer express their needs through the framework of treaty they agreed to, withdrawal clauses are a last-resort tool allowing them to unilaterally pull out without incurring responsibility for violation of international law.[143]

III. Analyzing Withdrawal through the Lens of the Principle *Pacta Sunt Servanda*

Whenever domestic interests collide with international commitments, withdrawal clauses represent an *extrema ratio* in treaty maintenance that every state can legally use. In a system that lacks centralized enforcement, withdrawal may end up being used for opportunistic purposes, shifting from a cooperative act to a noncooperative one. As withdrawal assumes noncooperative features it triggers an ontological incoherence, given its legality. Indeed, this may undermine states' obligation to perform treaty obligations in good faith, in line with the general principle of international law *pacta sunt servanda*.[144]

In the words of Ronald Dworkin, the good-faith principle represents aspirational guidance of states' behavior.[145] In the context of the international law of treaties, good faith grounds behavioral study of states' decisions in treaty making and treaty maintenance. Therefore, it can be used as an indicator to test the cooperativeness of a state's exercise of its right to withdraw.

See List of Parties to the Convention, UN FRAMEWORK CONVENTION ON CLIMATE CHANGE, https://unfccc.int/process/parties-non-party-stakeholders/parties-convention-and-observer-states (last updated Aug. 7, 2018).

141 The UNFCCC was signed in 1992 at the United Nations Conference on Environment and Development.

142 The Kyoto Protocol and the Paris Agreement represent two main efforts of the international community to curb global warming. *See* JENNI KAUPPILA, *Transnational Advocacy Networks in International Climate Policy: The Challenge of Raising the Voices of the Marginalised Effectively Without Compromising Their Legitimacy*, *in* INTERNATIONAL CLIMATE CHANGE LAW AND POLICY: CULTURAL LEGITIMACY IN ADAPTION AND MITIGATION 138 (Thoko Kaime ed., 2014).

143 *See infra*, Chapter 6, Part I.A (understanding withdrawal as last resort tools in treaty making and treaty maintenance).

144 *See supra*, Chapter 2, Part I.C (questioning the general cooperativeness of withdrawal).

145 *See* RONALD DWORKIN, TAKING RIGHTS SERIOUSLY 25 (1977); *see also* Kolb, *supra* note 4, at 7.

The following section establishes that there is a direct relationship between the absence of good faith in a withdrawal and the politicization of the decision to pull out. First, it defines good faith in relation to withdrawal to understand its influence on treaty maintenance. Second, it classifies opportunistic behavior that may hinder good faith and define a shift from cooperative to noncooperative outcomes in the decision of pulling out—namely, geopolitical strategies and domestic politicization.

A. *From Cooperative to Noncooperative Outcomes*

Though withdrawal clauses are legal tools, their impact on interstate cooperation is questionable. Understanding withdrawal clauses under the lens of good faith allows identifying the direct relationship between the politicization of commitment and withdrawal and to weigh it against the principle *pacta sunt servanda*.[146]

Pacta sunt servanda is a core principle of the VCLT that applies to every treaty, without exception, and in all stages of treaty life, from entry into force to termination—including withdrawal.[147] This principle must be honored in good faith; it requires parties to uphold the spirit and the letter of a treaty. It applies only to existing obligations, not to anything that occurred before the formation of an agreement or after its termination.[148] Good faith imposes a responsibility to abstain from calculated acts that could frustrate the object and purpose of an international agreement.[149] Since the classic international legal scholarship of Christian von Wolff[150] and Emer de Vattel,[151] the principles of good faith and *pacta sunt servanda* have been deeply interconnected, the former being a precondition for the latter.[152] Article 26 of the VCLT,[153] which codifies the principle *pacta sunt servanda*, upholds the binding force of

146 *See supra*, Chapter 1, Part II.A (analyzing withdrawal in general international law, with a focus on the principle *pacta sunt servanda*).

147 *See* Humphrey Waldock, *Special Rapporteur on the Law of the Treaties, Sixth Report on the Law of the Treaties*, 2 UNYBILC 60, ¶ 1 (1966).

148 ILC Report 1966, 2 UNYBILC 211, ¶ 4 (1966). For case law analysis of international jurisprudence, see *Land and Maritime Boundary (Cameroon v. Nigeria)*, Judgment, 1998 I.C.J. 301 (June 11).

149 *See* MARK E. VILLIGER, COMMENTARY ON THE 1969 VIENNA CONVENTION ON THE LAW OF TREATIES 365–67 (2009).

150 *See generally* CHRISTIAN VON WOLFF, INSTITUTIONES IURIS NATURAE ET GENTIUM, ch. VII, ¶ 389 (1750).

151 *See generally* EMER DE VATTEL, LE DROIT DES GENS OU PRINCIPES DE LA LOI NATURELLE, Book II, ch. XIV (1758).

152 *See* Kolb, *supra* note 4, at 10–11.

153 Vienna Convention on the Law of Treaties, May 23, 1969 1155 U.N.T.S. 331, 8 I.L.M. 679 (1969).

international treaties, which parties to them are required to perform in good faith.[154]

The study of good faith is a particularly difficult task. In this regard, Robert Kolb affirmed that good faith cannot be defined but must be understood in context.[155] Good faith represents an essential element of the performance of legal obligations and interstate cooperation. At the jurisprudential level, in the *Nuclear Test Case*,[156] the ICJ explicitly connected good faith to trust and confidence in foreign policy:

> One of the basic principles governing the creation and performance of legal obligations ... is good faith. Trust and confidence are inherent in international cooperation, in particular in an age when this cooperation in many fields is becoming increasingly essential.

In the law of treaties, good faith represents a general principle for the interpretation of states' obligations that guides states' behavior in their decision-making process.[157] Article 31(1) of the VCLT[158] states that a treaty "shall be interpreted in good faith in accordance with the ordinary meaning to be given to the terms of the treaty in their context and in the light of its object and purpose." Article 31(2) narrows the purpose of interpretation of each treaty, including its context and preamble.[159] The ICJ also confirmed the relevance

---

154 *See supra,* Chapter 1, Part II.A (defining withdrawal under general principles of international law).

155 *See* Robert Kolb, *Apercus sur la Bonne Foi en Droit International Public* 54 RHDI 1, 7 (2001).

156 Request for an Examination of the Situation in Accordance with Paragraph 63 of the Court's Judgment of 20 December 1974 in the *Nuclear Tests* (*New Zealand v. France*) Case, Order, 1995 I.C.J. 288 (Sept. 22).

157 Historically, the principle of good faith can be traced back to the Roman law principle contractus bonae fidei, which imposed a requirement of integrity in relations between different juridical subjects. It integrated an objective element based on behavioral obligations and a subjective element based on knowledge of the counterparts' rights. Since the time of Grotius (1552–1645), this principle has become one of the pillars of the architecture of the law of treaties. *See* HUGO GROTIUS, DE JURE BELLI AC PACIS, Book II, Cap. XVI (1625). In modern international law, it represents a general principle of international law or, in the words of the preamble of the VCLT, it is defined as a universally recognized principle. *See* DWORKIN, *supra* note 145, at 25.

158 VCLT, art. 31 ("General rule on interpretation").

159 The object and purpose of a treaty are usually embedded in its preamble. *See generally* Carter & Weiner, *supra* note 126, at 86; *see also* Case Concerning Rights of Nationals of the United States of America in Morocco (France v. United States of America), Judgment I.C.J. Rep. (1952) (Aug. 27), 183, 184.

of good faith in withdrawal procedures in the *Gabčikovo-Nagymaros* case.[160] While attesting that the procedural articles embedded in the VCLT (Articles 65–68) on withdrawal do not codify existing customary law, the Court assessed that they are grounded on the obligation to execute treaties in good faith. With regard to withdrawal, this is a key parameter to be followed to disincentive unilateral arbitrary decisions.[161]

Treaty making and treaty maintenance do not occur in a vacuum but must be pictured in their social, economic, and political milieu. As the conditions that led contracting parties to join an agreement change over time, remaining in or leaving an agreement are the result of a precise policy choice. If it is true that every policy decision entails a political stance, the politicization of the decision to leave an agreement may end up instrumentalizing withdrawal clauses, triggering a noncooperative act against good faith.

The following illustration shows the direct relationship between the politicization of commitment and non-cooperativeness in states' behaviors, which results in trend toward withdrawal:

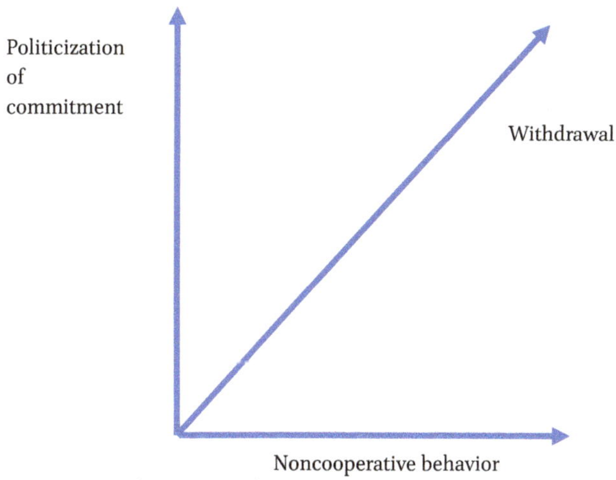

FIGURE 1 Politicization of commitment, states' noncooperative behaviors, and withdrawal

Commitment and withdrawal being two faces of the same coin, they reflect the will of the parties at the moments of treaty entry and exit.[162] Withdrawal

160 In the *Gabčikovo Nagymaros Project* case, the ICJ found that the Hungary notification, on May 19, 1992, of its termination of the 1977 bilateral treaty with Czechoslovakia was premature, since it was to take effect six days later. Gabčíkovo-Nagymaros Project (Hungary v. Slovakia), 1997 Judgment I.C.J. Reports 7, Sept. 25, 1997, p. 66, para. 109.

161 ROBERT KOLB, THE LAW OF TREATIES, AN INTRODUCTION 253 (2016).

162 *See supra,* Chapter 2, Part I.C (understanding withdrawal in comparison with breach).

clauses respond to the contracting parties' need for flexibility so they can adapt to changing circumstances. However, whenever these clauses are abused, the principle of good faith may be questioned. Thus, even though withdrawal is a legal tool, it may end up representing a noncooperative tool in practice.

To test good faith in withdrawal decisions, it is paramount to identify criteria that indicate use of withdrawal clauses inconsistent with the purpose of withdrawal. Understanding the intent of withdrawal sheds light on the cooperativeness of a state's decision. A lack of good faith in withdrawal from international agreements tends to be directly proportional to the politicization of the decision to pull out. As a result, whenever the driving force behind the withdrawal decision is political strategy, it may create an abuse of withdrawal. In other words, politicized withdrawals entail manipulation of the withdrawn treaty or institution as a way to exert state power. This can either seek to harness the denounced treaty or organization in a way that is more aligned with national goals or weaken the stability of the denounced agreement. The first scenario generally corresponds with geopolitical strategies, the latter with domestic politicization.

The described trend can potentially turn withdrawal from a cooperative act to address risk to a noncooperative act to promote a national political agenda in foreign policy.[163] The unilateral action frustrates the original goal that contracting parties were seeking to address during treaty negotiations, short-circuiting parties' good faith obligation. Notwithstanding the fact that political factors are behind any treaty action, the next section identifies two main categories of withdrawal with a deep political rationale: national geopolitical strategy and domestic politicization of the issue.

i. Geopolitical Strategy

Withdrawal as a national geopolitical strategy represents a tool of foreign policy used as leverage for conveying national interests at the supranational level. It has been mainly related to the trend of denunciation of multilateral organizations during the Cold War, disengagement from Israeli-Palestinian conflict-related agreements, and the collective withdrawal of African states from the International Criminal Court.

During the Cold War, withdrawal was not really used as a mechanism to address risk related to the agreement, but rather as way to adjust the withdrawn agreement to the national prerogatives or ideology of each bloc.[164] This phenomenon primarily involved, on the one hand, the Soviet bloc's withdrawal,

---

163 *See* Bilder, *supra* note 2, at 52 (analyzing withdrawal clauses under the light of risk management in international agreements).

164 *See supra,* Chapter 1, Part I.B (understanding the progressive codification of withdrawal clauses in states' practice, which emerged during the Cold War years).

during the 1950s, from UN specialized agencies, such as UNICEF, WHO, UNESCO, and the World Bank Group (WBG), and on the other hand, the Western bloc's withdrawal, between the 1970s and 1980s, from organizations like ILO and UNESCO.[165]

The acts of denunciation by the U.S.S.R. and the United States represented a political strategy enacted through the legal channel of withdrawal.[166] A latent trend of exerting national power through withdrawal was emerging in international relations. Indeed, the two blocs used withdrawal to orient the substantive focus of the organizations they were parties to and rejoined years later. Most of these cases of withdrawal were followed by a reaccession of the organization once key points of national interest of the withdrawn state had been addressed. For this reason, it is possible to define those examples as "boomerang withdrawals."

Similarly, withdrawal as a geopolitical action has involved cases of denunciation of international treaties in relation to the Israeli-Palestinian conflict. Indeed, the United States and Israel openly denounced international forums allegedly upholding the Palestinian cause. For instance, this trend included the withdrawal of the United States and Israeli from UNESCO in 2017 and from the UN Human Rights Council in 2018.[167]

Moreover, the pledge of the African Union (AU) for collective disengagement of African countries from the International Criminal Court (ICC) also entailed a geopolitical strategy to control the activity of the organization.[168] Indeed, the AU sought to defer the prosecution of the Sudanese president, Omar Al-Bashir,[169] following an ICC arrest warrant, due to the peace process in

---

165 *See infra,* Chapter 4, Part I.B.i (exploring cases of withdrawal from UN agencies during the Cold War period).

166 Analyzing primary governmental sources helps in reconstructing the dynamics of the two blocs during the Cold War with regard to withdrawal. The U.S. decision to withdraw from UNESCO in 1984 was supported by a National Intelligence study on possible Soviet responses to various scenarios of U.S. withdrawal or staying in: "If we stay in the UNESCO it should be at the price of very far-reaching accommodation on the management of the reforms. And we ought to set up a plan for replacing its Director, Mr. M'bow, when his term expires in a few years. If we leave, we should aim to bring the organization to a moribund state, through denial of funds and legitimacy, and then press for its revival on a more sound basis." National Intelligence Council, Memorandum for: Directors of Central Intelligence, NIC #05506–84, (Sept. 25, 1984), https://www.cia.gov/library/readingroom/docs/cia-rdp89b00423r000300370007-6.pdf.

167 *See infra,* Chapter 4, Part III.A.iii (assessing instances of withdrawal as reactions to a perception of bias or unfairness).

168 *See infra,* Chapter 4, Part I.A (exploring African countries' collective disengagement from the ICC).

169 The ICC began its investigations on the Sudanese President Omar Al-Bashir based on a Security Council referral. S.C. Res. 1593 (Mar. 31, 2005).

Sudan. As the AU could not achieve its goal through diplomatic negotiations in the UN Security Council,[170] it first encouraged its member states not to cooperate in the ICC's arrest warrant and then called for a collective withdrawal.[171]

ii. Domestic Politicization

Conceiving of withdrawal as a result of domestic politicization of international issues reflects the backlash of nationalism against internationalism.[172] From a political standpoint, the global expansion of international governance has generated a reaction domestically that aims at reestablishing the status quo ante, drawing a line between the domestic sphere and the international one. From a legal perspective, the backlash of nationalism against internationalism frequently uses the instrument of withdrawal from international treaties as states seek disengagement from core international values.

Governments tend to take a step back whenever international agreements expand into areas that clash with domestic political agendas.[173] This is particularly relevant in those fields where the expansionist interpretation given by international tribunals or the application of international organizations' practice created a norm shift. Where the consequences of the implementation of the agreement ex post produce a burden that was not foreseeable ex ante, parties tend to seek treaty exit as a risk management technique to preserve the perimeters of their domestic jurisdiction.[174]

Since the dawn of the modern international community, the growth of the international legal and political spheres has encroached on states' sovereignty

---

170 AU Assembly, 13th Ordinary Session, *Decision on the Meeting of African States Parties to the Rome Statute of the International Criminal Court (ICC) Doc. Assembly/AU/13(XIII)*, AU Assembly Doc. Dec. 245 (XIII) Rev. 1, ¶ 10 (July 1–3, 2009), https://au.int/sites/default/files/decisions/9560-assembly_en_1_3_july_2009_auc_thirteenth_ordinary_session_decisions_declarations_message_congratulations_motion_0.pdf.

171 AU Assembly, 28th Ordinary Session, *Decision on the International Criminal Court (ICC) Doc. EX.CL/1006(XXX)*, AU Assembly Doc. Dec.622 (XVIII), ¶ 8 (Jan.30–31, 2017), https://www.au.int/web/sites/default/files/decisions/32520-sc19553_e_original_-_assembly_decisions_621-641_-_xxviii.pdf.

172 *See infra,* Chapter 3, Part I.B.iii (analyzing global retrenchment to internationalism). *See* Eric A. Posner, *Liberal Internationalism and the Populist Backlash*, 49 ARIZ. ST. L.J. 759 (2017) (analyzing the "backlash" against liberal cosmopolitanism); *see also* Martti Koskenniemi, *Less Is More: Legal Imagination in Context*, 31 LEIDEN J. INT'L L. 469, 469–72 (2018) (analyzing disengagement from global connection).

173 *See infra,* Chapter 5, Part I.B (conceptualizing withdrawal as a reactionary decision due to the expansion of international bodies into the realm of states' domestic jurisdiction).

174 *See* Laurence R. Helfer, *Overlegalizing Human Rights: International Relations Theory and the Commonwealth Caribbean Backlash Against Human Rights Regimes*, 102 COLUM. L. REV. 1832, 1887 (2002).

to the extent of obligations they have contracted to accept. Domestic jurisdiction is a corollary of states' sovereignty. It recognizes an exclusive competence of a state within its territory over all matters subject to legislative, executive, and judicial powers, without external limitations.

Historically, it is possible to point out three phases in the evolution of the principle of domestic jurisdiction. Before the outbreak of World War I, states could autonomously determine the breadth of domestic jurisdiction with regard to their own territory. Later, with the advent of the League of Nations, international law began playing a more cogent role in setting the balance between the international and domestic spheres.[175] States began entering into agreements on matters previously contemplated as being within domestic jurisdiction, such as agreements relating to labor law or the treatment of minorities.[176]

This phenomenon entailed the internationalization of specific issues, providing the right of intervention to other states through diplomatic channels or international institutions. Eventually, in the aftermath of World War II, states decided to codify this principle to delimit the scope of domestic jurisdiction. Article 2(7) of the UN Charter[177] regulates domestic jurisdiction with a view to peaceful cooperation between states. The treaty language excludes a priori UN intervention on issues covered by domestic jurisdiction unless they are related to the Security Council's role in the maintenance of international security under Chapter VII of the UN Charter. As a result, preservation of peace, an absolute and intangible principle, sets the limits for the invocation of domestic jurisdiction.[178]

---

175 *See* Jean Siotis, *The Institutions of the League of Nations,* in THE LEAGUE OF NATIONS IN RETROSPECT: UN LIBRARY AND GRADUATE INSTITUTE OF INTERNATIONAL STUDIES SYMPOSIUM 19, 28 (Walter De Gruyter ed., 1983).

176 A jurisprudential analysis sheds light on the view of the Permanent Court of International Justice on domestic jurisdiction, in a dispute between Tunis and Morocco, concerning nationality decrees. Whether subject matter relates to domestic jurisdiction is an issue that depends on interstate relations. Questions of nationality are, in principle, of domestic concern. However, a question that involves the interpretation of international instruments is not of domestic concern. *Nationality Decrees Issued in Tunis and Morocco* 4, Advisory Opinion Permanent Court of International Justice Series B, No. 4 (Feb. 7, 1923), http://www.refworld.org/cases,PCIJ,44e5c9fc4.html.

177 Article 2(7) of the UN Charter provides: "Nothing contained in the present Charter shall authorize the United Nations to intervene in matters which are essentially within the domestic jurisdiction of any state or shall require the Members to submit such matters to settlement under the present Charter; but this principle shall not prejudice the application of enforcement measures under Chapter VII."

178 *See* HANS KELSEN, THE LAW OF THE UNITED NATIONS, A CRITICAL ANALYSIS OF ITS FUNDAMENTAL PROBLEMS, 770 (1950); *see also* LELAND GOODRICH, EDVARD HAMBRO & ANNE

Today, as a result of globalization, we are experiencing an increasing interplay between domestic and international politics.[179] As a result, withdrawal can be used to exit agreements and delimit the boundaries between what is domestic and what is beyond the interests of the national sphere. Consequently, the role of domestic jurisdiction is being challenged. The tension between nationalism and internationalism in many countries worldwide have reignited the debate around this topic, which may strike a new balance between an ever-growing international sphere vis-à-vis growing national appeals for noninterference.

Nationalism promised to revive the status quo ante in the world order before the arrival of globalization.[180] Withdrawal crystallizes a precise moment in the world order, resulting in a polarized political agenda on internationally relevant topics. If we consider commitment and withdrawal as symmetrical moments, then we should recognize the politicization of withdrawal as a result of the politicization of commitment.[181] Politicized decisions of withdrawal end up reflecting political parties' change. Nationalist governments started using withdrawal as an instrument of propaganda to respond to their internal electorate. Therefore, as governments change at home, the internal political shift reflected its impact at the international level through unilateralism. Especially when it comes to agreements regulating issues of global concern—in the fields of human rights, climate change, international criminal law, arms control, international development, etc.—the disengagement of one party potentially affects the global action of the whole international community.[182] In this case, withdrawal no longer represents a tool to mitigate risk, but rather a tool that confronts multilateralism. Disengaging from multilateral cooperation ends up being the ultimate goal of withdrawal, and this undermines the essence of good faith in the law of treaties.

SIMONS, THE CHARTER OF THE UNITED NATIONS – COMMENTARY AND DOCUMENTS 67–68 (3rd ed., 1969); FREDERIC L. KIRGIS, INTERNATIONAL ORGANIZATIONS IN THEIR LEGAL SETTING (2d ed. 1993).

179 *See infra,* Chapter 3, Part I.B.iii (analyzing how the nationalist narrative envisions universal regulations and transnational regimes as ways of limiting states' sovereignty).

180 *See generally* IAN BREMMER, US VS. THEM, THE FAILURE OF GLOBALISM (2018).

181 *See supra,* Chapter 2, Part I.B.ii (shedding lights on the politicization of international commitments in modern treaty making).

182 For instance, the process of collective withdrawal of African states from the International Criminal Court represents, in the view of the ICC prosecutor, Mr. Fatou Bensouda, a regression from what contracting parties sought to achieve in Rome at the time of constituency. This was a global action to create a supra-national court that would have international jurisdiction for atrocious crimes. See Robbie Gramer, *Why Russia Just Withdrew from the ICC*, Foreign Policy (Nov. 16, 2016), https://foreignpolicy.com/2016/11/16/why-russia-just-withdrew-from-icc-putin-treaty-ukraine-law/.

Alternation between international-oriented versus domestic-oriented governments has always been present at the national level, with consequences for states' treaty actions.[183] Nonetheless, the globalization era benchmarks a polarization between governments oriented to commit and those oriented to disengage from international cooperation. This phenomenon resulted in peaking withdrawal from multilateral agreements.[184]

With an "America first" agenda,[185] the Trump administration inaugurated a new foreign policy doctrine in the United States—one oriented to nationalism and isolationism—a paradigm shift relative to the Obama administration.[186] The United States' conduct entailed withdrawal from core international commitments and progressive disengagement from multilateral cooperation.[187] President Trump denounced or announced denunciation from several multilateral and bilateral agreements, also ending participation in multilateral organizations. In 2017, the U.S. government pulled out of UNESCO,[188] the

---

183 Since the period between the two world wars, the U.S. system has alternated between nationalism and internationalism. American President Woodrow Wilson envisioned a system based on liberal values, through democracy and an international organization, as a prelude for peace and stability. Nonetheless, the Wilsonian model of the League of Nations—which was eventually rejected by US domestic politics—was labeled early on as idealist, as it embodied a form of legal moralism that would prove utopian in practice. The succeeding Harding administration brought the U.S. political agenda to a "return to normalcy," shifting from internationalism to nationalism. This narrative dismantled the Wilsonian embryonic promise of multilateralism, restoring the conditions that existed before World War I, which focused on domestic interests. *See generally* GEORGE KENNAN, AMERICAN DIPLOMACY, 1900–1950 (1951).

184 *See infra,* Chapter 3, Part II (benchmarking withdrawal through a quantitative study to understand the evolution of its significance over time).

185 "America first" represents U.S. foreign policy vision during the Trump Administration (2016–2020). It entails a policy stance oriented to isolationism. This motto became popular in American culture in the aftermath of World War I, when President Warren G. Harding called for a "return to normalcy" to end the liberal internationalism of the Wilson administration. The slogan was later used by the America First Committee, a non-interventionist pressure group that advocated for isolationism against American entry into World War II. *Mutatis mutandis,* such an expression was later used during the 2016 presidential campaign by then-candidate Donald Trump, who after he was elected defined it as the "major and overriding theme" of his administration and made it official foreign policy doctrine during his mandate.

186 *See supra,* Chapter 2, Part I.B.ii (analyzing legal strategies for securing international commitments during the Obama administration).

187 *See generally* Jean Galbraight, *Contemporary Practice of the United States Related to International Law,* 113 AJIL 813 (2019).

188 Constitution of the United Nations Educational, Scientific and Cultural Organization (UNESCO), Nov. 16, 1945 4 U.N.T.S. 275.

Trans-Pacific Partnership (TTP),[189] and the Joint Comprehensive Plan of Action (JCPOA)[190] and announced denunciation of the Paris Agreement, which was completed in 2019. In 2018, it pulled out of the UN Human Rights Council,[191] the US-Iran Treaty of Amity,[192] and the Optional Protocol to the Vienna Convention on Diplomatic Relations,[193] both conferring jurisdiction to the ICJ. In 2019, it denounced the Intermediate-Range Nuclear Forces (INF) bilateral treaty with Russia[194] and the UN Arms Trade Treaty;[195] and in 2020, it announced withdrawal from the WHO.[196]

Similarly, the United Kingdom sought disengagement from European integration and cooperation through the so-called Brexit, triggering a withdrawing procedure that lasted from 2016 to 2020.[197] As the terms of withdrawal from the EU were not satisfactory at home, the process of pulling out stalled in a political impasse. The duration of negotiations—between the government and the parliament and between the government and the EU—implies the government's aim of setting optimal conditions for withdrawal and future relations with the EU.[198] After the agreed date of withdrawal, March 29, 2019, passed with no solution, the British government reached an agreement with the European Council, signed on October 17, 2019, and in force since February 1,

---

189 The Trans-Pacific Partnership was a proposed free trade agreement between twelve Pacific-rim countries. The deal, negotiated during the Obama administration, was expected to be one of the largest free trade deals ever. However, with the U.S. withdrawal under the Trump administration in 2017, it never entered into force. *See infra,* Chapter IV, Part V (analyzing the U.S. signatory withdrawal from the TTP).

190 United Nations Security Council, *Joint Comprehensive Plan of Action (JCPOA) on the Islamic Republic of Iran's Nuclear Programme*, S.C. Res. 2231 (Jul. 20, 2015). Though the JCPOA was concluded as a political commitment that was not legally binding, its legal nature was questioned since it was supported by the UN Security Council Resolution 2231, a binding source of international law.

191 The Human Rights Council is a UN body comprised of many states that promotes and protects human rights worldwide.

192 Treaty of Amity, Economic Relations, and Consular Rights, Aug. 15, 1955 284 U.N.T.S. 93.

193 Optional Protocol concerning the Compulsory Settlement of Disputes, Apr. 24, 1963, 596 U.N.T.S. 487.

194 Treaty Between the United States of America and the Union of Soviet Socialist Republics on the Elimination of Their Intermediate-Range and Shorter-Range Missiles, U.S.-U.S.S.R., Dec. 8, 1987, T.I.A.S. No. 12101.

195 Arms Trade Treaty, C.N.266.2013. Treaties-XXVI.8 (Apr. 2, 2013).

196 Constitution of the World Health Organization (WHO), Jul. 22, 1946, 14 U.N.T.S. 185.

197 *See infra,* Chapter 4, Part II.D (analyzing the process of British disengagement from the EU).

198 *See* Brexit Brief, *Dreaming of Sovereignty*, The Economist (Mar. 19, 2016) (mentioning the Tory Prime Minister Edward Heath's analysis on sovereignty), https://www.economist.com/britain/2016/03/19/dreaming-of-sovereignty.

2020.[199] That agreement set a transitional period until December 31, 2020, to define future relations between the withdrawing party and the EU on a different set of aspects.[200] On December 31, 2020, the British Parliament approved the "deal," to become effective on January 1, 2021.[201] A "no deal" scenario, which would inevitably have caused uncertainty with regard to life, work, business, and investments in the UK, was avoided.[202]

Also at the regional level, Venezuela, in 2017, disengaged from cooperation with the Organization of the American States (OAS). As the OAS stemmed the general situation of human rights violations in the country, the Venezuelan government decided to withdraw to avoid suspension or sanctions.[203]

The examples above reflect the antagonism of unilateralism vis-à-vis multilateralism, which in turn reflects an inherent tension in the world order. Nationalism worldwide has interpreted domestic will for reviving national sovereignty as a shield against international interference. As a result, withdrawal serves as an instrument to draw a line between what is national and what is international. Since withdrawal responds to domestic politicization of international issues, not only do nationalist governments seek opportunistic behaviors in foreign policy, but they also openly declare their ideological disengagement from multilateral cooperation.

B. *Lawfulness and Cooperativeness of Withdrawal*

Even though withdrawal clauses authorize a lawful act de jure, they can trigger noncooperative outcomes de facto or unlawful outcomes. As a result, withdrawal can be defined through different categories, based on the degree of cooperation of the denouncing state and the legal effects of the withdrawing

---

199 *See* UK Government, Department from Exiting the European Union, *Policy Paper: New Withdrawal Agreement and Political Declaration* (Oct. 19, 2019), https://www.gov.uk/government/publications/new-withdrawal-agreement-and-political-declaration.

200 Future relations between the UK and the EU are mainly related to trade, law enforcement, data sharing and security, aviation standards and safety, access to fishing waters, supplies of electricity and gas, and licensing and regulation of medicines. *See* Tom Edgington, *Brexit: What is the Transition Period?*, BBC (Jan. 31, 2020), https://www.bbc.com/news/uk-politics-50838994.

201 The House of Commons voted 521 for and 73 against; then the House of Lords approved the deal and eventually the Queen sealed it.

202 Especially with regard to trade, as the UK left the single market and customs union, if a new free trade agreement could not be reached in time the UK had to face the immanent possibility of trading with European partners with no deal. *See* Amanda Sloat, *What Next for Brexit: Britain Plays the Ultimate Game of 'Deal or No Deal,'* BROOKINGS (Mar. 7, 2019), https://www.brookings.edu/blog/order-from-chaos/2019/03/07/what-next-for-brexit-britain-plays-the-ultimate-game-of-deal-or-no-deal/.

203 *See infra,* Chapter 4, Part II.D (analyzing the case of the Venezuelan withdrawal from the OAS).

procedure. Testing withdrawal in relation to the level of respect for interstate cooperation and lawfulness of the exit procedure ultimately sheds light on the different outcomes and legal consequences for the denouncing state.

First, whenever there is misalignment with good faith obligations under the law of treaties, there is a shift from cooperation to noncooperation. Indeed, the increasing politicization of states' commitments in the phase of treaty entrance has affected good faith in the invocation of withdrawal clauses. Therefore, even though they are conceived of as cooperative instruments, withdrawal clauses may end up hindering interstate cooperation grounded in the agreement to be denounced.

Second, withdrawal may be legal or illegal, depending on compliance with the procedures that govern withdrawal. The treaty itself regulates the procedure and, subsidiarily, general rules of international law apply to define core conditions, along with the VCLT[204] or customary international law. Therefore, a state that effectively follows the withdrawal procedure cannot incur sanctions or international responsibility before an international tribunal. Moreover, whenever conditions for withdrawal are not met, the withdrawing State will find itself in violation of international law and still bound by the law of the treaty or the organization it attempted to exit.

Using cooperation and legality as indicators for defining categories of withdrawal, it is possible to identify four different tiers: (a) legal, cooperative withdrawal; (b) illegal, cooperative withdrawal; (c) legal, noncooperative withdrawal; and (d) illegal, noncooperative withdrawal.

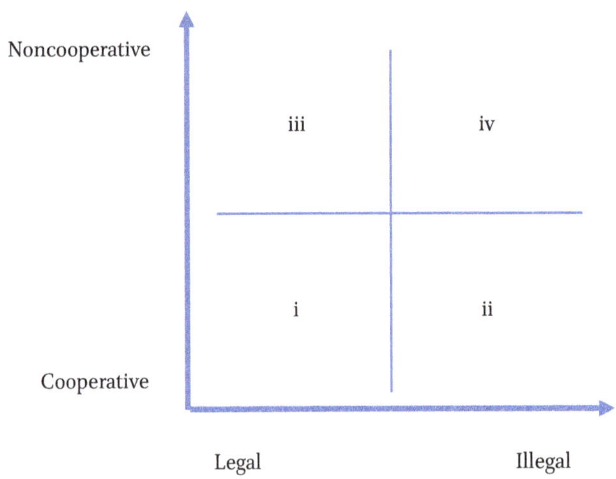

FIGURE 2 Categories of withdrawal: lawfulness vs. cooperation

204 VCLT, art. 54 ("Termination of or withdrawal from a treaty under its provisions or by consent of the parties"), U.N.T.S., 1155, 331 (23 May 1969).

i. Legal, Cooperative Withdrawal

Legal, cooperative withdrawal is a category that is triggered whenever the denouncing state complies with the duties of the exit procedure defined in the treaty that is the object of denunciation and pursues cooperative behavior with the other party states. Indeed, if we consider the right of withdrawal as insurance to join an agreement, then every state has the right to leave without incurring legal consequences.[205]

Withdrawal is intended to be and, most of all can be, a cooperative act. Since treaties do not operate in a static environment, withdrawal allows legal termination of treaty-based cooperation whenever it is no longer consistent with national interests or the interests of the parties.[206] These two circumstances give rise to different outcomes in terms of withdrawal. In the former, a state can unilaterally withdraw while still being compliant with its good-faith obligations. Indeed, withdrawal may serve to denounce obsolete treaties, as in the aftermath of World War II, or commodities agreements in the aftermath of decolonization.[207] The latter circumstance falls under the category of collective withdrawal: all member states to a treaty decide to exit but only in order to join a new agreement.[208] For instance, in the 1990s, the parties to the General Agreement for Tariffs and Trade (GATT)[209] decided to denounce that treaty to move quickly toward the creation of the World Trade Organization (WTO).[210] Similarly. Between the 1970s and 1990s, European states decided to collectively denounce the European Free Trade Agreement (EFTA) to join the European Union.

ii. Illegal, Cooperative Withdrawal

Illegal, cooperative withdrawal occurs when a denouncing state violates the treaty's rules to exit, notwithstanding cooperative behavior. In this circumstance, good faith may be met, but legal requirements for withdrawal are not met. Therefore, even if the act of withdrawal is in line with the object and purpose of an international agreement, it is a procedural breach.[211]

---

205 *See* Helfer, *supra* note 3, at 631.

206 *See* Briggs, *supra* note 3; *see also* Helfer, *supra* note 3, at 626; Helfer, *supra* note 5, at 1581.

207 *See infra,* Chapter 3, Part III.B.ii (examining how withdrawal evolved over time).

208 *See infra,* Chapter 5, Part II.D (exploring categories of collective withdrawal for establishing alternative consensus).

209 General Agreement on Tariffs and Trade, Oct. 30, 1947, 55 U.N.T.S. 194; 61 Stat. pt. 5; T.I.A.S. No. 1700.

210 Marrakesh Agreement Establishing the World Trade Organization, Apr. 15, 1994, 1867 U.N.T.S. 154; 33 I.L.M. 1144 (1994).

211 *See* VILLIGER, *supra* note 149, at 365–67.

First, in this case, the withdrawing state may incur responsibility due to its violation of international law. Second, it will still be bound by the treaty or the organization it attempted to exit since procedural conditions for withdrawal were not met. In practice, states have generally avoided this kind of withdrawal, as its illegal component may be eventually sanctioned as breach and the state will not benefit from exit prerogatives.[212]

iii. Legal, Noncooperative Withdrawal

Legal, noncooperative withdrawal occurs when a denouncing state exits a treaty following procedural standards while hindering its cooperative duties. When a state that follows the rules set in the withdrawal clause complies with legal requirements but then uses withdrawal clauses in an opportunistic way, it may undermine the stability of cooperation in the international community along with certainty and predictability in international law. In this view, when an international legal tool ends up serving unilateral strategies, it weakens interstate cooperation grounded in the agreement that is the object of denunciation.[213] Therefore, noncooperative practices hinder not only the structure of international obligations and commitments but also the essence of the international law of treaties grounded in the principle *pacta sunt servanda.*

Non-cooperativeness may affect not only the interests of the other contracting parties but also the general public interest of the international community. Whenever the agreement protects the general public interest, the whole international community is at stake. For instance, the denunciation of environmental and human rights treaties and arms control agreements, as well as withdrawal from UN agencies and international tribunals, all represent cases of unilateral withdrawal hindering general public interests. A massive denunciation of these categories of international agreements may ultimately hinder the core values of multilateralism.[214] Indeed, as we conceive multilateralism as a system able to protect fundamental principles among nations, then withdrawal represents a disengagement from high-profile commitments that define the pillars of the international legal order.[215]

---

212 *See supra*, Chapter 2, Part I.C (discussing the illegal element of breach, which is absent in cases of withdrawal).

213 *See* CLARENCE W. JENKS, A NEW WORLD OF LAW? A STUDY OF THE CREATIVE IMAGINATION IN INTERNATIONAL LAW 180 (1969).

214 *See* HAROLD H. KOH, THE TRUMP ADMINISTRATION AND INTERNATIONAL LAW 49 (2018) (assessing the potential impact of U.S. withdrawal from core international agreements on the stability of international relations).

215 *See infra,* Chapter 4, Part III (analyzing instances of withdrawal from high-profile commitments).

Even if noncooperative behaviors do not trigger legal consequences per se, they still have reputational effects for the denouncing state. Thus, noncooperative withdrawal may be close to breach in terms of its costs.

iv. Illegal, Noncooperative Withdrawal

The last category entails pulling out of an international agreement in a way that is neither legal nor cooperative. The withdrawing state breaches not only the legal procedure regulating exit but also its cooperative duties.

For instance, this was the case when North Korea denounced the International Covenant on Civil and Political Rights[216] in 1997, notwithstanding the lack of an ad hoc clause. Both the UN Human Rights Committee and the UN Secretary-General rejected the North Korean claim, due, respectively, to the nature of the interests the Covenant protects and the state's unlawfulness under Article 54 of the VCLT.[217]

Illegal, noncooperative withdrawal triggers reputational and legal consequences. The reputational effect, matched with direct sanctions, provides a solid framework for compliance similar to the effect of breach.[218] Not only do sanctions prevent noncompliance, they also modify the cost-benefit analysis of each party that is a rational agent that acts to pursue an identifiable set of interests.[219] Therefore, states being rational actors, they have generally avoided falling into this category, as illegal, noncooperative withdrawal can be publicly revealed and adequately sanctioned.

216 International Covenant on Civil and Political Rights, Dec. 16, 1966, 999 U.N.T.S. 171; S. Exec. Doc. E, 95–2 (1978); S. Treaty Doc. 95–20; 6 I.L.M. 368 (1967).

217 *See infra,* Chapter 4, Part III.A (analyzing the North Korean denunciation of the International Covenant on Civil and Political Rights).

218 *See* Guzman, *supra* note 35, at 1827.

219 *See infra, Chapter 6,* Part I.C (analyzing the impact of a sanctions' regime on withdrawal decisions). *See* Mitchell, *supra* note 64; *see also* Zaelke, Kaniaru & Kruzikova, *supra* note 65.

CHAPTER 3

The Evolution of Withdrawal

> "There is nothing more difficult to carry out, nor more doubtful of success, nor more dangerous to handle, than to initiate a new order of things."
>
> NICCOLÒ MACHIAVELLI

Introduction

Evaluating the impact of the trend of withdrawal from multilateral treaties requires an examination of the legal and political framework in which withdrawal operates. This chapter places withdrawal from international agreements in its sociopolitical context and describes its historical and theoretical framework. The evolution of the international community has affected its unity—the unity that allows a plurality of heterogeneous sovereign states to coexist and cooperate in an international community—ultimately leading to the reaction of withdrawal. The effects of the crisis of unity within the legal order have been expressed through the phenomenon of withdrawal.

The interplay between law and politics has progressively determined new paradigms in international negotiations, and, consequently, in the international law of treaties. The international legal theory has defined treaty-making and treaty-maintenance processes, mainly through functionalism, constructivism, and rationalism. Eventually, the rise of liberal theories at the domestic and international level fostered a different approach in international law, one meant to transform parties' perceptions and calculations of interests.[1] On

1 *See generally* Anne-Marie Slaughter Burley, *International Law and International Relations Theory: A Dual Agenda*, 87 AJIL 205 (1993) [hereinafter "*Dual Agenda*"]; *see also* Anne-Marie Slaughter Burley, *International Law in a World of Liberal States*, 6 EJIL 503, 504 (1995) [hereinafter "Liberal States"]; Kalevi J. Holsti, *Governance Without Government: Polyarchy in Nineteenth Century European International Politics*, *in* GOVERNANCE WITHOUT GOVERNMENT 30 (James M. Rosneau & Ernst-Otto Czempiel eds., 1992); DAVID A. WELCH, JUSTICE AND THE GENESIS OF WAR 212–14 (1995); ROBERT O. KEOHANE, INTERNATIONAL INSTITUTIONS AND STATE POWER vii (1989).

 | DOI:10.1163/9789004467644_004

the verge of globalization, it led to the advent of new subjects, processes, and instruments, redefining the contours of international law with a progressive pulverization of states' sovereignty.[2] Nonetheless, the diffusion of the liberal model was not the "end of history," as Fukuyama predicted.[3] The pulverization of sovereignty came with a price—a backlash against internationalism—and withdrawal represents the tip of this iceberg.

The crisis of unity in international relations mirrors the different waves of withdrawal from multilateral treaties. Through a quantitative study, this chapter also reviews instances of withdrawal from and denunciations of all multilateral treaties deposited with the UN Secretary-General between 1945, with the foundation of the United Nations, and December 2020. The study aims to shed light on the significance of withdrawal and its evolution over time, identify withdrawing states, and illuminate on the growing trend of withdrawal from high-profile commitments. The empirical results ultimately show how withdrawal evolved in states' practice from being a legal act consistent with interstate cooperation to being a noncooperative tool.

I. From Unity to Disengagement in the International Legal Order

Since the formation of the modern international community, from the post-World Wars era to the post-globalization era, the international system has undergone structural changes that have repeatedly brought into question the stability of its unity. Withdrawal has emerged as disengagement from agreements that were no longer consistent with unity. As the international community progressively evolved to become a global community, its negotiations framework and treaty-making and treaty-maintenance processes changed over time. Law and diplomacy were tasked with finding the most suitable form for international agreements to take to further interstate cooperation and adjust to the new models of unity in the international community and new forms of cooperation in international relations.

A. *The Concept of Unity*

Exploring the concept of unity sheds light on the factors that help states to coexist peacefully rather than continually clash. Throughout the centuries,

2 *See* Phillip Trimble, *Globalization, International Institutions and the Erosion of National Sovereignty*, 95 MICH. L. REV. 1944–46 (1997); *see also* Jack Goldsmith, *Sovereignty, International Relations Theory, and International Law*, 52 STAN. L. REV. 959 (2000).

3 *See* FRANCIS FUKUYAMA, THE END OF HISTORY AND THE LAST MAN (1992).

unity has changed its essence, determining not just changes but real mutations in the international system. Great transformations in history have greatly affected international relations. From the medieval Christian ethos to the Westphalian community to the modern multilateral post-World Wars order, it is possible to perceive the evolution of international unity. In the modern international community and, especially, in the globalized present, unity has been challenged and the line between national and international law has been contested. This has led, as was inevitable, to a crisis in the multilateral order, of which withdrawal is a symptom.

Unity in international law represents the international community's raison d'être.[4] It responds to a basic ontological question: what can bind individuals together? The answer is, a common power that can make each person equal, creating the conditions necessary for everything we value in human society. From this perspective, unity is intended as the essence and nature of the authority that ultimately represents the foundation of a global universal order that allows coexistence of individuals and thus of states.[5]

Since Dante Alighieri, international scholars have striven to find unity in the international system. The medieval system was grounded on a religious sense of unity that could allow the realization of individual free will. Unity was a divine creation that humans could realize and discover. It entailed a universal sense of order dependent on God while embodied in a monarch.[6] The turning point from medieval to modern scholarship can be found in Hugo Grotius, who envisioned unity as a form of natural legal order that led to the formation of states as an expression of perfect societies. In the aftermath of the Treaty of Westphalia (1648),[7] Grotius envisioned a new model for the organization of

---

4 Unity can be interpreted as the foundation of every order. *See* CARL SCHMITT, THE CONCEPT OF THE POLITICAL 95 (1932) (discussing that legal unity presupposes political unity, which is established by a sovereign decision between friends and enemies); *see also* GEORG JELLINEK, GENERAL THEORY OF THE STATE 144 (1900) (conceptualizing the classic assessment of states' unity with regard to three elements: territorial unity, people, and effective governmental control).

5 *See generally* MARIO PROST, THE CONCEPT OF UNITY IN PUBLIC INTERNATIONAL LAW (2012).

6 *See generally* DANTE ALIGHIERI, MONARCHY (Cambridge Texts in the History of Political Thoughts, 1st ed., 1996).

7 The Peace of Westphalia ended the Thirty Years' War. This war was fought primarily in Central Europe between 1618 and 1648 and, therefore, was one of the longest and most destructive conflicts in human history. Initially, the war involved Protestant versus Catholic states in the fragmented Holy Roman Empire. It progressively became a more general conflict involving most of the great powers and reflecting the dynamics of the France-Habsburg rivalry for European dominion. *See generally* PETER H. WILSON, EUROPE'S TRAGEDY: A NEW HISTORY OF THE THIRTY YEARS WAR 787 (2010).

the Old Continent: the establishment of a modern system of states.[8] This was a time when temporal and secular powers were crumbling in Europe, with the collapse of the traditional power of the papacy and the Holy Roman Empire and the beginning of a new world order.[9] Westphalia is considered the starting point in the historical development of international law.[10] With the formal recognition of states as sovereign and independent political units, the international system became an association of sovereign states.[11]

Grounding unity in a system of states represented the continuation of medieval religious unity. Harmonious relations in Europe were no longer maintained by the Christian ethos but rather by a system of diplomacy that allowed the maintenance of *jus publicum europaeum*.[12] With the establishment of the international community as a community of sovereign states arose the issue of what legal instrument would suitably further the maintenance of unity. Grotius grounded the essence of the "law of nations" on treaty law, replacing the medieval instruments of natural law and Roman law.[13] Universal natural order was a precondition for societies to flourish, and agreements could make

---

8 *See* CHARLES S. EDWARDS & HUGO GROTIUS: THE MIRACLE OF HOLLAND: A STUDY IN POLITICAL AND LEGAL THOUGHT 104 (1981).

9 *See* Leo Gross, *The Peace of Westphalia 1648–1948*, 42 AJIL 20, 28 (1948) (writing that Westphalia marked the end of one epoch—the ancien régime—and the opening of another; in the political arena, it represented the end of a hierarchical structure of European society and the beginning of a new system characterized by the coexistence of a multiplicity of states); *see also* LEO GROSS, 1 ESSAYS ON INTERNATIONAL LAW AND ORGANIZATION (1984).

10 *See* DIONISIO ANZILOTTI, COURS DE DROIT INTERNATIONAL 5 (1929); *but see* ROBERT REDSLOB, HISTOIRE DES GRANDS PRINCIPES DU DROIT DES GENS – DEPUIS L'ANTIQUITÉ JUSQU'À LA VEILLE DE LA GRANDE GUERRE 213 (1923) (stating that Westphalia represented the moment of the rise of international law; each sovereign state was deemed equal to every another and free from any external authority); RICHARD A. FALK, LAW IN AN EMERGING GLOBAL VILLAGE: A POST-WESTPHALIAN PERSPECTIVE 4 (1998) (pointing out that only a century later, after the contribution of Grotius, it seemed possible to appreciate that Westphalia had represented a defining moment of transition from the medieval to the modern).

11 *See* T. M. FRANCK, THE EMPOWERED SELF: LAW AND SOCIETY IN THE AGE OF INDIVIDUALISM 5 (1999). For a succinct account of the main points, see also Amos S. Hershey, *History of International Law Since the Peace of Westphalia*, 6 AJIL 30, 30–69 (1912) (outlining the most salient events in the development of the international legal system from 1648 to the beginning of the twentieth century).

12 *See* CARL SCHMITT, THE NOMOS OF THE EARTH IN THE INTERNATIONAL LAW OF JUS PUBLICUM EUROPAEUM (1950) (describing the origin of the Eurocentric global order until its decline at the end of the nineteenth century).

13 *See* HUGO GROTIUS, DE JURE BELLI AC PACIS, Prolegomena, ¶ 46 (1625) (analyzing the law of nations based on the law of nature).

relations between states easier.[14] As the affairs of states became more intertwined, the number of international agreements increased and their scope broadened, and international agreements became the primary instruments for regulating interstate relations.[15]

Studying the progressive development of international law is helpful not only in understanding the most recent practices that lie at the heart of multilateralism but also in defining the scope of the change in the international legal order. Every significant change in the concept of unity ultimately created an ontological challenge for the international community, with withdrawal being used to disengage from international commitments that were no longer deemed necessary or useful.[16]

The history of the rise and fall of political and legal orders mirrors the rise and fall of unity. The progressive formation of a global community at the supranational level has been counterbalanced by a quest for national identity at the domestic level in many countries. From the post-World Wars era to the postcolonial era to the post-Cold War era to the globalization (or post-globalization) era, a crisis of unity in the international community has coincided with a trend toward withdrawal from international agreements. This implies that law and diplomacy have adapted to the evolving sociopolitical framework to find the most suitable forms of treaty making and treaty maintenance, which will be discussed in the following section.

B. *International Legal Theory and the Treaty-making Process*

The evolution of the concept of unity in the international order reflects the interplay between international relations theories and the international legal theory. The question of whether law and politics constitute two different, separate fields or one overlapping but not conterminous sphere ignited vigorous scholarly debate that ultimately influenced the treaty-making and treaty-maintenance processes.[17] The subsections below map the substantive and procedural aspects of the evolution of the international law of treaties from the rise of modern multilateralism and connect them with trends of withdrawal over time.

---

14 *See* Charles S. Edwards, Hugo Grotius: The Miracle of Holland: A Study in Political and Legal Thought 104 (1981) (in the absence of relevant data on international treaties, Grotius, in his reconstruction of the "law of the nations," mostly analyzed customary sources of law).

15 *See* Guyora Binder, Treaty Conflict and Political Contradiction: The Dialectic of Duplicity 27 (1988); *see also* Mario Toscano, The History of Treaties and International Politics 50 et seq. (1966).

16 *See* Mario Prost, The Concept of Unity in Public International Law 131–32 (2012).

17 *See* Slaughter Burley, *Dual Agenda*, *supra* note 1, at 213.

i. Toward a Global International Community

The quest to give the international legal system a role beyond that of being merely an epiphenomenon in the international order has influenced theoretical scholarship in the fields of international law and international relations.[18] Analyzing the legal theories and diplomatic techniques behind international agreements fosters understanding of the forces behind treaty making and treaty maintenance, which have been tailored to an evolving concept of unity.[19]

With the creation of the United Nations system, international agreements and legal institutions were particularly weak and had to readjust to the formation of the modern international community that arose in the aftermath of World War II. International agreements that became obsolete in the post-war period were progressively denounced, and sovereign states developed new goals and techniques in relation to the international law of treaties.[20] Diplomacy developed an associative paradigm that replaced a system that had been based on a balance of power.[21] The concept of unity evolved to multilateralism, in which the newly constituted United Nations shaped treaty making and treaty maintenance.[22] The multilateral context became a technical forum

---

18 *See* Stepan Wood, Anne-Marie Slaughter Burley & Andrew S. Tulumello, *International Law and International Relations Theory: A New Generation of Interdisciplinary Scholarship*, 92 AJIL 367, 369 (1998) (identifying the main points of interconnection between international legal theory and international relations theory; international lawyers rely on international relations studies for three main purposes: to detect substantive problems and frame better legal solutions, to explain the structure or processes behind a given norm or institution, and to reconceptualize a given norm or institution).

19 Throughout the evolution of international relations, international scholars expressed their concern about empowering international law. *See* Keith E. Whittington, R. Daniel Kelemen & Gregory A. Caldeira, *Overview of Law and Politics, The Study of Law and Politics*, *in* THE OXFORD HANDBOOK OF POLITICAL SCIENCE (Robert E. Godin ed., 2009); *see also* DAVID TRUBEK & ALVARO SANTOS, THE NEW LAW AND ECONOMIC DEVELOPMENT: A CRITICAL APPRAISAL (2006); Richard. A. Falk, *The Relevance of Political Context to the Nature and Functioning of International Law: An Intermediate View*, *in* THE RELEVANCE OF INTERNATIONAL LAW 133, 142 (Karl. W. Deutsch & Stanley Hoffman eds., 1968) (discussing the need for liberating international law from the perception of futility).

20 *See infra*, Chapter 3, Part II.B.ii (analyzing the evolution of withdrawal over time).

21 The balance-of-power theory was typical of nineteenth-century international relations; it provided that states may secure their coexistence by preventing any one from acquiring sufficient power to dominate the others. *See generally* MICHAEL SHEEHAN, THE BALANCE OF POWER: HISTORY AND THEORY (2000); *see also* RICHARD LITTLE, THE BALANCE OF POWER IN INTERNATIONAL RELATIONS: METAPHORS, MYTHS AND MODELS (2007).

22 The United Nations was established in the aftermath of World War II, succeeding the League of Nations. With the adoption of the UN Charter on June 25, 1945, as a result of the San Francisco Conference, the United Nations began its operations, mainly aiming at maintaining international peace and security, developing friendly relations

where sovereign states could create new policy instruments for collective cooperation, triggering exponential growth in the number of international negotiated instruments. The treaty-making process reflected the evolution of the international community, and a model developed that focused not only on rules but also on processes. Rules aim to regulate behaviors and provide for sanctions; processes have a broader scope, including as they do communication, reassurance, and monitoring.[23] Shifting to an approach grounded on processes, international legal scholars sought to reconceptualize international law and its relationship with international politics.

The New Haven School, with the contributions of Myres McDougal and Harold Lasswell, initiated a new approach to international law with a policy-oriented perspective and reformist ambitions. Conceiving of international law as the "law of foreign affairs," international lawyers were trained as policy makers with a domestic and global mission. They used theories from domestic law and domestic politics to rethink international law.[24] First, international lawyers were tasked with raising sovereign nations from the ashes of World War II. Second, they had to foster the development of a better legal system to advance and safeguard fundamental rights and human dignity.[25] As the international order is an anarchic system with no hierarchies or enforcement bodies, the functions and forms of international law cannot be analogous to domestic ones. International law, then, should be a system to foster and protect common values rather than restrain behaviors.[26] Therefore, international treaties were meant to be perpetual tools, without withdrawal clauses, with which to secure a world order around core values through established institutions.[27]

---

among nations, protecting human rights, promoting social progress, and upholding international law.

23 *See* Slaughter Burley, *Dual Agenda*, *supra* note 1, at 209; *see also* ABRAM CHAYES, THOMAS EHRLICH & ANDREAS F. LOWENFELD, INTERNATIONAL LEGAL PROCESS: MATERIALS FOR AN INTRODUCTORY COURSE xiii–xv (1968).

24 *See* Slaughter Burley, *Liberal States*, *supra* note 1, at 508–09 (analyzing domestic regime types as the basis for liberal theories).

25 *See* Myres S. McDougal & Michael W. Reisman, *International Law in Policy Oriented Perspective*, *in* THE STRUCTURE AND PROCESS OF INTERNATIONAL LAW 103 (Ronald St. J. Macdonald & Douglas M. Johnston eds., 1983); *see generally* MYRES S. MCDOUGAL & ASSOCIATES, STUDIES IN WORLD PUBLIC ORDER (1960); MICHAEL REISMAN, THE VIEW FROM THE NEW HAVEN SCHOOL OF INTERNATIONAL LAW, INTERNATIONAL LAW IN CONTEMPORARY PERSPECTIVE (1992).

26 *See* RICHARD A. FALK, THE STATUS OF LAW IN INTERNATIONAL SOCIETY 14 (1970).

27 *See supra*, Chapter 1, Part 1.B (analyzing the progressive codification of withdrawal clauses in international law); Myres S. McDougal & Harold D. Lasswell, *The Identification and Appraisal of Diverse Systems of Public Order*, in STUDIES IN WORLD PUBLIC ORDER (Myres S. McDougal & Associates eds., 1960). *But see* FALK, *supra* note 26, at 41–49 (discussing the impossibility of a community of values in the international order).

International lawyers' struggle to empower international law vis-à-vis politics evolved through a more pragmatic approach—the so-called functionalist approach[28]—that furthered systemic stability rather than ethics and morality.[29] This approach focused on how international legal norms would perform functions that are congruent with the self-interest of states and their political actions. With this framework, stability became essential as a shield against impending crises, especially in the Cold War years. By analyzing the core functions of international law, functionalism sought to demonstrate that the international legal system does not rest only on minimum rules for world order but also on cooperative regimes grounded on multilateral treaties and the law-oriented bureaucracies that maintain them. The strength of functionalism relies on the fact that it is in states' interests for there to be a self-contained international order with a specific toolkit of rules.[30] It connects the dots between crisis and decision-making.[31]

Functionalism is based on the institutionalization of international law, as it envisions the international organization as maximizing democratic legitimacy in the law-making process. International agreements and international institutions are tools for overcoming crises at the supranational level, establishing common standards and pursuing common interests through international cooperation.[32] Therefore, law provides the rules of the game in international relations, along with the definitions of the actors and the instruments available for interaction of states.[33] This approach brought particular attention

28 Based on the precepts of McDougal and Lasswell, Richard Falk of Princeton University pushed the legal response to realism toward a functional approach that is reflected in his world order models.

29 If international lawyers were seeking to demonstrate the impact of international law on politics, political scientists were focused on proving the opposite. This approach led to a systems theory in which international law represents the intersection of the political and legal systems. As a result, international law represents a set of rules regulating the international political system, with the former contained and constrained by the latter. *See* MORTON A. KAPLAN & NICHOLAS KATZENBACH, THE POLITICAL FOUNDATION OF INTERNATIONAL LAW 348–51 (1961) (recognizing the potential value and effectiveness of international law); *see also* Andrew T. Guzman, *A Compliance-Based Theory of International Law*, 90 CAL. L. REV. 1823, 1847–57 (2002) (illustrating formal and substantial commitments in international law for the achievement of an agreement between contracting parties).

30 *See* BURNS H. WESTON, RICHARD A. FALK & ANTHONY D'AMATO, INTERNATIONAL LAW AND WORLD ORDER (2nd ed., 1990) (analyzing political problems at the international level and the solutions contained in the international legal system).

31 *See* Slaughter Burley, *Liberal States*, *supra* note 1, at 503 (analyzing the rules of the international political process that lead from crises to decision-making to shed light on how nations behave).

32 *See* CHAYES, EHRLICH & LOWENFELD, *supra* note 23, at xii.

33 *See* LOUIS HENKIN, HOW NATIONS BEHAVE: LAW AND FOREIGN POLICY 20–21 (2nd ed., 1979).

to compliance theories in treaty making.[34] The negotiation and ratification processes behind international agreements are key to creating the possibility of states' compliance. According to strategic theory,[35] states' behavior is dictated by a calculation of advantages. Therefore, treaties are meant to strengthen states' propensity to be compliant—or, in other words, to make the agreement work.[36]

ii. From Top-down to Bottom-up Diplomacy

With the expansion of the number of sovereign states in the postcolonial period,[37] the entire international community, comprising almost two hundred states,[38] joined the channels of summit diplomacy such that they had the potential to enter into multilateral commitments and international agreements.[39] Under the aegis of the United Nations, international conferences progressively drew in a greater majority of states around sensitive topics and became global conferences.[40] Along with the founding of multilateral organizations and specialized agencies, the international treaty-making

---

34 *See supra,* Chapter 2, Part I.A.ii (analyzing compliance and the progressive focus of international lawyers on this matter).

35 Strategic theory is a method of analysis that includes game theory, operations research, systems analysis, and related disciplines to analyze rational behavior and its motivations. *See* Abram Chayes, *An Inquiry into the Workings of Arms Control Agreements*, 85 Harv. L. Rev. 905, 905–06 (1972).

36 Especially with regard to arms control, compliance strategies need to be tailored to find consistency of the treaty with national interests. *See* id. at 934.

37 With the rise of the voice of developing states in the multilateral context, the problem of "false universalism" emerged as a priority in the scholarly debate. The UN system was tasked with the challenge of promoting collective interests and greater negotiating capacity. *See* B.S. Chimni, *Third World Approaches to International Law: Manifesto*, 8 Int'l Commun. L. Rev. 3, 4 (2006); *see also* José E. Alvarez, *Hegemonic International Law Revisited*, 97 AJIL 881 (2003).

38 The United Nations is considered a planetary international organization, as it mostly embraces the universality of countries at a global level. Today, it has 193 members. The data are available online at http://www.un.org/en/sections/member-states/growth-united-nations-membership-1945-present/index.html.

39 Today, almost every sector of international relations is regulated in a multilateral context. Collective issues, such as social, economic, and environmental problems, began to be the main focus of the legislative process of the international organization system. *See* Oscar Schachter, *International Legislation, in* 7 International Encyclopedia of the Social Sciences (1968).

40 *See* Douglas M. Johnston, Consent and Commitment in the World Community: The Classification and Analysis of International Instruments 21–22 (1997) (discussing "megaconference diplomacy").

process changed.[41] From traditional ministerial diplomacy, the treaty-making process evolved, through multilateral conferences, into an ever-increasing number of multilateral agreements.[42] International scholars debated the shifting paradigms in the international treaty-making process and, in turn, the functional role that the law of treaties plays in the context of summit diplomacy.[43]

The postcolonial period brought a wave of withdrawal as states disengaged from international agreements related to colonialism.[44] It was time to find a balance between pluralities of legal cultures, which resulted in a new model of unity. Traditionally, international law reflected the interplay between civil law and common law systems. The Romano-Germanic tradition, with its uniform system of rules for the peaceful settlement of interstate disputes through a litigation model, influenced the architecture of the international legal system.[45] The establishment of the International Court of Justice, which replaced the Permanent Court of International Justice, along with the rise of international arbitration in various forms, entrenched a model of adjudication based on the application of relevant legal rules and principles.[46] Legal cultures not based on civil law and common law systems have a less litigious tradition, which has significantly shaped the evolution of international law. Though the litigation model could persist in transactional sectors, such as trade and economics, this was not feasible in nonreciprocal areas of international law that regulate

41 At the end of the Cold War, NATO Secretary-General Manfred Wörner addressed the changing paradigms in international diplomacy with a statement about the Old Continent: "Europe has a basic choice: either it lapses back into the old power politics and balance of power diplomacy of past centuries or it moves ahead along the road leading to a new order of peace and freedom, whether this be based on multinational or supranational cooperation. Our choice is clear: we are going forward." Manfred Wörner, NATO Secretary-General, Address to the Bremer Tabaks Collegium in Brussels: The Atlantic Alliance and the European Security in the 1990s (May 17, 1990), www.nato.int/docu/speech/1990/s900517a_e.htm.

42 *See* JOHNSTON, supra note 40, at 16 (analyzing the changing ratio between bilateral and multilateral agreements in the evolution of the international community).

43 Associative diplomacy furthered the model of top-level conferences—where states publicly express their commitment—so vigorously that scholars have identified the category of summit diplomacy. The solemnity and publicity of the ceremony achieve a particular political significance, reinforcing states' pledges. *See* id. at 20.

44 *See infra,* Chapter 3, Part II.B.iv (analyzing instances of withdrawal in the postcolonial time).

45 *See* JOHNSTON, supra note 40, at 82–83.

46 *See generally* SHABTAI ROSENNE, THE LAW AND PRACTICE OF THE INTERNATIONAL COURT OF JUSTICE (3rd ed., 1985).

the public good. For most international scholars, insisting on the litigation model—one based on judicial or arbitral forms—remained a utopian view.[47]

The need for a new paradigm for the international law of treaties led to the formation of an operational model based on a problem-oriented approach that sought prevention rather than remedy. Treaty-making and treaty-maintenance processes progressively encompassed managerial strategies, wherein international norms serve as models of conduct in foreign policy and the means for development of international policies. The operational model deemphasized the need for clarity, certainty, and predictability to seek uniform and universally accepted rules. The system of multilateral treaties shifted from a paradigm based on binding obligations to a model of widely accepted definitions, guidelines, and policy recommendations embedded in a legal form.[48]

During the Cold War, withdrawal was primarily used as an instrument of geopolitical strategy to seek national advantages with respect to the text of international agreements or in the internal balance of international organizations.[49] At the end of this period, a new model of unity arose that overcame the bipolar system. Any ideology that was an alternative to liberalism collapsed. Fascism was eradicated with the end of World War II, while communism ended with the implosion of the U.S.S.R. The international legal system became more effective; its rules, procedures, and institutions more visible. Constructivist theories sought to reconceptualize international law through the practices of international organizations and through the lens of international governance.[50] They reinforced the power of shared ideas and the influence of culture in international agreements, as shared interests were socially constructed.[51] Thomas Franck's theory of legal legitimacy supported the fairness and inherent qualities of norms. Norms emanating from a fair process that allocated resources equitably through an equal law-making process were meant to outweigh the

---

47 Utopia is envisioned in the struggle to tackle what is perceived as a systemic evil in the international system. *See* JOHNSTON, supra note 40, at 82–83; *see also* TREVOR TAYLOR, UTOPIANISM IN INTERNATIONAL RELATIONS: BRITISH AND AMERICAN PERSPECTIVES, 93–95 (1985).

48 *See* Prosper Weil, Toward Relative Normativity in Law?, 77 AJIL 413, 415 (1983).

49 *See supra,* Chapter 2, Part III.A.i (understanding withdrawal as a geopolitical strategy).

50 *See* Friederich Kratochwill & John G. Ruggie, *International Organization: A State of the Art on an Art of the State,* 40 Int'l Org. 753, 762–73 (1986).

51 *See* Philip A. Karber, *Constructivism as a Legal Method in International Law, in* 94 Proceedings of the Annual Meeting (American Society of International Law) 189, 189–92 (2000); *see also* DAVID B. HUNTER, JAMES SALZMAN & DURWOOD ZAELKE, INTERNATIONAL ENVIRONMENTAL LAW AND POLICY 374 (2011).

realist interests that characterized the Cold War, which brought a new wave of withdrawals.[52] Compliance was reaffirmed as a form of procedural justice that embraced both the treaty-negotiation and treaty-maintenance phases.[53] States would comply even in the absence of enforcement, as only illegitimacy and complexity were to hinder compliance. Consultations, transparency, and persuasion were conceived of as producing better results than coercion in the international system, given its anarchic nature, because they could enhance parties' willingness to comply.[54] Nonetheless, the treaty-making process had to cope with the challenge of ambiguity of the legal argot—the so-called constructivist ambiguity—which reflected the heterogeneity of the contracting parties.[55] Even though these limitations hindered the relevance of international law, the international legal system was still a tool to influence political circumstances.[56]

Negotiation settings evolved from ministerial diplomacy with closed summits to a global network of public diplomacy. States' delegations began to be composed of heterogeneous forces in multilateral forums, with a plurality of stakeholders communicating different interests.[57] In addition to traditional ministerial officers, different subnational institutions represented differentiated national interests, while civil society representatives advocated for nongovernmental interests and industrial representatives defended business

52 *See supra,* Chapter 2, Part III.A.i (analyzing the use of withdrawal as a geopolitical strategy during Cold War). States commit and comply with a norm whenever they perceive it as a "social norm." *See* THOMAS M. FRANCK, THE POWER OF LEGITIMACY AMONG NATIONS (1990); *see also* THOMAS M. FRANCK, FAIRNESS IN INTERNATIONAL LAW AND INSTITUTIONS (1995).

53 In the constructivist view, norms entail a meaningful sense of obligation for each state that is capable of influencing groups' or individuals' behaviors. *See* Timothy F. Malloy, *Regulation, Compliance and the Firm,* 76 TEMP. L. REV. 451, 464–65 (2003).

54 *See* HUNTER, SALZMAN & ZAELKE, *supra* note 51, at 365.

55 *See* Peter H. Sand, *Institution-Building to Assist Compliance with International Environmental Law: Perspectives,* 56 HEIDELBERG J. INT'L L. 3, 776, 776–92 (1996).

56 *See* Stanley Hoffmann, *International Law and the Control of Force, in* THE RELEVANCE OF INTERNATIONAL LAW 21 (Karl W. Deutsch & Stanley Hoffman eds., 1968).

57 The role of foreign offices has shifted toward that of coordinators of a plurality of domestic interests in pre-negotiation phases and also of administrative tasks regarding the maintenance of diplomatic records and the publication of official documents. *See* Frank Biermann et al., *Studying the Influence of International Bureaucracies: A Conceptual Framework,* in MANAGERS OF GLOBAL CHANGE, THE INFLUENCE OF INTERNATIONAL ENVIRONMENTAL BUREAUCRACIES 37, 53 (Frank Biermann & Bernd Siebenhuner eds., 2009) (analyzing the role of international bureaucracies in complex negotiation situations as they offer their services as neutral mediators).

interests.[58] The world order evolved through this new concept of public diplomacy, forging the principles that govern the international community.[59] This change was eventually reflected in the law of treaties, which involves a plurality of actors in the law-making task.[60] The renewed approach to international negotiations was tailored as a trade-off of juridical form for pragmatism, with parties preferring to secure political engagement rather than legal obligations.[61]

The scholarly effort to find a juridical form for multilateral agreements institutionalized the diplomats' task as being to find a minimum common denominator between parties and the lawyers' task as being to translate it into common standards. Through rational choice theory, the rationalist approach created an ad hoc framework that introduced a problem-solving method in multilateral treaty-making processes based on regimes.[62] Aiming at optimizing states' behaviors, the rationalist approach developed regime theories.[63] Regimes are defined as principles, rules, and procedures to regulate

---

58 *See* Johnston, *supra* note 40, at 18–19 (analyzing the role of sovereign and non-sovereign entities in the formation of international agreements); *see also* Charles Lipson, *Why Are Some International Agreements Informal?*, 45 Int'l Org. 495 (1991) (shedding light on the pros and cons of informal procedures, such as memoranda of understandings, in the international treaty-making process: on the one hand, they entail flexibility, speed, and confidentiality, and on the other, they usually lack dispute settlement clauses because they are purely non-binding instruments).

59 *See* Johnston, *supra* note 40, at 10–11 (focusing on the evolution and classification of diplomatic functions).

60 *See* Bertrand Ramcharan, The International Law Commission: Its Approach to Codification and Progressive Development of International Law (1977) (analyzing the evolution of the codification process in the international community).

61 *See* Nadia Von Bassewitz, *International Climate Change Policy: Where Do We Stand?*, in Climate Change: International Law and Global Governance, Volume ii: Policy, Diplomacy and Governance in a Changing Environment 101, 119–21 (Oliver C. Ruppel et al. eds., 2013) (analyzing the evolution of diplomatic technique a from top-down to a bottom-up strategy); *see also* Pamela Chasek, Earth Negotiations: Analyzing Thirty Years of Environmental Diplomacy (2001); William Zartman & Maureen Berman, The Practical Negotiator (1982).

62 Grounded on microeconomic models, rational choice theory seeks to identify cost-effective decisions for rational agents. The theory is that based on the available information, probabilities of future events, and the potential costs and benefits related to preferences, an agent will act consistently at the moment of determining the best choice of action. *See generally* Patrick Dunleavy, Democracy, Bureaucracy and Public Choice: Economic Models in Political Science (1991) (analyzing rational choice theory applied to the political context.

63 The rationalist approach began applying theories of neoclassical economics to identify the legal implications of maximizing behavior based on states' preferences. *See generally* Jack L. Goldsmith & Eric A. Posner, The Limits of International Law (2006).

international cooperation around given topics while reducing transactional costs.[64]

With the creation of special regimes, the international legal system evolved through specialization. Regimes were divided along the lines of their point and purpose, pursuing their strategic choices in different functional areas, such as trade law, human rights law, environmental law, security law, international criminal law, European Union law, and others.[65] Decision-making occurred within the regimes' institutions, which created the conditions for systematic multilateral negotiations between parties, thereby increasing the quality of information.[66] The rationalist approach developed a methodology based on compliance while creating the conditions for decentralized enforcement.[67] International regimes were not meant to impose upon states particular conduct; they were to have a facilitative purpose.[68] This system eventually enhanced monitoring procedures within international treaties, exposing the actions of one state to the eyes of the others.[69]

Moreover, regimes were meant to adapt international treaties to changing circumstances in the life of a state. In the 1997 *Gabčikovo-Nagymaros Project* case,[70] the ICJ explained international regimes using the concept of flexibility. The treaty provisions at issue identified a joint investment project between Hungary and Slovakia, establishing a regime. In the opinion of the Court,

---

64 *See* Ronald B. Mitchell, *Sources of Transparency: Information Systems in International Regimes*, *in* 42 INT'L STUD. Q. 109, 109–10 (1988).

65 Martti Koskenniemi envisions functional regimes in the role that sovereign states used to play in international relations. Globalization has brought changes in how to approach new challenges as political engagement shifted from sovereign states to functional regimes. *See* Martti Koskenniemi, *The Politics of International Law – 20 Years Later*, 20 EJIL 7, 12–14 (2009).

66 Regimes facilitate linkages, connecting different spheres within the same regime and connecting different regimes. *See* ORAN R. YOUNG, INTERNATIONAL COOPERATION: BUILDING REGIMES FOR NATURAL RESOURCES AND THE ENVIRONMENT (1989); *see also* Oran R. Young, *International Regimes: Toward a New Theory of Institutions*, 39 WORLD POL. 104 (1986).

67 *See* Slaughter Burley, *Dual Agenda*, *supra* note 1, at 220 (charting featured points on international norms and institutions from the perspective of regime theorists and international lawyers).

68 Regimes are meant to simplify conveying domestic interests at the international level while ensuring cooperation. *See* ROBERT O. KEOHANE, AFTER HEGEMONY: COOPERATION AND DISCORD IN THE WORLD POLITICAL ECONOMY 246 (1984).

69 Not only did the regime system hinge on the principle of reciprocity due to a diffuse controlling system, it also fostered the role of reputation in guiding states' behavior. *See* id. at 244–45.

70 Gabčíkovo-Nagymaros Project (Hungary v. Slovakia), Judgment I.C.J. Rep. 1997 (1) (Sept. 25).

because economic and environmental circumstances changed while the treaty was in force, adjustments to the regime were necessary to guarantee an equitable balance of interests between contracting parties.[71] In the absence of relevant data, the Court invited the parties to renegotiate on the basis of results produced by technical experts.[72] The decision of the Court reflected a trend of shifting from a legal to a managerial approach, with disputes being addressed as managerial problems and taking into account technical or economic considerations. This entailed an interdisciplinary approach allowing for the combination of legal techniques with empirical findings in social science and economics.[73]

The application of rational choice to international governance brought international law to less legalist forms and a greater focus on efficiency and transparency. It fostered recourse to soft legal mechanisms in international agreements as a way to create for states nonbinding systems for compliance rather than binding structures that must be committed to. This approach has proven particularly relevant in the law of treaties in the fields of human rights, climate change, and arms control. It aimed at placing the treaty-making process in a regime context, giving rational sovereign states more incentives to participate and comply.[74] It ultimately generated a trend of states remaining in regimes they joined while withdrawing from agreements or protocols under the regime umbrella.[75]

iii. Liberalism: the End of History?

On the verge of globalization, liberal theories, through democratic institutions and free markets, spread their message worldwide.[76] They fostered a different approach in international law, one meant to transform parties' perceptions and calculation of interests and make it possible to engage with new subjects, processes, and instruments.[77]

---

71 *See* id. at 80 at [146].

72 *See* id. at [147].

73 *See* Martti Koskenniemi, *The Fate of Public International Law: Between Technique and Politics*, 70 Mod. L. Rev. 1, 14 (2007); *but see* J. Klabbers, *The Relative Autonomy of International Law, or the Forgotten Politics of Interdisciplinarity*, 1 J. Int'l L. & Int'l Rel. 35 (2005) (criticizing interdisciplinarity in legal science).

74 *See* Slaughter Burley, *Dual Agenda, supra* note 1, at 224–25 (analyzing the use of regime theory in different fields of international law and questioning its deficiencies).

75 *See infra*, Chapter 4, Part iv (exploring cases of states withdrawing from international agreements regulated under a regime framework while remaining in the regimes).

76 Liberal theories became the "common heritage of mankind." *See* Fukuyama, supra note 3.

77 *See generally* Slaughter Burley, *Dual Agenda, supra* note 1; *see also* Slaughter Burley, *Liberal States, supra* note 1, at 504; Holsti, *supra* note 1, at 30; Welch, *supra* note 1, at 212–14; Keohane, *supra* note 1, at vii.

In the last decades, the liberal agenda has changed the contours of international law and cooperation.[78] As Anne Marie Slaughter affirmed, in the post-Cold War era, a rapprochement between international law and international relations helped achieve relative stability in the world order.[79] Democratic values were the primary factor that allowed states to coexist and cooperate. Human rights became the core mission of foreign policy. The rule of law confirmed its preeminence in domestic democratic legal systems. International organizations served as the main channel for spreading and consolidating this message. As liberalism conveyed a single political, economic, and legal model, the world order progressively embraced this model.[80]

To echo a Kantian affirmation, liberal states are more likely to adopt and observe international norms.[81] In a system without coercion and central enforcement, such as the international one, rules are tailored to shape international politics while crystallizing sovereign behaviors and expectations.[82] Mutatis mutandis, the modern liberal model, sought to secure what has been defined as the "liberal peace."[83] This does not mean that liberal states are more prone to pacifism than non-liberal ones. Convergence factors underlying the interests that states have in common, based on political, legal, and economic paradigms, reduce the likelihood of military conflicts.[84] Globalization enhanced the spread of the liberal model, easing the flow of capital, services, goods, and people and generating a shift from an international paradigm to a

78 *See* Trimble, *supra* note 2, at 1944–46; *see also* Goldsmith, *supra* note 2.

79 *See generally* Slaughter Burley, *Liberal States*, *supra* note 1.

80 *See* William C. Bradford, In The Minds of Men: A Theory of Compliance with the Laws of War 9 (2004).

81 Kant wanted to maintain the "perpetual peace" as a real possibility. With that aim, he envisioned perfection of the international legal order through a federation of republican states based on rationality. Homogeneity of constitutions and legal orders at the national level would eventually allow a proper system of rights and legal relations between states and beyond states to emerge. *See* Immanuel Kant, Perpetual Peace: A Philosophical Sketch (1795).

82 *See* Robert O. Keohane, International Institutions and State Power vii (1989).

83 The "liberal peace" model does not entail liberal states being more prone to pacifism than non-liberal ones, but it creates the conditions that render it unlikely that they would wage war against one another. *See* Slaughter Burley, *Liberal States*, *supra* note 1, at 509 (stating that liberal states have never waged war against one another); *but see* Bruce M. Russett, Grasping the Democratic Peace: Principles for a Post–Cold War World 11–23 (1993).

84 Liberal theories have shaped the world order around a model of "common marketization" of international relations with the possible achievement of homeostasis. *See* Fukuyama, *supra* note 3.

transnational one.[85] However, this process triggered a progressive pulverization of states' sovereignty, ultimately undermining the concept of unity.

Liberal international relations theory assumes a circular system with states' commitments at the international level determined by their domestic political, social, and economic situations.[86] Through institutionalization and patterned interactions, the liberal model furthered a fair distribution of costs and benefits among parties.[87] First, it presumes that states enter into agreements willing to comply with them. Indeed, as economic and political interdependence among states increases, cooperative models have a greater impact on compliance strategies.[88] Second, monitoring and sanctioning procedures promote the reliability of all actors through the activity of independent institutions.[89] Nations that trust each other will deal with the risk of nonperformance by relying on voluntarism and assistance.[90]

Under the liberal model, international law is no longer the law of nations, as it used to be in the Westphalian model; it regulates activities that take place beyond territorial orders. International agreements represent the evolution, coordination, and harmonization of interstate dialogue between relevant actors, including non-state actors. Through regime theories,[91] liberalism sought to secure commitment and compliance over time. Regimes are not

---

85 *See* Yuval Noah Hariri, *We Need a Post-Liberal Order Now*, The Economist (Sept. 26, 2018), www.economist.com/open-future/2018/09/26/we-need-a-post-liberal-order-now.

86 Having democratically elected governments grounded on rule-of-law standards along with economic interdependence reflects the beneficial influence of democracy on international peace. Democratic states, organized around rules and institutions, are more likely to accept and observe rules of international law. *See* Burley, *Liberal States, supra* note 1, at 532.

87 *See* Henkin, supra note 33.

88 The role of international law is to influence domestic systems through the vertical internalization of international norms and the horizontal relations of interstate cooperation. The "vertical internalization" of norms within states furthers compliance with international agreements, triggering transnational relations between the main agents. *See* Harold Hongju Koh, *Why Do Nations Obey International Law?*, 106 Yale L.J. 2599, 2599–659 (1997) (criticizing the managerial approach taken by Chayes and the legitimacy model of Franck).

89 Based on liberal theories, states are more likely to comply under the aegis of a neutral institution rather than under the check of another party. *See* Beth A. Simmons, *Capacity, Commitment, and Compliance: International Institutions and Territorial Disputes*, 46 J. Conflict Resol. 829, 829–56 (2002).

90 The liberal theoretical framework draws a causal link between states' behavior at the international level and their internal political, social and economic conditions. *See* Bruce Russett, *Politics and Alternative Security: Towards a More Democratic, Therefore More Peaceful World, in* Alternative Security: Living Without Nuclear Deterrence 107, 111 (Burns H. Weston ed., 1990).

91 *See supra,* Chapter 2, Part 1.B.ii (understanding the functioning of international regimes).

just legal treaties but political institutions as a whole.[92] Therefore, not only do regimes implement rules, they also develop policies and programs. These strategies are tailored to respond to particular issue areas covered by a treaty, promoting behavioral changes and an enhanced environment for compliance. Stakeholders' participation—through states, subnational governments, international organizations, NGOs, and individuals—is key in the treaty-making and treaty-maintenance process.

This phenomenon reflects the evolution of non-state actors from law-takers to law-makers.[93] In the field of climate change, this is the result of experience with the Kyoto Protocol[94] and the Paris Agreement,[95] with which non-state actors participated as relevant stakeholders. Through this mechanism, within the United Nations Framework Convention on Climate Change (UNFCCC),[96] the Conference of Parties consecrated the need for a combination of various relevant actors concerned with multifaceted aspects of climate change.[97] In the field of international trade, the Trans-Pacific Partnership (TPP)[98] negotiations

---

92 *See* Oran R. Young & Marc A. Levy, *The Effectiveness of International Environmental Regimes, in* THE EFFECTIVENESS OF INTERNATIONAL ENVIRONMENTAL REGIMES 1, 3–6 (Oran R. Young ed., 1999) (claiming that regimes that are politically effective are not necessarily also legally effective).

93 *See* Cedric Ryngaert, *State Responsibility and Non-State Actors, in* NON-STATE ACTOR DYNAMICS IN INTERNATIONAL LAW: FROM LAW-TAKERS TO LAW-MAKERS 163, 183 (Math Noortmann & Cedric Ryngaert eds., 2010); *see also* Paul B. Stephan, *Privatizing International Law,* 97 VA. L. REV. 1573, 1577 (2011) (discussing a cost-benefit study on the participation of non-state actors in the treaty-making process); Peter J. Spiro, *NGOs in International Environmental Lawmaking: Theoretical Models,* Temple University Legal Studies Research Paper 26, 2–3 (2006) (measuring the influence of non-state actors in the law-making process). For an analysis of the role of non-state actors in treaty maintenance, see *infra,* Chapter 5, Part II.B.

94 Kyoto Protocol to the United Nations Framework Convention on Climate Change, Dec. 10, 1997, 2303 U.N.T.S. 148.

95 Conference of the Parties, Adoption of the Paris Agreement, Dec. 12, 2015, U.N. Doc. FCCC/CP/2015/L.9/Rev/1 (Dec. 12, 2015).

96 United Nations Framework Convention on Climate Change, May 9, 1992 1771 U.N.T.S. 107.

97 *See* Rafael Leal-Arcas & Antonio Morelli, *The Resilience of the Paris Agreement: Negotiating and Implementing the Climate Regime,* 31 GEO. ENVTL. L. REV. 1 (2018); *see also* Daniel Bradlow, What Paris Climate Deal Can Teach Us about Solving the World's Most Complex Problems, THE CONVERSATION (Dec. 17, 2015), https://theconversation.com/what-paris-climate-deal-can-teach-us-about-solving-the- worlds-most-complex-problems-52162.

98 The Trans-Pacific Partnership (TPP) negotiations began in 2008, under the Obama administration. There were 19 rounds of formal negotiations that resulted in the final text of the agreement being announced on October 5, 2015. The TPP was signed on February 4, 2016, but with the U.S. disengagement under the Trump Administration in 2017, it never entered into force.

represented a moment for constructive dialogue between the public and the private sector for the achievement of a shared agreement.[99]

With liberalism, the international treaty-making process evolved based on normative principles rather than legal obligations. Following the managerial path, the liberal approach grounded and measured the effectiveness of international agreements through normative values, such as the rule of law, good governance, justice, participation, and sustainability. In shifting from legal obligations to normative principles, this model created global regulatory practices. In order to develop a driver for innovation, it used indicators for assessment of compliance with treaty standards. Transforming normative frameworks into global technical standards and benchmark indicators, rankings, and ratings has represented a turn in policy making. Laws and policies that conform to a given prototype produce an index score in line with the measurement of the indicator.[100] This prototypical instrument has guided different stakeholders in their compliance with international standards in a globalized system of knowledge.[101] The metrological claim for measurement allowed a process of standardization through quantification, making normative values comparable and establishing horizontal relations between different regimes.[102]

The liberal ideal of spreading a liberal model around the world did not come without a price. The dilemma of globalization was polarization, with an intrinsic political tension in international relations between internationalism and nationalism as two latent forces that determine the evolution of the world order.[103] The link between issues traditionally related to foreign policy—such as climate change, energy security, international trade, and regulation of the

---

99 *See* Melissa J. Durkee, *The Business of Treaties*, 63 UCLA L. REV. 264 (2016).

100 *See* Nehal Bhuta, *Governmentalizing Sovereignty: Indexes of State Fragility and the Calculability of Political Order, in* GOVERNANCE BY INDICATORS: GLOBAL POWER THROUGH QUANTIFICATIONS AND RANKINGS 132 (Kevin Davis et al. eds., 2012).

101 *See* SALLY ENGLE MERRY, THE SEDUCTION OF QUANTIFICATION: MEASURING HUMAN RIGHTS, GENDER VIOLENCE AND HUMAN TRAFFICKING 21 (2016) (analyzing how a globalized system of knowledge can be tested locally through indicators).

102 *See generally* THEODORE PORTER, TRUST IN NUMBERS: THE PURSUIT OF OBJECTIVITY IN SCIENCE AND PUBLIC LIFE (1995).

103 "Winners" and "losers" of globalization have polarized the world order. On one hand, the middle class of developing countries and the world's rich arose as the "winners"; on the other, the neediest populations of the most indigent countries, along with the middle class of the Western world, ended up being the "losers." Not only do these categories represent different segments of the world population, but they also espouse a different view of world order, triggering a real dilemma concerning the effects of globalization. *See generally* IAN BREMMER, US VS. THEM, THE FAILURE OF GLOBALISM (2018); *see also* BRANKO MILANOVIC, GLOBAL INEQUALITY: A NEW APPROACH FOR THE AGE OF GLOBALIZATION (2016).

financial markets—and domestic political agendas became increasingly tighter.[104] Eventually, this interconnection resulted in a global retrenchment of internationalism that found its legal expression through withdrawal or, in several cases, high-profile withdrawal from multilateral agreements.[105] Martti Koskenniemi and Eric Posner viewed this political trend as a backlash to internationalism[106]—a trend that aims to reverse the effects of globalization and reestablish the paradigms of the traditional Westphalian order.[107] As the line between national and international law shifted in the globalized present, a new trend of withdrawal reappeared as not only a way to step back from a commitment but also as a way to define momentum in foreign policy. It is an act typical of sovereignty that emanates from a monolithic state authority—the executive power—reaffirming its sovereign prerogatives.

II. Quantitative Study on Withdrawal

The crisis of unity in international relations is reflected in the trend of withdrawal from multilateral treaties, which has occurred with varying frequency and for different reasons over time.[108] The quantitative analysis in this chapter is intended to demonstrate the significance of withdrawal with respect to commitment to multilateralism. This section reviews the cases of withdrawals from and denunciations of all multilateral treaties deposited with the UN Secretary-General between 1945, with the foundation of the United Nations, and December 2020. The study's aim is to shed light on four main aspects of

---

104 *See* Andrea Bianchi, *The Fight for Inclusion: Non-State Actors and International Law*, *in* FROM BILATERALISM TO COMMUNITY INTEREST: ESSAYS IN HONOR OF JUDGE BRUNO SIMMA 41 (Ulrich Fastenrath et al. eds., 2011); *see also* Julie Mertus, *Considering Non-State Actors in the New Millennium: Toward Expanded Participation in Norm Generation and Norm Application*, 32 N.Y.U. J. INTL. L. & POL. 537 (2000) (analyzing the paradigms of the doctrine of subjects through the social fabric and structure of international law and international relations, whose confines become increasingly more blurred); ANTONIO FRANCESCHET, KANT AND LIBERAL INTERNATIONALISM 88 (2002) (affirming that the global market economy has replaced anarchy in international relations).

105 *See infra*, Chapter 3, Part II.B.iv (analyzing the increasing impact of withdrawal on states' international commitments).

106 *See* Eric A. Posner, *Liberal Internationalism and the Populist Backlash*, 49 ARIZ. ST. L.J. 759 (2017) (analyzing the backlash against liberal cosmopolitanism); *see also* Martti Koskenniemi, *Less is More: Legal Imagination in Context*, 31 LEIDEN J. INT'L L. 469, 469–72 (2018) (analyzing disengagement from global connection).

107 *See* Trimble, *supra* note 2, at 1944–46 (1997); *see also* Goldsmith, *supra* note 2.

108 *See supra*, Chapter 3, Part I.A (defining the concept of unity).

the phenomenon: (a) the significance of withdrawal in states' practice; (b) the evolution of withdrawal over time; (c) the identity of withdrawing states; and (d) the increasing trend of withdrawal from high-profile commitments.[109] The study reveals the evolution of the purposes behind withdrawal decisions, which must be understood in their changing sociopolitical context.

A. *Defining the Population of Interest and the Goals*

Analyzing the whole spectrum of multilateral treaties is a very difficult task for any scholar. Indeed, it is difficult to estimate the number of international agreements concluded in a decades-long period of time, and any attempt to do so confronts the fallacy of arbitrary selection.[110] The challenge in quantitatively studying international treaty law is to achieve consistency in making treaty calendars. Comprehensiveness in the analysis is important to meaningful results. Therefore, it is important to determine what to include and what to exclude in the definition of the group of multilateral treaties to be subjected to scrutiny.[111]

The existing literature in the field contains very few attempts to quantify cases of withdrawals from international treaties. In 2005, Lawrence Helfer conducted a study of withdrawal that included cases of withdrawal upon notice to intergovernmental organizations, a treaty depository, or other treaty parties between 1945 and 2005. His goal was to demonstrate how withdrawal is a regular component of modern treaty practice.[112] In 2010, Barbara Koremenos and Allison Nau followed a different empirical approach: they collected a sample of 142 international agreements from the United Nations Treaty Series (UNTS). They analyzed the number of withdrawal clauses in their sample, along with the length of notice periods and wait periods, to demonstrate how they were rationally designed.[113]

---

109 For the purpose of this book, the "high-profile commitment" is used in reference to those commitments that are core in the international legal system, as they protect fundamental values of the international community.

110 *See* JOHNSTON, *supra* note 40, at 4–9 (analyzing efforts to determine what to include in and what to exclude from a treaty law analysis).

111 Although quantitative studies entail probabilistic outcomes and are not deterministic, they nevertheless allow consolidating the validity of the hypothesis. *See* MICHAEL NICHOLSON, CAUSES AND CONSEQUENCES IN INTERNATIONAL RELATIONS: A CONCEPTUAL STUDY 146 (1996).

112 *See* Laurence R. Helfer, *Exiting Treaties*, 91 VA. L. REV. 1579, 1601–07 (2005).

113 *See* Barbara Koremenos & Allison Nau, *Exit, No Exit*, 81 DUKE J. COMP. & INT'L. L. 81, 100 et seq. (2010).

Here, my study to quantify withdrawals is intended to show how this phenomenon progressively affected commitment, culminating in high-profile withdrawals from multilateral agreements within the last decade. Quantitative studies demonstrate the evolution of withdrawal over time, how often and under what circumstances states actually have invoked withdrawal provisions, and what states have been primarily involved in this practice.

To carry out such an analysis, this section takes into account all cases of withdrawal and denunciation of multilateral treaties deposited with the Secretary-General of the United Nations.[114] The population of interest in my study comprises a sample of over 560 major multilateral instruments, including the following:[115]

- All multilateral treaties deposited with the Secretary-General (presently over 560 treaties);
- The Charter of the United Nations, which confers certain depositary functions upon the Secretary-General (although the Charter itself is deposited with the U.S. government);
- Multilateral treaties formerly deposited with the Secretary-General of the League of Nations to the extent that formalities or decisions affecting them have been brought within the framework of the United Nations; and
- Certain pre-United Nations treaties, other than those formerly deposited with the Secretary-General of the League of Nations, that were amended by protocols adopted by the General Assembly of the United Nations.

Though this study does not pretend to be all-encompassing, it analyzes a spectrum of multilateral agreements particularly significant in interstate cooperation. By including all the multilateral agreements deposited with the UN Secretary-General, the study seeks to overcome the problem of cherry-picking to create a population of cases. It focuses on multilateral treaties with a global scope, excluding a priori regional agreements, or agreements related to particular functional areas of subject matters. This procedure makes it possible to get an accurate picture of the global withdrawal trend, avoiding variables that may obscure the significance of the study.

---

114 All data collected for this study are included in a table that can be found in the Appendix of this book: Table of Withdrawals.

115 The United Nations Treaty Collection makes available a database for access to multilateral treaties deposited with the Secretary-General of the United Nations. The information and the data are available online at https://treaties.un.org/pages/Content.aspx?path=DB/MTDSGStatus/pageIntro_en.xml.

Based on this sample, this section classifies all the cases of withdrawal and denunciation from the formation of the United Nations in 1945 through December 2020. It seeks to:

i. Quantify withdrawals;
ii. Test the significance of withdrawal over time;
iii. Identify the states that have been most prone to withdrawal; and
iv. Demonstrate the increasing impact of withdrawal on states' commitment.

B. *Empirical Results*

Quantitative data shed light on a field that is blurred and unexplored. Withdrawal represents a treaty-related action that always existed in the international legal order but that has evolved over time. The rich array of examples from states' practice shows how withdrawal clauses can be used differently in foreign policy as states balance their domestic needs with international prerogatives. The empirical results ultimately show how withdrawal evolved from being a legal act consistent with cooperation to a substantive tool for disengagement from multilateral cooperation.

i. Withdrawal Cases

In the more than 560 multilateral treaties in the study population, there were 230 cases of withdrawal or denunciation. This number is particularly significant when we remember that, conventionally, international lawyers tend to consider withdrawal a sporadic event in international treaty law.[116]

The last decade, from 2011 through 2020, registered the highest rate of withdrawals and denunciations in the past fifty years (since the 1960s). These data show that withdrawal is reemerging as a prominent trend in states' practice. However, does it represent the same phenomenon that it used to? Analyzing the evolution of withdrawal over time, it is possible to identify different phases of withdrawal.

The following illustration shows the overall significance of withdrawal practice from 1945 through 2020:

116 *See* Helfer, *supra* note 105, at 1608–09 (arguing that, despite the scares scholarly attention, the international legal practice shows that states quit multilateral treaties quite regularly. Nonetheless, only few cases of withdrawal gain momentous, especially if they attract political attention. By contrary the so-called "housekeeping" denunciations fall below the political radar screen).

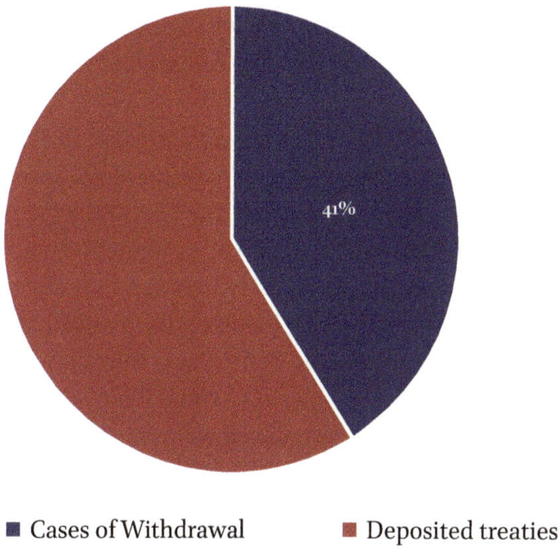

FIGURE 3 The significance of withdrawal (1945–2020)

ii. Test the Significance of Withdrawal over Time

To understand the temporal evolution of the phenomenon from 1945 through 2020, benchmarking each decade illuminates the most salient variables. This period of time includes a half decade from 1945 through 1950 and seven decades from 1951 through 2020.

During the first half decade of activity of the United Nations from 1945 through 1950, only three withdrawals were deposited with the UN Secretary-General, all of them from treaties from the League of Nations period.

The following two decades, from 1951 through 1970, contained two peaks, with 41 and 49 cases of withdrawal and denunciation. Especially from 1951 through 1960, this practice was strictly related to a progressive disengagement with World War II agreements that were still in force. Therefore, withdrawal originally served as a tool to normalize international relations in times of peace. In the second decade, from 1961 through 1970, withdrawal mainly represented a way to terminate League of Nations agreements. The international community was about to enter a new generation of agreements, and withdrawal represented a step in the process of transitioning multilateral cooperation from the League of Nations to the United Nations.[117] Withdrawal was

117 From 1951 through 1970, a significant number of denunciations of League of Nations multilateral treaties were registered (64 of the 90 total cases of denunciation and withdrawal during these years).

meant to be a lawful act in interstate cooperation, and it was primarily used as such, first easing the transition to peacetime and then the transition to the UN multilateral system.

The next two decades, from 1971 through 1990, saw a paradigm shift in relation to withdrawal. Those years reflect the progressive expansion of the international community, with newly independent states having been created in the aftermath of decolonization. In those years, a significant number of withdrawing states, more than 20% of the total, were recently independent developing countries.[118] Though the majority of denunciations still involved the category of League of Nations multilateral treaties, there was a trend toward denunciation of commodity agreements.[119] This suggests a trend of developing countries disengaging from the status quo ante to achieve emancipation from agreements they had not independently signed.

The third period of analysis stretches from 1991 through 2010. Here, data show an emerging trend of high-profile withdrawal, with withdrawal from treaty categories that included human rights treaties, international trade and development agreements, agreements on the status of women and privileges and immunities, and educational and cultural agreements. Withdrawal in these categories amounted to approximately 30% of the total in this period.[120] However, in those decades, withdrawal does not appear to have been definitive action. Indeed, those two decades saw the highest rate of withdrawn denunciations, or re-accession to the denounced treaty: 12% of the total withdrawals and denunciations.[121]

The last decade, from 2011 through 2020, continued the growing trend of high-profile withdrawals. Indeed, more than 70% of denounced and withdrawn treaties embraced sensitive fields, such as privileges and immunities, penal matters, law of the sea, educational and cultural matters, international trade and development, the environment, and narcotic drugs and psychotropic

118 The two decades from 1971 through 1990 registered 46 cases of withdrawal. Of those, 10 came from newly independent developing countries, including Egypt, Iraq, Saint Vincent and the Grenadines, India, Sri Lanka, Fiji, Senegal, and Malawi.

119 Among the 46 cases of withdrawal and denunciation registered from 1971 through 1990, 13 involved commodities agreements.

120 From 1991 through 2010, there were 17 registered cases of high-profile withdrawal out of 55 denunciations.

121 In the two decades from 1990 through 2010, there were 4 cases of re-accession to withdrawn treaties, 2 cases of withdrawn denunciations, and 1 rejection of a withdrawal, in an total population of 55 multilateral treaties.

substances. This trend reveals the progressive disengagement of sovereign states from high-profile commitments.[122]

The following chart shows the evolving significance of withdrawal over the decades from 1945 through 2020:

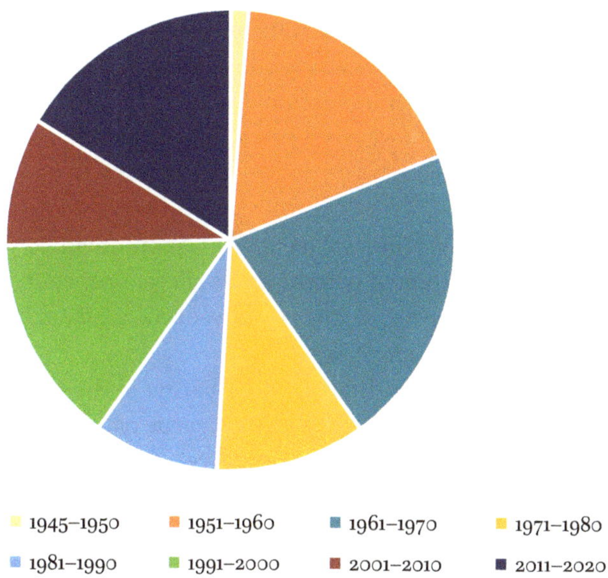

FIGURE 4 The evolution of withdrawal over time (1945–2020)

iii. Identification of States Most Prone to Withdrawing

Quantitative analysis of withdrawal also shows which states have been more prone to using this tool. Historically, France and the Netherlands are the two states with the highest rates of withdrawal, with 13 registered cases each. Regionally, since 1945, European Union countries have registered the highest rate of denunciations, with 94 cases.[123] The Americas registered 33 cases of

122 In the period from 2011 through 2020, 27 of the 36 denounced agreements pertained to high-profile commitments. For the purposes of this book, the term "high-profile commitment" is used to refer to commitments that go to the core of the international legal system because they protect fundamental values of the international community.

123 The EU countries included in this list are the 27 member states as of 2020, namely Austria, Belgium, Bulgaria, Croatia, Republic of Cyprus, Czech Republic, Denmark, Estonia, Finland, France, Germany, Greece, Hungary, Ireland, Italy, Latvia, Lithuania, Luxembourg, Malta, Netherlands, Poland, Portugal, Romania, Slovakia, Slovenia, Spain, and Sweden. The United Kingdom, which is not included in this list, alone had 10 cases of withdrawal.

denunciations,[124] Southeast Asian countries registered 32 cases of denunciations,[125] and South Asian countries registered 16 cases.[126] African countries registered 14 cases;[127] while Middle Eastern and North African countries registered 6 cases each.[128]

If we focus solely on the last decade, the United States and Canada are the states with a highest score. Nevertheless, given the plurality of states that sought disengagement from multilateral agreements in this period, it is reasonable to conclude that high-profile withdrawal from treaties deposited with the UN Secretary-General is a generalized trend more than a symptomatic reaction by just one or a few countries.

iv. The Increasing Impact of Withdrawal on States' Commitment

The quantitative data show the evolution of withdrawal as a legal cooperative act to a legal noncooperative act. Analyzing withdrawal over time allows us to understand the different phases of the phenomenon.

In the first period of analysis, withdrawal was a functional act in the evolution of treaty making from war to peacetime and from the League of Nations to the United Nations. In the second period, it began progressively involving more states as a result of decolonization. Postcolonial states that believed the status quo was illegitimate began to disengage from multilateral agreements of the previous administration.[129] Thus, withdrawal represented a way to terminate

---

124 The American countries that withdrew from one or more treaties deposited with the UN Secretary-General were the United States, Canada, Colombia, Brazil, Bolivia, Dominican Republic, Ecuador, Jamaica, Trinidad and Tobago, Barbados, Guyana, and Saint Vincent and the Grenadines.

125 The Southeast Asian countries that withdrew from one or more treaties deposited with the UN Secretary-General were Australia, China, New Zealand, Indonesia, Myanmar, Malaysia, Philippines, Singapore, Thailand, North Korea, and Fiji Islands.

126 The South Asian countries that withdrew from one or more treaties deposited with the UN Secretary-General are India, Pakistan, Bhutan, and Sri Lanka.

127 The sub-Saharan African countries that withdrew from one or more treaties deposited with the UN Secretary-General are South Africa, Senegal, Uganda, Malawi, Burundi, and Gambia.

128 The Middle Eastern and North African countries that withdrew from one or more treaties deposited with the UN Secretary-General are: Egypt, Iraq, Lebanon, and Palestine.

129 In the years of postcolonialism, the New International Economic Order represented a strategy set forth by developing countries breaking free from colonialism. Through the United Nations Conference on Trade and Development, they openly rejected the status quo of the Bretton Woods system, promoting a revision of the international economic system in favor of Third World countries. Specifically, they sought to advance their interests by improving their terms of trade, development assistance and by other means.

multilateral agreements related to colonialism, especially in the field of commodities. In the third period, withdrawal appeared to be an embryonic tool for noncooperative behavior. However, it often represented a mere threat that did not ultimately hinder the dynamics of multilateralism. Only in the fourth period—the latest one—did withdrawal emerge as clear disengagement from multilateralism. This period registered the highest peak of withdrawals and denunciations since the 1960s and, for the first time, included treaties regulating fundamental values of the international community. Therefore, not only does withdrawal now signal states' will to terminate the application of some multilateral treaties, it also appears to be an instrument that undermines multilateralism *tout court*.

The following figure shows the impact of withdrawal from high-profile commitments in the most recent decade, 2011 through 2020:

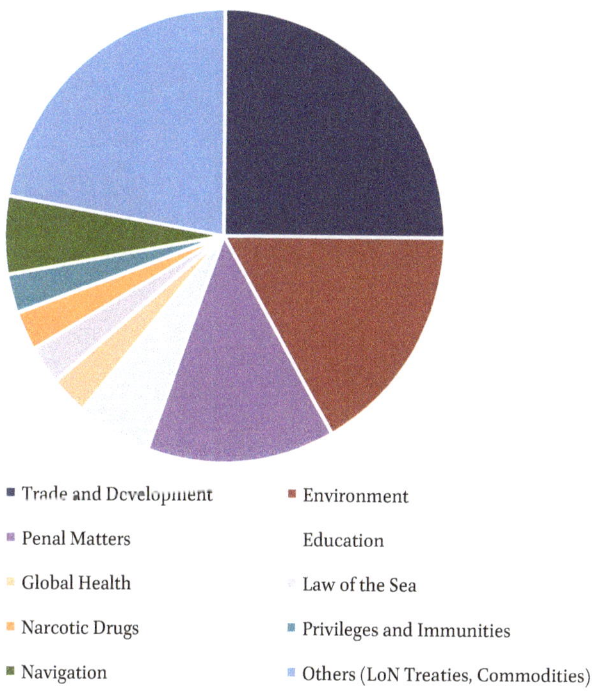

FIGURE 5 Impact of withdrawal from high-profile commitments (2011–2020)

The trend of the impact of withdrawal on states' commitment is particularly significant if we compare the data on withdrawal with the data on accession and entry into force. Indeed, 2018 and 2019 registered more cases of withdrawal than of entries into force of multilateral treaties,[130] which indirectly reflects the nature of the trend regarding states' commitment to multilateralism.

130 Among the treaties deposited with the UN Secretary-General in 2018, there were registered 3 cases of withdrawal and 1 case of entry into force; in 2019, there were registered 6 cases of withdrawal and 3 cases of entry into force.

CHAPTER 4

Categories of Withdrawal

> "We should remember to learn from cartographers the simultaneity between liberty and rigor."
>
> ALESSANDRO BARICCO

Introduction

Analyzing withdrawal in its empirical context allows for drawing a map of the evolution of this phenomenon through the years. This chapter takes into account the most salient instances of withdrawal since the formation of modern multilateralism with the foundation of the UN system, creating a taxonomy with different categories. With this aim, it shows how domestic decisions can hinder multilateralism and how involved parties would favor or disfavor such a course of action. Where the magnitude of the analysis is too vast for a detailed analysis, it is possible to identify the most relevant examples of withdrawal, taking into account exit from international tribunals and quasi-judicial bodies, exit from international organizations, and exit from high-profile commitments related to global issues in the international community.[1] Moreover, it is possible to identify instances of withdrawal from multilateral treaties and signature withdrawals, which constitute particular instances of disengagement from multilateral cooperation. The thread that connects different withdrawals is an interruption in the alignment between domestic needs and international prerogatives. If commitment captured the moment of coincidence between the national and supranational sphere, withdrawal redraws the line of separation between them.

This chapter first examines the category of withdrawal from international tribunals, specifically the International Court of Justice (ICJ), the International Criminal Court (ICC), and the UN Human Rights Committee. Second, it sheds light on the category of withdrawal from international organizations

1 High-profile commitments refer to those international agreements regulating core topics in the international community, including human rights, trade, arms control, and climate change.

 | DOI: 10.1163/9789004467644_005

and related sovereignty issues. It examines attempts to withdraw from the United Nations and from UN specialized agencies and international financial institutions. Then, it considers regional organizations, with a particular focus on Brexit. Moreover, this taxonomy explores withdrawal from the most salient multilateral commitments dealing with global topics, mainly those related to peace and security, arms control, human rights, and climate change. It also discusses withdrawing from operational agreements under a regime's umbrella while remaining in the framework treaty and, finally, signature withdrawals.

I. International Tribunals and Committees

The expanding role of international tribunals and quasi-judicial bodies has created a phenomenon called "judicial globalization," which has progressively shaped domestic jurisprudence and, in turn, led to harmonization of legal standards in the multifaceted legal order of the international community.[2] The permeability of domestic legal systems to international influence through the judiciary has triggered conflicting reactions. On the one hand, appreciation of this phenomenon has been expressed by international magistrates and commentators. For instance, the Canadian Supreme Court applauded increasing harmonization with respect to human rights standards of domestic tribunals due to their review of decisions from other jurisdictions, including international courts. On the other hand, the legitimacy of this phenomenon has been questioned based on the principle of domestic jurisdiction. Indeed, its impact on domestic legal systems has led governments to invoke withdrawal with the aim of preserving domestic jurisdiction in the face of international judicial scrutiny.[3]

The criticism of international judicial review has had different outcomes in states' practice, depending on the jurisdiction, generating instances of withdrawal from judicial and quasi-judicial bodies. The present analysis focuses on withdrawals from the jurisdiction of the ICJ and the International Criminal

2 *See* Anne-Marie Slaughter Burley, *Judicial Globalization*, 40 VA. J. INT'L. L. 1103, 1104 (2000) (analyzing the phenomenon in the European context, whereas the ECJ and the ECtHR are tasked to review domestic complaints in member States while enhancing compliance towards EU treaties and the European Convention on Human Rights); *see generally* Joost Pauwelyn & Rebecca Hamilton, *Exit from International Tribunals*, 9 J. INT'L DISP. Settlement 679 (2018) (providing a comprehensive overview of the different categories of withdrawal from international tribunals over the past decade).

3 *See* Claire L'Heureux-Dubé, *The Importance of Dialogue: Globalization and the International Impact of the Rehnquist Court*, 34 TULSA L.J. 15, 16 (1998); *see also* Yogesh Tyagi, *The Denunciation of Human Rights Treaties*, *in* 79 BYIL 86 (2009).

Court, as well as withdrawal from quasi-judicial bodies in the UN system of human rights protection.

A. *The International Court of Justice*

Analyzing and understanding withdrawal and denunciation of the ICJ requires a preliminary assessment of its jurisdiction. Under Article 93 of the UN Charter, all 193 UN members are ipso facto parties to the Statute of the International Court of Justice (ICJ Statute).[4] However, being a party to the ICJ statute is not sufficient to establish the ICJ's competence because its jurisdiction must be expressly accepted by its members.[5] Therefore, withdrawing from the act that voluntarily gives jurisdiction to the Court implies that the Court lacks competence with respect to the withdrawing state.[6]

The United States' withdrawal from the ICJ is an example of permanent disengagement from its jurisdiction. The United States accepted the general compulsory jurisdiction of the ICJ in 1946[7] under the Truman administration. It withdrew its consent decades later, in 1985, in order to be shielded from

4 Article 35, paragraph 1, of the ICJ Statute provides that the Court shall be open to the states that are parties to the Statute, and Article 93, paragraph 1, of the Charter of the United Nations provides that all Members of the United Nations are ipso facto parties to the Statute.

5 The competence of the Court relies on previous acceptance of its jurisdiction, based on the following options: (a) an ad hoc agreement that submits the dispute to the Court; (b) a jurisdictional clause, which typically applies when the parties had previously joined an agreement that, in the event of a disagreement over its interpretation or application, conferred jurisdiction on the Court; (c) declarations made under Article 36, paragraph 2 of the Statute, where every party to the dispute had previously accepted the compulsory jurisdiction of the Court in the event of a dispute with another State that had made an analogous declaration. Therefore, the jurisdiction of the Court depends on its voluntary prior acceptance by member states.

6 By the combined application of Article 36, paragraph 1, of the ICJ Statute and Article 38 of the Rules of the Court, the pleading State must indicate the provision of the international agreement that establishes the Court's jurisdiction. Article 36, paragraph 2, of the Statute, which regulates the nature of legal disputes in relation to which such compulsory jurisdiction may be recognized, reads as follows: "The states parties to the present Statute may at any time declare that they recognize as compulsory *ipso facto* and without special agreement, in relation to any other state accepting the same obligation, the jurisdiction of the Court in all legal disputes concerning (a) the interpretation of a treaty; (b) any question of international law; (c) the existence of any fact which, if established, would constitute a breach of an international obligation; (d) the nature or extent of the reparation to be made for the breach of an international obligation."

7 International Court of Justice: United States Recognition of Compulsory Jurisdiction of the United States signed August 14, 1946; Senate advice and consent deposit August 2, 1946; deposited with the United Nations August 26, 1946, https://www.loc.gov/law/help/us-treaties/bevans/m-ust000004-0140.pdf.

international judicial interpretations.[8] With that decision, the ICJ's jurisdiction over the United States became contingent on specific treaty provisions. Withdrawing from the underlying treaty conferring jurisdiction on the Court implicitly undermined the Court's competence.

A second disengagement occurred in 2005. The U.S. withdrew from the Optional Protocol to the Vienna Convention on Consular Relations (VCCR),[9] which confers jurisdiction on the ICJ with regard to the subject matter covered by the agreement. The decision resulted from the desire of the U.S. government to be shielded from the ICJ's unexpected interpretation of the Vienna Convention. Continuing on this path, on October 3, 2018, the U.S. government announced its decision to withdraw from the Optional Protocol to the Vienna Convention on Diplomatic Relations (VCDR),[10] which confers compulsory jurisdiction on ICJ over related disputes. That U.S. decision is closely related to the U.S. announcement, in 2018, that it was withdrawing from the 1955 U.S.-Iran Treaty of Amity,[11] which similarly confers jurisdiction on the ICJ. When Iran brought a case before the ICJ that was grounded on violation of the Treaty of Amity, the United States responded with the withdrawal.[12] This position reinforced the United States' disengagement from dialogue with Iran in the aftermath of the denunciation of the Joint Comprehensive Plan of Action (JCPOA)[13] and was part of a cascade of treaty denunciations.[14]

---

8 Termination by the United States of America of the declaration recognizing as compulsory the jurisdiction of the Court, in conformity with Article 36, paragraph 2, of the Statute of the International Court of Justice, UN Treaties and International Agreements registered or filed and recorded with the Secretariat of the United Nations, Vol. 1408, I. Nos. 23569–23582 (1985) p. 270.

9 Optional Protocol to the Vienna Convention on Consular Relations concerning the Compulsory Settlement of Disputes, Apr. 24, 1963 21 U.S.T. 77, 596 U.N.T.S. 487.

10 Optional Protocol concerning the Compulsory Settlement of Disputes, Apr. 24, 1963, 596 U.N.T.S. 487.

11 Treaty of Amity, Economic Relations, and Consular Rights, Aug. 15, 1955, 284 U.N.T.S. 93.

12 In the words of U.S. Secretary of State Mike Pompeo: "I'm announcing that the United States is terminating the 1955 Treaty of Amity with Iran. This is a decision, frankly, that is 39 years overdue. In July, Iran brought a meritless case in the International Court of Justice alleging violations of the Treaty of Amity. Iran seeks to challenge the United States decision to cease participation in the Iran nuclear deal and to re-impose the sanctions that were lifted as a part of that deal. Iran is attempting to interfere with the sovereign rights of the United States to take lawful actions necessary to protect our national security. And Iran is abusing the ICJ for political and propaganda purposes and their case, as you can see from the decision, lacked merit." U.S. Department of State, Remarks to the Media, Oct. 3, 2018, https://www.state.gov/secretary/remarks/2018/10/286417.htm.

13 Joint Comprehensive Plan of Action (Jul. 14, 2015), http://www.state.gov/e/eb/tfs/spi/iran/jcpoa/.

14 *See infra,* Chapter 4, Part III.B (analyzing U.S. policy of disengagement from arms control agreements under the Trump administration).

Consistently with this policy, the Trump administration announced it would "commence a review of all international agreements that may still expose the United States to purported binding jurisdiction in the International Court of Justice."[15]

B. *The International Criminal Court*

The U.S. and Russian withdrawals from the ICC, along with a new trend of denunciation among African countries, are part of the phenomenon of disengagement from "judicial globalization."

The ICC was the outcome of years of negotiations to establish a permanent international tribunal to prosecute individuals accused of major international crimes, including crimes of genocide, crimes against humanity, and war crimes. With the aim of finalizing an agreement about the Court, in 1998 the United Nations General Assembly convened a diplomatic conference in Rome, which resulted in the Rome Statute.[16]

Though the United States did not vote to adopt the statute, it signed it later, in 2000.[17] The Clinton administration decided to observe and assess the functioning of the Court over time before becoming subject to its jurisdiction through ratification.[18] The treaty was never ratified by Congress and remained in a sort of limbo between signature and ratification.[19] Once the Rome Statute achieved its *de minimis* conditions for going into effect in 2002, the United States decided to pull out. President George W. Bush's administration declared

15 White House, Press Briefing by Press Secretary Sarah Sanders, Small Business Administrator Linda McMahon, and National Security Advisor (Oct. 3, 2018), https://www.whitehouse.gov/briefings-statements/press-briefing-press-secretary-sarah-sanders-small-business-administrator-linda-mcmahon-national-security-advisor-100318/. *See also* Scott R. Anderson, *Walking Away from the World Court*, Lawfare (Oct. 5, 2018), https://www.lawfareblog.com/walking-away-world-court.

16 The Rome Statute was adopted by a vote of 120 to 7, with 21 countries abstaining; the seven "no" votes were those of China, Iraq, Israel, Libya, Qatar, Yemen, and the United States. Rome Statute of the International Criminal Court, July 17, 1998, 2187 U.N.T.S. 90; 37 I.L.M. 1002 (1998).

17 Roy S. Lee, *The Rome Statute and Its Contributions to International Law*, *in* THE INTERNATIONAL CRIMINAL COURT AND THE MAKING OF THE ROME STATUTE 1 (Roy S. Lee ed., 1999); *see also* Michael P. Scharf, *Results of the Rome Conference for an International Criminal Court*, 10 ASIL Insights 3 (Aug. 11, 1998), https://www.asil.org/insights/volume/3/issue/10/results-rome-conference-international-criminal-court.

18 Clinton's Statement on War Crimes Court, BBC (Dec. 31, 2000), http://news.bbc.co.uk/2/hi/1095580.stm.

19 Considering that the act of signature represents a *prima facie* endorsement of an international agreement, the time between signature and withdrawal may serve, as in the U.S. case with the Rome Statute, as time to examine the treaty domestically and consider ratifying it.

that not only would the United States not ratify the Rome Statute, it would also withdraw its signature so that its intention to not become a party to it would be reflected in the UN depository's list. That way, the United States was free from any signatory obligation to refrain from acts that would defeat the statute's objective and purpose.[20]

More recently, following the U.S. pattern, the Russian Federation withdrew from the ICC. Russia signed the Rome Statute in 2000 but never became a member since it failed to ratify it. In November 2016, Russian President Vladimir Putin issued an order of withdrawal from the Rome Statute. The decision was announced after the ICC ruling on Russia related to the Crimean issue.[21] Since the United States and the Russian Federation were neither members of nor donor countries to the ICC, their withdrawal had a mainly symbolic effect, which nonetheless undermined the legitimacy of the institution.

With regard to African countries' membership in the ICC, there is an ongoing trend of seeking withdrawal from the Rome Statute.[22] The first country to express its intention to terminate its membership was South Africa. The South African government presented its withdrawal notification to the ICC in 2016, but that decision was eventually nullified by a judicial decision. As a member state of the ICC, South Africa failed to execute an ICC arrest warrant against Sudanese President Omar Al Bashir during his 2015 visit to the country.[23] The Pre-Trial Chamber of the ICC considered this a breach of the country's duties under the Rome Statute.[24] Consequently, the South African government sent its

---

20 VCLT art. 18 ("Obligation not to defeat the object and purpose of a treaty prior to its entry into force") states that: "A State is obliged to refrain from acts which would defeat the object and purpose of a treaty when: (a) it has signed the treaty or has exchanged instruments constituting the treaty subject to ratification, acceptance or approval, until it shall have made its intention clear not to become a party to the treaty; or (b) it has expressed its consent to be bound by the treaty, pending the entry into force of the treaty and provided that such entry into force is not unduly delayed."

21 The ICC defined the status of Russia in Crimea, which arose in 2014, as an ongoing occupation.

22 Rome Statute of the International Criminal Court, July 17, 1998, 2187 U.N.T.S. 90; 37 I.L.M. 1002 (1998).

23 The South African government experienced rebukes in domestic and international fora for failing to detain and render to the ICC the Sudan President Omar Al Bashir during his June 2015 visit. *See* Hannah Woolaver, *Domestic and International Limitations on Treaty Withdrawal: Lessons from South Africa's Attempted Departure from the International Criminal Court, in* AJIL UNBOUND, 450, 455 (2017); *see also* Curtis A. Bradley & Laurence R. Helfer, *Treaty Exit in the United States: Insights from the United Kingdom or South Africa?*, in 111 AJIL UNBOUND 428, 433 (2017).

24 Prosecutor v. Omar Hassan Ahmad Al-Bashir, Decision Under Article 87(7) of the Rome Statute on the Non-Compliance by South Africa with the Request by the Court for the Arrest and Surrender of Omar Al-Bashir, ICC-02/05–01/09 (July 6, 2017).

notification to withdraw from the Rome Statute to the UN Secretary-General. Since the Rome Statute requires a one-year notification period, the denunciation was challenged before South African domestic courts.[25] The High Court of South Africa ordered the government to revoke its notification because it was constitutionally invalid. Even if the domestic constitution does not include an express provision for treaty denunciation, the Court concluded, the executive should be tasked with treaty signature while the legislature should be tasked with treaty ratification and, as *acte contraire*, withdrawal.[26] The South African government complied with the judicial decision but also expressed an intention to end its membership in the ICC.[27]

Additionally, the African Union made an appeal to African countries to pull out of the ICC due to an alleged bias in its operations. In the Court's history, it has mainly dealt with cases in the African region, which resulted in a call from the African Union for the preservation of sovereignty and criticizing unfair targeting. This triggered a debate about collective withdrawal from the institution.[28] In addition to South Africa, the Republic of Gambia and Burundi decided to withdraw. However, the first two of these countries withdrew their denunciation and only the third actually pulled out.[29] Kenya, Namibia, and Uganda also considered joining the exodus based on bias.[30] In the words of the ICC chief prosecutor, Fatou Bensouda, this consolidating trend of withdrawal is a regression from what all countries wanted to achieve in Rome at the time of constituency: justice for atrocious crimes.[31]

---

25 The Democratic Alliance (DA), the official party in opposition to the South African government, raised the question of constitutionality of withdrawal based on two arguments: First, the notification did not receive legislative approval. Second, withdrawing from the ICC would result in a substantive breach of the Bill of Rights. *See* Democratic Alliance v. Minister of International Relations and Cooperation 2017 (3) SA 212 (G.P.) (S. Afr.).

26 Democratic Alliance v. Minister of International Relations and Cooperation 2017 (3) SA 212 (G.P.) ¶ 51–57 (S. Afr.).

27 *See* Gia Nicolaides, *ANC Set on Withdrawing from the ICC*, EYE WITNESS NEWS (Jul. 5, 2017), https://ewn.co.za/2017/07/05/anc-dead-set-on-withdrawing-from-icc.

28 *See* Elise Keppler, *AU's 'ICC Withdrawal Strategy' Less Than Meets the Eye, Opposition to Withdrawal by States*, Human Rights Watch News (Feb. 1, 2017), https://www.hrw.org/news/2017/02/01/aus-icc-withdrawal-strategy-less-meets-eye.

29 *See infra,* Chapter 4, Part I.C (analyzing African countries' collective withdrawal from the ICC as a reaction to perceived bias by the tribunal).

30 *See* Emmanuel Igunza, *African Union Backs Mass Withdrawal from ICC*, BBC (Feb. 1, 2017), https://www.bbc.com/news/world-africa-38826073.

31 *See* Robbie Gramer, *Why Russia Just Withdrew from the ICC*, FOREIGN POL'Y (Nov. 16, 2016) https://foreignpolicy.com/2016/11/16/why-russia-just-withdrew-from-icc-putin-treaty-ukraine-law/.

Similarly, in March 2018, the Philippines denounced the Rome Statute after the ICC began examining alleged crimes against humanity occurring in the context of the "war on drugs."[32] The underlying rationale for the withdrawal, which became effective one year later, in March 2019, was the decision of the Philippines' President, Rodrigo Duterte, to avoid an examination by the Court of the extrajudicial killings that occurred pursuant to the national policy against drug dealers and users that the Duterte administration launched in 2016.[33]

C. *The UN Human Rights Committee*

The United Nations Human Rights Committee[34] is a United Nations treaty body with quasi-judicial functions that was established in one of the primary agreements in the international human rights system, the International Covenant on Civil and Political Rights (ICCPR).[35] During the 1990s, the UN Human Rights Committee registered several instances of denunciation by Caribbean states. Jamaica, Trinidad and Tobago, and Guyana[36] sought disengagement from the Committee despite their relatively positive record in human rights protection.[37] By ratifying both the ICCPR[38] and the American Convention of Human Rights (ACHR),[39] they had accepted grievance mechanisms through the UN Human

32 According to a United Nations estimate, more than 27,000 extrajudicial killings occurred in the Philippines during the "war on drugs" period. *See High Commissioner Bachelet Calls on States to Take Strong Action Against Inequalities*, United Nations Human Rights Office of the High Commissioner (UNOHCHR) (Mar. 6, 2019), https://www.ohchr.org/EN/NewsEvents/Pages/DisplayNews.aspx?NewsID=24265&LangID=E.

33 In February 2018, the ICC prosecutor, Fatou Bensouda, announced that the Court would begin examining the extrajudicial killings that had occurred in the Philippines since the beginning of the Duterte administration in 2016. *See Statement of the Prosecutor of the International Criminal Court, Fatou Bensouda, on Opening Preliminary Examinations into the Situations in the Philippines and in Venezuela*, International Criminal Court (ICC) (Feb. 8, 2018), https://www.icc-cpi.int/Pages/item.aspx?name=180208-otp-stat.

34 The Human Rights Committee is formed by eighteen independent experts, and it oversees the ICCPR implementation, monitoring parties' compliance with human rights standards and the norms embedded in it. Its competence relies on its First Optional Protocol, ratified by 116 of the 172 parties of the ICCPR, and it can receive petitions from individuals.

35 International Covenant on Civil and Political Rights, Dec. 16, 1966, 999 U.N.T.S. 171; S. Exec. Doc. E, 95–2 (1978); S. Treaty Doc. 95–20; 6 I.L.M. 368 (1967).

36 Jamaica, Trinidad & Tobago, and Guyana are independent nations that are part of the Caribbean Commonwealth and that used to be colonies of the United Kingdom.

37 *See* Rose-Marie B. Antoine, *Opting Out from the Optional Protocol – Is this Inhumane?*, 3 Caribbean L. Bull. 28, 37 (1998) (analyzing the Caribbean scenario, where the role of international tribunals was stigmatized under the rhetoric of "judicial imperialism").

38 International Covenant on Civil and Political Rights, Dec. 16, 1966, 999 U.N.T.S. 171; S. Exec. Doc. E, 95–2 (1978); S. Treaty Doc. 95–20; 6 I.L.M. 368 (1967).

39 American Convention on Human Rights "Pact of San Jose, Costa Rica," Nov. 22, 1969 S. Treaty Doc. No. 95–21; 1144 U.N.T.S.123; O.A.S.T.S. No. 36; 9 I.L.M. 99 (1970).

Rights Committee and the Inter-American Commission (IACmHR).[40] Nevertheless, since Commonwealth Caribbean nations had never abolished the death penalty and maintained "death rows" for prisoners, in the early 1990s an increasing number of death row petitions reached international bodies. This led to a de facto abolition of the death penalty in the Caribbean States when the international bodies requested that the death penalty be commuted for "humanitarian reasons."[41]

On October 23, 1997, Jamaica denounced the ICCPR's First Optional Protocol[42] in order to end the right of individuals to petition the Human Rights Committee.[43] Thereafter, Jamaica did not attempt to again accede to the denounced agreement, but neither did it withdraw from the ACHR. On the one hand, such a governmental decision kept open a channel by which individuals could file petitions at the supranational level. On the other, it allowed the country to remain in the regime.[44]

Trinidad and Tobago withdrew from both the Optional Protocol and the American Convention on May 26, 1998.[45] The government asked to be permitted to rejoin the Optional Protocol, conditioned on a reservation on the Human Rights Committee's competence with regard to capital defendants' petitions.[46] The Committee declared that the reservation was invalid because

---

40 *See* Anthony Payne, *Westminister Adapted: The Political Order of the Commonwealth Caribbean*, *in* DEMOCRACY IN THE CARIBBEAN: POLITICAL, ECONOMIC AND SOCIAL PERSPECTIVES 57, 60 (Jorge Dominguez et al. eds., 1993); *see also* Laurel B. Francis, *Caribbean Community States and State Succession*, *in* CARIBBEAN PERSPECTIVES ON INTERNATIONAL LAW AND ORGANIZATIONS, 84, 85–87 (Bertrand Ramcharan Laurel B. Francis eds., 1989).

41 *See, e.g.*, Earl Pratt and Ivan Morgan v. Attorney General for Jamaica and the Superintendent of Prisons, Saint Catherine's Jamaica, Privy Council Appeal No. 10, 1993, Judgment, Nov. 2, 1993, 33 ILM 364 (1993) (upholding ruling that prolonged detention on death row constituted cruel and unusual punishment).

42 Optional Protocol to the International Covenant on Civil and Political Rights, Dec. 16, 1966, 999 U.N.T.S. 171; 6 I.L.M. 368 (1967).

43 Pursuant to Article 12 of the Optional Protocol, Jamaica's withdrawal became effective three months after the denunciation, on January 23, 1998.

44 Since Jamaica never accepted the jurisdiction of the Court, the individual petitions could result only in recommendations by the Commission, never binding legal decisions. *See* Natalia Schiffrin, *Jamaica Withdraws the Right of Individual Petition Under the International Covenant on Civil and Political Rights*, 92 AJIL 563 (1998); *see also* Laurence R. Helfer, *Overlegalizing Human Rights: International Relations Theory and the Commonwealth Caribbean Backlash Against Human Rights Regimes*, 102 COLUM. L. REV. 1832, 1881 (2002).

45 Trinidad and Tobago denounced the Optional Protocol pursuant to its Article 12 and the American Convention pursuant to its Article 78. The denunciation of the Optional Protocol took effect on August 26, 1998 and the denunciation of the American Convention took effect on May 26, 1999, one year after it was deposited.

46 The reservation proposed by Trinidad and Tobago affirmed that "Trinidad and Tobago re-accedes to the optional Protocol to the international covenant on civil and Political

it was incompatible with the object and purpose of the Optional Protocol and, therefore, inadmissible.[47] In response, Trinidad and Tobago again denounced the Optional Protocol as a whole on March 27, 2000.[48]

Guyana ratified the Optional Protocol because the national government, while distrusting the domestic judiciary, wanted international remedies for human rights abuses to be available. The Human Rights Committee issued its first decision against Guyana in March 1988, and in 1999 the government decided to pull out of the Agreement, alleging that it hampered national sovereignty. Then, it re-acceded to the treaty, but with a death penalty reservation.[49]

Even though the denunciations by the three Caribbean states concerned only capital punishment issues, their echoes, which hindered the system of human rights protection in the region, were far broader. Not only did they narrow the opportunities for supranational review of human rights violations, they also altered the position of domestic courts about international sources of law, creating a more inward-looking system.[50]

II. International Organizations

Since 1946, George Orwell's work has captured the endemic tension between internationalism and national sovereignty with regard to international organizations, as they are—in his words—at the same time independent of their member states and fundamentally dependent on them.[51] Withdrawal from international organizations mirrors this tension. States tend to withdraw, or threat to withdraw, whenever their interests are not represented equally

rights with a reservation to Article 1 thereof to the effect that the human rights committee shall not be competent to receive and consider communications relating to any prisoner who is under sentence of death in respect of any matter relating to his prosecution, his detention, his trial, his conviction, his sentence or the carrying out of the death sentence on him and any matter connected therewith."

47 Kennedy v. Trinidad & Tobago, Communication No. 845/1999, UN GAOR, Hum. Rts. Comm., 55th Sess., Supp. No. 40 vol. 2, at 266, UN Doc. A/55/40 (2000).

48 The denunciation of the First Optional Protocol of the ICCPR became effective on June 27, 2000. *See* Thomas Buergenthal, *The U.N. Human Rights Committee*, *in* MAX PLANCK UNYB 341, 384–85 (2001); *see also* Glenn McGory, *Reservation or Virtue? Lessons from Trinidad and Tobago's Reservation to the First Optional Protocol*, 23 HUM. RTS. Q. 769, 772 (2001).

49 Yasseen v. Guyana, Communication No. 676/1998, UN GAOR, Hum. Rts. Comm., Supp. No. 40 vol. 2, at 162, UN Doc. A/53/40 (1998).

50 *See* Helfer, *supra* note 44, at 1884.

51 *See* GEORGE ORWELL, THE COLLECTED ESSAYS, JOURNALISM AND LETTERS OF GEORGE ORWELL, VOLUME 4: IN FRONT OF YOUR NOSE, 1945–1950, at 1952, 1953 (1968).

anymore, or whenever they want to create a leverage to reorient the organization. In the context of a persisting Westphalian model of international community, traditional state-centric sovereignty is operating as a bulwark for nationalism against the autonomy of the international system and supranational institutions.[52]

The phenomenon of withdrawal can be analyzed at different levels within international organizations. Some organizations, including the United Nations, did not have withdrawal clauses available to them from the beginning, and others did, or, instead, included them as amendments to constituency agreements. The analysis on withdrawal from international organizations allows for shedding lights on the evolution of negotiations of withdrawal clauses.

A. *United Nations*

The only attempt to withdraw from the United Nations has been by Indonesia. In 1965, Indonesia objected to the creation of Malaysia and criticized the creation of a nonpermanent Malaysian seat in the Security Council as an act of neocolonialism. By telegram, President Sukarno withdrew Indonesia's membership, also canceling $50 million in economic and technical aid already allocated to Malaysia. The situation changed one year later when, due to a change in government, Indonesia resumed cooperation with the UN.[53] Because the UN had never formally acknowledged Indonesia's denunciation, the return was accepted and the Indonesian delegation allowed to return. The UN had not formally recognized the withdrawal notice—though they treated the case as one of noncooperation—in order to avoid creating a precedent for exit.[54]

Historically, the United States has introduced several bills to review its membership in the UN. Especially when the organization took positions misaligned with the United States' domestic agenda on sensitive topics such as the Israeli-Palestinian issue and the environment, the United States has proposed

---

52 *See* Jochen Herbst, *Observations on the Right to Withdrawal from the EU: Who Are the Masters of Treaties*, 6 GERMAN L.J. 1755, 1759 (2005).

53 General Suharto seized power in a coup and notified the Secretary-General that Indonesia would rejoin the United Nations.

54 In a letter addressed to the Secretary-General on January 20, 1965, the First Deputy Prime Minister and Minister for Foreign Affairs of Indonesia informed the Secretary-General that "Indonesia has decided at this stage and under the present circumstances to withdraw from the United Nations." In his reply of February 26, 1965, after noting the contents of the letter from the government of Indonesia, the Secretary-General expressed "the earnest hope that in due time [Indonesia] will resume full cooperation with the United Nations." For the text of the letter from Indonesia and the Secretary-General's reply, see document A/5857 and Corr.1 and A/5899.

bills to defund the organization or leave it. Since 1997, a bill has been introduced in every Congress to revise U.S. membership, but those bills have never moved beyond referral to a standing committee.[55]

B. *UN Agencies*

Like the UN Charter,[56] other international organizations excluded *a priori* withdrawal clauses from their constituency agreements in order to ensure permanent instruments that would remain in force *ad libitum*. The architecture of the specialized agencies that was created under the UN umbrella mirrored the will of policy makers to avoid withdrawal by not including an ad hoc provision.

Nonetheless, instances of denunciations started appearing as collateral outcomes of Cold War dynamics.[57] In 1949, the Soviet Union—and later, in 1950, eight of its Eastern European allies,[58] plus China[59]—withdrew from the World Health Organization (WHO) and the United Nations Children's Fund

---

55 In line with this trend, in 2017, on the very first day of the 115th Congress, House Representative Mike Rogers introduced H.R. 193, the American Sovereignty Restoration Act. American Sovereignty Restoration Act of 2017, H.R.193, 115th Cong. (2017). The bill would allow the president to terminate membership in the UN and its related agencies, pull out of financial and peacekeeping support, and retract the related headquarters agreements for the U.S.-based institutions. The current legislation has attracted more cosponsors than others in the past. *See* Tracy Nelson, *Exiting the United Nations: Paths and Potential*, YALE J. INT'L L. (Mar. 2, 2017), http://www.yjil.yale.edu/exiting-the-united-nations-paths-and-potential/. Without any doubt, U.S. withdrawal from the UN would leave the international system of cooperation vulnerable and unstable, echoing the post-World War I situation, when the United States was not part of the League of Nations. Even though the League of Nations was ideologically the fruit of the Wilsonian vision, the Wilson administration was unable to convince the U.S. Senate to commit to membership in the new organization. *See generally* NORMAN A. GRAEBNER & EDWARD M. BENNETT, THE VERSAILLES TREATY AND ITS LEGACY: THE FAILURE OF THE WILSONIAN VISION (2011); *see also* JEAN BAPTISTE DUROSELLE, HISTOIRE DIPLOMATIQUE DE 1919 À NOS JOURS, (1994).

56 Charter of the United Nations, 24 Oct. 1945, 1 U.N.T.S. XVI.

57 *See supra*, Chapter 2, Part III.A.i (analyzing withdrawal as a geopolitical strategy during the Cold War).

58 After its withdrawal, the U.S.S.R. demanded that other socialist countries of Europe follow its decision. Bulgaria, Romania, Albania, Czechoslovakia, Hungary, and Poland withdrew. They all restored their membership years later in 1957.

59 In May 1950, the Chinese government gave notice of its withdrawal from WHO. It rejoined the organization two years later in 1952. It is worth noticing that notwithstanding the denunciation, the Chinese government affirmed that it would continue to adhere to the purpose and principles of the organization in the field of global health. *See* THE FIRST TEN YEARS OF THE WORLD HEALTH ORGANIZATION 80 (1958).

(UNICEF).[60] Between 1952 and 1953, Poland,[61] Hungary,[62] and Czechoslovakia[63] withdrew from the United Nations Educational Scientific and Cultural Organization (UNESCO).[64]

Similarly, in the 1970s and 1980s the United States denounced the agreements establishing the International Labor Organization (ILO)[65] and UNESCO[66] and rejoined them later, once each organization had addressed important issues of domestic concern.[67]

In 1977, the United States announced the termination of its forty-three-year membership in the ILO. Allegedly, the organization dealt selectively with human rights issues, ignored due process in its proceedings, and suffered increasing politicization. Even though that decision was made during President Ford's administration, the Carter administration upheld it, demonstrating shared domestic view between Republican and Democratic parties on that issue. Confrontational dynamics due to the rise of the Group of 77, the limits of Cold War détente strategy, and Carter's agenda on human rights were decisive in the U.S. decision.[68] The United States rejoined the ILO three years later, in 1980, once salient points were addressed.

In 1984, at the peak of the Cold War, the Reagan administration announced the United States' withdrawal from UNESCO. Allegedly, the organization's corruption and an ideological bias in favor of the Soviet Union drove the American decision. Later, in 2003, the United States rejoined UNESCO under President George W. Bush.

---

60 Constitution of the World Health Organization (WHO), Jul. 22, 1946, 14 U.N.T.S. 185.

61 Poland denounced UNESCO on November 5, 1952 with a communication to the Acting Director General of the Organization.

62 Hungary denounced UNESCO on December 31, 1952.

63 Czechoslovakia denounced UNESCO on January 29, 1953.

64 *See* Nathan Feinberg, *Unilateral Withdrawal from an International Organization*, 39 BYIL 189, 204–11 (1963); *see also* Polish National Commission for UNESCO Review, Bulletin 5, 22–23 (2014), http://www.unesco.pl/fileadmin/user_upload/pdf/Biuletyn_2014_ENG.pdf.

65 Constitution of the International Labour Organization (ILO), May 10, 1944, 15 U.N.T.S. 40. Article 1(5) regulates withdrawal.

66 Constitution of the United Nations Educational, Scientific and Cultural Organization (UNESCO), Nov. 16, 1945, 4 U.N.T.S. 275; 41 AJIL Supp. 1. Article II(6) regulates withdrawal.

67 *See generally* MARK F. IMBER, THE USA, ILO, UNESCO AND IAEA: POLITICIZATION AND WITHDRAWAL IN THE SPECIALIZED AGENCIES (1989); *see also* Sean D. Murphy, *Contemporary Practice of the United States Relating to International Law*, 97 AJIL 962, 977 (2003).

68 *See* Richard A. Melson, *Human Rights and the American Withdrawal from the ILO*, 1 Universal Hum. Rts. 43 (1971).

In 1985, the UK and Singapore withdrew from UNESCO, as it allegedly had become "harmfully politicized," generating disagreement over management.[69] After the withdrawal, the organization's budget dropped considerably. Britain rejoined in 1997; Singapore in 2007.[70] The Republic of South Africa withdrew from UNESCO in 1956, claiming that the organization interfered in the country's racially based system of apartheid. The state rejoined the organization in 1994 during the leadership of Nelson Mandela.

In the abovementioned examples of withdrawal from international organizations—including United States and U.S.S.R. withdrawal from specialized agencies—the withdrawing states rejoined the organizations after a limited period of time. As a result, their acts have often been characterized as a temporary cessation of membership rather than withdrawal.[71]

More recently, during the Trump administration, the United States withdrew again from UNESCO and from the UN Human Rights Council, alleging anti-Israel bias, and subsequently from the WHO due to its alleged bias in favor of China.

With regard to UNESCO, in 2011, the Obama administration proceeded to cut the organization's budget, complying with domestic regulations, in reprisal for Palestine's membership.[72] Due to a diplomatic *differendo* related to Israeli-Palestinian issues and to being consistently in arrears with the organization, on October 12, 2017, the United States decided to withdraw,[73] and its lead was followed by Israel.[74]

69 *See* Michael Getler, *UNESCO Withdrawal Weighed by Thatcher*, WASH. POST (Nov. 21, 1984), https://www.washingtonpost.com/archive/politics/1984/11/21/unesco-withdrawal-weighed-by-thatcher/ba4bb65a-a6c0-4f9d-ad46-615f317e4e72/; *see also Britain Following Lead of U.S., Will Withdraw from UNESCO*, L.A. TIMES (Dec. 5, 1985), http://articles.latimes.com/1985-12-05/news/mn-371_1_unesco-membership.

70 For an overview of UNESCO history, see data available online at http://www.unesco.org/new/en/unesco/about-us/who-we-are/history/milestones/.

71 Some scholars have argued that there is sufficient states' practice to demonstrate that international law prohibits withdrawal when there is no withdrawal provision. *See* Michael Akehust, *Withdrawal from International Organizations*, 32 CURRENT LEGAL PROBS. 143, 146 (1979).

72 The United States cut the budget by over $80 million a year, about 22% of its entire budget for UNESCO. The cut was due to a 1990s-era law prohibiting the United States from funding any UN agencies recognizing Palestinian statehood. *See* Colum Lynch, *U.S. to Pull Out of UNESCO, Again*, FOREIGN POL'Y (Oct. 11, 2017), https://foreignpolicy.com/2017/10/11/u-s-to-pull-out-of-unesco-again/.

73 Pursuant to Article II (6) of the UNESCO Constitution, U.S. withdrawal was to take effect on December 31, 2018, until which the United States would remain a full member of UNESCO.

74 Despite the budgetary cut, by 2017, the United States had accrued more than $500 million in arrears with UNESCO. The strain that led the United States to withdraw was related to

Similarly, the United States has opposed the Human Rights Council (HRC) due to the Israeli-Palestinian conflict. The U.S. decision to pull out of it essentially reinstated the original position taken during the George W. Bush presidency, which declined to join the HRC at the time of its constituency in 2006. The United States joined the HRC in 2009 under the Obama administration.[75] On June 19, 2018, the Trump administration announced its intention to exit the HRC due to the organization's alleged anti-Israeli bias and allegedly flawed membership policies in relation to countries such as China, Cuba, Venezuela, and the Democratic Republic of Congo that have poor human rights records.[76]

On May 29, 2020, President Donald Trump announced the United States' withdrawal from the WHO,[77] which was followed by notification of the denunciation to the UN Secretary-General on July 6, 2020,[78] to be effective one year later.[79] The U.S. withdrawal represented a denunciation of an alleged China-centrism of the organization, which can be interpreted broadly as an act of disengagement from the multilateral approach to the COVID-19 pandemic crisis.[80]

C. *International Financial Institutions*

An example of an international organization's constituency agreements embedding a withdrawal clause from the beginning can be traced back to the Bretton

the UNESCO position with regard to Israel. *See* U.S. Dep't of State, *The United States Withdraws from UNESCO*, Press Statement of Heather Nauert, Department Spokesperson (Oct. 12, 2017), https://www.state.gov/r/pa/prs/ps/2017/10/274748.htm; *see also Israel Withdraws from UNESCO*, AL JAZEERA (Dec. 30, 2017), https://www.aljazeera.com/news/2017/12/israel-withdraws-culture-education-body-171230062947508.html.

75 *See* Jack L. Goldsmith, *The Contributions of the Obama Administration to the Practice and Theory of International Law*, 57 HARV. INT'L L.J. 1, 11 (2016).

76 *See* Ted Piccone, *U.S. Withdrawal from UN Human Rights Council Is 'America Alone,'* Brookings (Jun. 20, 2018), https://www.brookings.edu/blog/order-from-chaos/2018/06/20/u-s-withdrawal-from-u-n-human-rights-council-is-america-alone/].

77 *See* Donald G. McNeil Jr. & Andrew Jacobs, *Trump Says US Is Leaving WHO, but Experts Aren't So Sure*, NY Times (May 30, 2020), https://www.nytimes.com/2020/05/29/health/virus-who.html.

78 *See* Emily Rauhala, Karoun Demirjian & Toluse Olorunnipa, *Trump Administration Sends Letter Withdrawing US from World Health Organization Over Coronavirus Response*, WASH. POST (Jul. 7, 2020), https://www.washingtonpost.com/world/trump-united-states-withdrawal-world-health-organization-coronavirus/2020/07/07/ae0a25e4-b550-11ea-9a1d-d3db1cbe07ce_story.html.

79 When the United States joined WHO in 1948, it passed a joint congressional resolution, which declared that withdrawal would be permissible if the withdrawing member both provided one year's notice and fully met its financial obligations for the current year.

80 In order to address the COVID-19 pandemic, WHO developed public health measures for the international community to allow countries to prepare for and to respond to the global health crisis.

Woods negotiations for the constitution of the first International Financial Institutions (IFIS) in 1944. The *travaux préparatoires* that led to the IBRD Articles of Agreement demonstrate that the contracting parties sought to regulate liability on security issues and guarantees on callable capital.[81] The result was Article VI of the World Bank IBRD's Articles of Agreements, which authorizes membership denunciation at any time by giving notice of withdrawal.[82]

During the early years of operation of the World Bank, a group of developing countries from Eastern Europe, Latin America, and East Asia decided to end their membership as a result of Cold War strategies (most later rejoined).[83] In the 1950s, Poland and Czechoslovakia withdrew from the International Bank for Reconstruction and Development (IBRD), in line with Eastern bloc priorities. After a long absence, Poland rejoined the Bank in 1986, and Czechoslovakia did so in 1990.[84] Cuba, in the wake of the 1959 Cuban Revolution and its inclusion in Cold War strategies, withdrew from the World Bank Group (WBG) on November 14, 1960, never to rejoin.[85]

---

81 IBRD Articles of Agreement, Article VI, Withdrawal and Suspension of Membership: Suspension of Operations. Article VI regulates liability for *pro rata* share of the capital on obligations and liquidation process after the denunciation is operative. *See* Henry J. Bittermann, *Negotiations of the Articles of Agreement of the International Bank for Reconstruction and Developments*, 5 THE INT'L L. 59, 80–81 (1971) (analyzing the debate during the *travaux preparatoires* of Article VI of the IBRD Articles of Agreement); *see also* Daniel Bradlow, *International Law and the Operations of the International Financial Institutions* 1, *in* INTERNATIONAL FINANCIAL INTUITIONS AND INTERNATIONAL LAW (Daniel Bradlow & David B. Hunter eds., 2010); *see generally* ENRIQUE R. CARRASCO, FUNDAMENTALS OF INTERNATIONAL FINANCE AND DEVELOPMENT (2015).

82 Membership may also terminate for a member suspended by a majority of the governors for failure to fulfill treaty obligations, if that member has not been restored to good standing by a specular majority within a year after suspension occurred.

83 *See* Alejandro Reuss, *What's Behind the Withdrawals from the World Bank, IMF?*, NACLA (Sept. 4, 2007), https://nacla.org/news/what's-behind-withdrawals-world-bank-imf; *see also* Nations Encyclopedia, *The World Bank Group – International Bank for Reconstruction and Development (IBRD)*, http://www.nationsencyclopedia.com/United-Nations-Related-Agencies/The-World-Bank-Group-International-Bank-For-Reconstruction-And-Development-IBRD.html#ixzz5IWIGmjXE.

84 On June 27, 1986, Poland rejoined the Bank, bringing total IBRD membership to 150; on September 20, 1990, Czechoslovakia rejoined the Bank, IFC, and IDA, bringing the total membership of IBRD to 152, IFC membership to 136, and IDA membership to 138. Czechoslovakia also joined MIGA, becoming the sixty-first member. *See* WORLD BANK GRP., WORLD BANK GROUP ARCHIVISTS' CHRONOLOGY 1944–2013, http://pubdocs.worldbank.org/en/186241442500110286/PDF-World-Bank-Group-Archivists-Chronology-1944-2013.pdf.

85 Fidel Castro entered Havana and ousted the incumbent President, Fulgencio Batista, proclaiming the Cuban Revolution and assuming the role of prime minister. As a result of the new domestic strategy, Cuba withdrew its membership from both IBRD and IFC, bringing the total number of IBRD members to 67 and of IFC members to 59. *See* id.

In 1960, the Dominican Republic withdrew its membership from the IBRD and the International Finance Corporation (IFC). It rejoined on September 18, 1961.[86] On November 6, 1961, Indonesia withdrew from the IFC, and it withdrew from the IBRD on August 17, 1965. Between 1967 and 1968, Indonesia rejoined both institutions, also becoming part of International Centre for Settlement of Investment Disputes (ICSID)—the international arbitral institution within the WBG—which had been created in 1966.[87]

D. *Brexit and Regional Organizations*

Debate on withdrawal from regional organizations was rekindled in scholarly and political circles with the phenomenon of "Brexit." In June 2016, the British people voted on a membership referendum that opened the door for the country to leave the European Union.[88] The decision resulted in the current negotiations between the government of the UK and the EU, under the aegis of the European Commission, regarding the conditions of the withdrawal as the basis for future relationships.

The Treaty on the European Union[89] originally had no withdrawal clause, but amendments eventually introduced the possibility of withdrawal. The debate on whether there should be a clause allowing withdrawal from the EU can be traced to the Spinelli Report[90] in 1984, at which time the EU was an embryonic idea.[91] The right to withdraw was later developed through the process of negotiating the unratified Constitutional Treaty of 2004. At that time, states

86 The Dominican Republic rejoined the World Bank Group in September 18, 1961, becoming its seventy-second member. *See* id.

87 On April 13, 1967, Indonesia rejoined IBRD, becoming its 106th member; on April 23, 1968, Indonesia rejoined IFC, becoming its eighty-sixth member; and on October 1968, Indonesia also became the forty-second member of ICSID. *See* id.

88 From a political point of view, this was the result of the Conservative Party manifesto commitment. Once the decision to leave was taken, the leadership of the country passed from Mr. David Cameron to Ms. Theresa May, within the Conservative Party.

89 Treaty on European Union [TEU, Maastricht Treaty], Feb. 7, 1992, 1992 O.J. (C191) 1; 31 I.L.M. 253 (1992).

90 Draft Treaty Establishing the European Union ["Spinelli Report"], Feb. 14, 1984, 1984 O.J. (C 77/33) 1.

91 The Spinelli Report was a treaty proposal, developed on the basis of the 1941 Manifesto di Ventotene, echoing the idea of a United States of Europe. The report aimed at designing a new institutional asset for the Community, corroborating a system for human rights protection, and developing the subsidiarity principle and the principle of *primauté* of the communitarian law, all while strengthening common defense and external action. In other words, it started the process of constitutionalization of the European Union. *See* Paolo Ponzano, *The 'Spinelli Treaty' of February 1984: The Start of the Process of Constitutionalizing the EU*, *in* EU FEDERALISM AND CONSTITUTIONALISM: THE LEGACY OF ALTIERO SPINELLI 3–10 (Andrew Glencross & Alexander H. Trechsel eds., 2010).

seeking European Union membership were called to participate in the *travaux préparatoires* in conjunction with the EU member states and succeeded in securing the inclusion of a withdrawal clause.[92] Though the European Constitution project failed, the Treaty of Lisbon[93] incorporated ninety-five percent of its provisions. Article 50 of the Treaty on European Union (TEU) currently regulates the right to exit the EU.[94]

The British government's decision to pull out of the EU reflected the outcome of the Brexit referendum held on June 23, 2016.[95] On March 29, 2017, the UK initiated the official withdrawal process, which initially was to be concluded by March 30, 2019, but which was subject to numerous prorogations, ended on December 31, 2020, until a "deal" was reached between the EU and the UK. Brexit is propelled by a dual impetus arising out of a domestic political shift. First, it seeks disengagement from a regional commitment in order to gain a free hand with regard to foreign policy. Second, it represents a response to domestic pressure, based on popular will to terminate the agreement as expressed in a democratic instrument, the referendum.[96]

After decades together since the UK's entry into the EU in 1972, membership termination creates many challenges for the parties negotiating the exit agreement. Former EU Commissioner Michel Barnier was appointed under Article 50 of the TEU as chief negotiator of the Task Force for the Preparation and Conduct of the Negotiations with the United Kingdom, which operates

---

92 On May 1, 2004, ten new countries entered the European Union: Cyprus, Czech Republic, Estonia. Hungary, Latvia, Lithuania, Malta, Poland, Slovakia, and Slovenia. Since most of these countries had experienced the regime of the Warsaw Pact, which left no room for withdrawal, they decided to advocate for a withdrawal clause in the negotiation process for the 2004 Constitutional Treaty. For more information regarding states' membership in the European Union over time, see *Countries*, Eur. Union, https://europa.eu/european-union/about-eu/countries_en.

93 Treaty of Lisbon Amending the Treaty on European Union and the Treaty Establishing the European Community, Dec. 13, 2007, 2007 O.J. (C 306) 1.

94 *See* Rafael Leal-Arcas, *Three Thoughts on Brexit*, Queen Mary University of London School of Law Legal Studies Research Paper No. 249, 1, 3 (2016).

95 On December 7, 2016, the UK House of Commons voted 461 to 89 in favor of the government's plan to trigger Article 50 TEU by the end of March 2017. On January 24, 2017, the UK Supreme Court ruled in the Miller case that parliament must pass legislation to authorize the triggering of Article 50. On January 26, 2017, the UK government introduced a 137-word bill in parliament to empower the government to initiate the Brexit procedure by triggering Article 50, which received bipartisan support. Eventually, on March 16, 2017, the bill received Royal Assent by the Queen. Only at the end of this process was the British government able to notify the EU Commission about the decision to withdraw.

96 *See infra,* Chapter 6, Part II.A.ii (discussing constitutional mechanisms for containment of popular passions in domestic treaty maintenance).

with the support of the Council in the process of clarifying or updating the guidelines.[97] This process serves as a blueprint for restructuring balance at a regional level after a withdrawal following a long-lasting cooperation.

In the regional context, another high-profile instance of withdrawal from an international organization was the Venezuelan denunciation of the Organization of the American States (OAS). In 2017, the Venezuelan government announced its withdrawal from the OAS. In the seventy-year history of the organization, Venezuela is the first country to voluntarily denounce its membership. The new diplomatic balance within the OAS was the result of recent changes in political parties in power in countries traditionally friendly to the Bolivarian Republic, such as Brazil and Argentina. The OAS responded to the general situation of human rights violations in Venezuela with Permanent Council Resolution CP/RES 1078 of April 3, 2017, declaring a "violation of the constitutional order" in Venezuela. The organization was urged to apply the mechanisms for the preservation and defense of representative democracy provided for by Articles 20 and 21 of the Inter-American Democratic Charter[98] in order to restore democratic order.[99] Because the OAS could activate the procedure for sanctions, including membership suspension, the Venezuelan

---

97 *See* Judith Resnik & Clare Ryan, *Global Constitutionalism 2017, Reconstructing Constitutional* Order, A Part of the Gruber Program for Global Justice and Women's Rights of Yale Law School 1-27 (2017); *see also* Alex Hunt & Brian Wheeler, *Brexit: All You Need to Know About the UK Leaving the EU*, BBC (Nov. 22, 2018), https://www.bbc.com/news/uk-politics-32810887.

98 The Inter-American Democratic Charter was signed in Lima, Peru, on September 11, 2001, to respond to Peruvian government abuses during the Fujimori's mandate that led to the dissolution in Congress in 1992, along with an unconstitutional run for a third term in 2000. Then, the Democratic Charter was purported to limit not only military coups, but also threats to democratic governance. The Democratic Charter regulates core aspects of representative democracy, such as the separation of powers, transparency in electoral proceedings, and the rule of law. In the event of breach of the Charter's provisions, a procedure can be activated, under Articles 20 and 21, to support the noncompliant country in restoring the democratic order. With regard to Venezuela, it had already been applied in reaction to the 2002 coup against Hugo Chávez, when the OAS foreign ministers condemned the alteration of the constitutional regime. OAS, *Inter-American Democratic Charter* (Sept. 11, 2001), http://www.oas.org/charter/docs/resolution1_en_p4.htm.

99 On April 3, 2017, the Permanent Council of the Organization of American States (OAS) held a special meeting to consider "recent events in Venezuela," declaring, "The decisions of the Supreme Court of Venezuela to suspend the powers of the National Assembly and to arrogate them to itself are inconsistent with democratic practice and constitute an alteration of the constitutional order of the Bolivarian Republic of Venezuela." *See* OAS Press Release E-022/17 (Apr. 3, 2017), http://www.oas.org/en/media_center/press_release.asp?sCodigo=E-022/17; *see also* OAS Press Release S-032/18 (Jun. 5, 2018), http://www.oas.org/en/media_center/press_release.asp?sCodigo=S-032/18.

government decided to withdraw preemptively rather than risk suspension.[100] On April 28, 2017, it gave notice of its intention to withdraw from the OAS, which became effective two years later.[101]

In the context of regional protection of human rights, two significant withdrawals were the Greek denunciation of the Council of Europe and the Peruvian denunciation of the jurisdiction of the Inter-American Court of Human Rights (IACtHR).

Greece withdrew from the Council of Europe in 1969 during the Colonels' regime. After the Greek coup in 1967, the Council of Europe was faced with an important crisis because of flagrant violations by the dictatorship. The Committee of Ministers of the Council of Europe, in collaboration with the Parliamentary Assembly, activated the procedure for expulsion under Article 8 of the statute.[102] In December 1969, shortly before the expulsion decision, the Greek government notified the Council of Europe of its intention to withdraw[103] under Article 7 of the Statute.[104] Greece rejoined the organization only when democracy was restored in 1974.[105]

---

100 The Venezuelan decision follows the path of criticism of the OAS by the Bolivarian government since 1999, when Hugo Chavez became president, followed by his successor Nicolas Maduro. *See* Jennifer L. McCoy, *Venezuela Withdraws from the Organization of American States After Being Cited for Violation of the Inter-American Democratic Charter*, Scholar Strategic Network (May 2017), https://scholars.org/sites/scholars/files/ssn_basic_facts_mccoy_on_the_oas.pdf.

101 Note from the Permanent Mission of the Bolivarian Republic of Venezuela Enclosing a Copy of the Letter Denouncing the Charter of the Organization of American States (OAS) Pursuant to Article 143 and Initiating the Permanent Withdrawal of the Bolivarian Republic of Venezuela from the Organization. OEA/Ser.G CP/INF. 7707/17 29 (Apr. 28, 2017).

102 Statute of the Council of Europe, 5V.1949 E.T.S. 1, (1949). Article 8 states: "Any member of the Council of Europe which has seriously violated Article 3 may be suspended from its rights of representation and requested by the Committee of Ministers to withdraw under Article 7. If such member does not comply with this request, the Committee may decide that it has ceased to be a member of the Council as from such date as the Committee may determine."

103 Though Greece was the only country to withdraw from the Council of Europe, the procedure for suspension was activated twice: (a) Turkey, in 1980, following the military coup—Turkey regained its voting right in the Council of Europe Parliamentary Assembly only after democratic elections in 1984; and (b) Russia, from 2000 to 2001, as a result of its policies on Chechnya.

104 Article 7 of the Statute of the Council of Europe states: "Any member of the Council of Europe may withdraw by formally notifying the Secretary-General of its intention to do so. Such withdrawal shall take effect at the end of the financial year in which it is notified, if the notification is given during the first nine months of that financial year. If the notification is given in the last three months of the financial year, it shall take effect at the end of the next financial year."

105 *See* Kathryn Sikkink, *The Power of Principled Ideas: Human Rights Policies in the United States and Western Europe*, *in* IDEAS AND FOREIGN POLICY: BELIEFS, INSTITUTIONS AND

In 1999, during Alberto Fujimori's presidency, Peru denounced the jurisdiction of the IACtHR. When the country returned to democratic rule with the transitional government of Valentín Paniagua, Peru acceded again to the Court's jurisdiction in 2001.[106]

To shed light on the scope and consequences of withdrawal from a regional system of human rights, in May 2019, the Colombian government requested a consultative opinion[107] by the IACtHR.[108] In its request, Colombia raised three questions. First, it asked what human rights obligations a member of the OAS[109] would still be bound to after it denounced the American Convention on Human Rights.[110] Second, it asked what human rights obligations it would be bound to if it also withdrew from the Organization. Third, it asked, in the event of human rights violations by a state that had denounced the American Convention and the Charter of the OAS, (a) what human rights obligations the remaining OAS member states would have, (b) how OAS member states could enforce those obligations, and (c) what international human rights protection mechanisms could be activated by persons subject to the jurisdiction of the denouncing state.

As the request was couched in abstract and broad terms, and given the general application of the questions proposed, the Opinion of the Court may prove to be of permanent value, and it provides guidance to the OAS and

POLITICAL CHANGE 130, 149 (Judith Goldstein, Robert O. Keohane eds., 1993); *see also* Raquel Valls, *Withdrawal, Expulsion and Suspension of a Member State of the Council of Europe*, CVCE (Jul. 8, 2016), https://www.cvce.eu/content/publication/2006/1/9/f9b31f98-f1a1-407c-97ad-7e92363117fd/publishable_en.pdf.

106 *See* Douglas Cassel, *Does International Human Rights Law Make a Difference?*, Chi. J. Int'l. L. 121, 128 (2001); *see also* International Bar Ass'n, *Peru's Withdrawal from the Jurisdiction of the Inter-American Court*, IBA (Aug., 1999), https://www.ibanet.org/Human_Rights_Institute/About_the_HRI/HRI_Activities/HRI_Media/HRI_Interventions/archive/000899_Peru.aspx.

107 Request for a Consultative Opinion Presented by the Republic of Colombia with Regard to Obligations in Matters of Human Rights of a State That Has Denounced the *American Convention on Human Rights*, and Attempts to Withdraw from the OAS (April 2019), https://www.corteidh.or.cr/docs/opiniones/sol_oc_26_ing.pdf.

108 The Colombian *petitum* to the Inter-American Court of Human Rights defines the scope of the request as follows: "This Request refers to the mechanisms for the international protection of human rights available in those countries which claim to abandon the Inter-American System of Human Rights ['the Inter-American System'], and for this purpose, denounce the Convention and likewise denounce the Charter of the Organization of American States itself ['the Charter' and 'the OAS', respectively], and therefore attempt to cease to be members of that regional organization." *See* id.

109 Charter of the Organization of American States art. 112, Apr. 30, 1948, 119 U.N.T.S. 3, 2 U.S.T. 2394.

110 American Convention on Human Rights "Pact of San Jose, Costa Rica," Nov. 22, 1969, S. Treaty Doc. No. 95–21; 1144 U.N.T.S.123; O.A.S.T.S. No. 36; 9 I.L.M. 99 (1970).

all its member states regarding the parameters of withdrawal from regional agreements under the umbrella of the inter-American system of human rights protection.

Both the American Convention on Human Rights and the Charter of the OAS include withdrawal clauses that allow parties to pull out. Therefore, whenever a state chooses to exercise its right to withdraw from those instruments, it is released from any treaty obligation from the date withdrawal becomes effective. Nonetheless, the denouncing state remains bound to other human rights obligations based on customary international law and treaty law, the latter depending on the human rights instruments in which that state participates.[111]

Though the Colombian request to the Court was phrased in the abstract, it clearly applies to the Venezuelan denunciation of the OAS and to similar cases that may arise in the region. As the situation may generate a vacuum, particularly with regard to the system of human rights protection, the reply of the Court will help the remaining member states in their attempts avoid and react to any serious and systematic human rights violations by the withdrawing state.[112]

III. High-profile International Commitments

Withdrawal from high-profile international commitments implicates spheres of international law related mainly to highly politicized topics. These fields tend to expand their application and invade the sphere of domestic jurisdiction. For this reason, these fields have tended to be progressively politicized at home, so much so that national governments have tailored their political agenda to reestablish nationalism domestically.

It is crucial to take into account the functional area covered by the treaty subject to denunciation. For instance, withdrawal from treaties regarding peace and security entails significant outcomes for the international community as a whole. It is relevant to mention that more than half of security agreements do not include a withdrawal clause so the effectiveness of the agreement will be maintained. On the other hand, highly domestic politically

111 Written Observations of the United States regarding Request for a Consultative Opinion by the Republic of Colombia, CDH-SOC-1–2019/002 (Inter-American Court of Human Rights), https://www.corteidh.or.cr/sitios/observaciones/oc26/3_estadosunidos.pdf.

112 *See* Eleanor Benz, *The Inter-American Court's Advisory Function Continues to Boom – A Few Comments on the Requests Currently Pending*, EJIL:TALK! (Nov. 25, 2019), https://www.ejiltalk.org/the-inter-american-courts-advisory-function-continues-to-boom-a-few-comments-on-the-requests-currently-pending/.

related agreements, such as human rights agreements, often contain a withdrawal clause to assure contracting parties of flexibility.[113]

A. *Agreements Derogating from Norms of* Jus Cogens

Withdrawal from a multilateral agreement is particularly significant if the agreement codifies peremptory norms.[114] *Jus cogens* can be defined as peremptory norms of general international law from which no derogation is permitted due to their nature.[115] They mirror a concept of natural law, embedding a moral foundation, due to the inherent significance of the values they protect: fundamental rights of the human person and peace and equality between states.[116]

The Vienna Convention on the Law of Treaties (VCLT),[117] in relation to *jus cogens*, uses the following definition:

> [A] peremptory norm of general international law is a norm accepted and recognized by the international community of States as a whole as a norm from which no derogation is permitted and which can be modified only by a subsequent norm of general international law having the same character.[118]

The VCLT does not provide a catalog of *jus cogens* norms, but it establishes a test for their identification. First, a *jus cogens* norm is one that has been accepted and recognized by the international community as a whole, and

---

113 *See* Barbara Koremenos & Allison Nau, *Exit, No Exit*, 81 DUKE J. COMP. & INT'L L. 81, 106 (2010) (analyzing the impact of withdrawal clauses in given issue areas).

114 *See* Mark W. Janis, *The Nature of Jus Cogens*, 3 Conn. J. Int'l L. 359, 359 (1988).

115 The ILC explores in Draft Article 50 the emergence of *jus cogens* norms and their effects on the law of treaties. Draft Articles on the Law of Treaties with Commentaries, Adopted by the International Law Commission at its Eighteenth Session, *in U.N. Conference on the Law of Treaties, 1st & 2nd Sess., Vienna, 26 March–24 May 1968 and 9 April–22 May 1969*, at 67, ¶ 2(M), U.N. Doc. A/CONF.39/11/Add.2 (1971).

116 *See generally* MAURIZIO RAGAZZI, THE CONCEPT OF INTERNATIONAL OBLIGATIONS ERGA OMNES (1995); *see also* Markus Petsche, *Jus Cogens as a Vision of the International Legal Order*, 29 PENN ST. INT'L L. REV. 233, 238 (2010); M. Cherif Bassiouni, *International Crimes: Jus Cogens and Obligatio Ega Omnes*, 59 LAW & CONTEMP. PROBS. 63, 67 (1997) (affirming the highest hierarchical position of *jus cogens* norms amongst the international legal sources); *see also* Christian A. Levesque, *The International Covenant on Civil and Political Rights: A Primer for Raising a Defense Against the Juvenile Death Penalty in Federal Courts*, 50 AM. U. L. REV. 756, 765 (2001).

117 Vienna Convention on the Law of Treaties (VCLT), May 23, 1969 1155 U.N.T.S. 331, 8 I.L.M. 679 (1969).

118 VCLT art. 53 ("Treaties Conflicting with a Peremptory Norm of General International Law").

therefore has universal value. Second, it is not subject to derogation, which triggers nullity for all treaties conflicting with it. Third, it can be modified only by a subsequent norm having the same character and therefore protecting the same core values in the international legal system.[119]

The analysis of withdrawal when peremptory norms are involved entails two different considerations. First, one should question whether a state may withdraw from a treaty that derogates peremptory norms. Second, one should question whether a state may withdraw from a treaty whose language reflects one or more *jus cogens* norms.

Article 53 of the VCLT resolves the first issue, as it deems void any treaty conflicting with a *jus cogens* norm. Regarding the second issue, of paramount importance is maintaining a distinction between the withdrawn-from agreement and the content of the peremptory norm. Whenever a *jus cogens* norm is embedded in a treaty provision, the norm will be governed not only by general international law—or customary law—but also by the law of the treaty, insofar as it codifies customary law. A state party can denounce the agreement, but it will still be bound by the rule of general international law that is *jus cogens*. Therefore, the act of withdrawal may be a meaningless effort in that it will disengage the withdrawing state from the international agreement to which it was a party but not from the peremptory norm, which, by definition under Article 53 of the VCLT, is accepted and recognized by the international community as a whole. In other words, though a state can withdraw from a treaty, it cannot withdraw from a *jus cogens* norm.

An example of withdrawal from an international agreement reflecting peremptory norms is the attempted denunciation of the ICCPR[120] by North Korea in 1997. The ICCPR is a milestone in human rights protection. It was originally drafted with the aim of generating a global commitment in regard to fundamental rights in the civil and political sphere and aimed to be valid in perpetuity; therefore, it included no withdrawal clause.[121] The ICCPR codifies

---

119 *See* MAURIZIO RAGAZZI, THE CONCEPT OF INTERNATIONAL OBLIGATIONS ERGA OMNES (1995); *see also* Maurizio Ragazzi, *International Obligations Erga Omnes: Their Moral Foundation and Criteria of Identification in Light of Two Japanese Contributions*, *in* THE REALITY OF INTERNATIONAL LAW. ESSAYS IN HONOUR OF IAN BROWNLIE 455–77 (Guy S. Goodwin-Gill & Stefan Talmon eds., 1999).

120 International Covenant on Civil and Political Rights, Dec. 16, 1966, 999 U.N.T.S. 171; S. Exec. Doc. E, 95–2 (1978); S. Treaty Doc. 95–20; 6 I.L.M. 368 (1967).

121 As of 2018, the Covenant has 172 parties and six more signatories without ratification. *See Status of Ratification of Human Rights Treaties*, OHCHR, http://indicators.ohchr.org/.

several *jus cogens* norms, among them *habeas corpus* (Article 6)[122] and the prohibition against torture (Article 7).[123] Notwithstanding the lack of an ad hoc clause, in 1997, North Korea tried to denounce the ICCPR, allegedly due to an attack on its sovereignty.[124]

The UN Human Rights Committee rejected this attempt and issued a general comment criticizing any attempt to withdraw from the ICCPR.[125] It noted that countries that had ratified the ICCPR could not exit the covenant, as those rights had already vested. Since the rights protected by the ICCPR belong to the people, they cannot be denounced.[126] Also, the UN Secretary-General rejected the withdrawal of North Korea, which it claimed violated Article 54 of the VCLT with respect to requesting all parties' consent.[127] North Korea impliedly accepted the invalidity of withdrawal from ICCPR beginning in 2000, when it submitted its overdue second periodic report to the Human Rights Committee.[128]

---

122 U.S. jurisprudence made explicit reference to the ICCPR to ground the peremptory nature of the *habeas corpus*, consisting of an absolute prohibition against arbitrary deprivation of life. *See, e.g.*, Alejandre v. Republic of Cuba, 996 F. Supp. 1239, 1252 (S.D. Fla.1997).

123 The U.S. jurisprudence also made explicit reference to the ICCPR to ground the peremptory nature of the prohibition against torture. *See, e.g.*, Siderman de Blake v. Republic of Argentina, 965 F.2d 699, 714–17 (9th Cir. 1992).

124 *See* Thomas Buergenthal, *The U.N. Human Rights Committee*, *in* MAX PLANCK UNYB 341, 362 (2001). *See also* Elizabeth Evatt, *Democratic People's Republic of Korea and the ICCPR: Denunciation as an Exercise of the Right of Self Defence?*, in 5 AUST. J. HUM. RTS. 215, 219 (1998) (analyzing the Human Rights Committee decision regarding withdrawal in spite of the lack of an express treaty provision).

125 General Comment No. 26 (Continuity of Obligations), by the Human Rights Committee, adopted on 29 October 1997, reproduced in: "Compilation of General Comments and General Recommendations Adopted by Human Rights Treaty Bodies," Doc. HRI/GEN/1/Rev.5 of 26 April 2001, at 163.

126 The General Comment No. 26 by the Human Rights Committee states, "The rights enshrined in the Covenant belong to the people living in the territory of the State party. The Human Rights Committee has consistently taken the view [...] that once the people are accorded the protection of the rights under the Covenant, such protection devolves with the territory and continues to belong to them, notwithstanding a change in government of the State party, including dismemberment in more than one State or State succession or any sub-sequent action of the State party designed to divest them of the rights guaranteed by the Covenant."

127 The Danish government sent a Notification to the UN Secretary-General, upholding its interpretation of the North Korean case under Article 54 of the VCLT and expressing its lack of consent to North Korean unilateral act. *See* Hans Klingenberg, *Elements of Nordic Practice 1998: Denmark*, 68 NORDIC J. INT'L L. 163, 164 (1999).

128 *See* Ed Bates, *Avoiding Legal Obligations Created by Human Rights Treaties*, 57 INT'L & COMP. L. Q. 751, 755 (2008).

B. *Arms Control Agreements*

The denunciation of arms control agreements can be analyzed based on North Korean disengagement from the Nuclear Non-Proliferation Treaty (NPT) and U.S. withdrawal from the Joint Comprehensive Plan of Action (JCPOA), the Anti-Ballistic Missile (ABM) Treaty, the Intermediate-Range Nuclear Force (INF) Treaty, and the UN Arms Trade Treaty (ATT).

The withdrawal of North Korea from the NPT[129] in 2003 triggered important consequences in the field of arms control. The NPT is a landmark international treaty that, since 1968, has been a bulwark preventing development of nuclear weapons and weapons technology. With this purpose, it has furthered cooperation with regard to peaceful use of nuclear energy while promoting progressive nuclear disarmament.

North Korea joined the NPT in 1985 as a non-nuclear-weapons state. Article III of the NPT imposes a safeguards agreement on non-nuclear-weapons states through an agreement with the International Atomic Energy Agency (IAEA) to monitor compliance.[130] North Korea entered into its safeguards agreement with the IAEA in 1992. Nonetheless, it pulled out of the IAEA in 1994 and out of the NPT in 2003 and consequently (under Article X of the NPT) out of the safeguards agreement.[131]

As the NPT is the only binding multilateral commitment with the goal of disarmament by the nuclear-weapons states, its effectiveness was undermined by North Korean denunciation. Since North Korea was barred by the treaty from producing nuclear weapons, it sought denunciation so it would be free to do so. It followed the procedures set out in Article X of the NPT to pull out with immediate effect in 2003, blaming U.S. aggression for its decision. That action triggered long-lasting consequences for international nuclear security,

129 Treaty on the Non-proliferation of Nuclear Weapons (NPT), Jul. 1, 1968, 729 U.N.T.S. 161; 7 I.L.M. 8809 (1968); 21 UST 483. The Nuclear Non-Proliferation Treaty is a global agreement on arms control. Only four other countries—Cuba, India, Israel, and Pakistan—are not signatories, and Cuba participates in the treaty establishing a nuclear-free zone in Latin America.

130 The safeguards agreement with the International Atomic Energy Agency (IAEA) is meant to verify compliance with the obligations to refrain from manufacturing or acquiring nuclear explosive devices under Article II.

131 Article X of the NTP regulates withdrawal procedure: "Each Party shall in exercising its national sovereignty have the right to withdraw from the Treaty if it decides that extraordinary events, related to the subject matter of this Treaty, have jeopardized the supreme interests of its country. It shall give notice of such withdrawal to all other Parties to the Treaty and to the United Nations Security Council three months in advance. Such notice shall include a statement of the extraordinary events it regards as having jeopardized its supreme interests."

generating a North Korean crisis that is still dramatically present today.[132] In this case, withdrawal hid the geopolitical strategy of North Korea to undertake a nuclear program. It tested nuclear weapons repeatedly from 2006 to 2017.[133] As its actions threaten global peace and security, it was subjected to international sanctions through UN Security Council resolutions.[134]

In the United States, on October 13, 2017, the Trump administration declared its intention to withdraw from the JCPOA,[135] which is related to the Iranian nuclear program. This decision had implications for both arms control and international security. The JCPOA was concluded in 2015 between Iran, six other nations—the United States, the United Kingdom, France, Russia, China, and Germany[136]—and the European Union, as a "plan of action" grounded on voluntary measures.[137] Though not formally binding, the deal gave Iran relief from sanctions under U.S. law, EU law, and UN regulations in exchange for Iranian implementation of measures for the peaceful adaptation of its nuclear program. The Obama administration approved the JCPOA by following the nonbinding procedure, thus avoiding the necessity for congressional or senatorial consent.[138]

---

132 *See* Frederic L. Kirgis, *North Korea's Withdrawal from the Nuclear Non-Proliferation Treaty*, 2 ASIL INSIGHTS 8 (2003), https://www.asil.org/insights/volume/8/issue/2/north-koreas-withdrawal-nuclear-nonproliferation-treaty.

133 North Korea has conducted six nuclear tests: one each in 2006, 2009, and 2013, two in 2016, and one in 2017.

134 The full implementation of the Joint Statement represents the main goal of the Six Party Talks. *See* U.S. Delegation to the 2010 Nuclear Non-Proliferation Treaty Review Conference, Treaty on the Non-Proliferation on Nuclear Weapons (2010), https://www.state.gov/documents/organization/141503.pdf.

135 Joint Comprehensive Plan of Action (JCPOA) (Jul. 14, 2015), http://www.state.gov/e/eb/tfs/spi/iran/jcpoa/.

136 The counterparts to Iran in the deal were collectively known as P5+1, as they included the five permanent members of the UN Security Council, plus Germany.

137 The JCPOA was concluded as a political commitment, with no provision for ratification or entry into force. Therefore, it must be considered as not legally binding and based on contracting parties' voluntary measures. Nonetheless, as it was supported by the UN Security Council Resolution 2231, some commentators have questioned the non-binding nature of the agreement. *See* STEPHEN P. MULLIGAN, WITHDRAWAL FROM INTERNATIONAL AGREEMENTS: LEGAL FRAMEWORK, THE PARIS AGREEMENT, AND THE IRAN NUCLEAR AGREEMENT, 7 CONGRESSIONAL RSCH. SERV. (2018).

138 *See* Executive Order 13716 of January 16, 2016, Revocation of Executive Orders 13574, 13590, 13622, and 13645 with Respect to Iran, Amendment of Executive Order 13628 with Respect to Iran, and Provision of Implementation Authorities for Aspects of Certain Statutory Sanctions Outside the Scope of U.S. Commitments Under the Joint Comprehensive Plan of Action of July 14, 2015, 81 Fed. Reg. 3693 (Jan. 21, 2016); *see also* Jack L. Goldsmith, *The Contributions of the Obama Administration to the Practice and Theory of International Law*,

Thus, the succeeding Trump administration was able to declare that it could terminate the deal "at any time."[139]

Notably, domestic and international regulatory frameworks overlap. After the United States' domestic approval of the deal, the UN Security Council unanimously approved Resolution 2231[140] annexing the JCPOA, thereby terminating sanctions against Iran. From an international legal perspective, the termination of the JCPOA leaves open the matter of the mandatory nature of Resolution 2231, which could give indirect enforceability to the deal. Indeed, as a Security Council resolution has mandatory effectiveness, it may give continuous application to the withdrawn agreement, making the United States indirectly bound to it.[141]

Also in the area of arms control, it is worth considering the U.S. withdrawal from the Anti-Ballistic Missile (ABM) Treaty in 2002, and, more recently, the U.S. denunciation of the Intermediate-Range Nuclear Forces (INF) Treaty, in 2019. The former was denounced due to the temporal inadequacy of the instrument; the latter, due to alleged noncompliance by the other party. Even though they are both bilateral agreements between United States and Russia, they have a global impact on security. In 2019, the United States also denounced the UN Arms Trade Treaty (ATT),[142] a multilateral deal regulating common international standards that must be met before states authorize transfers of conventional weapons or export ammunition and weapons parts and components. President Trump "unsigned" the agreement,[143] which had been joined by the United States during the Obama Administration, in 2013 before congressional ratification was completed.[144]

In 2002, the U.S. government, under the Bush administration, decided to denounce the 1972 ABM Treaty.[145] That decision was made so that missile

---

57 HARV. INT'L L.J. 1, 11 (2016) (analyzing the legal effects of non-binding political commitments).

139 Remarks by the President on Iran Strategy (Oct. 13, 2017), https://www.whitehouse.gov/briefings-statements/remarks-president-trump-iran-strategy/.

140 UN Security Council, *Joint Comprehensive Plan of Action (JCPOA) on the Islamic Republic of Iran's nuclear programme*, U.N. SC Resolution 2231 (Jul. 20, 2015), http://www.refworld.org/docid/55b9e2084.html.

141 S.C. 2231, ¶ 2: "Calls upon all Members States ... to take such actions as may be appropriate to support the implementation of the JCPOA, including by taking actions commensurate with the implementation plan set out in the JCPOA and this resolution and by refraining from actions that undermine implementation of commitments under the JCPOA[.]"

142 Arms Trade Treaty, C.N.266.2013. Treaties-XXVI.8 (Apr. 2, 2013).

143 Depositary Notification from the UN Secretary-General, UN Doc. C.N.314.2019.Treaties-XXVI.8 (Jul. 19, 2019).

144 Jean Galbraight, *Contemporary Practice of the United States Related to International Law*, 113 AJIL 813, 813–18 (2019).

145 Limitation of Anti-Ballistic Missile Systems, May 26, 1972, U.S.-U.S.S.R., 23 U.S.T. 3435.

defenses could be deployed to protect against "growing missile threats" in the aftermath of 9/11. Changes in domestic priorities, along with changing technological threats, made the deal anachronistic from the United States' point of view. President Bush and other senior officials had previously described the ABM Treaty as a relic of the Cold War that conflicted with one of the administration's top priorities: strengthening missile defense.[146]

The legitimacy of the United States' withdrawal from the ABM Treaty was considered by the United States District Court for the District of Columbia in *Kucinich v. Bush*.[147] Thirty-two members of the House of Representatives brought the action to challenge President Bush's unilateral decision, which had been made without seeking congressional approval. The court dismissed the case due to the nonjusticiability of the issue. Many questions arising in connection with international treaties have been held to be nonjusticiable in the U.S. legal system. Most of these questions involved unilateral statements of the government's view. Therefore, issues related to international treaties are mainly political questions that are in the domain of the executive branch of government. In the case of denunciation of the ABM Treaty, not only had the plaintiffs not asserted deprivation of a constitutional right, but also the group of congressmen brought the issue to the court at the end of the six-month notice period required by the Treaty itself for denunciation. The notice of termination may have generated action in foreign countries who were relying on the U.S. government's declaration. Despite the bilateral nature of the agreement, the United States' withdrawal from the ABM Treaty had important consequences for nuclear rearmament due to its status as a global superpower.

Similarly, on February 2, 2019, the U.S. government notified its denunciation of the INF Treaty. Signed in 1987, the treaty prohibited possessing, producing, or test-flying ground-launched ballistic and cruise missiles with a range of 500 to 5,500 kilometers and their launchers. The Trump administration alleged Russian violations were the reason for denunciation, reiterating accusations of Russian noncompliance. Since 2014, the State Department's Annual Report on Adherence to and Compliance with Arms Control, Non-proliferation, and Disarmament Agreements and Commitments[148] has reported Russian violations of the INF Treaty. The United States expressed its concern that one-way adherence to the INF Treaty would eventually jeopardize not only the United

146 *See* Wade Boese, *US Withdraws from ABM Treaty, Global Response Muted*, Arms Control Today (Jul. 1, 2002), https://www.armscontrol.org/act/2002_07-08/abmjul_aug02.

147 Kucinich v. Bush, 236 F. Supp. 2d 1 (D.D.C. 2002).

148 Department of State, Bureau of Arms Control, Verification and Compliance, Annual Report on "Adherence to and Compliance with Arms Control, Non-proliferation, and Disarmament Agreements and Commitments" (Jul. 2014), https://www.state.gov/documents/organization/230108.pdf.

States' strategic position with respect to Russia, but also its capacity to contain the INF-class missile threat posed by other actors, such as China, who were not parties to the treaty.

From a legal perspective, if Russian violations were confirmed, the United States could either suspend or terminate the deal based on a material breach by the other party, Russia. On December 4, 2018, the United States officially gave Russia a sixty-day ultimatum for complying with the agreement, with denunciation as the only alternative, and on February 2, 2019, it notified its withdrawal, to be become effective six months later, on August 2, 2019.[149]

As previously discussed, the legality of the termination of a bilateral arms control agreement without legislative approval went before a federal court in *Kucinich v. Bush*.[150] Since the court declined to address the merits of the issue on justiciability grounds, there is little reason to expect that the INF denunciation will be declared invalid if it should be challenged in court.[151] From a geopolitical standpoint, the United States' decision to withdraw from the INF Treaty could undermine other long-standing international arms-control agreements, as it could be held up as a precedent by other actors who wish to opt out of such agreements.

C. *Climate Change Agreements*

Withdrawal from international climate change agreements can be analyzed by considering the Kyoto Protocol and the Paris Agreement.[152]

The Kyoto Protocol and the Paris Agreement are instruments negotiated within the UN Framework Convention on Climate Change (UNFCCC).[153] In a harmonization of law and politics, the UNFCCC—created in 1992 under the UN umbrella to provide climate solutions—[154] developed an array of instru-

---

149 *See* Julian Borger, *US Says It Will Pull Out of INF Treaty If Russia Does Not Comply Within 60 Days*, GUARDIAN (Dec. 4, 2018), https://www.theguardian.com/world/2018/dec/04/us-inf-russia-nuclear-treaty-deadline; *see also* U.S. Dep't of State, *U.S. Withdrawal from the INF Treaty on August 2, 2019*, Press Statement, Michael R. Pompeo, Secretary of State (Aug. 2, 2019), https://www.state.gov/u-s-withdrawal-from-the-inf-treaty-on-august-2-2019/.

150 Kucinich, 236 F. Supp. 2d 1.

151 *See* Hilary Hurd & Elena Chachko, *U.S. Withdrawal from INF Treaty: The Facts and the Law*, Lawfare (Oct. 25, 2018), https://www.lawfareblog.com/us-withdrawal-inf-treaty-facts-and-law.

152 Both denunciations of the Kyoto Protocol and the Paris Agreement on Climate Change saw withdrawals from the deal but not from the underlying regime. *See infra,* Chapter 4, Part IV (analyzing trends of disengagement from agreements but not from regimes).

153 The UNFCCC was signed in 1992 at the United Nations Conference on Environment and Development ("UNCED").

154 The UNFCCC today is composed of 197 parties, including the major contributors to climate change, and represents a global framework for the whole international community. *See*

ments within the annual Conference of Parties (COP), setting ad hoc principles for international climate deals.[155] The Kyoto Protocol and the Paris Agreement represent two major deals produced within the Framework convention and protocol approach of the UNFCCC, resulting from different negotiating strategies—top-down and bottom-up approaches, respectively.

The Kyoto Protocol was signed in 1997 in Kyoto, Japan, as part of COP 3, but did not come into force until years later in 2005. Negotiators were enthusiastic about the top-down approach of the so-called "cap and trade" system. This system sought to obtain mitigation commitments by relying on science to define global emissions caps and allowing states to negotiate about the caps and how they would be implemented.[156] Unfortunately, this model led to the disengagement of some of the most relevant actors in the field, including the United States and Canada.

Though the United States signed the Kyoto Protocol, it was never ratified by the Senate. The Bush administration decided to withdraw the U.S. signature from the document, disengaging from its international commitment on climate change.[157]

The U.S. withdrawal had important implications for both the effectiveness and the efficiency of the deal. Indeed, other countries, including Japan, New Zealand, and Russia, participated in Kyoto's first round but did not take on new targets in the second commitment period, which was negotiated in Doha in 2012.[158] On December 12, 2011, during COP 17, the Canadian government announced its withdrawal from the Kyoto Protocol, effective December 15,

---

List of Parties to the Convention, UNITED NATIONS FRAMEWORK CONVENTION ON CLIMATE CHANGE, https://unfccc.int/process/parties-non-party-stakeholders/parties-convention-and-observer-states (last updated Aug. 7, 2018).

155 *See* JENNI KAUPPILA, *Transnational Advocacy Networks in International Climate Policy: The Challenge of Raising the Voices of the Marginalised Effectively Without Compromising their Legitimacy*, *in* INTERNATIONAL CLIMATE CHANGE LAW AND POLICY: CULTURAL LEGITIMACY IN ADAPTION AND MITIGATION 138 (Thoko Kaime ed., 2014).

156 The "cap and trade" system is based on a threshold "cap," which is the total amount of greenhouse gases that can be emitted within a given system, and it allows a carbon dioxide emissions market to develop in which pollution credits could be bought and sold.

157 During the Clinton administration, in 1998, the former vice president, Al Gore signed the Kyoto accord on behalf of the United States. Later, in 2001, Condoleezza Rice, the national security adviser, announced that the United States considered the Kyoto accord "dead." *See* Julian Borger, *Bush Kills Global Warming Treaty*, GUARDIAN (Mar 29, 2001), https://www.theguardian.com/environment/2001/mar/29/globalwarming.usnews.

158 The Doha Amendment, negotiated in Doha in 2012, defined the second commitment period to the Kyoto Protocol. It set targets binding until 2020 and was joined by 37 countries: Australia, the European Union and its 28 member states, Belarus, Iceland, Kazakhstan, Liechtenstein, Norway, Switzerland, and Ukraine.

2012. Greenhouse gas emissions in Canada greatly exceeded what the government had committed to.[159] The Harper administration in charge at that time prioritized fossil fuels investments over climate prerogatives, with oil sands development occurring in Alberta. Eventually, to avoid the cost of liability for breaching the agreement, the government opted for pulling out.[160]

In order to overcome the problems that led to withdrawals from the Kyoto Protocol, contracting parties promoted new negotiating policies within the UNFCCC. Following a trend already apparent at the Copenhagen Climate Change Conference (COP 15) in 2009,[161] COP 21 introduced new strategies that led to the adoption of the Paris Agreement. The role of each country in reducing greenhouse gas emissions is no longer the result of a top-down approach, but instead follows a voluntary bottom-up approach. In UNFCCC negotiations, multilateral consensus for treaties relating to climate change is achieved through a new "pledge and review" process. As part of the COP 21 results, this model facilitated the construction of a legal framework around nation-states' "pledges" to mitigate greenhouse gas emissions. This model represents a renovated system in which governments are able to propose or pledge actions, policies, and goals unilaterally, and "review" them over time.[162]

The Paris Agreement is the first universal climate agreement to contain binding mitigation commitments.[163] It was adopted by 196 countries at COP 21

---

159 The Canadian government committed to cutting its greenhouse emissions to 6% below 1990 levels by 2012. Nonetheless, in 2009, emissions were actually 17% higher than in 1990.

160 *See Canada's Withdrawal from Kyoto Protocol Regrettable – UN Climate Official*, UN NEWS (Dec 13, 2011), https://news.un.org/en/story/2011/12/398142; *see also Canada Pulls Out of Kyoto Protocol*, GUARDIAN (Dec 13, 2011), https://www.theguardian.com/environment/2011/dec/13/canada-pulls-out-kyoto-protocol.

161 The Copenhagen Climate Change Conference, representing the 15th session of the Conference of the Parties to the UNFCCC, took place in Copenhagen and was hosted by the government of Denmark in December 2009. *COP 15*, UNITED NATIONS FRAMEWORK CONVENTION ON CLIMATE CHANGE, https://unfccc.int/process-and-meetings/conferences/past-conferences/copenhagen-climate-change-conference-december-2009/cop-15.

162 *See* Joseph E. Aldy & William A. Pizer, *Comparability of Effort in International Climate Policy Architecture*, Harvard Kennedy Sch. Working Paper 3 (2014).

163 The Paris Agreement has been referred to as the first-ever universal, legally binding global climate deal. *See Paris Agreement*, EUROPEAN COMM'N, https://perma.cc/2Q5D-KYUQ. By hosting the 21st Session of the Conference of the Parties ("COP 21") in 2015, Paris served as the stage for the global revolution on climate change. When COP 21 adopted the Paris Agreement in December that same year, the world celebrated. On April 22, 2016, at a ceremony convened by UN Secretary-General Ban Ki-moon in New York, 174 states and the European Union signed the Paris Agreement. UN Framework Convention on Climate Change, *Adoption of the Paris Agreement*, UN Doc. FCC/CP/2015/L.9/Rev.1 (Dec. 12, 2015).

in Paris,[164] on 12 December 2015 and entered into force on 4 November 2016.[165] However, the United States' position on climate change, under Trump administration, posed risks to the Paris Agreement's future and the degree of its success. On June 1, 2017, U.S. President Donald Trump fulfilled his campaign promise to leave the deal by announcing his intention to pull out of it. The Trump administration claimed that the Paris Agreement allowed other countries to gain a financial advantage over the United States, while imposing "draconian" financial burdens on the American people.[166] This announcement undermined the stability of the Paris Agreement as a whole, and international efforts to curb global warming consequently seem threatened.

Withdrawal clauses of the Kyoto Protocol (Article 27)[167] and Paris Agreement (Article 28)[168] were framed identically to secure cooperation at least for the three years after the entry into force of the deal, plus a one-year notice period from the date of notification of withdrawal to the depositary. Thus, the U.S. denunciation of the Paris Agreement will have to follow a formal procedure that will make the denunciation effective in 2020, one day after the end of the Trump administration mandate.[169]

---

164 *Paris Agreement – Status of Ratification*, UNITED NATIONS FRAMEWORK CONVENTION ON CLIMATE CHANGE, http://unfccc.int/paris_agreement/items/9444.php.

165 The Paris Agreement replaced the Kyoto Protocol, which remained in a transitional period until the prior became fully effective. *See* Sophie Power, *Paris Climate Agreement: A Quick Guide*, PARLIAMENT OF AUSTL. RSCH. PUBL'NS (Nov. 10, 2017), https://www.aph.gov.au/About_Parliament/Parliamentary_Departments/Parliamentary_Library/pubs/rp/rp1718/Quick_Guides/ParisAgreement.

166 *See* Kevin Liptak & Jim Acosta, *Trump on Paris Accord: 'We're Getting Out,'* CNN (June 2, 2017), https://perma.cc/CX93-J226.

167 Article 27 of the Kyoto Protocol affirms that "1. At any time after three years from the date on which this Protocol has entered into force for a Party, that Party may withdraw from this Protocol by giving written notification to the Depositary. 2. Any such withdrawal shall take effect upon expiry of one year from the date of receipt by the Depositary of the notification of withdrawal, or on such later date as may be specified in the notification of withdrawal. 3. Any Party that withdraws from the Convention shall be considered as also having withdrawn from this Protocol."

168 Article 28 of the Paris Agreement affirms that "1. At any time after three years from the date on which this Agreement has entered into force for a Party, that Party may withdraw from this Agreement by giving written notification to the Depositary. 2. Any such withdrawal shall take effect upon expiry of one year from the date of receipt by the Depositary of the notification of withdrawal, or on such later date as may be specified in the notification of withdrawal. 3. Any Party that withdraws from the Convention shall be considered as also having withdrawn from this Agreement."

169 *See* Timmon Roberts, *One Year Since Trump's Withdrawal from the Paris Climate Agreement*, Brookings (Jun. 1, 2018), https://www.brookings.edu/blog/planetpolicy/2018/06/01/one-year-since-trumps-withdrawal-from-the-paris-climate-agreement/.

The U.S. decision to withdraw from the Paris Agreement, reinforced by its blunt disengagement from climate commitments, may create imbalances in the global effort to halt climate change, as other parties will be called upon to strengthen pledges in order to reach the original goal set in Paris. Moreover, the United States being a pivotal state with regard to climate action, its withdrawal would hinder the overall resilience of the climate regime.[170]

IV. Withdrawing from the Agreement, Remaining in the Regime

The evolution of the international legal system through the establishment of regimes for different functional areas makes it important to reconsider the impact of withdrawal within the regimes context. A state may decide to withdraw from the whole framework covered by the regime—including a broad array of instruments and institutional forums—or to just withdraw from operational agreements under the regime's umbrella.

The decision to unilaterally pull out triggers consequential outcomes for the institutional framework of the regime, altering membership and participation. The withdrawing state is no longer able to have delegates in the treaty conferences or within the organization, nor may it enjoy the privileges of membership with respect to information, monitoring procedures, and resolution of disputes. A withdrawing state has no power in the decision-making process within international organizations and treaty regimes.[171] As the benefits embedded in a regime are greater, there are fewer incentives for pulling out.[172] Because regimes provide a framework for cooperation, states may decide to remain within the regime while pulling out of operational agreements. Remaining in a treaty regime while pulling out of a substantial agreement within its framework is behavior by a sovereign state that seeks to maintain benefits and shed obligations. This behavior has a dual effect on inter-state cooperation. On one hand, it negatively affects cooperation because of the pulling out of operational agreements; on the other, it may be good for cooperation because it maintains participation in a multilateral forum. Only monitoring the withdrawing party's behavior in such a situation will reveal the

---

170 *See* Rafael Leal-Arcas & Antonio Morelli, *The Resilience of the Paris Agreement: Negotiating and Implementing the Climate Regime*, 31 Geo. Envtl. L. Rev. (2018).

171 *See* Laurence R. Helfer, *Exiting Treaties*, 91 Va. L. Rev. 1579, 1613–14 (2005).

172 Membership benefits generally allow adjusting regime regulations to the evolving needs of its members. Whenever a party withdraws from the regime, it loses the inherent benefit of future regulation in the functional area covered by the regime. *See* Ronald B. Mitchell, *Sources of Transparency: Information Systems in International Regimes*, 42 Int'l Stud. Q. 109, 109–10 (1988).

effect on cooperation in the end. This, obviously, would entail a case-by-case assessment. Though maintaining engagement in future agreements may be an indicator of cooperativeness by a state, using the regime platform exclusively to take advantage of membership benefits or to secure domestic prerogatives in future protocols may be a sign of bad faith.

This is particularly relevant in the context of climate change. The U.S. government's decision to pull out of the Paris Agreement[173] was not accompanied by a decision to withdraw from the UNFCCC. The Trump Administration explored the option of withdrawing from the UNFCCC as a whole under Article 24[174] as a way to overcome the four-year delay between denunciation and exit imposed by the Paris Agreement (the three-year period beginning with its entry into force plus the one-year notice period beginning with notification of withdrawal). If it had withdrawn from the umbrella commitment to the UNFCCC, the United States would have automatically disengaged from the operational commitment of Paris Agreement. Since the United States has been a party to the UNFCCC since 1992, it would have been able to disengage from both commitments within a one-year time frame. However, it preferred the strategy of disengaging from the protocol while staying in the regime.

Denouncing an agreement while remaining in the regime entails a precise policy strategy. Withdrawal from protocols or subsequent agreements, in a regime context, allows a state to get out of specific obligations while still holding membership in the regime framework to maintain—or even increase—its voice in a given functional area. The United States' rejection of the Paris Agreement is an example of this phenomenon: it gets to maintain influence on future climate treaties by continuing to be a party to UNFCCC (that is, maintaining membership in the regime).

V. Signatory Withdrawal

Non-cooperativeness is not evident only when parties seek to withdraw from international treaties during the implementation phase. Similar dynamics

173 Conference of the Parties, Adoption of the Paris Agreement, Dec. 12, 2015 U.N. Doc. FCCC/CP/2015/L.9/Rev/1 (Dec. 12, 2015).

174 Article 24 of the UNFCCC affirms that "1. At any time after three years from the date on which the Convention has entered into force for a Party, that Party may withdraw from the Convention by giving written notification to the Depositary. 2. Any such withdrawal shall take effect upon expiry of one year from the date of receipt by the Depositary of the notification of withdrawal, or on such later date as may be specified in the notification of withdrawal. 3. Any Party that withdraws from the Convention shall be considered as also having withdrawn from any protocol to which it is a Party."

characterize contracting parties that announce they do not intend to ratify a treaty they had signed, effectively withdrawing their consent. This practice particularly characterized the U.S. and Russian behavior of "unsigning" treaties under consideration for ratification. Signatory withdrawal implies an underlying commitment issue due to a changing cost-benefit calculus or changed domestic politics.

Notwithstanding the fact that a treaty that has been signed but not ratified is not fully binding upon the signatory state, it still has some legal effects. Signing parties have an affirmative duty to not defeat the treaty's object and purpose before its entry into force. This is stated by Article 18 of the VCLT:

> A State is obliged to refrain from acts which would defeat the object and purpose of a treaty when:
>
> it has signed the treaty or has exchanged instruments constituting the treaty subject to ratification, acceptance or approval, until it shall have made its intention clear not to become a party to the treaty; or
>
> it has expressed its consent to be bound by the treaty, pending the entry into force of the treaty and provided that such entry into force is not unduly delayed.

Article 18 of the VCLT reflects a rule of customary international law that postulates an obligation of refraining in good faith from frustrating the object of a treaty, even before its entry into force.[175] The obligation imposed is effective between the moment of signature and the ratification of the treaty.[176] The act of signature entails a *prima facie* endorsement of an international agreement, which starts the clock running on a time frame for examination of the treaty domestically to consider ratification. Though a mere signature does not trigger binding obligations, it nevertheless imposes an *interim* obligation to not defeat the treaty's object and purpose up to the moment of ratification.[177] As Olivier Dörr pointed out, this is an autonomous obligation under international law

175 Article 18 of the VCLT codified international law as it existed at the time of its adoption, mainly reflecting decisions of international tribunal and states' practice. MICHAEL J. GLENNON, CONSTITUTIONAL DIPLOMACY 171–72 (1990); Martin A. Rogoff, *The International Legal Obligations of Signatories to an Unratified Treaty*, 32 ME. L. REV. 263, 284 (1980).

176 *See* David C. Scott, *Presidential Power to Un-Sign Treaties*, 69 U. CHI. L. REV. 1447, 1456 (2002).

177 Article 18 of the VCLT establishes an "interim obligation" for states to refrain from acts that would defeat the object and purpose of a treaty between its signature and ratification, which has been recognized in states' practice in various international legal regimes. *See* Paul Gragl & Malgosia Fitzmaurice, *The Legal Character of Article 18 of the Vienna Convention on the Law of Treaties*, 68 INT'L & COMP. L. QUART. 699 (2019); *see also* Rogoff, *supra* note 175, at 269.

with prospective (*ex nunc*) effects.[178] Therefore, any act contrary to the *interim* obligation related to the treaty may constitute a violation of international law on internationally wrongful acts, triggering responsibility in the sense of Article 13 of the Draft Articles on the Responsibilities of States.[179] Only by "unsigning" a treaty does a state terminate its interim obligations, as doing so makes clear its intention to not become a party to the treaty. Since the treaty is not binding upon the signatory parties until its ratification is concluded, one may argue that the basis for "unsigning" a treaty is a governmental decision to be free from the interim obligation.[180]

The legal effect of signature has been attested in a number of international decisions. Since the *Mavrommatis Palestine Concessions* case[181] and the Advisory Opinion on Reservations to the Convention on the Prevention and Punishment of the Crime of Genocide,[182] the ICJ has affirmed the case-by-case nature of this issue. A signature represents the first step of contracting parties' participation in the international agreement or convention they signed, establishing a provisional status in favor of the signatories. Due to its interim character before the treaty's entry into force, the signature confers a provisional status on the treaty and, as a precautionary measure, gives contracting parties the opportunity to raise objections. The risk of defeating the object and purpose of the treaty before its ratification is particularly pertinent with regard to multilateral treaties because it may upset the delicate balance achieved by the signatories during the negotiation process.[183]

International law protects legitimate expectations of states induced by another state under the doctrine of estoppel.[184] This is a rule of international

---

178 The effect of the signature is to be considered prospective (*ex nunc*), not retrospective (*ex tunc*). *See* Olivier Dörr, *Article 18, Obligation Not to Defeat the Object and the Purpose of a Treaty Prior to Its Entry into Force*, *in* VIENNA CONVENTION ON THE LAW OF TREATIES, A COMMENTARY 243, 245 (Olivier Dörr & Kirsten Schmalenbach eds., 2018).

179 Article 13 of the Draft Articles on the Responsibilities of States affirms that "[a]n act of a State does not constitute a breach of an international obligation unless the State is bound by the obligation in question at the time the act occurs."

180 Dorr, *supra* note 178, at 230–31 (explaining that only those states that have ratified the treaty in question may invoke responsibility for violations of the interim obligations of the "unsigning" state).

181 Mavrommatic Palestine Concessions (Greece v. Great Britain), 1924 P.C.I.J. Series A, No. 2 (Aug. 1924).

182 Reservations to the Convention on the Prevention and Punishment of the Crime of Genocide, Advisory Opinion, 1951 I.C.J. 15 (May 28).

183 *See* Rogoff, *supra* note 175, at 270.

184 *See, e.g.*, IAN BROWNLIE, PRINCIPLES OF PUBLIC INTERNATIONAL LAW 641 (1990); HERSCH LAUTERPACHT, PRIVATE LAW SOURCES AND ANALOGIES OF INTERNATIONAL LAW (WITH SPECIAL REFERENCE TO INTERNATIONAL ARBITRATION) (1970); I.C. MacGibbon, *Estoppel in International Law*, 7 INT'L & COMP. L.Q. 468 (1958).

law that bars a party from reinstating a status quo ante condition once its behavior has generated expectations or reliance by its counterparts.[185] Estoppel is now an established doctrine—largely considered as a general principle of international law pursuant to Article 38(l)(c) of the ICJ Statute[186]—grounded on the principle of good faith to protect expectations and reliance among states and to promote consistency in international relations. In the *Nottebohm* case,[187] the ICJ expressly addressed the validity of the estoppel doctrine:

> If one party has by any clear and unequivocal act or assertion led the other party to believe that that act is valid or that assertion true and in reliance upon that act or assertion the second party has acted or refrained from acting in a manner which results in detriment to that party, the first party is thereafter precluded from denying as against the second party the validity of that act or the truth of that assertion.

The fact that a country can decide not to proceed with ratification creates a dynamic of *de jure* legal authority contrasted with de facto political hostility from other states that expected a more cooperative posture from the withdrawing party.[188] This decision ultimately frustrates political expectations related to the subject matter of the unsigned treaty and affects interstate cooperation.[189] In this regard, Harold Koh remarked that any act of future cooperation of a state with the unsigned treaty may create a subsequent state practice inconsistent with the withdrawal of the signature. This may be considered a de facto repudiation or, at least, a conflicting practice undermining the force

185 The international rule of estoppel can be traced back to both Anglo-American common law and European civil law systems, which have an analogous concept of "*preclusion*" or "*foreclusion*." *See* Antoine Martin, *L'estoppel En Droit International Public*, in 9 INT'L J. L. LIBR. 130, 131 (1981) (reconstructing the different theories grounding the principle of estoppel from numerous municipal systems).

186 Article 38(l)(c) of the ICJ Statute encompasses the general principles of law recognized by civilized nations. *See* Temple of Preah Vihear (Cambodia v. Thail.), 1962 I.C.J. 6, 43 (June 15) (separate opinion of Judge Alfaro) ("I have no hesitation in asserting that this principle, known to the world since the days of the Romans, is one of the 'general principles of law recognized by civilized nations' applicable and in fact frequently applied by the International Court of Justice in conformity with Article 38, para. 1 (c) of its Statute").

187 Nottebohm (Liechtenstein v. Guatemala), 1955 I.C.J. 4 (Apr. 6).

188 By withdrawing its signature, not only does a state make it clear that it does not intend to become a party to that treaty, but it implies its intention to not be subject to any sort of obligation—including interim obligations—related to the unsigned treaty. *See* Scott, *supra* note 176, at 1474.

189 *See* Harold Hongju Koh, *Foreword: On American Exceptionalism*, 55 STAN L. REV., 1479, 1508 (2003).

of the "unsigning" act, based on cooperation outside the treaty framework on a case-by-case basis.[190]

Signatory withdrawal originated in the United States' practice when President George W. Bush "unsigned" the Kyoto Protocol on Climate Change in March 2001 and the Rome Statute in May 2002. The Bush Administration intended to be free of any legal obligation arising from the signing of those international treaties during the Clinton administration, which only had limited senatorial support.[191]

In the latter case, since the signature took place right before the end of Clinton's administration, it sparked a juridical debate domestically regarding its validity. The outgoing administration sought to give continuity to the treaty by signing it. The incoming administration responded with complete disengagement from the treaty through signature withdrawal. The Bush administration criticized Clinton's decision to put a "last-minute" signature on a treaty,[192] relying on the protection of Article 18 of the VCLT, which was binding on the incoming executive with regard to avoiding acts contrary to the object and purpose of the treaty.[193] To undo the consequences of Clinton's signature, in its letter of notification of signature withdrawal from the Rome Statute to the UN Secretary-General, the Bush administration affirmed that

> [t]he United States does not intend to become a party to the [International Criminal Court] Treaty. Accordingly, the United States has no legal obligations arising from its signature on December 31, 2000. The United States requests that its intention not to become a party, as expressed in this letter, be reflected in the depositary's status lists relating to this treaty.[194]

The Bush administration's signature withdrawals raised the issue that signing a treaty when it does not have congressional or parliamentary consideration

---

190 *See* id. at 1509 (analyzing the U.S. signature withdrawal from the Rome Statute, which left open opportunities for cooperation on a case-by-case base, such as a request for evidence to support an ICC prosecution or extradition of suspects located on U.S. soil).

191 The Clinton administration joined the Kyoto Protocol on November 12, 1998, and the Rome Statute on December 31, 2000.

192 *See Clinton's Words: "The Right Action,"* N.Y. TIMES (Jan. 1, 2001), https://www.nytimes.com/2001/01/01/world/clinton-s-words-the-right-action.html.

193 *See* John R. Bolton, *Should We Take Global Governance Seriously?*, 1 CHI. J. INTL' L. 205, 212 (2000) (especially criticizing Clinton's strategy of invoking Article 18 instead of submitting the treaty for congressional approval).

194 Letter from John R. Bolton, 3rd Under Secretary of State for Arms Control and International Security to Kofi Annan, U.N. Secretary-General (May 6, 2002), http://www.state.gov/r/pa/prs/ps/2002/9968.htm.

might eventually short-circuit the constitutional procedure of ratification, which is based on a shared power between the executive and legislative branches.[195] Such a shared power is present not only during the moment of ratification but also for signature withdrawal. Indeed, before "unsigning" a treaty under congressional consideration, the president must obtain the legislature's approval.

This was the case with the Comprehensive Test Ban Treaty,[196] an unratified international agreement prohibiting nuclear tests signed on September 25, 1996, under the Clinton administration. When the Bush administration sought to "unsign" it, the Senate did not consent to withdrawing the treaty from congressional consideration. Under U.S. domestic law, the president does not have the authority to unilaterally withdraw a disfavored treaty without the Senate's concurrence.[197] Without this preliminary step, the treaty is still under consideration and the president cannot proceed to signature withdrawal.

The practice of signature withdrawal was later resumed during the Trump administration, which "unsigned" the Trans-Pacific Partnership (TTP), and the ATT.[198]

The TTP represented one of the pillars of the Obama Administration trade policy and strategic pivot to Asia, aiming at becoming one of the world's largest free trade deal, embracing twelve Pacific-rib countries, and covering approximately 40 percent of the global economy.[199] Even if the agreement was signed on February 4, 2016 in Auckland, it never became effective, as it did not meet the ratification requirement provided in the treaty, which provided for ratification by all signatories or by at least six states corresponding to 85% of the GDP of the contracting parties, within two years from the signature. On January 23,

---

195 The U.S. Constitution provided for a shared power between the executive and legislative branches with regard to the process of joining international treaties to support the president with the Senate's advice and counsel through a checks-and-balances mechanism. Moreover, this provision represents a safeguard for each state, which have equal power in the treaty-making process. The so-called treaty clause of the U.S. Constitution provides that the president "shall have Power, by and with the Advice and Consent of the Senate, to make Treaties, provided two-thirds of the Senators present concur." U.S. CONST. art. 2, ¶ 2.

196 Comprehensive Nuclear Test Ban Treaty, S. Treaty Doc. No. 105–28, 105th Cong., 1st Sess. (1996), 35 I.L.M. 1439 (1996).

197 The State Department Legal Office advised the White House that, in these circumstances, based on a customary requirement, the president would lack the authority to act unilaterally. *See* Treaties and Other International Agreements: The Role of the United States Senate, S. Rep. No. 106–71, 106th Cong., 2nd Sess. 145 (2001).

198 Arms Trade Treaty, C.N.266.2013. Treaties-XXVI.8 (Apr. 2, 2013).

199 The contracting parties that negotiated the TPP were Australia, Brunei, Canada, Chile, Japan, Malaysia, Mexico, New Zealand, Peru, Singapore, Vietnam, and the United States.

2017. President Trump issued a presidential memorandum for the U.S. Trade Representative to withdraw as a signatory of the agreement,[200] which was followed by a letter to the TPP depositary reaffirming that the U.S. would have no legal obligation from its previous signature.[201] The remaining eleven contracting parties decided to revise the agreement and to proceed without the United States, forming the Comprehensive and Progressive Agreement for Trans-Pacific Partnership (CPTPP), signed on January 23, 2018 in Santiago, Chile, and effective since December 30, 2018.[202]

The ATT, signed during the Obama administration on September 25, 2013, was for the regulation of international trade in conventional arms and the prevention of illicit trade and diversion. After the announcement of the U.S. withdrawal, on April 26, 2019, President Trump issued a request to the Senate for the ATT's return, which was not formally approved. Nevertheless, on July 18, 2019, President Trump notified the UN Secretary-General of the United States' intention to not become a party to that treaty.[203] This incident represented an unprecedented case of U.S. signature withdrawal without the concurrence of the Senate.[204]

Echoing the U.S. example, on November 16, 2016, the Russian Federation "unsigned" the Rome Statute.[205] The Russian government explained its intention not to become a party to the ICC by citing lack of independence and high cost.[206] However, the signature withdrawal came two days after the publication of the ICC Prosecutor's Annual Report on Preliminary Examination Activities,

---

200 U.S. Memorandum of Jan. 23, 2017, Withdrawal of the United States from the Trans-Pacific Partnership Negotiations and Agreement (FR Doc. 2017–01845), https://www.federalregister.gov/documents/2017/01/25/2017-01845/withdrawal-of-the-united-states-from-the-trans--pacific-partnership-negotiations-and-agreement.

201 Letter from the Office of the United States Trade Representative to the Trans-Pacific Depositary (Jan. 30, 2017), https://ustr.gov/sites/default/files/files/Press/Releases/1-30-17%20USTR%20Letter%20to%20TPP%20Depositary.pdf.

202 James McBride, Andrew Chatzky & Anshu Siripurapu, *What's Next for the Trans-Pacific Partnership (TPP)?*, Council on Foreign Rels. (last updated Feb. 1, 2021, 7:00 EST), https://www.cfr.org/backgrounder/what-trans-pacific-partnership-tpp.

203 Depositary Notification from the UN Secretary-General, UN Doc. C.N.314.2019.Treaties-XXVI.8 (Jul. 19, 2019).

204 *See* Jean Galbraight, *Contemporary Practice of the United States Related to International Law*, 113 AJIL 813, 817 (2019).

205 Russia signed the Rome Statute on September 13, 2000. Later, on November 16, 2016, it "unsigned" the agreement, issuing the bylaw N. 361-rp, wich is available online at http://publication.pravo.gov.ru/Document/View/0001201611160018.

206 *Statement by the Russian Foreign Ministry*, Ministry of Foreign Affs. of the Russian Fed'n (Nov. 16, 2016), https://www.mid.ru/en/foreign_policy/news/-/asset_publisher/cKNonkJE02Bw/content/id/2523566.

which labeled the hostilities between Russia and Ukraine with regard to the situation in Crimea and Eastern Ukraine as international armed conflict.[207] The existence of an international armed conflict would involve the application of the ICC jurisdiction. Although the Rome Statute was merely signed, not ratified, under Article 126,[208] it still imposed an interim obligation to not defeat its object and purpose. By withdrawing its signature, the Russian government freed itself from international obligations deriving from it, thereby avoiding potential prosecutions before the ICC.

Signature withdrawal, like withdrawal, reveals a commitment issue. Whenever conditions are not right for a state to ratify an agreement, it may be compelled to withdraw its signature from it. From this perspective, a state's signature may be seen as a preliminary first step in a state's commitment before ratification. In any event, signature withdrawal serves as tool to reinstate the status quo ante. This may be the consequence of an unfavorable cost-benefit calculus, such as in the Russian case, or the result of an agreement with limited domestic support.

Through signature withdrawal, a government makes clear its intention not only not to become a party to that treaty but also not to be compliant with it. Once the status quo ante is reinstated via signature withdrawal, a government has eliminated Article 18 obligations, thus avoiding responsibility under international law.[209]

207 International Criminal Court, The Office of the Prosecutor, Report on Preliminary Examination Activities 35 para. 158 (Nov. 14, 2016), https://www.icc-cpi.int/iccdocs/otp/161114-otp-rep-PE_ENG.pdf.

208 Article 126.2 of the Rome Statute states: "For each State ratifying, accepting, approving or acceding to this Statute after the deposit of the 60th instrument of ratification, acceptance, approval or accession, the Statute shall enter into force on the first day of the month after the 60th day following the deposit by such State of its instrument of ratification, acceptance, approval or accession."

209 In the U.S. domestic system, when a president seeks to "unsign" a treaty that has already been deposited with the Senate for consideration, he must receive senatorial approval to do so. If the Senate does not grant that approval, the president cannot "unsign" the treaty—but he may find other ways to make clear his intention not to ratify the agreement. However, in these circumstances, obligations under Article 18 remain unabated. *See* David C. Scott, *Presidential Power to Un-Sign Treaties*, 69 U. Chi. L. Rev., 1447, 1475–76 (2002); *see also* Michael J. Glennon, Constitutional Diplomacy 174 (1990).

CHAPTER 5

Rationales for Withdrawal

> "There is no tyranny more cruel than that which is exercised within the shade of the law and with the colours of justice."
>
> MONTESQUIEU

Introduction

Withdrawal is a phenomenon that has significantly reshaped balance in the world order. Not only political but also legal and economic consequences follow from one country's decision to withdraw from an international commitment. Although it is not yet possible to determine all the ramifications of the trend of withdrawal, it is possible to examine the context in which withdrawal has occurred and its evolution since the formation of the current multilateral system. This methodology allows for systematizing withdrawals, depending on the rationale of the denunciation.

States' decisions to withdraw from a multilateral treaty can have different causes, depending on how changing political, economic, or social conditions at home match supranational trends. Using a heuristic approach, this chapter proposes a classification and identifies two main categories of withdrawal: withdrawal that is a reaction in domestic policy and withdrawal that is a proactive step in foreign policy.

It is important to study states' rationales for denunciation of international agreements. Is a state willing to take this step because it wishes to protect its sovereignty, because it wishes to amend or renegotiate the agreement, or because it wants to create an alternative agreement or institution to better serve domestic interests? Even though it is difficult and probably impossible to place multifaceted decisions in pure categories, systematizing the reasons behind withdrawal helps to reconstruct the behavioral patterns involved in states' exits. The rationales for denunciation represent the ideological link between the political decision to disengage from international cooperation and the legal procedure for pulling out without incurring the consequences of noncompliance. It is possible to create a taxonomy based on differing motivations for withdrawal.

 | DOI: 10.1163/9789004467644_006

Withdrawal may represent a reaction to an alleged intrusion into domestic policy or sovereignty or, instead, a proactive assertion of sovereign power.

I. Withdrawal as a Reaction in Domestic Politics

Withdrawal can be a reactive instrument of domestic policy whenever a state seeks to protect its sovereignty from external inferences. From this perspective, relevant factors to analyze are (a) economic factors behind withdrawal, (b) expansion of international jurisdiction ("mission creep"), (c) the perception of bias or unfairness of an international agreement, organization, or tribunal; and (d) shifts in domestic politics and the rise of populism.

The following table lists the most important instances of reactionary withdrawal and is followed by detailed analysis of each.

TABLE 2 Withdrawal as a reaction in foreign policy

	Reason	Cases	Countries	Year
Economic Costs	Unwillingness or inability to finance the regime	i. ECT	Italy	2015
		ii. UNESCO	USA	2017
Mission Creep	Expansion of international jurisdiction and judicial globalization	i. Optional Protocol Vienna Convention on Consular Relations	USA	2005
		ii. Optional Protocol Vienna Convention on Diplomatic Relations	USA	2018
		iii. UNCLOS	China (withdrawn)	2016
		iv. UN Human Rights Committee	Caribbean States	1997–2000
Bias	Perception of bias or unfairness	i. Cold War strategies: UNICEF, WHO, UNESCO, IFIS	Soviet bloc, Western bloc	1950s 1970s
		ii. Israeli–Palestinian Conflict: UNESCO, UN Human Rights Council	US, Israel	2018
		iii. African Union Plea: International Criminal Court	Burundi, South Africa (withdrawn), Gambia (withdrawn)	2016–2017
		iv. WHO	US	2020

A. *Economic Costs*

Often, the decision to withdraw involves a cost-benefit analysis. It is important to distinguish between states' decisions made for economic reasons and states decisions that seek to generate economic consequences.

Whenever the cost of membership overweighs its benefits, a state may be more inclined to denounce an agreement. Several states that denounced multilateral organizations' treaties justified their decision based on their unwillingness or inability to finance the regime system or international organization they had joined. For instance, in May 2015, the Italian government announced its decision to withdraw from the Energy Charter Treaty (ECT), which it justified by saying it was a consequence of a review of governmental spending.[1] Allegedly, the costs of remaining as a member would be too high because of Italy's domestic budgetary restrictions.[2]

Similarly, in 2017, the United States announced its intention to withdraw from UNESCO. Though the decision was formally grounded on political factors related to anti-Israel bias, economic factors played a major role. By the beginning of the Trump administration, the United States was more than $500 million in arrears with UNESCO. Moreover, the United States had lost its voting power within the UNESCO General Conference, the principal decision-making body, which approves budgets and makes decisions about programs in the fields of education, science, and culture.[3]

Different from withdrawal due to economic costs is withdrawal to produce an economic outcome. For instance, the 1977 U.S. decision to withdraw from the ILO—the oldest UN specialized agency—had a heavy impact on the organization. The ILO almost collapsed financially because the withdrawal of the United States and the associated termination of its financial contributions resulted in a 25 percent cut in the organization's budget. The United States rejoined two years later, which significantly strengthened the ILO's ability to carry out its mission.[4]

---

1 With regard to the Italian situation as a withdrawing party to the ECT, *see The Status of Member Countries in the ECT*, ECT, https://energycharter.org/who-we-are/members-observers/countries/italy/. *See also* Francesca Morra & Lorenzo Parola, *Any Consequences Stemming from Italy's Withdrawal from the Energy Charter Treaty*, ISPI (May 15, 2015), http://www.ispionline.it/it/energy-watch/any-consequences-stemming-italys-withdrawal-energy-charter-treaty-13323.

2 *See* Antonio Morelli, *Commentary to Article 47 of the Energy Charter Treaty*, *in* COMMENTARY TO THE ENERGY CHARTER TREATY 484, 486–87 (Rafael Leal Arcas ed., 2018).

3 *See* U.S. Dep't of State, *The United States Withdraws from UNESCO*, Press Statement of Heather Nauert, Department Spokesperson (Oct. 12, 2017), https://www.state.gov/r/pa/prs/ps/2017/10/274748.htm.

4 *See* Michael Akehust, *Withdrawal from International Organizations*, 32 CURRENT LEGAL PROBS. 143 (1979). *See also* Victor-Yves Ghebali, *The International Labour Organization: A Case*

Similarly, the U.S.S.R.'s decision in 1949 to leave the WHO had an impact on the organization's finances. The Soviet Union presented a notification of withdrawal jointly with the Ukrainian and Byelorussian Soviet Republics—which initially had independent seats in the World Health Assembly—and with Bulgaria, Romania, Albania, Poland, Czechoslovakia, and Hungary.[5] As withdrawal would end payment of membership contributions, WHO Director General Brock Chisholm decided on a conciliatory stance.[6] As the WHO statute did not include an exit provision, he officially considered the status of the communist countries to be "inactive" rather than "withdrawn."

In July 1955, two years after the death of Stalin, the Soviet Union formally expressed its intention to rejoin WHO, following Khrushchev's de-Stalinization trend. The organization facilitated the rejoining of the U.S.S.R. and Soviet-allied countries based on Chisholm's policy, asking for payment of only a small percentage of their back dues. The communist countries' reentry process ended in 1956.[7]

B. *Expansion of Jurisdiction ("Mission Creep")*

The decision to withdraw from international judicial or quasi-judicial bodies mirrors a trend in foreign policy of seeking to shield states' sovereignty from the expansion of supranational jurisdictions.

The progressive disengagement of the United States from the International Court of Justice (ICJ) represents a strategy of avoiding unexpected judicial rulings that undermine national decisions related to foreign policy. First, in 1985, the Reagan administration withdrew from the general compulsory jurisdiction of the ICJ after an unfavorable decision concerning American military intervention in Nicaragua.[8] Later, in 2005, the George W. Bush administration

---

Study on the Evolution of U.N. Specialised Agencies, *in* INTERNATIONAL ORGANIZATION AND THE EVOLUTION OF WORLD SOCIETY 103, 110–13 (Roberto Ago, Nicolas Valticos eds., 1989). *See also* Feinberg, *supra* note 64, at 204–11.

5 In February 1949, the WHO secretariat was informed of the withdrawal decisions by telegram; this was a few months before the Second World Health Assembly in Rome, Italy.

6 WHO was created as an organization of all nations. Russian physicians and health officials who joined the WHO staff encouraged Soviet countries to remain. *See* Charles-Edward A. Winslow, *International Health*, 41 AM. J. PUB. HEALTH 12 1455, 1458 (1951) (endorsing Chisholm's conciliatory stance with the following language: "The erring brothers have their seats waiting for them when they desire to mend their ways").

7 *See generally* Elizabeth Fee et al., *At the Roots of The World Health Organization's Challenges: Politics and Regionalization*, 106 AM. J. PUB. HEALTH 11 1912 (2016) https://www.ncbi.nlm.nih.gov/pmc/articles/PMC5055806/#bib5.

8 Case Concerning Military and Paramilitary Activities in and against Nicaragua (Nicaragua v. United States of America), Judgment I.C.J. Rep. (1984) (Nov. 26).

withdrew from the Optional Protocol to the Vienna Convention on Consular Relations (VCCR) after the ICJ heard three cases of foreign nationals sentenced to death row without consular notification.[9] In 2018, the Trump administration withdrew from the Optional Protocol to the Vienna Convention on Diplomatic Relations (VCDR) in connection with a case brought by Palestine challenging the United States' relocation of its embassy from Tel Aviv to Jerusalem.[10] At the same time, it withdrew from the U.S.-Iran Treaty of Amity,[11] which similarly provides for ICJ jurisdiction, after Iran brought a case before the ICJ alleging violations by the United States related to its decision to cease participation in the Iran nuclear deal.[12]

Similarly, the U.S. disengagement from the ICC, with the withdrawal of its signature to the Rome Statute, was a way to have a free hand in foreign policy without being bound to international criminal law in the aftermath of the 9/11 attacks.[13]

Russia withdrew from the ICC in response to the ICC's stance with regard to Russian policy in Crimea. Labeling the Crimean issue an armed conflict between Russia and Ukraine, the Court took jurisdiction of this issue.[14]

Similarly, in 2016, China threatened to withdraw from the UN Convention on the Law of the Sea (UNCLOS), signed in Montego Bay in 1982,[15] as a countermeasure against a ruling in an arbitration case brought by the Philippines with regard to territorial disputes in the South China Sea. The fact that China

---

9 *See* John Quigley, *The United States' Withdrawal from International Court of Justice Jurisdiction in Consular Cases: Reasons and Consequences*, 19 DUKE J. COMP. & INT'L. L. 263, 265 (2009) (as the U.S. government did not communicate a time period to the UN Secretary-General, it is possible it intended the act of withdrawal to have immediate effect); *see also* Frederic L. Kirgis, *President Bush's Determination Regarding Mexican Nationals and Consular Convention Rights*, ASIL INSIGHTS (Mar. 9, 2005).

10 *See* Roberta Rampton et al., *U.S. Withdrawing from Vienna Protocol on Dispute Resolution*, REUTERS (Oct. 3, 2018, https://uk.reuters.com/article/usa-diplomacy-treaty/u-s-withdrawing-from-vienna-protocol-on-dispute-resolution-bolton-idUKW1N1UJ0oV.

11 Treaty of Amity, Economic Relations, and Consular Rights, Aug. 15, 1955, 284 U.N.T.S. 93.

12 *See* U.S. Dep't of State, Remarks to the Media, Oct. 3, 2018, https://www.state.gov/secretary/remarks/2018/10/286417.htm.

13 *See infra*, Chapter 5, Part II.A (assessing how shifts in political leadership, as in the U.S. experience, can trigger withdrawal from international agreements joined by previous administrations).

14 Moreover, Russia had already been under investigation by the Court for the conflict in South Ossetia, ignited in 2008 with Georgia. *See* Robbie Gramer, *Why Russia Just Withdrew from the ICC*, Foreign Policy (Nov. 16, 2016), https://foreignpolicy.com/2016/11/16/why-russia-just-withdrew-from-icc-putin-treaty-ukraine-law/.

15 United Nations Convention on the Law of the Sea, Dec. 10, 1982 1833 U.N.T.S. 3, 397; 21 I.L.M. 1261 (1982).

ultimately did not denounce the UNCLOS suggests that the organization could effectively balance interests through diplomacy, preventing withdrawal.[16]

Withdrawal of Caribbean countries (Guyana, Jamaica, and Trinidad and Tobago) from the Optional Protocol to the International Covenant on Civil and Political Rights, which established the competence of the UN Human Rights Committee, involved similar dynamics. The Committee generated a de facto abolition of the death penalty in the Caribbean States. Caribbean governments started viewing human rights bodies as obstacles to capital punishment and international pleading systems as a loophole allowing avoidance of domestic procedures.[17] The international system's alteration of domestic judicial procedures for protecting human rights created a backlash against international human rights institutions in the Commonwealth Caribbean.[18]

States' disengagement from international jurisdictions must be seen to be a result of the perception domestic governments have of international bodies and tribunals. For instance, the U.S. government defined the current trend of judicial withdrawal as a "continued consistent policy of the United States to reject [international] jurisdiction."[19] This mirrors a backlash by sovereign states against the interference of international judicial interpretations with foreign policy.[20]

C. *Perception of Bias or Unfairness*

Among the factors that trigger misalignment between international and domestic spheres is members states' perception that international agreements, organizations, or tribunals are biased or unfair, which has occurred in

16 *See* Roncevert Ganan Almond, *U.S. Ratification of the Law of the Sea Convention*, DIPLOMAT (May 24, 2017), https://thediplomat.com/2017/05/u-s-ratification-of-the-law-of-the-sea-convention/.

17 According to the jurisprudence of the Inter-American Court and Commission and that of other international human rights tribunals, human rights instruments may properly be applied in respect of substantive and procedural norms under the treaty. Baruch Ivcher Bronstein v. Peru, Jurisdiction, Judgment, Inter-Am. Ct. H.R. (ser. C) No. 54, ¶ 37 (Sept. 24, 1999).

18 *See* Thomas Buergenthal, *The U.N. Human Rights Committee*, *in* MAX PLANCK UNYB 341, 384–85 (2001).

19 White House, Press Briefing by Press Secretary Sarah Sanders, Small Business Administrator Linda McMahon, and National Security Advisor (Oct. 3, 2018) (interviewing national security advisor John Bolton), https://www.whitehouse.gov/briefings-statements/press-briefing-press-secretary-sarah-sanders-small-business-administrator-linda-mcmahon-national-security-advisor-100318/.

20 *See* Joost Pauwelyn & Rebecca Hamilton, *Exit from International Tribunals*, 9 J. INT'L DISP. SETTLEMENT 679, 687 (2018); *see also* Zheng Wang, *China and UNCLOS: An Inconvenient History*, DIPLOMAT (Jul. 11, 2016), https://thediplomat.com/2016/07/china-and-unclos-an-inconvenient-history/].

three contexts. First, it occurred in connection with Cold War dynamics; disengagement from multilateral commitments was sought to enhance each bloc's strategies. Second, it has occurred in relation to the Israeli-Palestinian conflict, especially with regard to U.S. and Israel denunciations of multilateral forums upholding the Palestinian cause. Third, it is involved in the case of collective withdrawal of African countries from the International Criminal Court (ICC) due to perception of bias resulting in so-called "judicial imperialism."

During the Cold War, this was a recurring motivation for withdrawal. The Soviet Union withdrew from WHO[21] and UNICEF in 1949. Its decision was followed by the withdrawal of its Eastern European allies, namely Bulgaria, Romania, Albania, Czechoslovakia, Hungary, and Poland. Only Yugoslavia, which had previously broken off its relationship with the U.S.S.R., retained membership. These withdrawals fall within the logic of Cold War strategies and can be seen as an act of retaliation by one bloc against another. The U.S.S.R. had opposed the disestablishment of the United Nations Relief and Rehabilitation Administration (UNRRA), which provided considerable civil and economic aid to the war-affected Soviet-bloc countries.[22] Additionally, between 1952 and 1953, Poland, Hungary, and Czechoslovakia withdrew from UNESCO.[23] Their decision was a protest against the agency's actions, which were allegedly biased, in connection with the increasing Cold War tension globally and in Europe. The UNESCO General Conference sought to maintain cooperation within the framework of the agreement, but this was not very successful. Withdrawal from the organization merely crystallized a de facto disengagement that had already been ongoing since 1949 as a result of Eastern Europe polarization in the Cold War context.[24] Cooperation was restored a couple of years later, in the second half of 1954, by which time the international scene had changed.[25]

Moreover, as part of ideological disengagement during the Cold War, developing countries in the Soviet orbit pulled out of International Financial Institutions (IFIS) due to ideological bias. First, Poland and Czechoslovakia withdrew from the IBRD in 1959 and 1954, respectively, claiming that the institution

21 Constitution of the World Health Organization (WHO), Jul. 22, 1946, 14 U.N.T.S. 185.

22 *See* Leo A. Kaprio, *Forty Years of WHO in Europe: The Development of a Common Policy*, 40 WHO REGIONAL PUBLICATIONS 4 (1991).

23 *See* Feinberg, *supra* note 64, at 204–11; *see also* Hans N. Weiler, *Withdrawing from Unesco: A Decision in Search of an Argument*, in 30 COMP. EDUCATION REV. 1, 32, 34 (1986) (stating that the organization was labeled a "docile instrument of the cold war").

24 In 1949, Poland suspended payment of its contribution and its participation in the work of the Executive Board and the National Commission's activities.

25 Polish National Commission for UNESCO Review, Bulletin 5, 22–23 (2014), http://www.unesco.pl/fileadmin/user_upload/pdf/Biuletyn_2014_ENG.pdf.

was subservient to the Marshall Plan, thereby subordinating Europe to the economic influence of the United States.[26] Second, Cuba and the Dominican Republic withdrew from the World Bank Group (WBG) in 1960, followed by Indonesia in 1961.[27] In this way, the Eastern bloc was eroding the influence of the Western bloc in developmental multilateral forums while avoiding regime changes in the domestic political systems of developing countries. On the other side of the iron curtain, in 1985, the United States, United Kingdom, and Singapore withdrew from UNESCO, denouncing the organization for becoming progressively politicized.

The Israeli-Palestinian conflict also generated withdrawals based on perceptions of bias or unfairness. Indeed, after the United States rejoined UNESCO in 2003, it pulled out again in 2017, along with Israel. The organization welcomed Palestine as a member state in 2011. This act resulted in a decrease in the organization's budget because of a 1990s-era law prohibiting the United States from funding any UN agencies recognizing Palestinian statehood. Later, in 2017, the organization declared that the old city of Hebron in the West Bank was a Palestinian World Heritage Site; this generated a diplomatic *differendo* that resulted in the U.S. and Israeli withdrawal.[28] Similarly, the United States pulled out of the UN Human Rights Council in 2018. Because the Council voted to probe into the killing of Palestinians in Gaza, the United States withdrew, alleging "chronic bias" of the organization.[29]

Withdrawal due to an alleged underlying bias was also involved in the collective withdrawal of African countries from the ICC. At its thirtieth summit in January 2018, the African Union (AU) decided to seek an advisory opinion from the ICJ with regard to immunities of heads of state before the ICC.[30]

Most state parties to the Rome Statute come from the African region, and this is also the most investigated region due to self-referral mechanisms and the

26 On March 14, 1950, Poland denounced the IBRD Article of Agreements, while Czechoslovakia withdrew its membership on December 31, 1954. The World Bank replied that the governments' arguments were erroneous because the World Bank's operations were in accordance with its constituency agreements. *See World Bank Group* Historical Chronology, *supra* note 84.

27 *See* id.

28 In 2017, UNESCO supported a resolution denouncing Israel's policies regarding religious sites in East Jerusalem and the West Bank. This act had already provoked the withdrawal of the Israeli Ambassador before UNESCO. The following declaration regarding the Palestinian World Heritage Site generated a diplomatic breakdown. *See* Lynch, *supra* note 72.

29 *See* Piccone, *supra* note 76.

30 Assembly of the African Union [AU Assembly], 30th Ordinary Session, *Decision on the International Criminal Court*, AU Assembly Doc. Dec.672, ¶ 5(i) (Jan. 28–29, 2018), https://au.int/sites/default/files/decisions/33908-assembly_decisions_665_-_689_e.pdf.

prosecutor's initiative.[31] Though the AU supported creation of the ICC, the AU condemned the indictment of and associated arrest warrant for the head of state of Sudan, Omar Al-Bashir.[32] The AU had previously requested that the UN Security Council defer ICC proceedings on the case due to the peace process in Sudan, but this request was not heard.[33] As a result, the AU implemented a policy of noncooperation with the ICC, requesting its member states not to cooperate in the arrest of the Sudanese president and calling for a mass withdrawal from the tribunal.[34] While only Burundi has denounced the Rome Statute, South Africa also started withdrawal proceedings,[35] followed by Gambia,[36] without effective results. Other AU members, Kenya, Namibia, and Uganda, also considered withdrawing, for being biased against regional leaders,[37] while Botswana, Ghana, Nigeria, and Tanzania are still supporting the ICC.[38]

Another relevant case of disengagement from multilateral cooperation due to a perception of bias is the United States' withdrawal from the WHO. On May 29, 2020,[39] President Donald Trump announced the country's withdrawal from the organization,[40] and that was followed by a notification of the

---

31 *See* Priya Pillai, *The African Union, the International Criminal Court, and the International Court of Justice: At the Fault Lines of International Accountability*, 10 ASIL INSIGHTS 22 (Aug. 22, 2018), https://www.asil.org/insights/volume/22/issue/10/african-union-international-criminal-court-and-international-court.

32 The ICC began its investigations of Sudanese President Omar Al-Bashir based on a Security Council referral. S.C. Res. 1593 (Mar. 31, 2005).

33 AU Assembly, 13th Ordinary Session, *Decision on the Meeting of African States Parties to the Rome Statute of the International Criminal Court (ICC) Doc. Assembly/AU/13(XIII)*, AU Assembly Doc. Dec. 245 (XIII) Rev. 1, ¶ 10 (July 1–3, 2009), https://au.int/sites/default/files/decisions/9560-assembly_en_1_3_july_2009_auc_thirteenth_ordinary_session decisions_declarations_message_congratulations_motion_0.pdf.

34 AU Assembly, 28th Ordinary Session, *Decision on the International Criminal Court (ICC) Doc. EX.CL/1006(XXX)*, AU Assembly Doc. Dec. 622 (XVIII), ¶ 8 (Jan. 30–31, 2017), https://www.au.int/web/sites/default/files/decisions/32520-sc19553_e_original_-_assembly_decisions_621-641_-_xxviii.pdf.

35 After giving notice of its denunciation, South Africa had to revoke it due to a High Court decision.

36 After giving notice of its denunciation, Gambia reversed the decision after a change in its domestic administration.

37 Approximately 90% of the ICC cases pertained to alleged crimes in African countries. *See* Emmanuel Igunza, *African Union Backs Mass Withdrawal from ICC*, BBC (Feb. 1, 2017), https://www.bbc.com/news/world-africa-38826073.

38 *See* Joost Pauwelyn & Rebecca Hamilton, *Exit from International Tribunals*, 9 J. INT'L DISP. SETTLEMENT 679, 185 (2018) (assessing the allegations of tribunal bias in the backlash of African countries against the ICC); *see also* Priya, *supra* note 31, at 22.

39 *See supra*, Chapter 4, Part II.B (focusing on the U.S. withdrawal from the WHO).

40 *See* McNeil & Jacobs, *supra* note 77.

denunciation to the UN Secretary-General on July 6, 2020[41] to be effective one year later.[42]

Trump's decision was allegedly made for economic reasons, specifically the necessity of redirecting funds to national health priorities because of the coronavirus pandemic.[43] However, behind that decision lay the Trump administration's perception that the WHO was biased and accused it of being China-centric with regard to management of the COVID-19 pandemic. In April, the U.S. President sent a letter to the WHO Director General, Tedros Adhanom Ghebreyesus, asking for substantive improvements with regard to the organization's independence from China.[44] Allegedly due to the WHO's failure to undertake the requested reforms, the U.S. President ultimately decided to pull out.[45]

From this perspective, the U.S. withdrawal mirrors the U.S. disengagement from multilateralism, also in the global health field. Considering that the WHO was created for the purpose of setting common standards in public health and furthering collaboration among its members in health crises, the U.S. decision to withdraw its membership may constitute a risk to the organization from a political and health perspective. First, the absence of one of the major players in the international community hinders the global capacity of the WHO to respond to global emergencies, such as the COVID-19 pandemic, and serve as a facilitator in providing cures and tracing outbreaks. Second, the lack of U.S. funding may jeopardize the operational capacity of the organization, which may lose one of its largest funders in an unprecedented time of global health crisis.[46]

---

41 *See* Rauhala, Demirjian & Olorunnipa, *supra* note 78.

42 When the United States joined WHO in 1948, it passed a joint congressional resolution, which declared that withdrawal was permissible if the withdrawing member both provided one year's notice and fully met its financial obligations for the current year.

43 *See* Amy McKeever, *Here Is What We'll Lose If the U.S. Cuts Ties with WHO*, NAT'L GEOGRAPHIC (Jul. 10, 2020), https://www.nationalgeographic.com/science/2020/07/what-we-will-lose-if-united-states-cuts-ties-with-world-health-organization/.

44 Throughout the political management of the COVID-19 pandemic, President Trump repeatedly criticized WHO's response, which he characterized as doing favors for China and failing to hold Beijing accountable for the outbreak. *See* Steve Holland & Michelle Nichols, Trump *Cutting U.S. Ties with World Health Organization over Virus*, REUTERS (May 29, 2020), https://www.reuters.com/article/us-health-coronavirus-trump-who/trump-cutting-u-s-ties-with-world-health-organization-over-virus-idUSKBN2352YJ.

45 *See* Harold H. Koh & Lawrence O. Gostin, *How to Keep the United States in the WHO: Immediate Withdrawal Would Be a Global Health and a Legal Disaster*, FOREIGN AFFAIRS (June 5, 2020), https://www.foreignaffairs.com/articles/world/2020-06-05/how-keep-united-states-who.

46 In the years from 2018 to 2019, the United States was WHO's top donor, with a contribution of $893 million, which accounted for around 15% of the biennial budget of the organization. *See* McKeever, *supra* note 43.

II. Withdrawal as an Act of State Power

When withdrawal is a proactive instrument of sovereign power, exit serves four main purposes. First, it allows countries to have a free hand in foreign policy to gain more power in the functional areas covered by the treaty or organization previously joined. Second, announcing its intention to exit gives a party leverage to seek amendment of a treaty. Third, withdrawal furthers defense strategies, especially with respect to security. Fourth, it serves as a tool for forming consensus among the international community.

The following table lists the most important instances of withdrawal as an act of state power and is followed by detailed analysis.

TABLE 3 Withdrawal as an act of state power

	Reason	Cases	Countries	Year
Shift in domestic political leadership	Repudiate previous administrations' decisions	i. ICC ii. OAS iii. Trump Administration denunciations: UN Human Rights Council, UNESCO, JCPOA, Optional Protocol Vienna Convention on Diplomatic Relations, UN Arms Trade Treaty iv. EU	US Venezuela US UK	2001 2017 2017–2020 2020
Leverage for amending a treaty	Seek convergence with domestic interests	i. Cold War strategies: UNESCO, ILO, WHO ii. Re-accession with reservation: UN Human Rights Committee	Soviet Bloc Western Bloc Caribbean States	1950s 1970s 1997–2000
Defense strategy	Seek new balances in security arena	i. NPT ii. ABM iii. INF	North Korea US US, Russia	2003 2002 2019
Alternative consensus	Will to create new agreement	i. International Convention for Regulatory Whaling ii. GATT iii. EFTA	Iceland US, EU States UK, Denmark Portugal	1992 1994 1970s–1980s

A. *Shift in Domestic Political Leadership*

Withdrawal may reflect a significant shift in political leadership domestically that mirrors an ideological shift toward interests that collide with those embedded in the denounced agreement. Withdrawal extracts countries from previously assumed foreign policy commitments, freeing them to undertake different courses of action. This is particularly evident when it comes to politicized commitments. Governing parties may repudiate the decisions of previous administrations, and in doing so shift the balance between internationalism and isolationism. Even if is true that the recent rise of nationalism in many countries around the world reignited this phenomenon, withdrawal due to a shift in domestic political leadership has always occurred.

For instance, in the U.S. scenario, alternation between the Democratic and Republican parties on the national level has resulted in marked shifts in foreign policy.[47] Generally speaking, Democrats have been more prone to engage in internationalism, following the Wilsonian tradition, and Republicans have preferred a traditional isolationist strategy. The previous analysis of U.S. disengagement from international tribunals[48] showed that Republican administrations have repeatedly withdrawn from ICJ jurisdiction: this occurred under the Reagan administration, the George W. Bush administration, and the Trump administration. Similarly, George W. Bush denounced President Clinton's signature on the Rome Statute for the ICC[49] in order to have more freedom of action in the aftermath of 9/11. The same administration denounced the Kyoto Protocol on climate change[50] in 2001 in order to protect the U.S. economy. That decision was meant to shield the country from higher energy prices and avoid "free-riding" by other countries, in light of the agreement's unenforceability. In 2002, the United States withdrew from the 1972 Anti-Ballistic Missile (ABM) Treaty.[51] The United States also refused to join the UN Human Rights Council (HRC) at the time of its establishment in 2006.[52]

---

47 *See* Curtis A. Bradley & Jack L. Goldsmith, *Presidential Control Over International Law*, 131 HARV. L. REV. 1201, 1225 (2018) (analyzing U.S. presidents' power to terminate international agreements).

48 *See supra,* Chapter 4, Part I (analyzing U.S. policies of disengagement from international tribunals).

49 Rome Statute of the International Criminal Court, July 17, 1998, 2187 U.N.T.S. 90; 37 I.L.M. 1002 (1998).

50 Kyoto Protocol to the United Nations Framework Convention on Climate Change, Dec. 10, 1997 37 I.L.M. 22 (1998); 2303 U.N.T.S. 148; U.N. Doc FCCC/CP/1997/7/Add.1.

51 *See supra,* Chapter 4, Part III.B (focusing on US withdrawal from arms control agreements and the ABM Treaty).

52 *See supra,* Chapter 4, Part II.B (analyzing the US decision to withdraw from the UNHRC).

Since 2017, the Trump administration has followed the same line, reversing most of the foreign policy decisions of the Democratic Obama administration. The U.S. pattern under the Trump administration has echoed President Harding's "back to normalcy," which sought to reverse Wilsonian internationalism.[53] The Trump administration's foreign policy philosophy is "America first," which in application has resulted in the United States disengaging from most of its international commitments.[54] In the area of climate change, it withdrew from the Paris Agreement; in the area of human rights, from the HRC and UNESCO; in the area of security, from the Joint Comprehensive Plan of Action (JCPOA), the Intermediate-Range Nuclear Forces (INF) treaty, and the UN Arms Trade Treaty; and in the area of international law and diplomatic affairs, from the Optional Protocol to the Vienna Convention on Diplomatic Relations, which conferred jurisdiction on the ICJ.

In parallel, the UK sought to regain political independence by pulling out of the European Union (EU). Brexit takes the UK back to its nineteenth-century "splendid isolation." This was a diplomatic practice of avoiding permanent alliances or commitments with other Great Powers and having minimal involvement in European affairs.[55] From a nationalist perspective, Brexit is a way of asserting parliamentary supremacy vis-à-vis international organizations' policies and decisions. Though it is true that there is no question of eroding national sovereignty because the UK's Parliament has the power to repeal its commitments,[56] it is also true that maintaining commitment is a primary principle in international law. To gain a free hand in foreign policy by pulling out of the European Union, the UK must struggle through foreign policy negotiations. The difficulty of negotiations with the EU for an exit deal leaves open the question whether it is still possible to be splendidly isolated in a globalized world.

---

53 The "back to normalcy" doctrine can be summarized, in the words of President Harding, as follows: "America's present need is not heroics, but healing; not nostrums, but normalcy; not revolution, but restoration; not agitation, but adjustment; not surgery, but serenity; not the dramatic, but the dispassionate; not experiment, but equipoise; not submergence in internationality, but sustainment in triumphant nationality."

54 *See supra,* Chapter 2, Part III.A.ii (assessing withdrawal policies as a reaction to domestic politization).

55 The "splendid isolation" doctrine is perfectly described in the words of the Canadian politician George Eulas Foster: "In these somewhat troublesome days when the great Mother Empire stands splendidly isolated in Europe." *See* ANDREW ROBERTS, SALISBURY: VICTORIAN TITAN 629 (2000)*; see also* HAROLD WILLIAM V. TEMPERLEY, THE FOREIGN POLICY OF CANNING 1822–1827, at 342 (1925).

56 Brexit Brief, *Dreaming of Sovereignty*, THE ECONOMIST (Mar. 19, 2016) (mentioning the Tory Prime Minister Edward Heath's analysis of sovereignty), https://www.economist.com/britain/2016/03/19/dreaming-of-sovereignty.

B. *Leverage for Amending a Treaty*

States can use withdrawal or threats of withdrawal as leverage for amending a treaty to which they committed. This is a way to count more in a treaty-based negotiation forum or international organization.[57] For instance, in 1977 and 1984, the United States denounced the agreements establishing the ILO[58] and UNESCO[59] in order to reorient the substantive focus of the organizations. It rejoined ILO in 1980 and UNESCO in 2003 once each organization had addressed issues of concern to it.[60] In a similar fashion, in the 1950s the Soviet Union, along with its allies, temporally withdrew from WHO,[61] UNESCO, and the ILO, only to rejoin them years later.[62] In both cases, the denunciations had a dual goal. First, withdrawal was meant to create disengagement from a multilateral dialogue with the other bloc. Second, withdrawal concealed a strategy for amending agreements pursuant to each bloc's ideology and needs. Unsurprisingly, reentry of international agreements or organizations happened only after key issues for each bloc were addressed.[63]

Exit as a strategy for amending treaties has often occurred in the form of withdrawal and contextual reaccession to an international agreement with a reservation. An example is the withdrawal of Caribbean States (Guyana, Jamaica, and Trinidad and Tobago) from the UN Human Rights Committee in the 1990s.[64] They sought to denounce the underlying treaty—the ICCPR First Optional Protocol—and later rejoin it while presenting a reservation on the death penalty clause.[65]

Another example is Sweden's June 29, 2002 withdrawal from the Council of Europe Convention on the Reduction of Multiple Nationality and on Military Obligations in cases of Multiple Nationality.[66] It rejoined the next day with a

---

57 *See* ALBERT O. HIRSCHMANN, EXIT, VOICE AND LOYALTY: RESPONSES TO DECLINE IN FIRMS, ORGANIZATIONS, AND STATES 15 (1970).

58 Constitution of the International Labour Organization (ILO), May 10, 1944, 15 U.N.T.S. 40.

59 Constitution of the United Nations Educational, Scientific and Cultural Organization (UNESCO), Nov. 16, 1945, 4 U.N.T.S. 275; 41 AJIL Supp. 1.

60 *See* MARK F. IMBER, THE USA, ILO, UNESCO AND IAEA: POLITICIZATION AND WITHDRAWAL IN THE SPECIALIZED AGENCIES (1989); *see also* Sean D. Murphy, *Contemporary Practice of the United States Relating to International Law*, 97 AJIL 962, 977 (2003).

61 Constitution of the World Health Organization (WHO), Jul. 22, 1946, 14 U.N.T.S. 185.

62 *See* Feinberg, *supra* note 64, at 204–11.

63 *See supra,* Chapter 4, Part II.B (focusing on cases of withdrawal of each bloc from UN agencies).

64 *See supra,* Chapter 4, Part I.C (analyzing the policy of disengagement of the Caribbean States from the UN Human Rights Committee).

65 *See* Helfer, *supra* note 44, at 1881.

66 The Convention aims to reduce as much as possible the number of cases of multiple nationalities, as between parties. It lays down rules to reduce cases of multiple nationalities in the case of the acquisition of a new nationality or the renunciation of one nationality

reservation limiting the scope of the agreement's application to the military obligations regulated in Chapter 1 of the Convention, leaving the regulation of multiple nationalities to statutory provisions in each member state. Later, in 2007, the parties to the Convention adopted an interpretation agreement allowing denunciation of Chapter 1, thereby transforming the Swedish conduct into a general right of all members.[67]

On June 29, 2011, Bolivia denounced the 1961 Single Convention on Narcotic Drugs,[68] which had been ratified in 1976, after fruitless amendment attempts. Subsequently, the Bolivian government deposited its document of reaccession, conditional on a reservation that would allow the use of coca in its territory.[69] Since the reservation was objected to by fewer than one third of members—the *de minimis* requirement set in the Convention—Bolivia could rejoin with reservation.

The practice of denunciation with contextual reaccession followed by reservation to unilaterally modify treaty obligations raises several questions as to its validity and legal effects. In 1992, the Swiss Federal Tribunal contributed to such a discussion, analyzing the Swiss interpretative declaration on Article 6(1) of the European Convention on Human Rights (ECHR),[70] which had been declared invalid by the European Court of Human Rights in the *Belilos* case.[71] The Tribunal considered the strategy of denouncing and re-accessing

---

and the legal consequences for persons concerned, including minors. It also contains provisions on military obligations in cases of multiple nationality. Convention on the Reduction of Cases of Multiple Nationality and on Military Obligations in Cases of Multiple Nationality, E.T.S. 043 (1968).

67 *See* Bjorn Arp, *Denunciation Followed by Re-Accession with Reservations to a Treaty: A Critical Appraisal of Contemporary State Practice*, LXI NETHERLANDS INT'L L. REV 141, 157 (2014).

68 Single Convention on Narcotic Drugs, Mar. 25, 1961, Treaty Doc. C.N. 829.2011. 520 U.N.T.S. 151 (1961).

69 The text of the reservation reads as follow: "The Plurinational state of Bolivia reserves the right to allow in its territory: traditional coca leaf chewing; the consumption and use of the coca leaf in its natural state for cultural and medicinal purposes; its use in infusions; and also the cultivation, trade and possession of the coca leaf to the extent necessary for these licit purposes.
At the same time, the republic of Bolivia (*sic*) will continue to take all necessary legal measures to control the illicit cultivation of coca in order to prevent its abuse and the illicit production of the narcotic drugs which may be extracted from the leaf. The effective accession of Bolivia to the aforementioned convention is subject to the authorization of this reservation."

70 Switzerland signed the Convention on December 21, 1972, and ratified it on November 28, 1974, with an interpretative declaration on article 6(1).

71 Judgment of the European Court of Human Rights, July 29 1988, Belilos v. Switzerland, App. No. 10328/83.

the ECHR with a new reservation. It concluded that such a practice would be an abuse of the right to denounce.[72]

It is debatable whether withdrawing from and re-acceding to a convention with the sole purpose of presenting a reservation should be considered a late reservation or a new ratification. In the view of the UN Secretary-General, this practice falls in the latter category, as it allows a contracting party to decide on a case-by-case basis whether the treaty should enter into force or not, given the reservation. However, some states have firmly rejected this practice as being not in good faith under international law.[73] For instance, in the case of the Bolivian denunciation of the Single Convention on Narcotic Drugs, the United States[74] and some European countries[75]—Italy, Finland, the Netherlands, Ireland, Sweden, Portugal, and Romania—condemned the Bolivian behavior.

C. *Defense Strategy*

As a proactive tool in foreign policy, withdrawal may also further countries' defense strategies. This is particularly relevant in the area of security, where the affirmation of sovereign power can be exerted through the legal channel of withdrawal provisions.

This was the case in the North Korean 2003 withdrawal from the Nuclear Non-Proliferation Treaty (NPT) when the domestic program's clear policy disengagement from the international regulation was detected.[76] This strategy led to the nuclear rearmament of North Korea, which resumed missile testing, reactivated nuclear facilities, and expelled international inspectors from the

---

72 Judgment of the Second Civil Section, Dec. 17, 1992, Elizabeth B. v. Thurgau Canton Council of State, Bge 118 ia 488.

73 *See* Arp, *supra* note 67, at 164.

74 Objection by the United States of America to Bolivia's Reservation, UN Doc. C.N.361.2012. Treaties-VI.18 (Depositary Notification) (July 10, 2012).

75 Objection by Italy to Bolivia's Reservation, UN Doc. C.N.750.2012. Treaties-VI.18 (Depositary Notification) (Dec. 28, 1012); Objection by Finland to Bolivia's Reservation, UN Doc. C.N.95.2013. Treaties-VI.18 (Depositary Notification) (Jan. 8, 2013); Objection by the Netherlands to Bolivia's Reservation, UN Doc. C.N.102.2013. Treaties-VI.18 (Depositary Notification) (Jan. 8, 2013); Objection by Ireland to Bolivia's Reservation, UN Doc. C.N.101.2013. Treaties-VI.18 (Depositary Notification) (Jan. 9, 2013); Objection by Sweden to Bolivia's Reservation, UN Doc. C.N.723.2012. Treaties-VI.18 (Depositary Notification) (Dec. 21, 2012); Objection by the Portuguese Republic to Bolivia's Reservation, UN Doc. C.N.93.2013. Treaties-VI.18 (Depositary Notification) (Jan. 8, 2013); Objection by Romania to Bolivia's Reservation, UN Doc. C.N.91.2013. Treaties-VI.18 (Depositary Notification) (Jan. 22, 2013).

76 *See* Masahiko Asada, *Arms Control Law in Crisis? A Study of the North Korean Nuclear Issue*, 9 J. CONFLICT & SEC. L. 331, 341 (2004).

International Atomic Energy Agency (IAEA).[77] The reaction of the international community to the North Korean strategy led the UN Security Council to impose sanctions by passing Resolution 1718 of 2006, Resolution 1874 of 2009, Resolution 2087, and Resolution 2094 of 2013, and more recently with Resolution 2270 and 2321 of 2016, and Resolution 2371, and Resolution 2375 of 2017. North Korean rearmament created a crisis in international security that is still far from being solved.

U.S. disengagement from bilateral arms control agreements signed with Russia during the Cold War is part of a national defense strategy. The 2002 decision to pull out of the ABM Treaty and the 2018 announced denunciation of the Intermediate-Range Nuclear Forces (INF) raise questions about the new balance of powers in international security. Even though these are bilateral agreements, they sought to raise a global barrier to the spread of nuclear weapons. Overcoming a nonproliferation bulwark encourages unilateral armament and disincentivizes peaceful settlement of disputes. Moreover, it triggers a cascade effect—the decision to withdraw from arms control agreements may ultimately support countries' decisions to undertake nuclear programs for purposes of national security. Though securing arms control agreements took years of negotiations, withdrawal may end up being a rushed decision that needs to balance domestic security interests with regional and global interstate cooperation.

D. *Alternative Consensus*

Withdrawal may ultimately serve as a tool to generate an alternative consensus among the international community that is outside the scope of the withdrawn agreement.[78] For instance, Iceland denounced the International Convention for the Regulation of Whaling[79] in 1992 and, with the active support of other member states, created a new regime, the North Atlantic Marine Mammal Commission.[80]

---

77 *See* Frederic L. Kirgis, *North Korea's Withdrawal from the Nuclear Non-Proliferation Treaty*, 2 ASIL INSIGHTS 8 (Jan. 24, 2003), https://www.asil.org/insights/volume/8/issue/2/north-koreas-withdrawal-nuclear-nonproliferation-treaty.

78 *See* Helfer, *supra* note 171, at 1588.

79 International Convention for the Regulation of Whaling, Dec. 2, 1946 62 Stat. 1716; 161 U.N.T.S. 72.

80 *See* David D. Caron, *The International Whaling Commission and the North Atlantic Marine Mammal Commission: The Institutional Risks of Coercion in Consensual Structures*, 89 AJIL 154, 155 (1995).

Similarly, in the 1990s, the United States and European countries pursued an exit strategy to secure the effectiveness of trade talks at the Uruguay Round.[81] They decided to withdraw from the General Agreement for Tariffs and Trade (GATT)[82] and created the World Trade Organization (WTO),[83] an international organization that could bring together developed and developing nations under the same institutional umbrella.[84]

The exodus of European states from the European Free Trade Agreement (EFTA) to the EU also illustrates shifting consensus by way of alternative regional deals. EFTA is a regional trade organization and free-trade area established in 1960 as an alternative trade bloc for those European states unable or unwilling to join the European Economic Community.[85] As some of those states decided to join the European Communities, they pulled out of EFTA. This was the case with the United Kingdom and Denmark in 1972, Portugal in 1986, and Austria, Finland, and Sweden in 1995. As the UK is currently in the process of leaving the EU, there is an ongoing debate regarding the opportunity to rejoin EFTA. The UK would negotiate bilateral agreements with the EU for access to the single market on a sector-by-sector base, becoming subject to EFTA jurisdiction.[86] This raises an obvious question: would withdrawing from an organization to join another one be a real gain in terms of sovereignty?

81 Final Act Embodying the Results of the Uruguay Round of Multilateral Trade Negotiations, Apr. 15, 1994, 1867 U.N.T.S. 14; 33 I.L.M. 1143 (1994).

82 General Agreement on Tariffs and Trade, Oct. 30, 1947 55 U.N.T.S. 194; 61 Stat. pt. 5; T.I.A.S. No. 1700.

83 Marrakesh Agreement Establishing the World Trade Organization, Apr. 15, 1994, 1867 U.N.T.S. 154; 33 I.L.M. 1144 (1994).

84 *See* Richard H. Steinberg, *In the Shadow of Law or Power? Consensus-Based Bargaining and Outcomes in the GATT/WTO*, 56 INT'L ORG. 339, 358 (2002) (arguing that the withdrawal from GATT and the creation of the WTO represented an act of power of the United States and European countries, as the latter sought to secure in the WTO Agreement obligations in line with their domestic interests); *see also* Alan O. Sykes, *Protectionism as a "Safeguard": A Positive Analysis of the GATT "Escape Clause" with Normative Speculations*, 58 U. CHI. L. REV. 255, 279 (1991).

85 The founding members of EFTA were known as the "outer seven" in contrast with the "inner six" founders of the European Communities. The seven states were Austria, Denmark, Norway, Portugal, Sweden, Switzerland, and the United Kingdom. The current EFTA members are Norway and Switzerland, among the founders, along with Iceland and Lichtenstein, which joined later in 1970 and 1991, respectively. More information is available online at http://www.efta.int/About-EFTA/EFTA-through-years-747.

86 Rafael Leal-Arcas, *Three Thoughts on Brexit*, Queen Mary University of London School of Law Legal Studies Research Paper 249 (2016); *see also* David Phinnemore, *Could the UK Rejoin the European Free Trade Association (EFTA) After Brexit?*, CONVERSATION (Jul. 19, 2017), http://theconversation.com/could-the-uk-rejoin-the-european-free-trade-association-efta-after-brexit-81208; *see also* Philip Allott, *UK/EU Withdrawal Agreement: A Legal Speculation*, UK Constitutional Law Association (Nov. 7, 2018), https://ukconstitutionallaw.org/2018/11/07/philip-allott-uk-eu-withdrawal-agreement-a-legal-speculation/.

CHAPTER 6

Regulating and Enhancing Orderly Withdrawal from Multilateral Treaties

> "You can't change human nature, but you can change tools, you can change techniques. And that way you can change civilization."
>
> STEWART BRAND

Introduction

This chapter questions what role international law still plays in defining the rules of the game in a time of backlash against internationalism. The success of international negotiations does not depend on their capacity to create global agreements but rather on their capacity to secure their effectiveness and further to not create global agreements when commitment is premature and bilateral agreements or other forms of cooperation may be preferred by states. After identifying the bottleneck problem at the international and domestic levels, this chapter traces the way to regularize orderly withdrawal. It suggests policy responses for international lawyers, policy makers, and other relevant stakeholders who engage with international treaties and make recommendations at the international and domestic levels.

The alignment of domestic and international solutions with respect to commitment is key to regularizing orderly withdrawal and enhancing treaty maintenance in the multilateral system. Therefore, it is possible to conclude that international law still matters in the face of rising nationalism. International lawyers, scholars, policy makers, and, generally, all relevant stakeholders now have the task of contributing to the resilience of multilateral agreements, in line with the founding legal principle *pacta sunt servanda*.

 | DOI: 10.1163/9789004467644_007

I. International Solutions

In a system that lacks centralized enforcement, enhancing orderly withdrawal from multilateral treaties is a delicate process that requires balancing international and domestic prerogatives. The goal is to identify a toolkit of recommendations and solutions for strengthening commitment while providing necessary risk mitigation for states over the long term. This section analyzes the spectrum of international solutions available to further orderly withdrawal based on a wide array of best practices. States' commitment to multilateral treaties can be enhanced through defining withdrawal procedures, strengthening regimes' system, and providing substantive penalties and indirect sanctions.

First, conceptualizing the drafting of withdrawal clauses requires balancing the uncertainty endemic in the international law of treaties and the principle of good faith.[1] Defining a procedural safeguard can be achieved in different ways: requiring a rationale for withdrawal decisions, providing a time frame for exit, or encouraging negotiations.

Second, as withdrawal is viewed in its international contours, pulling out from a treaty does not disengage the withdrawing state from the legal, economic, and political environment in which the treaty operates.[2] This is particularly relevant in the case of international regimes.[3] Not only can they create higher stakes for members than a normal treaty, they also establish horizontal connections between different functional areas—through interlocking regimes systems—creating a safety net against the negative spillover effects of withdrawal.

Ultimately, in the face of withdrawal, substantive penalties and indirect sanctions are intended to make withdrawal as least as burdensome as breach. They can deflect states' noncooperative behaviors, creating specific protection for rights vested in international agreements.

A. *Securing Commitment through Withdrawal Procedure*

Treaty design is oriented to prescribing procedural steps, balancing states' needs vis-à-vis international prerogatives. Withdrawal clauses represent *lex*

---

1 *See supra,* Chapter 2, Part III.A (analyzing withdrawal under the lens of the principle of good faith to assess the evolution of this instrument from cooperative to noncooperative outcomes).

2 *See* Laurence R. Helfer, *Exiting Treaties*, 91 VA. L. REV. 1579, 1619 (2005).

3 *See* Richard R. Baxter, International Law in "Her Infinite Variety," 29 INT'L & COMP. L.Q. 549, 551 (1980) (assessing the functioning of international regimes, especially with regard to those treaties that cover delicate issues for a state, such as national security, regarding which governments' decisions would be more likely to further domestic prerogatives than international values); see also Steven R. Ratner, Does International Law Matter in Preventing Ethnic Conflict?, 32 N.Y.U. J. INT'L L. & POL. 591, 652 (2000).

specialis in the treaty framework in which they are included, as they define the contours for exit, by regulating states' actions in the moment of denunciation.[4]

Withdrawal clauses are meant to set clear rules ex ante to guide states' behavior ex post. Under this lens, the way withdrawal clauses are drafted is key in enhancing contracting parties' good faith within the treaty framework. Tailoring effective withdrawal clauses able to promote good faith in the treaty framework should mainly rely on four elements: (a) balancing good faith obligation with risk management needs; (b) requiring a reason to withdraw; (c) mandating negotiated requirements; and (d) including a time frame beginning with the denunciation and ending at the moment of pulling out.

i. Balancing Good Faith and Risk Management in Withdrawal Clauses

Withdrawal being voluntary, what parties consent to is the only limit on withdrawal.[5] Article 54 of the Vienna Convention on the Law of Treaties (VCLT) provides a basis for voluntary withdrawal, which may be either codified in a treaty provision or expressed through ad hoc consent.[6] For this reason, it is important for negotiators to frame clear exit clauses that provide formal and substantive guidance to contracting parties.

Withdrawal provisions make it possible to deal with uncertainty in treaty making and secure a flexible agreement.[7] They play a dual role. During negotiations of an international agreement, withdrawal clauses encourage a larger number of states to ratify or adhere to the agreement. During the implementation phase, withdrawal clauses make it easier for all contracting parties to openly address issues related to changed circumstances while avoiding breaches of treaty obligations and violations of international norms.[8]

Whenever the functional area touched by the agreement is too volatile or sensitive, withdrawal clauses can facilitate reaching consensus among

4 In the view of Jan Klabbers, politics can be guided, but never tamed. *See* JAN KLABBERS, INTERNATIONAL LAW 70 (2017).

5 *See* Timothy Meyer, *Good Faith, Withdrawal, and the Judicialization of International Politics*, 2 QUESTIONS OF INT'L L. 3, 5 (2014), http://www.qil-qdi.org/good-faith-withdrawal-and-the-judicialization-of-international-politics/.

6 VCLT art. 54 ("Termination of or withdrawal from a treaty under its provisions or by consent of the parties").

7 The techniques adopted in risk management are different and tend to limit risks through substantial or formal methods. In the first case, states will tend to limit the significance of the subject matter of the agreement to mitigate loss. In the latter case, states will opt for clauses that could scale down their obligations to perform. *See* RICHARD B. BILDER, MANAGING THE RISKS OF INTERNATIONAL AGREEMENTS 52 (1981); *see also* Herbert W. Briggs, *Unilateral Denunciation of Treaties: The Vienna Convention and the International Court of Justice*, 68 AJIL 51 (1974).

8 *See* HAROLD TOBIN, THE TERMINATION OF MULTIPARTITE TREATIES 202 (1993).

contracting parties.[9] On the one hand, contracting parties need to draft facilitative instruments to further participation and ratification. On the other, they must be careful that these instruments not end up being loopholes for states that find compliance no longer convenient. Withdrawal clauses that are tailored to restrict exit opportunities may discourage parties from reaching an agreement in the first place. Therefore, negotiators are tasked with accurately calibrating the costs and benefits of withdrawal clauses to produce optimal conditions ex ante while deterring opportunistic behaviors ex post.[10] Whenever negotiations are too premature to reach a multilateral agreement, parties should consider other forms of cooperation, such as bilateral agreements or political understandings.[11] This is a way to strengthen interstate cooperation with respect to sensitive topics and reach a binding commitment when the time is right for all the contracting parties. Beginning early in the negotiating phase, withdrawal should be understood as a last-resort tool, not as a wild card method of securing treaty closure.[12]

If a restrictive withdrawal clause would probably prevent the less engaged states from joining the agreement, a less restrictive clause may further broader participation without affecting the agreement's substantive commitments. However, while drafting withdrawal clauses that are too rigorous might eventually create a narrower platform of contracting parties, drafting broader ones may encourage opportunistic invocations.[13]

The principle of good faith limits withdrawing parties such that they must comply with the rules contained in the withdrawal clause of the treaty being denounced. The relevance of good faith in withdrawal procedures was

---

9 *See* Christian Downie, The Politics of Climate Change Negotiations, Strategies and Variables in Prolonged International Negotiations (2014); see also Stefan Persson, Deadlocks in International Negotiations, 29 Cooperation & Conflict 3, 211 (1994); Laurence R. Helfer, *Terminating Treaties*, *in* The Oxford Guide to Treaties 624, 637–38 (Duncan Hollis ed., 2020).

10 *See* Paul B. Stephan, *The New International Law—Legitimacy, Accountability, Authority and Freedom in the New Global Order*, 70 U. Colo. L. Rev. 1555, 1580 (1999); *see also* Ian Hurd, *Legitimacy and Authority in International Politics*, 53 Int'l Org. 379 (1999).

11 *See supra*, Chapter 2, Part II.A.ii (understanding risk management in multilateral negotiations).

12 *See* Christine Chinkin, *Normative Development in the International Legal System*, *in* Commitment and Compliance – The Role of Non-Binding Norms in the International Legal System 21 (Dinah Shelton ed., 2003); *see also* Wolfgang H. Reincke & Jan Martin Witte, *Challenges to the International Legal System Interdependence, Globalization, and Sovereignty: The Role of Non-binding International Legal Accords*, *in* Commitment and Compliance – The Role of Non-Binding Norms in the International Legal System 75 (Dinah Shelton ed., 2003) (exploring the role of non-binding legal sources as tools for progressive development in international law).

13 *See* Bilder, *supra* note 7, at 52.

established by the ICJ in the *Gabčikovo-Nagymaros* case,[14] which inspired the VCLT's procedural articles related to termination of international treaties in its Part V. The good faith parameter should inspire states' behaviors in international relations and discourage arbitrary unilateral solutions.[15] In framing withdrawal clauses, contracting parties should strive for a balance between good faith and risk management in each treaty negotiation so as to produce clauses that are neither too weak—allowing opportunistic behaviors—nor too strict—discouraging parties from joining.

ii. Requiring a Reason for Withdrawal

Requiring that a reason be provided for withdrawal is a strategy to enhance commitment by exposing the withdrawing state's decision to the other contracting parties and, more broadly, to the international community. Most withdrawal clauses impose no such requirement on withdrawing states.[16] The only exception can be mostly found in arms control treaties and labor law treaties.[17]

Arms control agreements tailor withdrawal clauses to particular factual contexts while leaving withdrawing parties to determine their occurrence.[18] For instance, the 1997 Convention on the Prohibition of the Use, Stockpiling, Production and Transfer of Anti-Personnel Mines and their Destruction[19] recognizes the right of withdrawal, conditional on a full explanation of a withdrawing party's reasons. Similarly, the 1972 Treaty of the Limitation of

---

14 In the *Gabčikovo Nagymaros Project* case, the ICJ found that the Hungary notification, on May 19, 1992, of its termination of the 1977 bilateral treaty with Czechoslovakia was premature, since it was to take effect six days later. Gabčíkovo-Nagymaros Project (Hungary v. Slovakia), 1997 Judgment I.C.J. Reports 7, Sept. 25, 1997, p. 66, para. 109.

15 *See supra,* Chapter 2, Part III (analyzing withdrawal under the lens of the principle of good faith in the execution of international agreements).

16 Notice of withdrawal usually consists of a brief letter, expressing the government's intention, addressed to the treaty depositary or secretariat. *See* HANS BLIX & JIRINA H. EMERSON, THE TREATY MAKER'S HANDBOOK 114 (1973) (providing examples of notice of withdrawal).

17 *See* Abram Chayes, *An Inquiry into the Workings of Arms Control Agreements*, 85 HARV. L. REV. 905, 957 (1972).

18 Usually, arms control agreements include withdrawal clauses in case extraordinary events related to the agreement impair important domestic interests.

19 Article 20(2) of the Convention provides: "Each State Party shall, in exercising its national sovereignty, have the right to withdraw from this Convention. It shall give notice of such withdrawal to all other States Parties, to the Depositary and to the United Nations Security Council. Such instrument of withdrawal shall include a full explanation of the reasons motivating this withdrawal." Convention on the Prohibition of the Use, Stockpiling, Production and Transfer of Anti-Personnel Mines and their Destruction (usually referred to as the Ottawa Convention on the Anti-Personnel Mine Ban Treaty), Sept. 18, 1997, 2056 U.N.T.S. 211.

Anti-Ballistic Missile Systems (ABM Treaty)[20]—a bilateral agreement between the U.S. and the U.S.S.R.—recognized the right to withdrawal only if either party decided that extraordinary events concerning the subject matter of the treaty had jeopardized its supreme interests and provided a contextual notification to the other party.[21] Similarly, in the international labor field, there is no stringent *de jure* requirement for justification, but the International Labour Organization (ILO) often asks governments to give their reasons after consulting with worker and employer representatives from that state.[22]

Even though states' practice mostly overlooks motivations for withdrawal, Article 65(1) of the VCLT expressly establishes such a requisite:[23]

> A party which, under the provisions of the present Convention, invokes either a defect in its consent to be bound by a treaty or a ground for impeaching the validity of a treaty, terminating it, withdrawing from it or suspending its operation, must notify the other parties of its claim. The notification shall indicate the measure proposed to be taken with respect to the treaty and the reasons therefor.

Though Article 65 does not reflect customary international law, it provides a procedural mechanism for withdrawal, as well as invalidity, termination, and suspension, which can be useful in enhancing orderly withdrawal.[24] First, it imposes a requirement of notification on states that pull out of an international agreement, which reflects a need for transparency and certainty in international relations.[25] Second, by requiring notification of the motivation for

---

20 Article XV(2) of the ABM Treaty provides: "Each Party shall, in exercising its national sovereignty, have the right to withdraw from this Treaty if it decides that extraordinary events related to the subject matter of this Treaty have jeopardized its supreme interests. It shall give notice of its decision to the other Party six months prior to withdrawal from the Treaty. Such notice shall include a statement of the extraordinary events the notifying Party regards as having jeopardized its supreme interests." Treaty of the Limitation of Anti-Ballistic Missile Systems art. XV, May 26, 1972, 23 U.S.T. 3435.

21 *See* Chayes, *supra* note 17, at 958.

22 *See* Kevin Widdow, *The Denunciation of International Labour Conventions*, 33 INT'L & COMP. L. Q. 1052, 1055 (1984) (analyzing ILO motivation requirements applicable to its member states in a case of withdrawal).

23 VCLT art. 65.

24 *See supra*, Chapter 1, Part II.B.iii. (analyzing Article 65 of the VCLT and its procedural requirements for justifying withdrawal decisions).

25 *See* Mario Prost, *Procedure to be Followed with Respect to Invalidity, Termination, Withdrawal from or Suspension of the Operation of a Treaty*, in THE VIENNA CONVENTION ON THE LAW OF TREATIES – A COMMENTARY 1486–90 (Olivier Corten & Pierre Klein eds., 2011).

withdrawal, the VCLT sets clear parameters to avoid arbitrary use of the instrument for the mere purpose of getting free of inconvenient treaty obligations. Article 65, in requiring a statement of "reasons," echoes the previous reference to "grounds" for termination in the draft Article 62 of the 1966 ILC report to the UN General Assembly.[26] These represent a bulwark for the security of a treaty as against arbitrarily denunciations. Requiring the reason for the decision to withdraw represents a check on unilateral, purely arbitrary denunciations.

However, withdrawal clauses are mostly framed in such a way that they do not require justification, which does not align well with a state having good faith obligations. Requiring a reason for withdrawal has a dual goal of furthering good faith and addressing risk management in international treaties. First, such a parameter compels a withdrawing state to publicly express the reasons that led to its final choice. This is a way to make evident the level of cooperativeness of the denouncing state, furthering transparency in withdrawal decision. Second, it prevents denunciation from ending up being a blank check in the hands of governments and exposes the withdrawing state to the reaction of the other parties to the agreement and the international community as a whole.

iii. Negotiation Requirements

Orderly withdrawal can be achieved through a negotiation mechanism involving dialogue by the parties. Negotiation is a tool for defining the procedural steps for withdrawal and also for defining the status of relationships after withdrawal is concluded. In this regard, withdrawal clauses may establish a mechanism to be triggered between the moment of the denunciation and the exit. Whenever a contracting party files a notice to withdraw, it should be required to initiate a dialogue with its counterparts.[27]

Based on the ICJ's *Advisory Opinion on the Interpretation of the Agreement of 25 March 1951 between the WHO and Egypt*, the duties to consult and negotiate, along with the period of notice for termination of a treaty, are to be defined on a case-by-case basis, subject to the obligation to act in good faith.[28] States can

---

26 Int'l Law Comm'n, Rep. on the Work of Its Sixty-Fourth Session, U.N. Doc. A/6309/Rev.1, at 261 (1966).

27 Campbell McLachlan, *The Assault on International Adjudication and the Limits of Withdrawal*, 68 INT'L & COMP. L.Q. 499 (2019) (assessing international adjudication in cases of disputes arising between the contracting parties to a treaty and the withdrawing party).

28 *See supra*, Chapter 1, Part II.B.iii. (analyzing the VCLT procedural framework for withdrawal, along with the doctrinal and jurisprudential views). In the *Advisory Opinion on the Interpretation of the Agreement of 25 March 1951 between the WHO and Egypt*, with regard to the possible transfer from Alexandria of a WHO regional office for the Eastern Mediterranean Region, the ICJ affirmed contracting parties' mutual obligation to consult and fulfill

either establish an ex ante mechanism during the treaty-making phase, or they can establish it ex post, once withdrawal is filed, through an ad hoc agreement between parties. For instance, at the EU level, Article 50 of the Treaty on European Union (TEU) provides a provisional procedure for withdrawal requiring a deal between the withdrawing state and the organization:[29]

> A Member State which decides to withdraw shall notify the European Council of its intention. In the light of the guidelines provided by the European Council, the Union shall negotiate and conclude an agreement with that State, setting out the arrangements for its withdrawal, taking account of the framework for its future relationship with the Union. That agreement shall be negotiated in accordance with Article 218(3) of the Treaty on the Functioning of the European Union. It shall be concluded on behalf of the Union by the Council, acting by a qualified majority, after obtaining the consent of the European Parliament.

With regard to Brexit, to enforce the procedural framework of Article 50 of the TEU, the EU Commission established a Task Force for the Preparation and Conduct of the Negotiations with the United Kingdom that operates with the support of the Council in carrying out negotiations for the definition of exit contours.[30] Since Article 50 was enacted, the TEU has solely represented a programmatic provision. A subsequent instrument, the withdrawal termination agreement, is tasked with establishing detailed procedures by which the withdrawal will take place; it defines the agreed terms and conditions for withdrawal.[31] Nonetheless, accession to and withdrawal from the EU are procedurally imbalanced with respect to negotiation. To join the EU, an acceding member must close an agreement with all EU member states. To exit the EU, however,

---

their obligations in good faith. *Interpretation of the Agreement of 25 March 1951 between the WHO and Egypt*, 1980 Advisory Opinion 1. C. J. Reports, May 28, 1980, p. 96, para. 49.

29 Treaty of Lisbon Amending the Treaty on European Union and the Treaty Establishing the European Community, Dec. 13, 2007, 2007 O.J. (C 306) 1.

30 The EU Task Force for the Preparation and Conduct of the Negotiations with the United Kingdom is guided by the former EU commissioner Michel Barnier. *See* Judith Resnik & Clare Ryan, *Global Constitutionalism 2017, Reconstructing Constitutional* Order, A Part of the Gruber Program for Global Justice and Women's Rights of Yale Law School 1-27 (2017); *see also* Alex Hunt & Brian Wheeler, *Brexit: All You Need to Know About the UK Leaving the EU*, BBC (Nov. 22, 2018), https://www.bbc.com/news/uk-politics-32810887.

31 *See* Jochen Herbst, *Observations on the Right to Withdrawal from the EU: Who Are the Masters of Treaties*, 6 GERMAN L.J. 1755, 1757 (2005).

the withdrawing member need only conclude an agreement with the EU; no negotiation with any single member state is required.[32]

Negotiation requirements serve two main goals in securing orderly withdrawal. First, they allow parties to mutually define the conditions that regulate the exit procedure in the event they were not set out in the treaty that is the object of denunciation or the treaty offers only a programmatic framework to be operationalized through further regulation. Second, they are meant to define a modus vivendi[33] for the withdrawing state and the remaining parties to the treaty. Both sides commit to their future coexistence with regard to the subject matter covered by the denounced treaty in a provisional or even more definitive way. A negotiations requirement eases orderly withdrawal by states and enhances interstate dialogue and stability in foreign policy, laying the groundwork for future cooperation.

iv. Time Frame for Withdrawal

A time frame for withdrawal is a way to create a "compensation chamber" for withdrawing states, diluting the political charge behind the decision to pull out. Including this mechanism in an international agreement is analytically equivalent to establishing the duration of the agreement, at least for the withdrawing state.[34]

Defining a time frame for withdrawal reflects a risk management need that has been present since the entry into force of the agreement: mitigation of opportunistic behaviors of counterparts. During the implementation phase of an agreement, once the ratification process has been accomplished, a multilateral treaty may enter into force in whatever time frame it defines.[35] Especially with multilateral agreements, defining a time frame for entry into force helps parties be ready for implementation. The entry into force can occur immediately after the deposit of a state's instrument of ratification, acceptance, approval, or accession. That was the case, for instance, with Article VIII

32 *See* Rafael Leal-Arcas, *Three Thoughts on Brexit*, Queen Mary University of London School of Law Legal Studies Research Paper No. 249, 1, 3 (2016).

33 *Modus vivendi* ("way of living") is a Latin phrase used to describe an agreement between parties with differences of opinion ("agreeing to disagree"). It can be use provisionally, referring to ad interim agreements between contending parties pending the final settlement. In most situations it is prepared in a rather informal way and is replaced by a more detailed and formalistic agreement.

34 *See* BILDER, *supra* note 7, at 53.

35 UN Office of Legal Affairs, Treaty Section, *Treaty Handbook*, U.N. Sales No. E.12.V.1, 1ISBN-13 978-92-1-055293-6 (Revised Edition of 2012) 22–23.

of the Protocol Relating to the Status of Refugees of 1967,[36] which established its immediate entry into force.[37] In other cases, a specific time frame after states' deposit of their instrument of ratification, acceptance, approval, or accession is set out. Article 44(1)(2) of the ECT[38] provides for a nineteen-day standstill period after the deposit of its thirtieth instrument of ratification before the agreement enters into force. Other multilateral agreements contain similar provisions, such as, for instance, the Rome Statute of the International Criminal Court of 1998,[39] which for provides a 60-day freeze before its entry into force.[40]

Though international treaties often include a time frame for their entry into force, there is no similar regularized practice regarding a time frame for exit, which is left to the will of the contracting parties.[41] A minimum period can be set—the so-called notice period—in which parties negotiate terms and conditions.[42] This period serves a dual purpose. First, it avoids opportunistic denunciations by states seeking to avoid accountability for violations of the agreement. Second, it creates a "compensation chamber" for the de-politicization of the decision to pull out.

Article 65(2) of the VCLT[43] requires a three-month standstill period from the date of notification of withdrawal before exit may be completed. Though this provision did not reflect the customary practice of law at the time of the codification of the VCLT,[44] through the years the treaty-making process has

36 UN General Assembly, *Protocol Relating to the Status of Refugees*, 31 January 1967, United Nations, Treaty Series, vol. 606, p. 267, http://www.refworld.org/docid/3ae6b3ae4.html.

37 Article VIII of the *Protocol Relating to the Status of Refugees, 1967*, states: "For each State acceding to the Protocol after the deposit of the sixth instrument of accession, the Protocol shall come into force on the date of deposit by such State of its instrument of accession."

38 Energy Charter Treaty, Dec. 17, 1994, 2080 U.N.T.S. 95.

39 UN General Assembly, *Rome Statute of the International Criminal Court* (last amended 2010), 17 July 1998, ISBN No. 92-9227-227-6, http://www.refworld.org/docid/3ae6b3a84.html.

40 Article 126(2) of the *Rome Statute of the International Criminal Court* of 1998 states: "For each State ratifying, accepting, approving or acceding to this Statute after the deposit of the 60th instrument of ratification, acceptance, approval or accession, the Statute shall enter into force on the first day of the month after the 60th day following the deposit by such State of its instrument of ratification, acceptance, approval or accession."

41 *See generally* Alain Pellet, *The Normative Dilemma: Will and Consent in International Law Making*, AUST. YBIL 26 (1983); *see also* Mehrdad Payandeh, *The Concept of International Law in the Jurisprudence of H.L.A. Hart*, 21 EJIL 967, 971 (2009).

42 *See* Herbst, *supra* note 31, at 1757.

43 Article 65(2) of the VCLT provides: "If, after the expiry of a period which, except in cases of special urgency, shall not be less than three months after the receipt of the notification, no party has raised any objection, the party making the notification may carry out in the manner provided in article 67 the measure which it has proposed."

44 *See* Mario Prost, *Procedure to be Followed with Respect to Invalidity, Termination, Withdrawal from or Suspension of the Operation of a Treaty*, *in* THE VIENNA CONVENTION ON

evolved along these lines; the effects of withdrawal are deferred for an amount of time agreed to by the contracting parties.[45]

Setting a time frame pushes the effects of withdrawal to the moment of exit—*ex nunc*—rather than the moment of the denunciation. Unilateral exit attempts that do not comply with these conditions or restrictions are considered ineffective.[46] During the notice period, the legal obligations of all contracting parties continue unchanged. The withdrawing party is still bound by the treaty, like every other party, and responsible for any breach that occurs before the withdrawal becomes legally effective. Moreover, under Article 43 of the VCLT,[47] the withdrawal of a party from a treaty does not affect its duty to fulfill those treaty obligations to which it would be bound under international law independent of the denounced treaty.[48]

Under Article 70 of the VCLT,[49] the decision to withdraw from an international agreement does not have retroactive effect.[50] Therefore, the withdrawing state will still be bound by obligations that accrued before the denunciation becomes effective.[51] This provision reflects the law on the consequences of treaty termination, as set out in the arbitral award of the *Rainbow Warrior* case.[52] The effects of a decision to withdraw apply from the date withdrawal is

---

THE LAW OF TREATIES – A COMMENTARY 1487 (Olivier Corten & Pierre Klein eds., 2011) (exploring the existence of customary law regarding a time frame for withdrawal at the time of the codification process for the VCLT).

45 *See supra,* Chapter 1, Part II.B.iii. (analyzing the VCLT procedural framework for withdrawal under Article 65).

46 *See* Helfer, *supra* note 10, at 631.

47 Article 43 of the VCLT ("Obligations imposed by international law independently of a treaty") affirms that "[t]he invalidity, termination or denunciation of a treaty, the withdrawal of a party from it, or the suspension of its operation, as a result of the application of the present Convention or of the provisions of the treaty, shall not in any way impair the duty of any State to fulfill any obligation embodied in the treaty to which it would be subject under international law independently of the treaty."

48 *See* Humphrey Waldock, *Special Rapporteur on the Law of the Treaties, Sixth Report on the Law of the Treaties,* 2 UNYBILC 266 (1966) (analyzing the relationship between Article 43 and Article 70 of the VCLT).

49 VCLT, Article 70(1)(b) ("Consequences of the termination of a treaty") affirms that the termination of a treaty "does not affect any right, obligation or legal situation of the parties created through the execution of the treaty prior to its termination."

50 *See* Stephan Wittich, *Article 70, Consequences of Termination of a Treaty, in* VIENNA CONVENTION ON THE LAW OF TREATIES, A COMMENTARY 1283, 1299 (Olivier Dörr & Kirsten Schmalenbach eds., 2018).

51 For instance, Article 8.A of the OPEC Statute imposes on contacting parties the obligation to meet all financial obligations accrued during their membership. OPEC Statute, Resolution II.6 (Jan. 1961).

52 This case involved the difference between New Zealand and France with respect to the interpretation or application of two agreements concluded on July 9, 1986 between

completed, not from the date of the notification. In *Question of the Delimitation of the Continental Shelf between Nicaragua and Colombia*,[53] the ICJ expressly clarified this point, affirming the principle of *perpetuatio jurisdictionis*, which precludes a withdrawal notification from being effective until the end of the notice period. Notwithstanding the Colombian denunciation of the American Treaty on Pacific Settlement (Pact of Bogotá),[54] the Court maintained jurisdiction over the dispute, as the Nicaraguan suit was filed during the one-year term established in the agreement.[55]

Similarly, in 1999, when Trinidad and Tobago denounced the American Convention on Human Rights,[56] the Inter-American Commission held that it retained jurisdiction over complaints of violations committed by the withdrawing state before the withdrawal became effective even if the effects of those violations continues or did not manifest until a later date.[57] In short, a withdrawing state remains responsible for violations that occur before or during the notice period, as it is still considered a member of the organization.

The notice period is also intended to create a "cooling off period" to depoliticize states' denunciations by discouraging precipitous or opportunistic decisions. Separating the moment of the decision and the moment of the action is

---

the two states that related to the problems arising from the Rainbow Warrior Affair. France-New Zealand Arbitration Tribunal, 82 I.L.R. 500, p. 251, para 75 (Apr. 30, 1990).

53 In *Question of the Delimitation of the Continental Shelf between Nicaragua and Colombia*, the ICJ rejected Colombia's preliminary objections against Nicaragua's claim for delimitation of its continental shelf extending beyond 200 nautical miles. Question of the Delimitation of the Continental Shelf between Nicaragua and Colombia (Nicaragua v. Colombia), Judgment, 2016 I.C.J., 100 (Mar. 17).

54 Under Article LVI of the Pact of Bogotá, "[t]he present Treaty shall remain in force indefinitely, but may be denounced upon one year's notice, at the end of which period it shall cease to be in force with respect to the State denouncing it, but shall continue in force for the remaining signatories. The denunciation shall be addressed to the Pan American Union, which shall transmit it to the other Contracting Parties. The denunciation shall have no effect with respect to pending procedures initiated prior to the transmission of the particular notification." American Treaty on Pacific Settlement (Pact of Bogotá), Apr. 30, 1948, 17 O.A.S.T.S. 61.

55 In the Order of November 15, 2017, with regard to its competence to hear counterclaims in the *Nicaragua v. Colombia* case, the Court found that it maintained jurisdiction even with regard to counterclaims presented after the termination of the treaty between the contracting parties; it had jurisdiction for the same reason it had jurisdiction over the principal claims. Alleged Violations of Sovereign Rights and Maritime Spaces in the Caribbean Sea (Nicaragua v. Colombia), Counter-Claims Order, 2017 I.C.J. 289 (Nov. 15).

56 American Convention on Human *Rights (Pact of San Jose, Costa Rica), Nov. 22, 1969, 1144 U.N.T.S. 123.*

57 Roodal v. Trinidad and Tobago, Case 12.342, Inter-Am. Comm'n HR 89, OEA/ser L/V/II114, doc 5 rev. (2001).

a way to insulate or at least dilute withdrawal from political passions.[58] Treaty-makers can tailor the time of withdrawal to a political cycle. For instance, with regard to the Paris Agreement,[59] contracting parties sought to frame a three-year standstill period from the date the agreement would enter into force plus a one-year notice period from the date of notification of withdrawal. Since the Paris Agreement had only just entered into force at the time of the Trump administration's decision to pull out in 2017, the U.S. decision to withdraw would not become effective until four years after the agreement entered into force. Though the notice period was not intended, during negotiations, to be a precise strategy for de-politicization, the four-year timeframe aligns with election cycles in many countries.[60]

The exercise of withdrawal can be tailored around different notice periods and different needs. Based on states' practices, we can identify an array of time frame provisions that operate in different ways: (a) the "advance-notice" model, (b) the "humanitarian" model, and (c) the "clock" model.

First, the most common time frame category is the "advance-notice" mechanism, which provides that withdrawal will be effective only after a particular period time after the notification of withdrawal. This clause is particularly common in international organizations' statutes. The North Atlantic Treaty Organization (NATO)[61] and the Food and Agriculture Organization (FAO)[62] provide a one-year time frame; the Organization of American States (OAS)[63] and ILO,[64] a two-year timeframe. Only the Bretton Wood institutions, namely the International Monetary Fund (IMF)[65] and the International Bank for Reconstruction and Development (IBRD),[66] provide for immediate withdrawal. The relevance

58 *See infra,* Chapter 6, Part II.A.ii. (exploring ways to tame popular passions related to foreign policy decisions in domestic legal systems).

59 Conference of the Parties, Adoption of the Paris Agreement, Dec. 12, 2015 U.N. Doc. FCCC/CP/2015/L.9/Rev/1 (Dec. 12, 2015).

60 *See* Timmon Roberts, *One Year Since Trump's Withdrawal from the Paris Climate Agreement*, BROOKINGS (June 1, 2018), https://www.brookings.edu/blog/planetpolicy/2018/06/01/one-year-since-trumps-withdrawal-from-the-paris-climate-agreement/.

61 North Atlantic Treaty art. 13, Apr. 4, 1949, 63 Stat. 2241, 34 U.N.T.S. 243.

62 Constitution of the Food and Agriculture Organization art. XIX, Oct. 16, 1945, CTS 1945/32; 40 AJIL Supp. 76.

63 Charter of the Organization of American States art. 112, Apr. 30, 1948, 119 U.N.T.S. 3, 2 U.S.T. 2394.

64 International Labour Organization Constitution art. 1.5, May 10, 1944, 15 U.N.T.S. 40, http://www.refworld.org/docid/3ddb5391a.html [accessed 4 October 2018].

65 Articles of Agreement of the International Monetary Fund (Bretton Woods Agreement) art. 15, Dec. 27, 1945, 60 Stat. 1401; 2 U.N.T.S. 39.

66 International Bank for Reconstruction and Development Articles of Agreement art. VI (1), Dec. 27, 1945, U.N.T.S. 2, 13.

of the notice period is particularly evident with regard to Brexit. Article 50 of the TEU, which regulates withdrawal from the European Union, prescribes that notification does not have a legal effect of immediate termination. A two-year renewable notice period was established to set a *de minimis* threshold for the withdrawal to be effective, during which time the legal relationship between the EU and the withdrawing state would remain in force.

Second, there are provisions that exclude denunciation whenever the treaty is enforced, such as those involving international humanitarian law. This is the case of Common Article 63 of the Geneva Conventions of 1949,[67] which limit the effects of withdrawal until the end of a conflict. Not only it requires the conclusion of peace, but also of the operations connected with the release and repatriation of the persons protected under the Conventions' umbrella.

Third, some treaties, especially those related to delicate subject matter, encompass a waiting period. To make it easier to obtain broad consent in the international community, the waiting period strengthens states' commitment over time and avoids the volatility of politicized decisions. For instance, this is the case with the Genocide Convention,[68] which cannot be denounced for ten years. This mechanism operates like a clock, impeding the contracting parties from pulling out during the waiting period set in the agreement.

B. *Enhancing Commitment through International Regimes*

Inasmuch as the international legal system has evolved through the establishment of regimes in each subject matter area, a discussion of the effects of withdrawal from multilateral treaties cannot overlook the context of regimes. Indeed, international regimes may be able to strengthen treaty commitments because of the benefits of regimes along with systems that create safeguard mechanisms across different epistemic communities.[69]

---

67 Geneva Convention Relative to the Protection of Civilian Persons in Time of War, Aug. 12, 1949, 75 U.N.T.S. 287; Geneva Convention Relative to the Treatment of Prisoners of War, Aug. 12, 1949, 75 U.N.T.S. 135.

68 Convention on the Prevention and Punishment of the Crime of Genocide, Dec. 9, 1948 78 U.N.T.S. 277.

69 *See supra,* Chapter 3, part 1.B.iii (analyzing the functioning of international regimes in international legal theory and their impact on the evolution of the treaty-making process); John G. Ruggie, *Epistemology, Ontology and the Study of International Regimes, in* CONSTRUCTING THE WORLD POLITY 85–101 (John G. Ruggie ed., 1998); *see also* Oran R. Young & Marc A. Levy, *The Effectiveness of International Environmental Regimes, in* THE EFFECTIVENESS OF INTERNATIONAL ENVIRONMENTAL REGIMES 1, 3–6 (Oran Young ed., 1999); Robert O. Keohane, *The Demand for International Regimes,* 36 INT'L. ORG. 325 (1982) (analyzing regime functioning in the utilitarian social contract tradition); Ronald B. Mitchell, *Sources of Transparency: Information Systems in International Regimes, in* 42 INT'L STUD. Q. 109, 109–10 (1988). At the jurisprudential level, in the 1997 *Gabčikovo Nagy-*

International regimes may help to overcome the weaknesses related to the dichotomy between reciprocal and nonreciprocal obligations in international law.[70] Reciprocal obligations entail mutual relations between parties, such as, for instance, prohibition of the use of force, immunity regulations, or trade and investment relations. Nonreciprocal obligations, collaborative in nature and weaker with respect to enforcement, are mainly related to the regulation of the public good, such as in the fields of human rights and environmental law.[71]

International regimes may foster better adherence to international commitment, even in the case of nonreciprocal agreements, in two ways: (a) institutionalizing governance procedures for the regulation of each functional area, with increased benefits for participation; and (b) establishing horizontal relations in multiple functional areas. In this way, regimes impose a costs-benefit analysis on the withdrawing party while creating a safety net against withdrawal.

i. Regimes' Benefits versus Withdrawal's Costs

Balancing regimes' benefits with withdrawal costs is a cost-benefit analysis that every government carries out in the moment of its decision to stay in or withdraw from an international treaty or, even more so, a regime. A way to enhance states' commitment in the context of international regimes is to create a system that incentivizes membership whilst dis-incentivizing unilateral action.

Multilateral treaty regimes have progressively institutionalized governance procedures for the regulation of different functional areas, increasing benefits

---

maros Project case, the International Court of Justice explained international regimes as being flexible, allowing adaptation to economic and environmental circumstances while the treaty is in force, to guarantee an equitable balance of interests between contracting parties. Gabčíkovo-Nagymaros Project (Hungary v. Slovakia), Judgment I.C.J. Rep. 1997 (I) (Sept. 25), 80 at 146.

70 On the one hand, reciprocal obligations entail mutual relations between parties, with all of them providing consideration. They usually pertain to outward-looking obligations that address the state in its conduct at the international level toward the community of states. For instance, prohibition of the use of force, immunity regulations, or trade and investment relations are core examples of reciprocal obligations. On the other hand, nonreciprocal obligations entail non-mutual relations that are collaborative in nature. Unlike reciprocal obligations, they usually refer to inward-looking obligations that require the state to implement conduct within its domestic jurisdiction. They are usually codified as "public good" treaties, since they are characterized by non-rivalry consumption and non-excludability of benefits. Specifically, they refer to human rights law, environmental law, prosecution and punishment of international crimes, and nonproliferation of weapons of mass destruction.

71 *See* Antonios Tzanakopoulos, *Domestic Court as the 'Natural Judge' of International Law: A Change in Physiognomy*, *in* Select Proceedings of the European Society of International Law, International Law 1989–2010, 155, 158–59 (James Crawford & Sarah Nouwen eds., 2010).

for participation as compared to a normal multilateral treaty.[72] A regime's structure creates higher stakes than treaties, encouraging a regime's member to remain instead of leaving. Indeed, the trend of withdrawal from multilateral treaties is not matched by an analogous one of withdrawal from regimes.[73] Regimes' membership should be tailored to create a negative link between withdrawal and a range of future negative outcomes of pulling out from the treaty. In other words, withdrawal from a regime should entail losing substantive regime benefits from the moment of becoming a nonparty to a treaty under the regime system. The balance of membership benefits and withdrawal costs has different outcomes in the context of reciprocal and nonreciprocal obligations.

A state that unilaterally pulls out of an agreement providing for reciprocal obligations—such as a trade agreement—will incur substantive losses when it moves from being a member to being a nonmember. It will no longer receive the benefits of its membership and, moreover, will have to deal with the impossibility of continuing to deal with its former counterparts. Because treaties and regimes covering reciprocal obligations are ipso facto more solid due to their enforceability, they have a positive direct effect on interstate cooperation, notwithstanding burdens on withdrawal clauses. In terms of risk management, stronger substantive obligations can correspond to weaker withdrawal clauses without hindering states' commitment. Thus, it is likely that treaty negotiators will opt for more permissive withdrawal clauses to promote broader participation, as the nature of the agreement itself restricts exit. The case of the WTO Agreement[74] provides a fitting example, inasmuch as even though it embeds a permissive withdrawal clause, it maintains high stakes for its members to invoke it.[75]

---

72 International regimes furthered a managerial approach in the law of the treaties, overcoming exegesis to promote problem solving. *See* John G. Ruggie, *Epistemology, Ontology and the Study of International Regimes, in* CONSTRUCTING THE WORLD POLITY 85–101 (John G. Ruggie ed., 1998); *see also See* Oran R. Young & Marc A. Levy, *The Effectiveness of International Environmental Regimes, in* THE EFFECTIVENESS OF INTERNATIONAL ENVIRONMENTAL REGIMES 1, 3–6 (Oran R. Young ed., 1999); DAVID B. HUNTER, JAMES SALZMAN & DURWOOD ZAELKE, INTERNATIONAL ENVIRONMENTAL LAW AND POLICY 364 (2011).

73 *See supra,* Chapter 4, Part IV (exploring states' practice of withdrawal from operational agreements or protocols while remaining in the framework regimes).

74 Marrakesh Agreement Establishing the World Trade Organization, Apr. 15, 1994, 1867 U.N.T.S. 154; 33 I.L.M. 1144 (1994).

75 The WTO Agreement includes permissive withdrawal clauses to balance the domestic prerogatives of interest groups with states' international commitment. *See* Richard H. Steinberg, *Judicial Lawmaking and WTO: Discursive, Constitutional and Political Constraints*, 98 AJIL 247, 267 (2004).

Nonreciprocal obligations tend to have a weaker structure and be more exposed to free-riding by contracting parties. If, in the long run, all the parties would benefit from the goals of nonreciprocal agreements, which pertain to the common good in the international community, in the short run they have incentives to engage in further opportunistic behavior.[76] A noncooperative withdrawal will not expose the denouncing state to responsibility. Nonetheless, the non-cooperativeness will be detrimental to the other contracting parties and, ultimately, to the international community as a whole, not only because it leaves unsolved the underlying problems the treaty sought to address but also because it ultimately hinders interstate cooperation.[77]

Leveraging membership benefits is particularly relevant in the context of agreements regulating public goods. For instance, the Montreal Protocol on Substances That Deplete the Ozone Layer[78] creates higher stakes for member parties than nonmember parties. By introducing regulatory measures to control ozone-depleting substances, it created a mechanism such that only those who are parties to the regime can trade in those substances. Thus, excluding nonparties to the trading system of the regime generates an indirect penalty, making withdrawal more costly.

There is a direct relationship between membership benefits and withdrawal costs that substantially affects the cost-benefit analysis of states considering withdrawal. Inverse effects of membership create burdensome outcomes of withdrawal proportional to the loss of pulling out. The way regimes are framed is key to furthering commitment, scaling the costs and benefits of membership depending on the reciprocal and nonreciprocal obligations they seek to regulate. A regime is strengthened as noncooperation becomes more costly.

ii. Interlocking Regimes

International regimes have evolved through specialization, creating functional differentiation between multiple legal spheres. An increasing trend of horizontal relations between regimes has furthered harmonization of different epistemic communities. Interconnectedness between regimes allows (a) the

---

76 Withdrawal may represent a way to secure domestic prerogatives through opportunistic strategies while taking advantage of other parties' performance. In the environmental context, this would trigger free-riding behavior. *See* TODD SANDLER, GLOBAL CHALLENGES: AN APPROACH TO ENVIRONMENTAL, POLITICAL, AND ECONOMIC PROBLEMS 30 (1997).

77 Campbell McLachlan, *The Assault on International Adjudication and the Limits of Withdrawal*, 68 INT'L & COMP. L. Q. 499 (2019) (assessing the collective interests of the contracting parties other than the withdrawing state to constrain withdrawal).

78 Montreal Protocol on Substances that Deplete the Ozone Layer, Sep. 16, 1987, 1522 U.N.T.S. 3.

traditional fragmentation in international law to be overcome[79] and (b) the establishment of safeguards that operate through different instruments.[80]

With regime systems, a plurality of regulations has emerged in different functional areas, with different institutions and different outcomes that deal with specific topics.[81] This phenomenon is described as "fragmentation" of international law, where self-contained systems embedded in international regimes set special rules for treaty making and treaty maintenance for each functional area.[82] Interlocking regimes provide an example of ways to overcome fragmentation while creating synergies between different functional areas, especially in the interplay between agreements containing reciprocal and nonreciprocal obligations.

Reciprocal agreements began including protection for issues of common concern normally regulated in nonreciprocal agreements. For instance, trade agreements began regulating sustainability-, environmental-, and human rights-related topics. With this aim, the World Trade Organization (WTO) and the EU have both served as a bridge between the fields of trade and environmental protection.

Since the mid-1990s, the EU has played a major role in furthering this effort. By using conditionality clauses, it operationalized environmental protection and the spread of democratic principles through regional trade agreements.[83] The example of the EU opened a path for promoting sustainability through trade agreements in different platforms as well. The North American Free

---

79 Fragmentation of International Law. Problem Caused by the Diversification and Expansion of International Law. Report of the Study Group of the International Law Commission. Finalised by Martti Koskenniemi, Apr. 13, 2006, UN Doc A/CN/L682.

80 *See* Martti Koskenniemi, *The Fate of Public International Law: Between Technique and Politics*, 70 MOD. L. REV. 1, 14 (2007) (analyzing the interplay in international regimes between legal technique and empirical findings in the fields of social science and economics).

81 Martti Koskenniemi envisions a model where international regimes proliferate in number of spheres to create separate systems, based on increasing specialization. Instead of generating unification in the international legal system, this model creates conflicts due to fragmentation. *See* id. at 22.

82 The Study Group on Fragmentation of International Law, established within the International Law Commission in 2003, analyzed the phenomenon of expanding fragmentation in the international legal system and produced an analytical report to provide guidelines for interpretation. Report of the Study Group of the International Law Commission A/CN4/L.682 (13 April 2006).

83 *See generally* LORAND BARTELS, HUMAN RIGHTS CONDITIONALITY IN THE EU'S INTERNATIONAL AGREEMENTS (2005); *see also* Lachlan McKenzie, *Overcoming Legacies of Foreign Policy (Dis)interests in the Negotiation of the European Union-Australia Free Trade Agreement*, 72 AUSTRALIAN J. INT'L. AFFS. 3, 255–71 (2018).

Trade Agreement (NAFTA),[84] signed in 1994, was the first preferential trade agreement to address issues like climate change, environmental protection, and energy security, including a specific side agreement—the North American Agreement on Environmental Cooperation.[85] Similarly, in 2015, the WTO passed the Environmental Goods Agreement to enhance environmental protection and long-term sustainability.[86]

Trade agreements evolved to further a dual purpose in line with both sustainability and enforceability. Indeed, not only did the new generation of trade agreements develop regulation fully consistent with the UN Sustainable Development Goals (SDGs), but they also strengthened regulation on public goods that would otherwise lack direct enforceability. The Trans-Pacific Partnership (TPP)[87] and the Comprehensive Economic and Trade Agreement (CETA)[88] have included a regulation favoring a low-emission economy that promotes the same ends as the Paris Agreement on climate change,[89] but with enforceable rights.[90] As environmental agreements lack a dispute-settlement mechanism, trade agreements may serve as a parallel tool to provide enforcement in relation to that subject matter.[91]

---

84 North American Free Trade Agreement, Can.-Mex.-U.S., Dec. 17, 1992, 32 I.L.M. 289 (1993).

85 *See* Gene M. Grossman & Alan B. Krueger, *Environmental Impact of a North American Free Trade Agreement*, *in* MEXICO-U.S. FREE TRADE AGREEMENT 15 (Peter M. Garber ed., 1993).

86 *See* Fabio C. Morosini, *Trade and Climate Change: Unveiling the Principle of Common but Differentiated Responsibilities from the WTO Agreements*, 42 GEO. WASH. INT'L L. REV. 713, 748 (2010). International trade law served, in addition, as a vehicle for promoting the use of renewable energies. *See* Yinka O. Omorogbe, *Promoting Sustainable Development Through the Use of Renewable Energy: The Role of the Law*, *in* BEYOND THE CARBON ECONOMY: ENERGY LAW IN TRANSITION 39 (Don Zillman, Catherine Redgwell, Yinka Omorogbe & Lila K. Barrera-Hernández eds., 2008).

87 Chapter 20 of the proposed text for the TPP incorporated provisions concerning environmental regulation.

88 Chapter 24 of the CETA included provisions regulating environmental protection. *See* Comprehensive Economic and Trade Agreement (CETA) between Canada on one side and the European Union and its member tates on the other, Jan 14, 2017, L. 11/23.

89 Conference of the Parties, Adoption of the Paris Agreement, Dec. 12, 2015, U.N. Doc. FCCC/CP/2015/L.9/Rev/1 (Dec. 12, 2015).

90 The new generation of trade agreements incorporated environmental provisions with specific chapters on sustainable development. For instance, the TPP and CETA have evolved in this direction, including environmental protections in Chapter 20 and Chapter 23, respectively. Similarly, RTAs between developing countries and OECD countries have used this model. *See* Grossman & Krueger, *supra* note 84, at 15; *see also* Rafael Leal-Arcas, *Mega-Regionals and Sustainable Development: The Transatlantic Trade and Investment Partnership and the Trans-Pacific Partnership*, 6 RENEWABLE ENERGY L. & POL'Y REV. 4, 248–64 (2015).

91 *Compare* TPP art. 20.15 and CETA art. 24.5 *with* Paris Agreement arts. 4(2), 6(4).

The example of the trade and environmental spheres shows the potential outcome of overlapping regimes with respect to furthering states' commitment to different functional areas at the same time. Not only does this mechanism increase the effectiveness of multiple objectives, it also creates safeguards against withdrawal.

As international regimes create intertwined connections between different subject areas, those can provide a safety net against those state behaviors contrary to good faith. If a state decides to pull out from one international agreement, it may still be bound to particular rules in that agreement by another instrument related to it. It may also be dissuaded from pulling out of an agreement if by doing so it would face negative pressure or consequences in another regime. In the regime context, the act of withdrawal may end up being an empty shell, as it may not overcome the regimes' interconnected governance of some of the same subject areas.

C. Substantive Penalties and Sanctions

Withdrawing from international agreements generally does not trigger sanctions or penalties. Nonetheless, to create leverage encouraging contracting parties to engage with treaty commitments, negotiators may opt for indirect operational mechanisms and sanctioning systems. From a rationalist standpoint, both mechanisms modify states' cost-benefit analysis regarding the choice to withdraw or stay. If contracting parties seek to provide continuity to a treaty, they could ultimately make the consequences of withdrawal more similar to the consequences of breach.[92] Such measures represent the latest step in deflecting states' noncooperative behaviors, closing the cyclical process of furthering commitment in the international legal sphere.

Based on the principle of states' voluntarism, Article 70 of the VCLT allows parties to provide in the agreement for post-withdrawal obligations.[93] This tool provides a way to hold states to their obligations when they seek to exit a treaty, since it operates as a substantive penalty. First, they tend to discourage contracting parties from denunciation because they tie states' right to

---

92 *See* Ronald B. Mitchell, *Compliance Theory: An Overview*, *in* IMPROVING COMPLIANCE WITH INTERNATIONAL ENVIRONMENTAL LAW 7 (Peter Roderick et al. eds., 1996) (analyzing states' behavior from a rationalist perspective in regard to the application of sanctions to noncompliance).

93 VCLT, Article 70(1) ("Consequences of the termination of a treaty") affirms that "[u]nless the treaty otherwise provides or the parties otherwise agree, the termination of a treaty under its provisions or in accordance with the present Convention: (a) releases the parties from any obligation further to perform the treaty; (b) does not affect any right, obligation or legal situation of the parties created through the execution of the treaty prior to its termination."

withdraw to protection of other vested interests in the agreement. Second, they impose a burden on the withdrawing state that represents an indirect cost of withdrawal, notwithstanding the legality of the instrument.

In the context of foreign investments, continuing-effect clauses—also referred to as sunset clauses—provide that a treaty continues to bind the withdrawing state for a further period from the date of termination with respect to investments made before withdrawal. These instruments require protection of investors even after termination of the agreement, extending as they do the application of the withdrawn treaty beyond denunciation. From a procedural standpoint, they serve as a tool to protect rights vested under the treaty after a withdrawal becomes effective. From a substantive standpoint, they impose a condition on withdrawal that acts as a substantive penalty. In other words, they make withdrawal more burdensome for the contracting parties.

This technique is especially present in bilateral investment treaties (BITS) that provide that investments made, acquired, or approved before an exit will still be protected under the law of the treaty for a further period, usually between ten to twenty years.[94] This type of provision has been included in energy agreements for the protection of investments. For instance, the ECT[95] encumbers states' decision to withdraw with investors' prerogatives.[96] If any party leaves the ECT, they remain bound by investment protection obligations for a twenty-year period beginning on the effective date of withdrawal. This provision is related to the arbitration clause in the same instrument.[97] Investors' protection clauses reflect the need for the private sector to have clear commitments from the public sphere. If a sovereign state reneges on its commitments, investors will still be protected by the agreement.

The dichotomy between sovereign voluntarism vis-à-vis investors' protection came to a head, in practical terms, with the first case of withdrawal from the ECT.[98] In May 2015, the Italian government announced its decision to withdraw,

---

94 *See* Jeswald W. Salacuse, *The Emerging Global Regime for Investment*, 51 HARV. INT'L L.J. 427, 471 (2010).

95 Energy Charter Treaty (ECT), Dec. 17, 1994, 2080 U.N.T.S. 95, 34 I.L.M. 360.

96 Article 47(3) of the ECT provides: "The provisions of this Treaty shall continue to apply to Investments made in the Area of a Contracting Party by Investors of other Contracting Parties or in the Area of other Contracting Parties by Investors of that Contracting Party as of the date when that Contracting Party's withdrawal from the Treaty takes effect for a period of 20 years from such date."

97 Article 26 of the ECT provides that parties must give unconditional consent for arbitration or conciliation clauses.

98 *See* August Reinisch, *The EU and the Investor-State Dispute Settlement*, *in* EYIEL 2017, 249, 249–51. (Marc Burgenger et al. eds., 2017).

justifying it as a consequence of a national spending review.[99] Allegedly, the costs of remaining a member would be too high given Italy's domestic budgetary restrictions. Nonetheless, investors' legitimate expectations were frustrated, so on the basis of the ECT's regulation they sought protection through alternative dispute settlement mechanisms. The International Centre for Settlement of Investment Disputes (ICSID) arbitral tribunal, in the *ESPF* case,[100] found that Italy breached its ECT obligations due to the modification of the domestic legal regime related to renewable energy incentives and ordered it to pay compensation to the claimants. Similar conclusions were reached by the Stockholm Chamber of Commerce in the *Greentech*[101] and *CEF*[102] cases, due to the Italian government's premature termination of investors' incentives after withdrawing from the ECT. These examples show that applying the withdrawal clause to investor–state dispute settlement mechanisms triggers a substantive penalty against the withdrawing state. A withdrawing party's cost-benefit analysis needs to take into account investors' rights, which remain vested even after withdrawal.[103]

Sanctions are the harshest strategy for countering wrongful acts and promoting deterrence, as they increase the costs of deflection.[104] Since withdrawal is a legal and legitimate act, it cannot be directly subject to international sanctions. However, a noncooperative invocation of a withdrawal clause may produce negative externalities on a member of the international community,

---

99 With regard to the Italian situation as a withdrawing party to the ECT, see *Italy*, INT'L ENERGY CHARTER, https://energycharter.org/who-we-are/members-observers/countries/italy/ (accessed Feb. 16, 2021). *See also* Francesca Morra & Lorenzo Parola, *Any Consequences Stemming from Italy's Withdrawal from the Energy Charter Treaty?*, ISPI (May 15, 2015), http://www.ispionline.it/it/energy-watch/any-consequences-stemming-italys-withdrawal-energy-charter-treaty-13323.

100 ESPF Beteiligungs, GmbH ESPF Nr. 2 Austria Beteiligungs GmbH, and Infra Class Energie 5 GmbH & Co. KG v. Italian Republic, ICSID Case No. ARB/16/5 (registered Mar. 8, 2016). In this case, the respondent was ordered to pay US$18,893,440, plus interests and expenses, to the claimants.

101 Greentech Energy Systems and Novenergia v. Italian Republic, SCC Case No. 095/2015 (registered Jul. 7, 2015). In this case, the respondent was ordered to pay US$13,600,000, plus interest and part of the claimants' expenses.

102 CEF Energia BV v. Italian Republic, SCC Case No. 158/2015 (registered Nov. 20, 2015). In this case, the respondent was ordered to pay US$10,750.512 in damages, plus compound interest, to the claimant.

103 *See* Antonio Morelli, *Commentary to Article 47 of the Energy Charter Treaty*, *in* COMMENTARY TO THE ENERGY CHARTER TREATY 486–87 (Rafael Leal Arcas ed., 2018).

104 *See* Abram Chayes, Antonia Handler Chayes & Ronald B. Mitchell, *Managing Compliance: A Comparative Perspective*, *in* ENGAGING COUNTRIES: STRENGTHENING COMPLIANCE WITH INTERNATIONAL ENVIRONMENTAL ACCORDS, 39, 44–45 (Edith Brown Weiss & Harold K. Jacobson eds., 2000).

which can be ultimately subject to sanctions in the event of a threat to international peace and security.

In the context of arms control, the 2003 withdrawal of North Korea from the Nuclear Non-Proliferation Treaty is an example of the functioning of indirect sanctions embedded in international regimes.[105] Because the withdrawal from the agreement, followed by a national rearmament plan, had direct consequences for the international nuclear weapons system, it triggered the mechanism under Chapter VII of the UN Charter.[106] The UN Security Council sanctioned North Korea with Resolution 1718[107] in 2006, Resolution 1874[108] in 2009, Resolution 2087[109] and Resolution 2094[110] in 2013, Resolutions 2270[111] and 2321[112] in 2016, and Resolutions 2371[113] and 2375[114] in 2017. Through this series of sanctions, the international community, under the UN umbrella,

---

105 The Director General of the International Atomic Energy Agency held that the North Korean denunciation of NPT did not completely disengage the withdrawing country from international scrutiny; the Security Council can still intervene whenever peace and security are at stake. *See* Helfer, *supra* note 2, at 1620; *see also* interview by Emma Belcher with Dr. Mohamed El Baradei, Director General, Int'l Atomic Energy Agency (Des. 2, 2003), 28 FLETCHER F. WORLD AFFS. 29, 37, 39 (2004).

106 Article 39 opens Chapter VII of the UN Charter, and states: "The Security Council shall determine the existence of any threat to the peace, breach of the peace, or act of aggression and shall make recommendations, or decide what measures shall be taken in accordance with Articles 41 and 42, to maintain or restore international peace and security."

107 S.C. Res. 1718 (Oct. 14, 2006) (establishing a Sanctions Committee (1718 Committee) and imposing an arms embargo, assets freeze, and travel ban on persons involved in the DPRK's nuclear program, as well as a ban on a range of imports and exports).

108 S.C. Res. 1874 (June 12, 2009) (expanding measures related to exports and imports of all arms and related items and calling upon member states for prevention and reporting).

109 S.C. Res. 2087 (Jan. 22, 2013) (expanding measures for seizing and destroying materials suspected of being connected to the DPRK's weapons development or research).

110 S.C. Res. 2094 (Mar. 7, 2013) (imposing targeted financial sanctions and expanding the prohibited items list concerning nuclear, ballistic missile, and other WMD-related items).

111 S.C. Res. 2270 (Mar. 2, 2016) (enforcing new cargo inspection and maritime procedures, including mandatory inspection of cargo destined to and originating from the DPRK, and a ban on DPRK chartering of vessels and aircraft).

112 S.C. Res. 2255 (Nov. 30, 2016) (expanding the arms embargo to the items listed in a new conventional arms dual-use list and strengthening the proliferation network, requiring member states to reduce the number of staff at DPRK diplomatic missions and consular posts).

113 S.C. Res. 2371 (Aug. 5, 2017) (introducing a full ban on coal, iron, and iron ore; banning the hiring and paying of additional DPRK laborers used to generate foreign export earnings; and prohibiting the deployment and use of chemical weapons).

114 S.C. Res. 2375 (Sept. 11, 2017) (introducing a full ban on the supply, sale, or transfer of all condensates and natural gas liquids to the DPRK and limiting the amount of refined petroleum products allowed).

imposed a progressive set of economic and diplomatic measures that progressively tied North Korea, with the aim of ending its nuclear program.[115]

Therefore, whenever withdrawal undermines the most important principle of interstate cooperation, global peace and security, it can give rise to UN Security Council intervention. Even though this is not a mechanism that directly sanctions withdrawal, it seeks protection of interstate cooperation while furthering commitment to those international agreements that preserve peace and security.

II. Domestic Solutions

An efficient system of treaty maintenance needs to look both at the international treaty-making process that frames withdrawal clauses and the constitutional model of member states that defines the rules of the game. Domestic constitutional systems are structured in a way that defines the procedures for joining international agreements but is mostly silent on withdrawal.[116] Such asymmetry often gives a blank check to the executive, which has tended more and more often to use withdrawal as an act of realpolitik meant to gain opportunistic advantages contrary to good faith in international law of treaties.[117]

To enhance orderly withdrawal, it is important to have clear rules at the domestic level that serve not only to define states' power internally but also to indicate states' credibility internationally. First, to secure good faith in treaty maintenance, domestic systems should extend the application of checks and balances to foreign policy to tame politicization of commitment and

115 *See* Antonio F. Perez, *Survival of Rights Under the Nuclear Non-Proliferation Treaty: Withdrawal and the Counting Right of International Atomic Energy Agency Safeguards*, 34 VA. J. INT'L L. 749, 797 (1994) (analyzing how withdrawal can be ineffective with regard to the NPT).

116 *See supra,* Chapter 1, Part II.C. (analyzing withdrawal in domestic legal systems). For a study of the main literature on this subject matter, see Pierre-Hugues Verdier & Mila Versteeg, *Separation of Powers, Treaty-Making, and Treaty Withdrawal: A Global Survey*, *in* THE OXFORD HANDBOOK OF COMPARATIVE FOREIGN RELATIONS LAW 18 (C.A. Bradley ed., 2019); *see also* Tom Ginsburg, *Locking in Democracy: Constitutions, Commitment, and International Law*, 38 N.Y.U. J. INT'L. L. & POL. 707, 722 (2006); *see also* Hannah Woolaver, *From Joining to Leaving: Domestic Law's Role in the International Legal Validity of Treaty Withdrawal,* 30 EJIL 73 (2019) (assessing treaty entry and exit procedures at the domestic level).

117 *See* Curtis A. Bradley, *Exiting Congressional-Executive Agreements*, 67 DUKE L.J. 1615 (2018); *see also* Curtis A. Bradley & Jack L. Goldsmith, *On Presidential Control Over International Law*, 131 HARV. L. REV. 1201 (2018).

opportunistic withdrawals. Second, domestically, systems that restrain political and popular passions should be promoted, such as, for instance, recourse to direct democratic instruments.

Finally, from a governance perspective, the global context in which withdrawal operates has generated resilient international cooperation between the main stakeholders involved. Non-state actors play a key role, through the business sector and civil society, in treaty making and treaty maintenance, and they could ultimately have the significant function of providing stability to international treaties.

A. *Regulating Domestic Treaty-making Power*

The classic approach to international treaties is grounded on the realist assumption that states are unitary actors in international relations. However, this approach overlooks domestic procedures concerning the role of internal powers.[118] This section explores ways to enhance orderly withdrawal through domestic regulation, identifying an underlying asymmetry in treaty making and suggesting constitutional and statutory reforms, in a way that responds to the domestic politicization of issues covered in international agreements.[119]

In the view of Humphrey Waldock, Special Rapporteur of the ILC on the Law of Treaties, entering and exiting an international agreement are two symmetrical treaty-making processes that generate effects on a domestic legal system beyond a singular political mandate.[120] The executive's primacy in foreign policy is counterbalanced by the compelling need to further the democratic sharing of international commitments among political branches.[121] The participation of national legislatives in the phase of joining international treaties reflects this democratic impulse, which is mostly absent in the exit phase.[122] Though the ILC envisioned rules authorizing states to leave a treaty analogous

118 *See* Ginsburg, *supra* note 116, at 711; *see also* Rachel Brewster, *The Domestic Origins of International Agreements*, 44 Va. J. Int'l. L. 501 (2004).

119 For an analysis of different approaches to withdrawal in domestic legal systems, *see supra,* Chapter 1, Part II.C.

120 Sir Humphrey Waldock defined the treaty-making power of sovereign states through both its components: the capacity to conclude treaties and to withdraw from or terminate them. Humphrey Waldock, *Special Rapporteur on the Law of the Treaties, Second Report on the Law of the Treaties*, 2 UNYBILC 85 (1963).

121 *See supra,* Chapter 1, Part II.C. (exploring domestic legal systems' different approaches on withdrawal procedures and an emerging trend in modern constitutionalism regarding legislatives' involvement in withdrawal decisions).

122 *See* Laurence R. Helfer, *Treaty Exit and Intra-Branch Conflict at the Interface of International and Domestic Law, in* THE OXFORD HANDBOOK OF COMPARATIVE FOREIGN RELATIONS LAW (C.A. Bradley ed., 2019).

to those regulating the expression of consent, this approach remained mostly unexplored in states' practice.[123]

International law leaves the legitimacy of joining and leaving international treaties to domestic regulation. Every constitutional system configures the state's powers with regard to international obligations at the domestic level. Whereas the procedures for treaty entry are defined, a vacuum often remains with regard to treaty revocation. This phenomenon generates an asymmetric architecture of states' powers in international relations that may encounter limits in the maintenance of multilateral commitments.[124] Regulating treaty-making power can be seen as an indicator of whether a state is serious about abiding by its international commitments.[125] *Mutatis mutandis*, just as central banks have established provisions to reassure financial markets that their operations will be immune to political influence for the sake of economic stability, domestic constitutions or statutory provisions are expressions of domestic credibility in international relations.[126]

The subsections below identify two ways to foster orderly withdrawal through a trustworthy constitutional and statutory mechanism: (a) operationalize checks and balances in foreign policy and (b) restrain political and popular passions regarding international agreements.

i. Separation of Powers in Foreign Policy

As multilateralism has progressively internationalized sovereign activities, on the verge of globalization, checks and balances cannot operate just at the domestic level; they should also embrace states' distribution of powers related to foreign policy decisions. The triad of states' powers—legislative, executive, and judiciary—play a crucial role in defining national external action. Establishing clear rules ex ante for commitment is reassuring with regard to building

---

123 In its commentaries to Draft Article 63 on the Law of Treaties, the ILC remarked the importance of having symmetrical provisions between the expression of states' consent to be bound by a treaty and to withdraw from it. Draft Articles on the Law of Treaties with Commentaries, Adopted by the International Law Commission at its Eighteenth Session, *in U.N. Conference on the Law of Treaties, 1st & 2nd Sess., Vienna, 26 March–24 May 1968 and 9 April–22 May 1969*, at 83, U.N. Doc. A/CONF.39/11/Add.2 (1971).

124 *See supra*, Chapter 1, Part II.C. (assessing the regulatory trend of withdrawal from international agreements in domestic legal systems).

125 *See* Barry Weingast, *Constitutions as Governance Structures: The Political Foundations of Secure Markets*, 149 J. INST. THEO. ECON. 286 (1993); *see also* Barry Weingast, *The Political Foundations of Democracy and the Rule of Law*, 91 AM. POL. SCI. REV. 245 (1997).

126 *See* Robert J. Barro & David B. Gordon, *Rules, Discretion and Reputation in a Model of Monetary Policy*, 12 J. MONETARY ECON. 101 (1983) (designing a credible architecture for central banks to gain credibility in financial markets).

and maintaining commitment ex post while meeting legal obligations. A rational constitutional design would encompass a mechanism of checks and balances that operates whenever the state engages in international activity.[127]

Checks and balances in constitutional law entail a long-standing principle of law and government: separating power among a state's branches prevents too much power being in one place.[128] This system reflects Montesquieu's model of a tripartite system in which the sovereign authority shares power with the legislative, executive, and judicial branches.[129] Constitutions provide for different settings for the treaty-making process, with different roles for the executive, legislative, and judicial branches.[130]

Domestic legal systems mold international commitment, as they set domestic rules for states' external action.[131] Some scholars refer to "pre-commitment" as the way domestic legal systems embed specific international policies or legal instruments in their constitutional text by limiting the options of policy makers.[132] As states' commitment progressively resulted in diluted forms of international treaties, treaty making and treaty maintenance consequently

---

127 *See* Ginsburg, *supra* note 116, at 722; *see also* Oliver Willismson, *Credible Commitments—Using Hostages to Support Exchange*, 73 AM. ECON. REV. 519 (1983).

128 The American constitutional system has provided solid examples of the functioning of checks and balances since the drafting of its first state constitutions. For instance, the Constitution of Virginia of 1776 provided: "The legislative, executive, and judiciary department shall be separate and distinct, so that neither exercise the powers properly belonging to the other; nor shall any person exercise the powers of more than one of them, at the same time[.]" VA. CONST. OF 1776, *reprinted in* 10 SOURCES AND DOCUMENTS OF UNITED STATES CONSTITUTIONS 52 (W. S. Windler ed., 1979). *See also* MASS. CONST. OF 1780, pt. first, art. XXX, *reprinted in* 10 SOURCES AND DOCUMENTS OF UNITED STATES CONSTITUTIONS, *see id.* at 96 ("In the government of this commonwealth, the legislative department shall never exercise the executive and judicial powers, or either of them; the executive shall never exercise the legislative and judicial powers, or either of them; the judicial shall never exercise the legislative and executive powers, or either of them; to the end it may be a government of laws, and not of men."); *see generally* M.J.C. VILE, CONSTITUTIONALISM AND THE SEPARATION OF POWERS (1967).

129 *See* CHARLES LOUIS DE SECONDAT, BARON DE MONTESQUIEU, THE SPIRIT OF LAWS (1748).

130 *See generally* LUZIUS WILDHABER, TREATY-MAKING POWER AND THE CONSTITUTION: AN INTERNATIONAL AND COMPARATIVE STUDY 44 (1971).

131 *See* Stephen Holmes, *Precommitment and the Paradox of Democracy, in* CONSTITUTIONALISM AND DEMOCRACY, 195 (Jon Elster & Rune Slagstad eds., 1988); *see also* STEPHEN HOLMES, PASSION AND CONSTRAINT: ON THE THEORY OF LIBERAL DEMOCRACY, 134–77 (1995); *see* John McGinnis & Michael B. Rappaport, *Symmetric Entrenchment: A Constitutional and Normative Theory*, 89 VA. L. REV. 385 (2003) (analyzing the burden sharing of domestic powers involved in foreign policy among political internal branches).

132 *See* Ginsburg, *supra* note 116, at 718; *see also* Steven R. Ratner, *Precommitment Theory and International Law: Starting a Conversation*, 81 TEX. L. REV. 2055, 2060 (2003).

became politicized, ultimately expanding the perimeter of power of the executive.[133] Applying checks and balances to treaty-making power may ultimately generate more balanced systems, with depoliticized decisions, to enhance orderly withdrawal.[134]

Scholarly debate has primarily addressed the democratic deficit regarding multilateralism, overlooking illegitimate denunciations due to breach of domestic provisions.[135] Recent states' practices have brought attention to this topic, given an increasing jurisprudential trend toward invalidating withdrawal decisions by the executive that contravene legislative approval requirements. Since national courts regularly review the internal allocation of authority among political branches, they play a fundamental role in overseeing domestic exit procedures.[136] Two high-profile examples of this trend came out of the supreme judicial authorities of the United Kingdom and South Africa, which sanctioned the need for parliamentary participation in the decision to pull out of the European Union[137] and the International Criminal Court, respectively.[138]

As the British government embarked on the Brexit procedure, the British Supreme Court, in *Miller v. Secretary of State*,[139] defined for the first time the constitutional procedure to follow to withdraw from an international agreement. Since Article 50(1) of the Treaty on European Union[140] provides that withdrawal is meant to take place in line with the domestic constitutional law of its member states, the Court ruled on the allocation of such political power between the executive and legislative branches. In the United Kingdom, the government is mainly responsible for foreign policy decisions, though it has a formal obligation to notify Parliament of acts of ratification of international

133 *See supra,* Chapter 2, Part 2.B.ii. (shedding light on the progressive politicization of states' commitment in the international law of treaties).

134 *See* Ginsburg, *supra* note 116, at 722; *see also* McGinnis & Rappaport, *supra* note 131.

135 *See* Giuliana Ziccardi Capaldo, La Competenza a Denunciare i Tratrati Internazionali 13 (1983) (shedding lights on the lack of doctrinal debate regarding domestic competences on withdrawal from multilateral treaties).

136 *See* Laurence R. Helfer, *Treaty Exit and Intra-Branch Conflict at the Interface of International and Domestic Law, in* The Oxford Handbook of Comparative Foreign Relations Law (C.A. Bradley ed., 2019).

137 *See supra,* Chapter 4, Part II. D. (focusing on the "Brexit" procedure).

138 *See supra,* Chapter 4, Part I. B (analyzing the South African case as part of the African countries' collective disengagement from the Rome Statute of the International Criminal Court).

139 Miller v. Secretary of State for Exiting the European Union, UKSC 2016/0196 R, Judgment (Jan. 24, 2017).

140 TEU art. 50(1) affirms that "[a]ny Member State may decide to withdraw from the Union in accordance with its own constitutional requirements."

agreements.[141] The Court established that absent an ad hoc domestic procedure, requirements for withdrawal are to be set on a case-by-case basis, depending on the domestic effects of pulling out. Though the general competence belongs to the executive, parliamentary approval is necessary if the decision to withdraw affects the domestic legal system. Under the European Communities Act 1972,[142] which provided for the accession of the United Kingdom to the European Communities, not only did European law have to be considered a source of British domestic law, it became primary.[143] Therefore, the Court ruled that the executive could proceed only with parliamentary approval to trigger the procedures of Article 50 of the TEU. As a result of the *Miller* decision, on January 26, 2017, the UK government introduced a bill in the legislature to initiate the Brexit procedure, which received, on March 16, 2017, Royal Assent by the Queen. Only at the end of this process, with the participation of the state's powers, was the British government able to notify the EU Commission about the decision to withdraw.

With regard to South Africa's notification of its intention to denounce the Rome Statute in 2016,[144] the High Court defined the procedure for withdrawal in *Democratic Alliance v. Minister of International Relations and Cooperations*.[145] Applying the *acte contraire* principle, withdrawal is defined in relation to its symmetry with treaty entry. Since Article 231 of the 1996 South African

141 The responsibility for concluding treaties in the United Kingdom lies with the government—specifically, the institution of the Secretary of State for Foreign, Commonwealth and Development Affairs. This institution must lay most treaties before the Parliament for 21 sitting days before ratification. Though the House of Commons cannot amend treaties, it can block ratification indefinitely. *See generally* Arabella Lang, *Parliament's Role in Ratifying Treaties*, 5855 House of Commons Library Briefing Papers (Feb. 17, 2017).

142 European Communities Act 1972, Chapter 68 (Oct. 17, 1972).

143 The principle of supremacy of EU law was confirmed in UK jurisprudence in *R. v. Secretary of State for Transport, ex parte Factotrame Ltd.* (No. 2) [1990] 3 WLR 818, which held that "[i]f the supremacy within the European Community of Community Law over national law of member states was not always inherent in the EEC Treaty it was certainly well established in the jurisprudence of the Court of Justice long before the United Kingdom joined the Community. Thus, whatever limitation of its sovereignty Parliament accepted when it enacted the European Communities Act 1972 was entirely voluntary. Under the terms of the 1972 Act it has always been clear that it was the duty of a United Kingdom court, when delivering final judgment, to override any rule of national law found to be in conflict with any directly enforceable rule of Community law."

144 *See supra*, Chapter 3, Part I. B. (analyzing the South African government's denunciation of the Rome Statute and the Court's decision to invalidate the denunciation).

145 Democratic Alliance v. Minister of International Relations and Cooperations, [2017] (3) SA 212 (S. Afr.).

Constitution[146] requires parliamentary authorization to ratify an international agreement, parliamentary authorization must be considered necessary for pulling out of it.[147] Procedurally, the High Court found that the failure to repeal the domesticating legislation of the Rome Statute before lodging the notification of withdrawal represented an act of prematurity and procedural irrationality.[148] For these reasons, it invalidated the executive's decision to withdraw, ordered it to revoke its notification, which it deemed unconstitutional and invalid. Moreover, it required any future withdrawal to be preceded by parliamentary approval and repeal of domestic law related to the subject matter of the denounced agreement.[149] Though this decision caused an outcome similar to that of the British Supreme Court's decision in *Miller v. Secretary of State*, it was based on a different paradigm. In *Democratic Alliance v. Minister of International Relations and Cooperations*, it was made clear that the legislative competence does not need to be assessed on a case-by-case basis; strict separation of powers should exist for both ratification of and withdrawal from an international agreement.[150] In compliance with the Court's order, the South African government notified the UN Secretary-General of the revocation of its instrument of withdrawal on March 17, 2017.[151]

---

146 Article 231(2) of the South African Constitution ("International Agreements") provides: "An international agreement binds the Republic only after it has been approved by resolution in both the National Assembly and the National Council of Provinces, unless it is an agreement referred in subsection (3)." GRONDWET VAN DIE REPUBLIEK VAN SUID-AFRIKA [CONSTITUTION OF THE REPUBLIC OF SOUTH AFRICA] Dec. 18, 1996.

147 Democratic Alliance v. Minister of International Relations and Cooperations, p. 26, ¶ 57.

148 *See* id. at. 31, ¶ 70.

149 *See* Hannah Woolaver, *Domestic and International Limitations on Treaty Withdrawal: Lessons from South Africa's Attempted Departure from the International Criminal Court*, *in* AJIL UNBOUND 450–52 (2018), https://www.cambridge.org/core/journals/american-journal-of-international-law/article/domestic-and-international-limitations-on-treaty-withdrawal-lessons-from-south-africas-attempted-departure-from-the-international-criminal-court/ca118db7a9bfb8afb079784b05259d7b.

150 *See* id. (examining the rationales of the British and South African decisions concerning withdrawal from international agreements on a comparative base).

151 South Africa Withdrawal of Notification of Withdrawal, UN Doc. C.N.121.2017. TREATIES-XVIII.10 (Mar. 17, 2017). Although the government complied with the High Court's decision, some commentators have questioned what outcomes would have occurred if the executive had defied the court and not revoked the notice of withdrawal. In that event, even if South Africa ceased to be a member of the ICC, the effects of the Rome Statute would have continued unabated, as the treaty would not have been abrogated under domestic law. *See* Laurence R. Helfer, *Treaty Exit and Intra-Branch Conflict at the Interface of International and Domestic Law, in* THE OXFORD HANDBOOK OF COMPARATIVE FOREIGN RELATIONS LAW (C.A. Bradley ed., 2019).

Notwithstanding the political character of withdrawal in the British and South African cases, domestic courts granted the participation of states' political powers based on their competences. Though foreign policy traditionally belongs to the executive, it cannot be ultra vires—beyond the constitutional scope of its authority.[152] Therefore, whenever withdrawal results in intrusions into the sphere of another power, governmental freedom of action in foreign policy can be limited. Considering the consequences that withdrawal may produce internally, the judiciary operates as a guarantor of respect for the balance of powers.

ii. Containment of Popular Passions

Checks and balances have a dual function in constitutional law. First, they operate as a way to constrain power; second, they represent a legal mechanism to restrain politics and, in turn, popular political passions.[153]

Recourse to direct democracy in setting a foreign policy agenda exposes states' commitment to the risk of being affected by popular passions. Brexit is a clear example: a popular referendum made the determination to leave the European Union.[154] On June 23, 2016, the British population was called to vote on the United Kingdom European Union Membership Referendum.[155] Despite the nonbinding nature of the referendum, with a 51.9% majority in favor of leaving the EU,[156] the British government began the negotiation procedure for withdrawal from the organization it had joined in 1972.[157]

In American constitutional scholarship, the Federalist Papers no. 48 and 49 discussed the need to contain popular political passions in the lawmaking

---

152 In reference to the acts of political branches, constitutions or other domestic regulations set the perimeter of the scope of power given to them, while the judiciary sanctions excesses "beyond the power" (ultra vires).

153 *See generally* William B. Gwyn, The Meaning of the Separation of Powers (1965).

154 *See supra*, Chapter 4, Part II.D (focusing on the Brexit process).

155 The 2016 "United Kingdom European Union membership referendum" was not the first British referendum on leaving the EU. Indeed, in 1975, the United Kingdom held its first national referendum on permanence in the European Communities. The governing Labour Party, led by Harold Wilson, promised the renegotiation of the terms of UK membership in the EC, which led to a referendum on whether to remain in the EC. Because the outcome of the vote was 67.2% in favor of staying, the United Kingdom remained a member of the EC. *See generally* Alex May, Britain and Europe Since 1945 (1999).

156 On March 29, 2017, the UK initiated the official withdrawal process, which was concluded on December 31, 2020. *See* Resnik & Ryan, *supra* note 30; *see also* Hunt & Wheeler, *supra* note 30.

157 *See supra*, Chapter 4, Part II.D (exploring Brexit in the context of withdrawal from regional organizations).

process.[158] To prevent this interference with foreign policy, some constitutions actually prohibit recourse to direct democratic instruments in foreign policy. This can be seen as a way to shield states' commitment to international agreement from political propaganda. For instance, Article 75 of the Italian Constitution[159] does not allow abrogative referendums with regard to international treaties. Constitutional and regulatory frameworks tailored to mitigate popular passions in foreign policy can operate as safeguards against politicized withdrawal and preserve the stability of states' international commitments.

B. *Socializing Commitment through a Multi-stakeholders' Approach*

The progressive participation of non-state actors in modern international law resulted in the expansion of the scope of commitment. The formalist scholarship largely neglected the role of non-state actors in the international law of treaties, as they are not primary subjects in international law. Nonetheless, shifting trends in international politics and legal theory have created a de facto condition of business corporations and NGOs playing a decisive role in treaty making and treaty maintenance.

Studying the role of non-state actors in crafting international law, multilateral forums constitute a valid example of transnational structures assessing multi-stakeholders approaches to global challenges.[160] Sovereign states have facilitated the participation of civil society and business entities in state delegations during treaty making. National governments, then, have included non-state actors as participants in their missions before international organizations[161] or international summits.[162] More broadly, this phenomenon reflects the evolution of non-state actors from law-takers to law-makers as a way of fostering dialogue and interaction between players in the international community.[163]

---

158 *See* James Madison, The Federalist 48, 49 (1788) (opining that political passion may drive people to act through majorities in an unwise fashion in the lawmaking process).

159 Costituzione della Repubblica Italiana [Constitution of the Italian Republic], Dec. 27, 1947.

160 *See* Daniel Bradlow, What Paris Climate Deal Can Teach Us About Solving the World's Most Complex Problems, The Conversation (Dec. 17, 2015), https://theconversation.com/what-paris-climate-deal-can-teach-us-about-solving-the-worlds-most-complex-problems-52162 (developing new arrangements in global governance to allow multi-stakeholder responses to global problems).

161 *See* José E. Alvarez, Are Corporations "Subjects" of International Law?, 9 Santa Clara J. Int'l L. 1, 5 (2011).

162 *See* Erika R. George, The Enterprise of Empire: Evolving Understandings of Corporate Identity and Responsibility, in The Business Landscape and Human Rights Landscape: Moving Forward, Looking Back 19, 28 (Jena Martin & Karen E. Bravo eds., 2005).

163 *See* Cedric Ryngaert, State Responsibility and Non-State Actors, in Non-State Actor Dynamics in International Law: From Law-Takers to Law-Makers 163, 183 (Math

Despite their lack of subjectivity, non-state actors have carved out a niche in international negotiations that is reflected in the moment of treaty maintenance. Their participation has resulted in a broader commitment to the functional areas covered in international treaties; treaty provisions are internalized in corporate strategies and advocated throughout civil society. As a result, the rise of non-state actors in international relations has blurred the perimeter for the application of withdrawal clauses in international law. To understand the significance of withdrawal, it is important to understand not only the procedural but also the substantive implications underlying withdrawal clauses in international agreements. The context in which withdrawal operates generates synergies between state and non-state actors that are key to enhancing commitment to multilateral treaties.

i. Business Participation in the Maintenance of Multilateral Agreements

The commitment underlying multilateral agreements implicates policies and measures to be implemented at a national level by state parties and, often, to be incorporated into business strategies at the corporate level.[164] For this reason, the socialization of multilateral agreements domestically through the business sector entails elements of maintenance of multilateral commitments. The evolution of international negotiations has progressively embraced the business sector in the formation of multilateral deals. On one hand, this has allowed advantage to be taken of the technical expertise of these actors while pushing for long-term strategies. On the other hand, this has created a democratic deficit problem that may benefit only the most influential or powerful entities in decision-making processes. Enhancing multilateral forums for business participation in treaty making at the international level is a way to enhance, in turn, mechanisms for treaty maintenance at domestic level.

Noortmann & Cedric Ryngaert, eds., 2010); see also Paul B. Stephan, Privatizing International Law, 97 VA. L. REV. 1573, 1577 (2011) (presenting a cost-benefit study on the participation of non-state actors in the treaty-making process); Peter J. Spiro, NGOs in International Environmental Lawmaking: Theoretical Models, Temple University Legal Studies Research Paper No. 26, at 2–3 (2006) (measuring the influence of non-state actors in the law-making process).

164 Climate Change: UN Expert Welcomes Historic Paris Agreement but Calls on States to Scale up Efforts to Meet the 1.5 °C Target (Apr. 21, 2016), UN HUM. RTS. OFF. OF THE HIGH COMM'R, www.ohchr.org/EN/NewsEvents/Pages/DisplayNews.aspx?NewsID=19850&LangID=E (expressing the concern of John Knox, Special Rapporteur on Human Rights and Environment, in regard to the Paris Agreement that "the commitments pledged by Governments to date are insufficient to meet this global target").

Businesses have built global corporate strategies and models to gain a competitive advantage, internalizing and then implementing what was previously negotiated multilaterally.[165] Taking into account business needs is key to the definition of states' pledges in international negotiations. As a result of globalization, a global market economy has progressively been substituted for anarchy in international relations.[166] The business sector has, consequently, claimed a right to broader participation in the treaty-making process, pushing for strategic agendas at the international level that will take into consideration corporate needs. So far, business participation in international law has emerged first as a practice in the environmental field and then in the trade and investment field, promoting substantial synergies but lacking procedural regulation.[167]

In collaboration with sovereign actors, the contributions of private actors in the treaty-making and treaty-maintenance processes have encouraged innovations through workable solutions based on their technical expertise in each functional area. This has created the opportunity to build up synergies between government and business entities, to implement public-private partnerships, and to foster investments on a broader scale.[168] This ex ante participation in treaty making reflects an ex post role in the enforcement of the agreement. From this perspective, the challenges addressed during negotiations mirror, at a corporate level, the business strategies that will be implemented for years to come. Often, corporations operate with long-term strategies that collide with the short-term agendas of domestic governments. Therefore, the socialization of multilateral agreements through the business sector allows for more solid commitments that include a forward-looking framework for implementation.

---

165 *See* Lauren Hepler & Barbara Grady, How Much Do Companies Really Care About COP21?, Green Biz (Sept. 9, 2015), https://www.greenbiz.com/article/how-much-do-companies-really-care-about-cop21; see also CEO Pulse on Climate Change, Countdown to a Deal on Climate Change: What Does This Mean for Business Success?, PWC Global (July 2015), http://download.pwc.com/gx/ceo-pulse/climatechange/index.htm.

166 *See* Antonio Franceschet, Kant and Liberal Internationalism 88 (2002).

167 *See* Lawrence E. Susskind, *New Corporate Roles in Global Environmental Treaty-Making*, 27 Colum. J. World Bus. 62, 71 (1992) (analyzing business accreditation in environmental regimes); *see also* Natasha Affolder, *The Market for Treaties*, 11 Chi. J. Int'l L. 159, 159 (2010); Stephan, *supra* note 163, at 1577 (analyzing business in international law-making process); Melissa J. Durkee, The Business of Treaties, 63 UCLA L. Rev. 264, 269 (2016) (analyzing the evolution of business accreditation in trade regimes).

168 CDP, Business and the Paris Agreement, Corporate Support for a Global Agreement on Climate Change 2 (Oct. 11, 2015), https://6fefcbb86e61af1b2fc4-c70d8ead6ced550b4d987d7c03fcdd1d.ssl.cf3.rackcdn.com/cms/reports/documents/000/000/826/original/corporate-support-global-agreement-on-climate-change.pdf?1471969971.

This trend generates resilience against governments' short-sighted decisions to withdraw.[169]

In the environmental field, companies have participated in the Conference of Parties (COP) negotiations under the UNFCCC umbrella.[170] They called for clear standards in the spheres of mitigation, adaptation, and resilience to be implemented, in turn, by governments at the national level in compliance with their intended nationally determined contributions, which define what steps they will undertake internally to address climate change.[171]

---

169 *See* Rafael Leal-Arcas & Antonio Morelli, *The Resilience of the Paris Agreement: Negotiating and Implementing the Climate Regime*, 31 GEO. ENV'T L. REV. (2018).

170 In the environmental sphere, business corporations pushed for strategies that aim to reduce greenhouse gas emissions while easing the transition to a low-carbon economy with climate-resilient solutions. See World Economic Forum, Open Letter from CEOs to World Leaders Urging Climate Action (Nov. 23, 2015). The World Economic Forum has been a major player in fostering public–private cooperation and leading the private sector toward a stronger commitment in climate change to secure a stronger world for all of us. In this framework, facilitated by the World Economic Forum, the CEOs of 79 different multinational corporations declared: "Climate change is one of the biggest global challenges that will shape the way we do business now and in the coming decades." *See* id. The complete text of the declaration expressing the executives' commitment is available online. These 79 CEOs Believe in Global Climate Action, WORLD ECON. F. (Nov. 23, 2015), https://www.weforum.org/agenda/2015/11/open-letter-from-ceos-to-world-leaders-urging-climate-action. As analytical reports prepared during the Paris Agreement negotiations point out, more than 800 of the largest registered companies worldwide have shown that they favor an agreement on climate change. CDP, supra note 168 (analyzing business strategies in reducing greenhouse gases emissions). Among the international players, Coca-Cola Enterprises takes a clear stand against climate change in the pursuit of a common long-term goal: "We believe that such a deal should include a clear and credible long-term goal, together with ambitious national commitments from all countries, clear and transparent accounting mechanisms and a timetable to revisit the goal to ensure that it is in line with climate science." *See* id.

171 Specifically, a benchmarking process has been created for collecting data necessary for monitoring, reporting, and verifying (MRV). The implementation of such a mechanism not only allows for the measurement of global accomplishments but also gives grounds for sovereign accountability. See CDP, supra note 168, at 2 (discussing the positions of various multinational corporations with regard to the MRV mechanism). The Belgian chemical group Solvay "urge[s] a strategic action agenda—supported by clear and consistent policies and robust monitoring, reporting and verification (MRV)—that will complement business efforts to stimulate innovation as well as collaborative actions across value chains, and to develop and scale up alternative and renewable energy sources, promote energy efficiency, end deforestation and accelerate other low carbon options and technologies such as ICT." *See* id. CDP is a not-for profit organization that currently holds the "largest collection globally of primary climate change, water and forest risk commodities information and puts these insights at the heart of strategic business, investment and

Similarly, in the international trade and investments field, business corporations actively participated in the TPP negotiations to further a mega-regional platform for one of the largest-ever business treaties.[172] This was a way to address corporate ambitions in a common direction to set the pace for multilateral agreements based on multi-stakeholder solutions.

While business participation in treaty making and treaty maintenance can bring positive outcomes substantively, it may generate democratic deficit problems procedurally. Concerns arise especially with regard to values in the public interest, which may be trumped by profit goals. Downgrading of private participation in public law-making may result in a democratic deficit and lack of transparency.[173] Consequently, international practice has progressively engaged in the regulation of this field to integrate private entities' participation as a functional element of decision-making processes. Specifically, international organizations and multilateral summits have embraced new standards, as in the case of the COPs or the TPP, to procedurally regularize business actors' participation in the environmental and commercial fields. As a result, international secretariats and subordinate bodies have facilitated time for multi-stakeholders' dialogue to provide more effective solutions in the preparation and implementation of international regulations.[174]

To capture the commitment to climate action of the non-state actors involved in the process, the United Nations launched an ad hoc initiative, Non-State Actors Zone for Climate Action (NAZCA). This constitutes a global platform launched in 2014, under the Peruvian presidency of COP 20, which served as a central tool in building momentum and support during the COP 21 negotiations to achieve the Paris Agreement.[175] Similarly, TPP negotiations involved

---

policy decisions." *See* id. For further information, consult CDP's website at www.cdp.net/en-US/Pages/HomePage.aspx.

172 *See* Durkee, supra note 167, at 303.

173 *See* Peter K. Yu, Six Secret (and Now Open) Fears of ACTA, 64 SMU L. REV. 975, 987 (2011) (regarding approaches to treaty negotiations).

174 *See* JEFFREY S. LANTIS, THE LIFE AND DEATH OF INTERNATIONAL TREATIES: DOUBLE-EDGED DIPLOMACY AND THE POLITICS OF RATIFICATION ON COMPARATIVE PERSPECTIVE 84 (2009); see also Linda C. Reif, Environmental Policy: The Rio Summit Five Years Later, in CANADA AMONG NATIONS 1998: LEADERSHIP AND DIALOGUE 269 (Fen Osler Hampson & Maureen Appel Molot eds., 1998) (expressing the influence of non-state actors on Canadian foreign policy at the 1992 Earth Summit in Rio de Janeiro, and later in the UNFCC framework, with regard to the Kyoto Protocol; in the formation and implementation process, the influence of non-state actors allowed social and economic concerns in environmental protection to be better addressed).

175 NAZCA embraced 2,364 cities, 167 regions, 2090 companies, 448 investors, and 236 civil society organizations. This program encourages and monitors evolution of climate action

consistent corporate involvement to influence the outcomes of the agreement, mainly with regard to the regulation of tariff and nontariff barriers applicable to goods and services.[176]

The environmental and trade regimes entail a rational model regulating and institutionalizing non-state actors' participation and aligning market and public interests. This is a way in which the private sector assumes a public role in treaty making and treaty maintenance, addressing commitment in a pluralist direction.[177] Companies encourage governments worldwide to set up a clear regulatory framework to be complying actors at the time of implementation, while governments are tasked with identifying and balancing common interests vis-à-vis market prerogatives, easing socialization of international commitments.

ii. The Role of Civil Society

An integrated model for the multi-stakeholders approach to enhancing commitment to multilateral agreements would seek the inclusion of civil society to further protect and promote public interests. The role of civil society in international treaty maintenance reflects their evolution in the international legal order. As ancillary actors in the international community, they have safeguarded the public interest through enhancing information production and improving reputational leverage.

Civil society regularly produces information to challenge national reports on given issues, especially in the fields of human rights and environmental law. Whenever there is a vacuum in centralized monitoring, nongovernmental organizations (NGOs) and research institutions, with an informal and decentralized system, tend to fill it.[178] Not only do they file their reports with treaty

by tracking the action and the mobilization necessary to implement the deal. See the global platform NAZCA, Accelerating Climate Action, at http://climateaction.unfccc.int/.

176 The parties to the agreement include key countries in both side of the Pacific Ocean, including Canada, the United States, Mexico, Peru, Chile, New Zealand, Australia, Brunei, Japan, Malaysia, Singapore, and Vietnam.

177 In the international literature, legal sociologists have studied the role of business corporations as non-state actors producing or influencing global regulation. See generally PETER NEWELL, CLIMATE FOR CHANGE: NON-STATE ACTORS AND THE GLOBAL POLITICS OF THE GREENHOUSE (2000); see also VIRGINIA HAUFLER, A PUBLIC ROLE FOR THE PRIVATE SECTOR: INDUSTRY SELF-REGULATION IN A GLOBAL ECONOMY (2001); Gregory Shaffer, How Business Shapes Law: A Socio-Legal Framework, 42 CONN. L. REV.147, 174–78 (2009) (determining the influence of the private sector on the public sphere with regard to shaping the sovereign decision-making and law-making process).

178 While international secretariats are often understaffed and receiving few resources from member states, some international NGOs and research centers are in a better position, as

institutions and secretariats, but they also expose them to public opinion, giving broader visibility to noncooperative behaviors.[179] From this perspective, NGOs tend to target both noncompliance and withdrawal as means of noncooperation.[180] Information disclosure on states' compliance leverages a "naming and shaming" system. With this system, traditional sanctions are supported with a reputational model.[181] Regardless of the existence of a central authority in the international system, this model uses reputation to leverage the self-interest of states with a long-term perspective.[182] Opportunistic behaviors of states through unilateral withdrawals from multilateral agreements may trigger reputational harm. From a rationalist standpoint, building a strong reputation entails for each state a cost-benefit analysis. As a result, whenever

---

they rely on autonomous sources. NGOs, such as the Federation of American Scientists, and research organizations, such as Jane's and the International Institute for Strategic Studies, have developed increasing standing as independent sources for trustworthy information. *See* John Lanchbery, *Long-Term Trends in Systems for Implementation Review in International Agreements of Fauna and Flora, in* The Implementation and Effectiveness of International Environmental Commitments: Theory and Practice 73 (David G. Victor, Kal Raustiala & Eugene B. Skolnikoff eds., 1998). *See* David B. Hunter, *International Law and Public Participation in Policy-Making at the International Financial Institutions, in* International Financial Intuitions and International Law 199 (Daniel Bradlow & David B. Hunter eds., 2010) (analyzing transparency in the development finance context through the lens of public participation).

179 *See* Xinyuan Dai, International Institutions and National Policies 62–63 (2007) (monitoring centralized compliance procedures in multilateral environmental treaties and arms control agreements).

180 Not only do NGOs allow for analyzing patterns of behavior at the domestic level and progress in the implementation phase of an agreement, they also trigger an external monitoring system. *See* Sheila Jasanoff, *Contingent Knowledge: Implications for Implementation and Compliance, in* Engaging Countries, Strengthening Compliance with International Environmental Accords 63 (Edith Brown Weiss & Harold K. Jacobson eds., 1998).

181 "Naming and shaming" is regarded as one of the most appropriate tools in international advocacy; it allows specialized organizations to tackle abuses. *See* James Meernik, Rosa Aloisi, Marsha Sowell & Angela Nichols, *The Impact of Human Rights Organizations on Naming and Shaming Campaigns*, 56 J. Conflict Resol. 233, 233–34 (2012). *But see* Emily M. Hafner-Burton, *Sticks and Stones: Naming and Shaming the Human Rights Enforcement Problem*, 62 Int'l Org. 689, 707 (2008) ("Naming and shaming is not just cheap talk. But neither is it a remedy for all abuses governments put in the global spotlight for violations often adopt better protections for political rights afterward, but they rarely stop or appear to lessen acts of terror. Worse, terror sometimes increases after publicity.").

182 *See* Robert Howse & Ruti Teitel, *Beyond Compliance: Rethinking Why International Law Really Matters, in* 1 Glob. Pol'y 2, 127, 128 (2010). *But see* Jack L. Goldsmith & Eric A. Posner, The Limits of International Law (2006) (arguing that it would be difficult to prove that compliance to a rule is undertaken contrary to national self-interest).

a country loses its reputation at the international table, the only way to regain it is through commitment and compliance with international norms. Enhancing and detracting from reputation are factors that are built over time through government decisions and actions.[183]

Long-term benefits vis-à-vis short-term gains draw the line between international shared values and internal domestic prerogatives.[184] First, by honoring their commitment to the international community, states move toward a reputational consolidation, which is important in bilateral and multilateral negotiations. Second, those countries that are more likely to disregard international commitments will eventually struggle to find partners and allies in international relations. In extreme cases, when mutual trust is no longer an option, international law will serve only as a vehicle for imposing sanctions on those countries that have destroyed their reputational capital. In this context, sanctions are to be intended as a global specter, from punishment and retaliation to diplomatic and economic measures to reputational costs for the country, including the possibility of making future commitments at the international level.[185]

183 *See* Matthew C. Steohenson, *Court of Public Opinion: Government Accountability and Judicial Independence*, 20 J.L. Econ. & Org. 379, 379–81. (2004) (analyzing ways of furthering states' accountability through the mechanism of the so-called court of public opinion); *see also* Bennett Freeman, Senior Counselor, Corporate Responsibility, Burson-Marsteller, *To What Extent Can Voluntarism Provide Answers?*, remarks at the Wilton Park Conference on Business and Human Rights: Advancing the Agenda (Oct. 11, 2005).

184 *See* Ian Johnstone, Treaty Interpretation: The Authority of Interpretive Communities, 12 Mich. J. Int'l L. 371, 391 (1991); see also Alan Mitchell Polinsky, An Introduction to Law And Economics 31 (2d ed. 1989).

185 *See generally* Johnstone, supra note 184, at 391 (analyzing states' compliance with treaty commitments); see also Robert O. Keohane, International Relations and International Law: Two Optics, 38 Harv. Int'l L.J. 487, 496–99 (1997) (analyzing countries' decisions to observe international norms); Louis Henkin, International Law: Politics, Values and Functions: General Course on Public International Law, in 216 Collected Courses of the Hague Academy of International Law 9, 27 (1989), revised and published as Louis Henkin, International Law: Politics, Values and Functions (1990).

Conclusion

Evaluating the impact of a political event on the course of history is always a hard task. Chinese Prime Minister Chou En-lai said when he was questioned about the impact of the French Revolution—an event that had occurred approximately two centuries before—that it was "too early to tell."[1] Chou's sagacity in taking a long view of history teaches us that it is important not to stumble into the fallacy of rushed conclusions. Analogously, the development of a trend toward withdrawal in the context of global retrenchment entails political, legal, and economic consequences that this book seeks to address by providing a map for consideration by the main actors involved in treaty making and treaty maintenance.

Withdrawal clauses are last-resort tools to be used if a treaty member is unable to have its needs adequately met within the framework of the treaty it joined. They are a corollary to the general principle of *pacta sunt servanda*. To understand the phenomenon of withdrawal, it is necessary to understand the legal framework in which it operates. Treaty adherence is narrowly construed to foster interstate cooperation while discouraging unilateral deviations. Nonetheless, since treaties do not operate in a static environment, withdrawal allows for legally terminating treaty-based cooperation that no longer serves national interests. From this perspective, withdrawal can be understood as the opposite of commitment: the latter entails entering into treaty-based cooperation, while the former entails pulling out of it. Even when withdrawal is a lawful act *de jure*, it can trigger noncooperative outcomes de facto whenever it misaligns with good-faith obligations under the law of the treaties. Indeed, the increasing politicization of states' commitments when joining international treaties has affected good faith in the invocation of withdrawal clauses. Therefore, though they begin as cooperative instruments, withdrawal clauses end up hindering interstate cooperation.

The book has set out a taxonomy of withdrawal to allow us to understand the categories and rationales that have led states to pull out of international

1 The Chinese Prime Minister said this in 1972, on the occasion of the historic visit of US President Richard Nixon to Beijing, capital of the People's Republic of China. *See, e.g.*, Martin Krygier, Civil Passion, Selected Writings 296 (2005) (assessing Chou En-lai's wisdom); *see also* Grazyna Skapska, From Civil Society to Europe: a Sociological Study on Constitutionalism after Communism 221 (2011); *contra* Rana Mitter, *1911: The Unanchored Chinese Revolution*, 208 China Quart. 1009 (2011) (disputing Chou's actual reference to French Protests of May 1968, instead of the Bastille revolution of July 14, 1789); *see also* Richard McGregor, *Zhou's Cryptic Caution Lost in Translation*, Fin. Times, June 10, 2011.

 | DOI:10.1163/9789004467644_008

treaties and to identify behavioral patterns in states' exits. This set the stage for a rich array of examples of states' practices with regard to withdrawal that demonstrate how this instrument can be used reactively or proactively in foreign policy, depending on how states balance domestic needs with international prerogatives.

A quantitative study tested the evolution of withdrawal over time to understand its impact on states' practices. It reviewed instances of withdrawal from and denunciation of all the multilateral treaties deposited with the UN Secretary-General between 1945, with the foundation of the UN, and end of 2020. This study revealed the progressive evolution of withdrawal, especially in the last ten years, from a cooperative act *de jure* to a noncooperative act *de facto*, entailing as it does a growing trend toward withdrawal from high-profile commitments protecting fundamental values of the international community.

Even though it is probably "too early to tell" the outcome of this trend, it is possible to identify strengths and weaknesses of withdrawal clauses and identify proper policy responses for regulating and enhancing orderly withdrawal. Withdrawal is no longer the legal instrument it used to be, able to disrupt multilateral cooperation, as it did in the early twentieth century with the collapse of the League of Nations. The evolution of the international legal system, along with the changed context in which withdrawal operates, burdened states' decisions in line with the idea of continuity in the international law of treaties, which inspired modern treaty making.

To preserve continuity also with regard to treaty maintenance, first, states' commitment can be fostered through well-tailored treaty clauses and through mechanisms embedded in the international regimes' systems. Second, domestic legal architecture is crucial in providing clear rules that serve to define states' powers internally, while indicating states' credibility internationally, taking into account the contributions of all relevant stakeholders. By aligning international and domestic solutions with regard to commitment, it is possible to enhance regulation of withdrawal that is in line with the foundational principle of the law of treaties—*pacta sunt servanda*.

Appendix: Table of Withdrawals

The following Table collects all the cases of withdrawal and denunciations of multilateral treaties deposited with the United Nations Secretary-General from January 1, 1946 to December 31, 2020.

Notification of withdrawal	Effective withdrawal	State	Treaty	Functional area
10 Sept 2020	10 Sept 2021	Uganda	Lusaka Agreement on Co-Operative Enforcement Operations Directed at Illegal Trade in Wild Fauna and Flora, Lusaka, 8 September 1994	Environment
6 Jul 2020	6 Jul 2021	USA	Constitution of the World Health Organization (WHO), Geneva, 22 July 1946	Global Health
4 Nov 2019	4 Nov 2020	USA	Paris Agreement on Climate Change, Paris, 12 December 2015	Environment
23 Oct 2019	23 Oct 2020	Belgium	Convention On A Code Of Conduct For Liner Conferences, Geneva, 6 April 1974	Navigation
15 Oct 2019	15 Oct 2019 (Withdrawal of the instrument of ratification)	Jamaica	Regional Agreement on Access to Information, Public Participation and Justice in Environmental Matters in Latin America and the Caribbean, Escazú, 4 March 2018	Environment

(*cont.*)

Notification of withdrawal	Effective withdrawal	State	Treaty	Functional area
9 May 2019	9 May 2020	Bhutan	Statutes Of The International Centre for Genetic Engineering and Biotechnology, Madrid, 13 September 1983	Educational and Cultural Matters
29 Apr 2019	29 Apr 2019 (Withdrawal of the instrument of accession)	Malaysia	Rome Statute of the International Criminal Court, Rome, 17 July 1998	Penal Matters
27 Feb 2019	27 Feb 2019 (Accession cancelled) Re-access: 7 Oct 2019	Estonia	Protocol to the 1979 Convention on Long-Range Transboundary Air Pollution to Abate Acidification, Eutrophication and Ground-Level Ozone, Gothenburg (Sweden), 30 November 1999	Environment
12 Oct 2018	12 Oct 2018	USA	Optional Protocol to the Vienna Convention on Diplomatic Relations, Concerning the Compulsory Settlement of Disputes, Vienna, 18 April 1961	Privileges and Immunities, Diplomatic and Consular Relations
2 Sept 2018	31 Dec 2018	Palestine	Food Assistance Convention, London, 25 April 2012	Commodities
17 Mar 2018	17 March 2019	Philippines	Rome Statute of the International Criminal Court, Rome, 17 July 1998	Penal Matters
22 Sept 2017	22 Sept. 2018	Poland	Convention Regarding the Measurement of Vessels Employed in Inland Navigation, Paris, 27 November 1925	League Of Nations Multilateral Treaties

(*cont.*)

Notification of withdrawal	Effective withdrawal	State	Treaty	Functional area
15 Sept 2017	15 Sept 2018	Colombia	Optional Protocol Of Signature Concerning The Compulsory Settlement Of Disputes Geneva, 29 April 1958	Law of the Sea
30 Dec 2016	30 Dec 2017	Poland	Statutes Of The International Centre For Genetic Engineering And Biotechnology, Madrid, 13 September 1983	Educational and Cultural Matters
21 Dec 2016	31 Dec 2017	Slovakia	Constitution of the United Nations Industrial Development Organization Vienna, 8 April 1979	International Trade and Development
10 Nov 2016	Withdrawn: 10 Feb 2017	Gambia	Rome Statute of the International Criminal Court Rome, 17 July 1998	Penal Matters
27 Oct 2016	27 Oct 2017	Burundi	Rome Statute of the International Criminal Court Rome, 17 July 1998	Penal Matters
19 Oct 2016	Withdrawn: 7 Mar 2017	South Africa	Rome Statute of the International Criminal Court Rome, 17 July 1998	Penal Matters
30 Dec 2015	31 Dec 2016	Greece	Constitution of the United Nations Industrial Development Organization Vienna, 8 April 1979	International Trade and Development
17 Dec 2015	31 Dec 2016	Denmark	Constitution of the United Nations Industrial Development Organization Vienna, 8 April 1979	International Trade and Development
1 May 2015	31 May 2015	Trinidad and Tobago	International Sugar Agreement, 1992, Geneva, 20 March 1992	Commodities

(*cont.*)

Notification of withdrawal	Effective withdrawal	State	Treaty	Functional area
9 Jan 2015	10 Jan 2016	Austria	Agreement Establishing The Common Fund For Commodities, Geneva, 27 June 1980	Commodities
28 Nov 2014	31 Dec 2015	Belgium	Constitution of the United Nations Industrial Development Organization, Vienna, 8 April 1979	International Trade and Development
30 Sept 2014	31 Dec 2015	Luxembourg	Agreement Establishing The Common Fund For Commodities, Geneva, 27 June 1980	Commodities
31 Dec 2013	31 Dec 2014	Portugal	Constitution of the United Nations Industrial Development Organization, Vienna, 8 April 1979	International Trade and Development
30 Sep 2013	31 Dec 2014	France	Constitution of the United Nations Industrial Development Organization, Vienna, 8 April 1979	International Trade and Development
14 Jan 2013	14 Apr 2013	Canada	International Tropical Timber Agreement, 2006, Geneva, 27 January 2006	Commodities
28 Mar 2013	20 Mar 2014 Re-access: 21 Dec 2016	Canada	United Nations Convention to Combat Desertification in Those Countries Experiencing Serious Drought and/or Desertification, Particularly in Africa, Paris, 14 October 1994	Environment
13 Dec 2012	31 Dec 2013	New Zealand	Constitution of the United Nations Industrial Development Organization Vienna, 8 April 1979	International Trade and Development

(*cont.*)

Notification of withdrawal	Effective withdrawal	State	Treaty	Functional area
10 Dec 2012	10 Dec 2013	Belgium	Agreement Establishing the Common Fund for Commodities, Geneva, 27 June 1980	Commodities
7 Sept 2012	7 Sept 2013	Japan	Agreement Establishing the Common Fund for Commodities, Geneva, 27 June 1980	Commodities
29 Dec 2011	31 Dec 2012	Lithuania	Constitution of the United Nations Industrial Development Organization Vienna, 8 April 1979	International Trade and Development
15 Dec 2011	15 Dec 2012	Canada	Kyoto Protocol to the United Nations Framework Convention on Climate Change Kyoto, 11 December 1997	Environment
25 Jul 2011	25 Jul 2012	Netherlands	Convention on a Code of Conduct for Liner Conferences Geneva, 6 April 1974	Navigation
29 June 2011	1 Jan 2012	Bolivia	Single Convention on Narcotic Drugs, 1961, as Amended by the Protocol Amending the Single Convention on Narcotic Drugs, 1961 New York, 8 August 1975	Narcotic Drugs and Psychotropic Substances
27 Apr 2011	31 Dec 2012	United Kingdom	Constitution of the United Nations Industrial Development Organization Vienna, 8 April 1979	International Trade and Development

(*cont.*)

Notification of withdrawal	Effective withdrawal	State	Treaty	Functional area
1 Dec 2010	1 Dec 2010	Switzerland	Agreement Establishing the Terms of Reference of the International Jute Study Group, 2001, Geneva, 13 March 2001	Commodities
22 June 2010	21 Aug 2010	Netherlands	Terms Of Reference Of The International Copper Study Group, Geneva, 24 February 1989	Commodities
27 Oct 2009	27 Oct 2009	France	Amendment to Annex B of the Kyoto Protocol to the United Nations Framework Convention on Climate Change, Nairobi, 17 November 2006	Environment
17 Apr 2009	17 Apr 2010	Denmark	Convention on a Code of Conduct for Liner Conferences, Geneva, 6 April 1974	Navigation
22 Dec 2008	22 Dec 2009	Bulgaria	Convention on a Code of Conduct for Liner Conferences, Geneva, 6 April 1974	Navigation
17 Dec 2007	31 Dec 2007	Ecuador	Grains Trade Convention, 1995, London, 7 December 1994	Commodities
9 Nov 2007	8 Jan 2008	Colombia	Agreement to Establish the South Centre, Geneva, 1 September 1994	International Trade and Development
16 Oct 2007	20 Oct 2008	United Kingdom	Convention on a Code of Conduct for Liner Conferences, Geneva, 6 April 1974	Navigation

(*cont.*)

Notification of withdrawal	Effective withdrawal	State	Treaty	Functional area
26 Sept 2007	26 Sept 2008	Germany	Convention on a Code of Conduct for Liner Conferences, Geneva, 6 April 1974	Navigation
12 July 2007	12 July 2008	Luxembourg	Convention on the Nationality of Married Women, New York, 20 February 1957	Status of Women
16 March 2005	14 June 2005	Monaco	International Agreement on Olive Oil and Table Olives, 1986, as Amended and Extended, 1993, Geneva, 1 July 1986	Commodities
7 March 2005	7 March 2005	USA	Optional Protocol to the Vienna Convention on Consular Relations Concerning the Compulsory Settlement of Disputes, Vienna, 24 April 1963	Privileges and Immunities, Diplomatic and Consular Relations
1 Sept 2004	31 July 2007	Australia	Agreement Establishing the International Fund for Agricultural Development, Rome, 13 June 1976	International Trade and Development
29 Sept 2003	28 Nov 2003	Canada	Terms of Reference of the International Nickel Study Group, Geneva, 2 May 1986	Commodities
29 Sept 2003	28 Nov 200	Canada	Terms Of Reference Of The International Copper Study Group, Geneva, 24 February 1989	Commodities
31 Jul 2003	29 Sept 2003	Indonesia	Terms Of Reference Of The International Copper Study Group, Geneva, 24 February 1989	Commodities

(*cont.*)

Notification of withdrawal	Effective withdrawal	State	Treaty	Functional area
22 Jul 2003	20 Sept 2003	United Kingdom	Terms Of Reference Of The International Copper Study Group, Geneva, 24 February 1989	Commodities
6 Dec 2003	4 Feb 2003	Japan	Terms of Reference of the International Nickel Study Group, Geneva, 2 May 1986	Commodities
25 Nov 2002	25 Dec 2004	Japan	International Sugar Agreement, 1992 Geneva, 20 March 1992	Commodities
31 Oct 2002	30 Dec 2002 Re-access: 12 Nov 2004	Japan	Terms Of Reference Of The International Copper Study Group, Geneva, 24 February 1989	Commodities
15 May 2001	Withdrawn: 9 May 2002	Brazil	Statutes Of The International Centre For Genetic Engineering And Biotechnology, Madrid, 13 September 1983	Educational and Cultural Matters
14 Jul 2000	12 Sept 2000	Norway	Terms Of Reference Of The International Copper Study Group, Geneva, 24 February 1989	Commodities
17 March 2000	27 June 2000	Trinidad and Tobago	Optional Protocol to the International Covenant on Civil and Political Rights, New York, 16 December 1966	Human Rights
3 Nov 1999	3 Feb 2001	Singapore	Convention Concerning Customs Facilities for Touring, New York, 4 June 1954	Transport and Communication
16 Jul 1999	16 Jul 2000	Sri Lanka	International Natural Rubber Agreement, 1995, Geneva, 17 February 1995	Commodities

(*cont.*)

Notification of withdrawal	Effective withdrawal	State	Treaty	Functional area
26 Mar 1999	26 Mar 2000	Thailand	International Natural Rubber Agreement, 1995, Geneva, 17 February 1995	Commodities
5 Jan 1999	5 Apr 1999 Re-access: 5 Apr 1999	Guyana	Optional Protocol to the International Covenant on Civil and Political Rights, New York, 16 December 1966	Human Rights
22 Dec 1998	22 Mar 1999	Thailand	International Agreement on Jute and Jute Products, Geneva, 3 November 1989	Commodities
15 Oct 1998	15 Oct 1999	Malaysia	International Natural Rubber Agreement, 1995, Geneva, 17 February 1995	Commodities
9 Oct 1998	7 Jan 1999	India	International Agreement on Jute and Jute Products, Geneva, 3 November 1989	Commodities
26 Aug 1998	24 Nov 1998	Turkey	International Agreement on Olive Oil and Table Olives, 1986, as Amended and Extended, 1993, Geneva, 1 July 1986	Commodities
26 May 1998	26 Aug 1998 Re-access: 26 Aug 1998	Trinidad and Tobago	Optional Protocol to the International Covenant on Civil and Political Rights, New York, 16 December 1966	Human Rights
23 Oct 1997	23 Jan 1998	Jamaica	Optional Protocol to the International Covenant on Civil and Political Rights, New York, 16 December 1966	Human Rights
25 Aug 1997	Rejected	Democratic People's Republic of Korea	International Covenant on Civil and Political Rights New York, 16 December 1966	Human Rights
7 Jul 1997	7 Oct 1997	Pakistan	International Agreement on Jute and Jute Products, Geneva, 3 November 1989	Commodities

(*cont.*)

Notification of withdrawal	Effective withdrawal	State	Treaty	Functional area
27 Mar 1997	Withdrawn: 26 Sept 1997	Trinidad and Tobago	Agreement Establishing the International Fund for Agricultural Development, Rome, 13 June 1976	International Trade and Development
27 Mar 1997	27 Jun 1997	Trinidad and Tobago	International Coffee Agreement, 1994 Adopted by the International Coffee Council on 30 March 1994	Commodities
23 Dec 1996	31 Dec 1997	Australia	Constitution of the United Nations Industrial Development Organization, Vienna, 8 April 1979	International Trade and Development
25 Jul 1996	24 Aug 1996	Austria	International Sugar Agreement, 1992 Geneva, 20 March 1992	Commodities
15 May 1996	15 May 1997	Canada	Convention on Certain Questions Relating to the Conflict of Nationality Laws, The Hague, 12 April 1930	League of Nations Multilateral Treaties
26 Jan 1996	25 Apr 1996	Australia	International Agreement on Jute and Jute Products, Geneva, 3 November 1989	Commodities
4 Dec 1995	31 Dec 1996	USA	Constitution of the United Nations Industrial Development Organization, Vienna, 8 April 1979	International Trade and Development
4 Dec 1995	2 Feb 1996	Philippines	Terms Of Reference Of The International Copper Study Group, Geneva, 24 February 1989	Commodities
27 Jun 1995	27 Jul 1995	Finland	International Sugar Agreement, 1992 Geneva, 20 March 1992	Commodities
23 Jun 1995	23 Jul 1995	Sweden	International Sugar Agreement, 1992 Geneva, 20 March 1992	Commodities

(*cont.*)

Notification of withdrawal	Effective withdrawal	State	Treaty	Functional area
1 Sep 1994	1 Oct 1994 Re-access: 27 Mar 2007	Barbados	International Sugar Agreement, 1992 Geneva, 20 March 1992	Commodities
29 Jul 1994	1 Aug 1995	Turkey	Agreement Establishing The Common Fund For Commodities, Geneva, 27 June 1980	Commodities
21 Mar 1994	19 Jun 1994	USA	International Agreement on Jute and Jute Products, Geneva, 3 November 1989	Commodities
15 Feb 1993	17 Feb 1994	New Zealand	Agreement Establishing The Common Fund For Commodities, Geneva, 27 June 1980	Commodities
29 Dec 1992	29 Dec 1993	Netherlands	Agreement Concerning Manned Lightships not on their Stations, Lisbon, 23 October 1930	League of Nations Multilateral Treaties
29 Dec 1992	29 Dec 1993	Netherlands	Agreement Concerning Maritime Signals, Lisbon, 23 October 1930	League of Nations Multilateral Treaties
3 Dec 1992	31 Dec 1993	Canada	Constitution of the United Nations Industrial Development Organization, Vienna, 8 April 1979	International Trade and Development
3 Jun 1992	9 Jun 1993	Canada	Agreement Establishing The Common Fund For Commodities, Geneva, 27 June 1980	Commodities
6 Jan 1992	16 Jan 1993	Netherlands	Convention on the Nationality of Married Women, New York, 20 February 1957	Status of Women
5 Aug 1991	20 Aug 1992	Australia	Agreement Establishing The Common Fund For Commodities, Geneva, 27 June 1980	Commodities

(*cont.*)

Notification of withdrawal	Effective withdrawal	State	Treaty	Functional area
24 Dec 1987	31 Dec 1988 Re-access: 1 Jan 1992	Australia	Constitution of the United Nations Industrial Development Organization, Vienna, 8 April 1979	International Trade and Development
24 Dec 1987	23 Jan 1988	Egypt	International Sugar Agreement, Geneva, 5 July 1984	Commodities
30 Nov 1987	30 Dec 1987	New Zealand	International Sugar Agreement, Geneva, 5 July 1984	Commodities
2 Jul 1987	30 Sept 1987	New Zealand	International Coffee Agreement, 1983 Adopted by the International Coffee Council on 16 September 1982	Commodities
17 Nov 1986	17 Nov 1987	Iraq	International Natural Rubber Agreement, 1979 Concluded at Geneva on 6 October 1979	Commodities
24 Jul 1986	24 Jul 1987	Greece	Agreement Concerning Maritime Signals, Lisbon, 23 October 1930	League of Nations Multilateral Treaties
1 Oct 1985	1 Oct 1986	Belgium	Agreement Concerning Maritime Signals, Lisbon, 23 October 1930	League of Nations Multilateral Treaties
30 Jul 1985	30 Jul 1986	Netherlands	Convention for the Suppression of the Circulation of, and Traffic in, Obscene Publications, Concluded at Geneva on 12 September 1923 and Amended by the Protocol Signed at Lake Success, New York, on 12 November 1947, New York, 12 November 1947	Obscene Publications

(*cont.*)

Notification of withdrawal	Effective withdrawal	State	Treaty	Functional area
24 Jul 1985	24 Jul 1986	United Kingdom	International Convention Concerning the Use of Broadcasting in the Cause of Peace Geneva, 23 September 1936	League of Nations Multilateral Treaties
17 May 1985	17 May 1986	Australia	International Convention Concerning the Use of Broadcasting in the Cause of Peace Geneva, 23 September 1936	League of Nations Multilateral Treaties
25 Feb 1985	25 May 1985	Saint Vincent and the Grenadines	International Cocoa Agreement, 1980 Concluded at Geneva on 19 November 1980	Commodities
25 Jul 1984	25 Oct 1984	India	Agreement Establishing the International Tea Promotion Association Geneva, 31 March 1977	Commodities
13 Apr 1984	13 Apr 1985	France	International Convention Concerning the Use of Broadcasting in the Cause of Peace Geneva, 23 September 1936	League of Nations Multilateral Treaties
11 Jul 1983	11 Jul 1984	France	Agreement Concerning Maritime Signals, Lisbon, 23 October 1930	League of Nations Multilateral Treaties
31 Dec 1982	31 Dec 1982	Singapore	International Sugar Agreement, Geneva On 7 October 1977	Commodities
26 Nov 1982	26 Nov 1983	Turkey	International Natural Rubber Agreement, 1979 Concluded at Geneva on 6 October 1979	Commodities

(*cont.*)

Notification of withdrawal	Effective withdrawal	State	Treaty	Functional area
11 Oct 1982	11 Oct 1983	Netherlands	International Convention Concerning the Use of Broadcasting in the Cause of Peace Geneva, 23 September 1936	League of Nations Multilateral Treaties
29 Sept 1982	28 Dec 1982	Sri Lanka	Agreement Establishing the International Tea Promotion Association Geneva, 31 March 1977	Commodities
1 Jun 1982	1 Jun 1983	Turkey	International Tin Agreement, Geneva, 21 June 1975	Commodities
23 Mar 1982	31 Dec 1981	Romania	International Tin Agreement, Geneva, 21 June 1975	Commodities
24 Dec 1981	24 Dec 1982	United Kingdom	Convention on the Nationality of Married Women, New York, 20 February 1957	Status of Women
7 Oct 1980	6 Nov 1980	Portugal	International Sugar Agreement, Geneva On 7 October 1977	Commodities
4 Mar 1980	4 Mar 1981	Bulgaria	Convention Regarding the Measurement of Vessels Employed in Inland Navigation, Paris, 27 November 1925	League of Nations Multilateral Treaties
14 Aug 1978	14 Aug 1979	Netherlands	Convention Regarding the Measurement of Vessels Employed in Inland Navigation, Paris, 27 November 1925	League of Nations Multilateral Treaties
5 Jan 1978	5 Jan 1979	Hungary	Convention Regarding the Measurement of Vessels Employed in Inland Navigation, Paris, 27 November 1925	League of Nations Multilateral Treaties

(*cont.*)

Notification of withdrawal	Effective withdrawal	State	Treaty	Functional area
31 Aug 1976	31 Aug 1977	Germany	Convention Regarding the Measurement of Vessels Employed in Inland Navigation, Paris, 27 November 1925	League of Nations Multilateral Treaties
9 Jun 1976	8 Jul 1976	Senegal	Convention on The Territorial Sea and the Contiguous Zone Geneva, 29 April 1958	Law of the Sea
24 May 1976	24 May 1977	Romania	Convention Regarding the Measurement of Vessels Employed in Inland Navigation, Paris, 27 November 1925	League of Nations Multilateral Treaties
1 Mar 1976	30 Mar 1976	Senegal	Convention on the Continental Shelf Geneva, 29 April 1958	Law of the Sea
28 Jul 1975	19 Apr 1975	Yugoslavia	Convention Regarding the Measurement of Vessels Employed in Inland Navigation, Paris, 27 November 1925	League of Nations Multilateral Treaties
13 Jun 1975	13 Jun 1976	France	Convention Regarding the Measurement of Vessels Employed in Inland Navigation, Paris, 27 November 1925	League of Nations Multilateral Treaties
7 Feb 1975	7 Feb 1976	Switzerland	Convention Regarding the Measurement of Vessels Employed in Inland Navigation, Paris, 27 November 1925	League of Nations Multilateral Treaties
19 Apr 1974	19 Apr 1975	Czechoslovakia	Convention Regarding the Measurement of Vessels Employed in Inland Navigation, Paris, 27 November 1925	League of Nations Multilateral Treaties

(*cont.*)

Notification of withdrawal	Effective withdrawal	State	Treaty	Functional area
25 Jan 1974	25 Jan 1975	Germany	Convention for The Suppression of the Circulation of and Traffic in Obscene Publications, Geneva, 12 September 1923	League of Nations Multilateral Treaties
8 Feb 1974	16 Aug 1974	United Kingdom	General Act of Arbitration (Pacific Settlement of International Disputes), Geneva, 26 September 1928	League of Nations Multilateral Treaties
2 Oct 1973	2 Oct 1974	Thailand	Convention and Statute on the International Regime of Maritime Ports Geneva, 9 December 1923	League of Nations Multilateral Treaties
12 Sept 1973	12 Sept 1973	China	Special Protocol Concerning Statelessness, The Hague, 12 April 1930	League of Nations Multilateral Treaties
20 Feb 1973	20 Feb 1974	France	Convention Establishing an International Relief Union, Geneva, 12 July 1927	League of Nations Multilateral Treaties
31 Oct 1972	31 Oct 1973	Fiji	International Convention Relating to the Simplification of Customs Formalities Geneva, 3 November 1923	League of Nations Multilateral Treaties
2 Oct 1972	2 Oct 1973	Thailand	Convention and Statute on the International Regime of Maritime Ports Geneva, 9 December 1923	League of Nations Multilateral Treaties
9 Mar 1972	9 Mar 1973	Belgium	Convention Regarding the Measurement of Vessels Employed in Inland Navigation, Paris, 27 November 1925	League of Nations Multilateral Treaties

(*cont.*)

Notification of withdrawal	Effective withdrawal	State	Treaty	Functional area
30 Jul 1971	28 Oct 1971	Thailand	International Sugar. Agreement, 1968 Open for Signature at New York: from 3 To 24 December 1968	Commodities
9 Jun 1971	8 Jul 1971	Senegal	Convention on Fishing and Conservation of the Living Resources of the High Seas Geneva, 29 April 1958	Law of the Sea
9 Jun 1971	8 Jul 1971	Senegal	Convention on the High Seas, Geneva, 29 April 1958	Law of the Sea
9 Jun 1971	8 Jul 1971	Senegal	Convention on the Territorial Sea and the Contiguous Zone, Geneva, 29 April 1958	Law of the Sea
26 May 1971	26 May 1972	Poland	Convention on the Taxation of Foreign Motor Vehicles, Geneva, 30 March 1931	League of Nations Multilateral Treaties
19 Mar 1969	19 Mar 1969	Malawi	Convention Providing a Uniform Law for Cheques, Geneva, 19 March 1931	League of Nations Multilateral Treaties
17 Dec 1968	1 Jan 1969	New Zealand	Protocol for Limiting and Regulating the Cultivation of the Poppy Plant, the Production of, International and Wholesale Trade in, and Use of Opium, New York, 23 June 1953	Narcotic Drugs and Psychotropic Substances
9 Oct 1968	9 Oct 1968	Portugal	Convention Providing a Uniform Law for Cheques, Geneva, 19 March 1931	League of Nations Multilateral Treaties
9 Oct 1968	9 Oct 1968	Sweden	Convention Providing a Uniform Law for Cheques, Geneva, 19 March 1931	League of Nations Multilateral Treaties
24 Apr 1968	24 Apr 1968	Japan	Convention Providing a Uniform Law for Cheques, Geneva, 19 March 1931	League of Nations Multilateral Treaties

(*cont.*)

Notification of withdrawal	Effective withdrawal	State	Treaty	Functional area
7 Mar 1968	7 Mar 1969	Denmark	Convention on the Taxation of Foreign Motor Vehicles, Geneva, 30 March 1931	League of Nations Multilateral Treaties
22 Mar 1968	22 Mar 1969	Malawi	Convention and Statute on the Regime of Navigable Waterways of International Concern, Barcelona, 20 April 1921	League of Nations Multilateral Treaties
22 Mar 1968	22 Mar 1969	Malawi	Convention Relating to the Status of Refugees Geneva, 28 July 1951	Refugees and Stateless Persons
22 Mar 1968	22 Mar 1969	Malawi	Convention Relating to the Status of Stateless Persons New York, 28 September 1954	Refugees and Stateless Persons
18 Oct 1967	18 Oct 1967	Belgium	Convention Relating to the Status of Stateless Persons New York, 28 September 1954	League of Nations Multilateral Treaties
18 Oct 1967	18 Oct 1967	Switzerland	Convention Relating to the Status of Stateless Persons New York, 28 September 1954	League of Nations Multilateral Treaties
15 Oct 1967	15 Oct 1967	Brazil	Convention Relating to the Status of Stateless Persons New York, 28 September 1954	League of Nations Multilateral Treaties
15 Oct 1967	15 Oct 1967	Greece	Convention Relating to the Status of Stateless Persons New York, 28 September 1954	League of Nations Multilateral Treaties
15 Oct 1967	15 Oct 1967	Hungary	Convention Relating to the Status of Stateless Persons New York, 28 September 1954	League of Nations Multilateral Treaties

(*cont.*)

Notification of withdrawal	Effective withdrawal	State	Treaty	Functional area
15 Oct 1967	15 Oct 1967	Indonesia	Convention Relating to the Status of Stateless Persons New York, 28 September 1954	League of Nations Multilateral Treaties
15 Oct 1967	15 Oct 1967	Monaco	Convention Relating to the Status of Stateless Persons New York, 28 September 1954	League of Nations Multilateral Treaties
14 Oct 1967	14 Oct 1967	Poland	Convention Relating to the Status of Stateless Persons New York, 28 September 1954	League of Nations Multilateral Treaties
13 Oct 1967	13 Oct 1967	Finland	Convention Relating to the Status of Stateless Persons New York, 28 September 1954	League of Nations Multilateral Treaties
8 Oct 1967	8 Oct 1967	Austria	Convention Providing a Uniform Law for Cheques, Geneva, 19 March 1931	League of Nations Multilateral Treaties
8 Oct 1967	8 Oct 1967	Denmark	Convention Providing a Uniform Law for Cheques, Geneva, 19 March 1931	League of Nations Multilateral Treaties
8 Oct 1967	8 Oct 1967	Italy	Convention Providing a Uniform Law for Cheques, Geneva, 19 March 1931	League of Nations Multilateral Treaties
8 Oct 1967	8 Oct 1967	Norway	Convention Providing a Uniform Law for Cheques, Geneva, 19 March 1931	League of Nations Multilateral Treaties
5 Oct 1967	5 Oct 1967	France	Convention Providing a Uniform Law for Cheques, Geneva, 19 March 1931	League of Nations Multilateral Treaties
16 Aug 1967	16 Aug 1968	Denmark	Convention for the Suppression of the Circulation of, and Traffic in, Obscene Publications, Concluded at Geneva on 12september 1923 and Amended by the Protocol Signed at Lake Success, New York, on 12 November 1947, New York, 12 November 1947	Obscene Publications

(*cont.*)

Notification of withdrawal	Effective withdrawal	State	Treaty	Functional area
10 Jul 1967	10 Jul 1968	Romania	Convention on the Taxation of Foreign Motor Vehicles, Geneva, 30 March 1931	League of Nations Multilateral Treaties
14 Dec 1965	14 Dec 1966	Netherlands	Convention for the Suppression of the Illicit Traffic in Dangerous Drugs Geneva, 26 June 1936, and Lake Success, New York, 11 December 1946	Narcotic Drugs and Psychotropic Substances
9 Oct 1965	Withdrawn: 29 Sept 1966	Indonesia	Convention on the International Maritime Organization Geneva, 6 March 1948	Law of the Sea
9 Jul 1965	9 Jul 1966	Pakistan	Convention for the Suppression of the Illicit Traffic in Dangerous Drugs, Geneva, 26 June 1936	Narcotic Drugs and Psychotropic Substances
2 Jun 1965	2 Jun 1966	Luxembourg	Convention on the Taxation of Foreign Motor Vehicles, Geneva, 30 March 1931	League of Nations Multilateral Treaties
2 Apr 1965	2 Apr 1966	Madagascar	Convention Relating to the Status of Stateless Persons, New York, 28 September 1954	Refugees and Stateless Persons
3 Feb 1965	1 Jan 1966	Norway	Agreement Providing for the Provisional Application of the Draft International Customs Conventions on Touring, on Commercial Road' Vehicles and on the International Transport of Goods by Road, Geneva, 16 June 1949	Transport and Communications
20 Jan 1965	19 Sept 1966	Indonesia	Charter of the United Nations	Charter of the United Nations and Statute of the International Court of Justice

(*cont.*)

Notification of withdrawal	Effective withdrawal	State	Treaty	Functional area
10 Aug 1964	1 Jan 1965	Turkey	Agreement Providing for the Provisional Application of the Draft International Customs Conventions on Touring, on Commercial Road' Vehicles and on the International Transport of Goods by Road, Geneva, 16 June 1949	Transport and Communications
10 Aug 1964	1 Jan 1965	Turkey	Agreement Providing for the Provisional Application of the Draft International Customs Conventions on Touring, on Commercial Road' Vehicles and on the International Transport of Goods by Road, Geneva, 16 June 1949	Transport and Communications
20 Apr 1964	20 Apr 1965	Luxembourg	Convention Establishing an International Relief Union, Geneva, 12 July 1927	League of Nations Multilateral Treaties
20 Feb 1964	1 Jan 1965	Italy	Agreement Providing for the Provisional Application of the Draft International Customs Conventions on Touring, on Commercial Road' Vehicles and on the International Transport of Goods by Road, Geneva, 16 June 1949	Transport and Communications
29 Jan 1964	1 Jan 1965	Yugoslavia	Agreement Providing for the Provisional Application of the Draft International Customs Conventions on Touring, on Commercial Road' Vehicles and on the International Transport of Goods by Road, Geneva, 16 June 1949	Transport and Communications

(*cont.*)

Notification of withdrawal	Effective withdrawal	State	Treaty	Functional area
24 Dec 1963	24 Dec 1964	Romania	Convention Establishing an International Relief Union, Geneva, 12 July 1927	League of Nations Multilateral Treaties
6 Nov 1963	6 Nov 1964	Greece	Convention Establishing an International Relief Union, Geneva, 12 July 1927	League of Nations Multilateral Treaties
15 Oct 1963	1 Jan 1965	Austria	Agreement Providing for the Provisional Application of the Draft International Customs Conventions on Touring, on Commercial Road' Vehicles and on the International Transport of Goods by Road, Geneva, 16 June 1949	Transport and Communications
18 Mar 1963	18 Mar 1964	Ireland	Convention on the Taxation of Foreign Motor Vehicles, Geneva, 30 March 1931	League of Nations Multilateral Treaties
14 Jan 1963	14 Jan 1964	United Kingdom	Convention on the Taxation of Foreign Motor Vehicles, Geneva, 30 March 1931	League of Nations Multilateral Treaties
30 Jul 1962	30 Jul 1963	Hungary	Convention Concerning the Unification of Road Signals, Geneva, 30 March 1931	League of Nations Multilateral Treaties
20 Oct 1961	1 Jan 1963	Poland	Agreement Providing for the Provisional Application of the Draft International Customs Conventions on Touring, on Commercial Road' Vehicles and on the International Transport of Goods by Road, Geneva, 16 June 1949	Transport and Communications

(cont.)

Notification of withdrawal	Effective withdrawal	State	Treaty	Functional area
15 Sept 1961	1 Jan 1962	Denmark	Agreement Providing for the Provisional Application of the Draft International Customs Conventions on Touring, on Commercial Road' Vehicles and on the International Transport of Goods by Road, Geneva, 16 June 1949	Transport and Communications
26 May 1961	26 May 1962	Romania	Convention Concerning the Unification of Road Signals, Geneva, 30 March 1931	League of Nations Multilateral Treaties
26 Apr 1961	26 Apr 1962	Russian Federation	Convention Concerning the Unification of Road Signals, Geneva, 30 March 1931	League of Nations Multilateral Treaties
10 Apr 1961	10 Apr 1961	Iraq	Convention Establishing an International Relief Union, Geneva, 12 July 1927	League of Nations Multilateral Treaties
27 Mar 1961	27 Sept 1961	France	European Agreement on the Application of Article 23 of the 1949 Convention on Road Traffic Concerning the Dimensions and Weights of Vehicles Permitted to Travel on Certain Roads of the Contracting Parties, Geneva, 16 September 1950	Transport and Communications
15 Sept 1960	1 Jan 1961	Netherlands	Agreement Providing for the Provisional Application of the Draft International Customs Conventions on Touring, on Commercial Road' Vehicles and on the International Transport of Goods by Road, Geneva, 16 June 1949	Transport and Communications

(*cont.*)

Notification of withdrawal	Effective withdrawal	State	Treaty	Functional area
7 Jul 1960	1 Jan 1961	Switzerland	Agreement Providing for the Provisional Application of the Draft International Customs Conventions on Touring, on Commercial Road' Vehicles and on the International Transport of Goods by Road, Geneva, 16 June 1949	Transport and Communications
16 May 1960	1 Jan 1961	France	Agreement Providing for the Provisional Application of the Draft International Customs Conventions on Touring, on Commercial Road' Vehicles and on the International Transport of Goods by Road, Geneva, 16 June 1949	Transport and Communications
2 March 1960	1 Jan 1961	Norway	Agreement Providing for the Provisional Application of the Draft International Customs Conventions on Touring, on Commercial Road' Vehicles and on the International Transport of Goods by Road, Geneva, 16 June 1949	Transport and Communications
30 Jul 1959	1 Jan 1960	United Kingdom	Agreement Providing for the Provisional Application of the Draft International Customs Conventions on Touring, on Commercial Road' Vehicles and on the International Transport of Goods by Road, Geneva, 16 June 1949	Transport and Communications

(*cont.*)

Notification of withdrawal	Effective withdrawal	State	Treaty	Functional area
25 Feb 1959	1 Jan 1960	Sweden	Agreement Providing for the Provisional Application of the Draft International Customs Conventions on Touring, on Commercial Road' Vehicles and on the International Transport of Goods by Road, Geneva, 16 June 1949	Transport and Communications
29 Oct 1958	30 Oct 1959	Poland	Convention Concerning the Unification of Road Signals, Geneva, 30 March 1931	League of Nations Multilateral Treaties
28 Feb 1958	28 Feb 1959	Spain	Convention Concerning the Unification of Road Signals, Geneva, 30 March 1931	League of Nations Multilateral Treaties
6 Jun 1957	6 Jun 1958	Portugal	Convention Concerning the Unification of Road Signals, Geneva, 30 March 1931	League of Nations Multilateral Treaties
2 May 1956	2 May 1957	Austria	Convention Concerning the Unification of Road Signals, Geneva, 30 March 1931	League of Nations Multilateral Treaties
26 March 1956	26 March 1957	India	Convention and Statute on the Regime of Navigable Waterways of International Concern, Barcelona, 20 April 1921	League of Nations Multilateral Treaties
8 Oct 1956	8 Oct 1957	Cuba	Convention Establishing an International Relief Union, Geneva, 12 July 1927	League of Nations Multilateral Treaties
10 Sept 1956	10 Sept 1957	Finland	Convention on the Taxation of Foreign Motor Vehicles, Geneva, 30 March 1931	League of Nations Multilateral Treaties
13 Sept 1955	13 Sept 1955 Access ICJ compulsory jurisdiction	South Africa	Statute of the Permanent Court of International .Justice, The Hague, 16 December 1920	League of Nations Multilateral Treaties

(*cont.*)

Notification of withdrawal	Effective withdrawal	State	Treaty	Functional area
1 Aug 1955	1 Aug 1956	Egypt	Convention Establishing an International Relief Union, Geneva, 12 July 1927	League of Nations Multilateral Treaties
30 Nov 1954	1 Dec 1955	Luxembourg	Convention Concerning the Unification of Road Signals, Geneva, 30 March 1931	League of Nations Multilateral Treaties
19 Oct 1954	20 Oct 1955	France	Convention Concerning the Unification of Road Signals, Geneva, 30 March 1931	League of Nations Multilateral Treaties
26 May 1954	27 Nov 1954	France	European Agreement on the Application of Article 3 of Annex 7 of the 1949 Convention on Road Traffic Concerning the Dimensions and Weights of Vehicles Permitted to Travel on Certain Roads of The Contracting Parties Geneva, 16 September 1950	Transport and Communications
29 May 1953	30 May 1954	Italy	Convention Concerning the Unification of Road Signals, Geneva, 30 March 1931	League of Nations Multilateral Treaties
18 May 1953	19 May 1954	Monaco	Convention Concerning the Unification of Road Signals, Geneva, 30 March 1931	League of Nations Multilateral Treaties
26 Dec 1952	27 Dec 1953	Netherlands	Convention Concerning the Unification of Road Signals, Geneva, 30 March 1931	League of Nations Multilateral Treaties
16 May 1952	7 Nov 1952	South Africa	Convention Concerning the Unification of Road Signals, Geneva, 30 March 1931	League of Nations Multilateral Treaties
31 Mar 1952	1 Apr 1953	Sweden	Convention Concerning the Unification of Road Signals, Geneva, 30 March 1931	League of Nations Multilateral Treaties

(*cont.*)

Notification of withdrawal	Effective withdrawal	State	Treaty	Functional area
24 Feb 1952	25 Aug 1952	Luxembourg	Agreement on Most-Favoured-Nation Treatment For Areas of Western Germany under Military Occupation, 14 September 1948	League of Nations Multilateral Treaties
20 Feb 1952	21 Aug 1952	Greece	Agreement on Most-Favoured-Nation Treatment For Areas of Western Germany under Military Occupation, 14 September 1948	League of Nations Multilateral Treaties
18 Feb 1952	19 Aug 1952	France	Agreement on Most-Favoured-Nation Treatment For Areas of Western Germany under Military Occupation, 14 September 1948	League of Nations Multilateral Treaties
4 Feb 1952	5 Aug 1952	China	Agreement on Most-Favoured-Nation Treatment For Areas of Western Germany under Military Occupation, 14 September 1948	League of Nations Multilateral Treaties
20 Dec 1951	21 Jun 1952	Dominican Republic	Agreement on Most-Favoured-Nation Treatment For Areas of Western Germany under Military Occupation, 14 September 1948	League of Nations Multilateral Treaties
14 Dec 1951	15 Jun 1952	Belgium	Agreement on Most-Favoured-Nation Treatment For Areas of Western Germany under Military Occupation, 14 September 1948	League of Nations Multilateral Treaties

(*cont.*)

Notification of withdrawal	Effective withdrawal	State	Treaty	Functional area
14 Dec 1951	15 Jun 1952	Canada	Agreement on Most-Favoured-Nation Treatment For Areas of Western Germany under Military Occupation, 14 September 1948	League of Nations Multilateral Treaties
14 Dec 1951	15 Jun 1952	Ceylon	Agreement on Most-Favoured-Nation Treatment For Areas of Western Germany under Military Occupation, 14 September 1948	League of Nations Multilateral Treaties
14 Dec 1951	15 Jun 1952	Denmark	Agreement on Most-Favoured-Nation Treatment For Areas of Western Germany under Military Occupation, 14 September 1948	League of Nations Multilateral Treaties
14 Dec 1951	15 Jun 1952	India	Agreement on Most-Favoured-Nation Treatment For Areas of Western Germany under Military Occupation, 14 September 1948	League of Nations Multilateral Treaties
14 Dec 1951	15 Jun 1952	Netherlands	Agreement on Most-Favoured-Nation Treatment For Areas of Western Germany under Military Occupation, 14 September 1948	League of Nations Multilateral Treaties
14 Dec 1951	15 Jun 1952	Norway	Agreement on Most-Favoured-Nation Treatment For Areas of Western Germany under Military Occupation, 14 September 1948	League of Nations Multilateral Treaties

(*cont.*)

Notification of withdrawal	Effective withdrawal	State	Treaty	Functional area
14 Dec 1951	15 Jun 1952	Pakistan	Agreement on Most-Favoured-Nation Treatment For Areas of Western Germany under Military Occupation, 14 September 1948	League of Nations Multilateral Treaties
14 Dec 1951	15 Jun 1952	United Kingdom	Agreement on Most-Favoured-Nation Treatment For Areas of Western Germany under Military Occupation, 14 September 1948	League of Nations Multilateral Treaties
14 Dec 1951	15 Jun 1952	USA	Agreement on Most-Favoured-Nation Treatment For Areas of Western Germany under Military Occupation, 14 September 1948	League of Nations Multilateral Treaties
13 Nov 1951	13 Nov 1952	Hungary	Convention Establishing an International Relief Union, Geneva, 12 July 1927	League of Nations Multilateral Treaties
1 Oct 1951	1 Oct 1952	Myanmar	Convention Establishing an International Relief Union, Geneva, 12 July 1927	League of Nations Multilateral Treaties
30 June 1951	30 June 1952	Czechoslovakia	Convention Establishing an International Relief Union, Geneva, 12 July 1927	League of Nations Multilateral Treaties
27 Dec 1950	27 Feb 1951	Lebanon	Protocol of Provisional Application of the General Agreement on Tariffs and Trade, Geneva, 5 October 1947	League of Nations Multilateral Treaties

(*cont.*)

Notification of withdrawal	Effective withdrawal	State	Treaty	Functional area
6 Mar 1950	5 May 1950	China	Protocol of Provisional Application of the General Agreement on Tariffs and Trade, Geneva, 5 October 1947	League of Nations Multilateral Treaties
4 May 1948	4 May 1949	United Kingdom	Convention Establishing an International Relief Union and Statute of the International Relief Union, Geneva, 12 July 1927	League of Nations Multilateral Treaties

Bibliography

I. Books

Akehurst, Michael Barton, The Law Governing Employment in International Organizations (1967).

Alighieri, Dante, Monarchy (Cambridge Texts in the History of Political Thoughts, 1st ed., 1996).

Alvarez, Jose, International Organizations as Law-Makers (2005).

Am. Law Inst., Restatement (Third) of the Foreign Relations Law of the United States (1987).

Am. Law Inst., Restatement (Fourth) of the Foreign Relations Law of the United States (2018).

Anzilotti, Dionisio, Cours de droit international (1929).

Arsanjani, Manhoush H., et al., Looking in the Future: Essays on International Law in Honor of W. Michael Reisman (2011).

Aust, Anthony, Handbook of International Law (2010).

Baricco, Alessandro, The Barbarians, An Essay on the Mutation of Culture (2006).

Bartels, Lorand, Human Rights Conditionality in the EU's International Agreements (2005).

Bilder, Richard B., Managing the Risk of International Agreement (1981).

Binder, Guyora, Treaty Conflict and Political Contradiction: The Dialectic of Duplicity (1988).

Blix, Hans & Emerson, Jirina H. The Treaty Maker's Handbook (1973).

Bradford, William C., In The Minds of Men: A Theory of Compliance with the Laws of War (2004).

Breitmeier, Helmut, et al., Analyzing International Environmental Regimes: From Case Study to Database (2006).

Bremmer, Ian, Us vs. Them, The Failure of Globalism (2018).

Brownlie, Ian, Principles of International Law (1973).

Carrasco, Enrique R., Fundamentals of International Finance and Development (2015).

Carter, Barry E. & Weiner, Allen S. International Law (6th ed., 2011).

Chasek, Pamela, Earth Negotiations: Analyzing Thirty Years of Environmental Diplomacy (2001).

Chayes, Abram & Handler Chayes, Antonia, The New Sovereignty: Compliance with International Regulatory Agreements (1995).

Chayes, Abram et al., International Legal Process: Materials for an Introductory Course (1968).

Clapham, Andrew, Human Rights Obligations of Non-State Actors (2006).

Coicaud, Jean Marc & Heiskanen, Veijo, The Legitimacy of International Organizations (2001).

Dai, Xinyuan, International Institutions and National Policies (2007).

Daugberg, Carsten & Swinbank, Alan. Ideas, Institutions, and Trade: The WTO & the Curious Role of EU Farm Policy in Trade Liberalization (2009).

Downie, Christian. The Politics of Climate Change Negotiations, Strategies and Variables in Prolonged International Negotiations (2014).

Downs, George & Rocke, David M., Optimal Imperfection? Domestic Uncertainty and Institutions in International Relations (1995).

Dunleavy, Patrick, Democracy, Bureaucracy and Public Choice: Economic Models in Political Science (1991).

Dupuy, Pierre-Marie, Droit International Public (1992).

Duroselle, Jean Baptiste, Histoire Diplomatique de 1919 à Nos Jours, (11th ed. 1994).

Dworkin, Ronald, Taking Rights Seriously (1977).

Eagleton, Clyde, International Government (1932).

Edwards, Charles S., Hugo Grotius: The Miracle of Holland, a Study in Political and Legal Thought (1981).

Elster, Jon, Ulysses Unbound: Studies in Rationality, Precommitments and Constraints (2000).

Falk, Richard A., Law in an Emerging Global Village: A Post-Westphalian Perspective (1998).

Falk, Richard A., The Status of Law in International Society (1970).

Finnis, John, Natural Law and Natural Rights (1980).

Franceschet, Antonio. Kant and Liberal Internationalism (2002).

Franck, Thomas M., Fairness in International Law and Institutions (1995).

Franck, Thomas M., The Empowered Self – Law and Society in the Age of Individualism (1999).

Franck, Thomas M., The Power of Legitimacy among Nations (1990).

Fukuyama, Francis, The End of History and the Last Man (1992).

Garnaut, Ross, The Garnaut Review 2011: Australia in the Global Response to Climate Change (2011).

Glennon, Michael J., Constitutional Diplomacy (1990).

Goldsmith, Jack L., and Posner Eric A. The Limits of International Law (2006).

Gomaa, Mohammed M., Suspension or Termination of treaties on the Ground of Breach (1996).

Goodrich, Leland, et al., The Charter of the United Nations – Commentary and Documents (3rd ed. 1949).

Graebner, Norman A. & Bennett, Edward M. The Versailles Treaty and Its Legacy: The Failure of the Wilsonian Vision (2011).

Gross, Leo, Essays on International Law and Organization (1984).

Grossman Claudio, et al., International Law and Reparations, The Inter-American System (2018).

Grotius, Hugo, De Jure Belli ac Pacis, Preliminary Speech (1625).

Guzzini, Stefano, Realism in International Relations and International Political Economy (1998).

Gwyn, William B., The Meaning of the Separation of Powers (1965).

Haraszti, Gyorgy, Some Fundamental Problems of the Law of the Treaties (1973).

Hart, Herbert L. A., The Concept of Law (2nd ed., 1994).

Haufler, Virginia, A Public Role for the Private Sector: Industry Self-Regulation in a Global Economy (2001).

Held, David, Democracy and the Global Order: From the Modern State to Cosmopolitan Governance (1995).

Henkin, Louis, How Nations Behave: Law and Foreign Policy (1979).

Henkin, Louis, International Law: Politics, Values and Functions (1990).

Hirschman, Albert O., Exit, Voice and Loyalty: Responses to Decline in Firms, Organizations and States (1970).

Holmes, Stephen, Passion and Constraint: On the Theory of Liberal Democracy (1995).

Hunter Miller, David, My Diary at the Peace Conference (1924).

Hunter, David B., et al., International Environmental Law and Policy (2011).

Imber, Mark F., The USA, ILO, UNESCO and IAEA: Politicization and Withdrawal in the Specialized Agencies (1989).

Janis, Mark, An Introduction to International Law (1998).

Jellinek, Georg, General Theory of the State (1900).

Jenks, Clarence W., A New World of Law? A Study of the Creative Imagination in International Law (1969).

Jessup, Philip, Transnational Law (1956).

Johnston, Douglas M., Consent and Commitment in the World Community: The Classification and Analysis of International Instruments (1997).

Kaplan, Morton A., Nicholas Katzenbach. The Political Foundation of International Law (1961).

Kegley, Charles W., and Wittkopf, Eugene R. World Politics: Trends and Transformation, 10th ed., 2005.

Kelsen, Hans, The Law of the United Nations, A critical Analysis of Its Fundamental Problems (1950).

Kennan, George, American Diplomacy – 1900–1950 (1951).

Kennedy, David, International Legal Structures (1987).

Keohane, Robert O. & Nye, Joseph S., Power and Interdependence (1977).

Keohane, Robert O., After Hegemony: Cooperation and Discord in the World Political Economy (1984).

Keohane, Robert O., International Institutions and State Power (1989).

Kirgis Frederic L., International Organizations in Their Legal Setting (2nd ed., 1993).

Kissinger, Henry, Diplomacy (1994).

Kissinger, Henry, Nuclear Weapons and Foreign Policy (1957).

Klabbers, Jan, International Law (2017).

Koh, Harold H., The Trump Administration and International Law (2018).

Kolb, Robert, The Law of the Treaties: An Introduction (2016).

Koskenniemi, Martti, From Apology to Utopia (1989).

Koskenniemi, Martti, The Gentle Civilizer of Nations, The Rise and Fall of International Law: 1870–1960 (2001).

Krasner, Stephen D., Sovereignty: Organized Hypocrisy (1999).

Krygier, Martin, Civil Passion, Selected Writings (2005).

Lantis, Jeffrey S., The Life and Death of International Treaties: Double-Edged Diplomacy and the Politics of Ratification on Comparative Perspective (2009).

Lauren, Paul G., Diplomacy: New Approaches in History, Theory and Policy (1979).

Lauterpacht, Hirsch, Private Law Sources and Analogies of International Law (1927).

Lauterpacht, Hirsch, The Function of Law in the International Community (2011).

Little, Richard, The Balance of Power in International Relations: Metaphors, Myths and Models (2007).

Lopez, Martin, XV Anuario de Derecho Internacional (1999).

Madison, James, The Federalist (1788).

May, Alex, Britain and Europe since 1945 (1999).

McDougal, Myres S., Studies in World Public Order (1960).

McGrew, Anthony, The Transformation of Democracy?: Globalization and Territorial Democracy (1997).

Merry, Sally Engle, The Seduction of Quantification. Measuring Human Rights, Gender Violence and Human Trafficking (2016).

Milanovic, Branko, Global Inequality: A New Approach for the Age of Globalization (2016).

Mintz, Alex & DeRouen, Karl Jr., Understanding Foreign Policy Decision Making (2010).

Mitchell Polinsky, Alan. An Introduction to Law and Economics (2nd ed., 1989).

Mitchell, Ronald B., Intentional Oil Pollution at Sea: Environmental Policy and Treaty Compliance (1994).

MORGENTHAU, HANS J., POLITICS AMONG NATIONS: THE STRUGGLE FOR POWER AND PEACE (4th ed., 1967).

MULLIGAN, STEPHEN P., WITHDRAWAL FROM INTERNATIONAL AGREEMENTS: LEGAL FRAMEWORK, THE PARIS AGREEMENT, AND THE IRAN NUCLEAR AGREEMENT, 7 CONGRESSIONAL RESEARCH SERV. (2018).

NEWELL, PETER, CLIMATE FOR CHANGE: NON-STATE ACTORS AND THE GLOBAL POLITICS OF THE GREENHOUSE (2000).

OPPENHEIM, LASSA F. L., INTERNATIONAL LAW. A TREATISE (1905).

POLAKIEWICZ, JORG. TREATY-MAKING IN THE COUNCIL OF EUROPE (1999).

PORTER, THEODORE, TRUST IN NUMBERS: THE PURSUIT OF OBJECTIVITY IN SCIENCE AND PUBLIC LIFE (1995).

PROST, MARIO, THE CONCEPT OF UNITY IN PUBLIC INTERNATIONAL LAW (2012).

RAFTOPOULOS, EVANGELOS, INTERNATIONAL NEGOTIATION: PROCESS OF RELATIONAL GOVERNANCE FOR INTERNATIONAL COMMON INTEREST (2018).

RAGAZZI, MAURIZIO, INTERNATIONAL RESPONSIBILITY TODAY: ESSAYS IN MEMORY OF OSCAR SCHACTER (2005).

RAGAZZI, MAURIZIO, THE CONCEPT OF INTERNATIONAL OBLIGATIONS ERGA OMNES (1995).

RAMCHARAN, BERTRAND, THE INTERNATIONAL LAW COMMISSION: ITS APPROACH TO CODIFICATION AND PROGRESSIVE DEVELOPMENT OF INTERNATIONAL LAW (1977).

RAMSEY, MICHAEL D., THE CONSTITUTION'S TEXT IN FOREIGN AFFAIRS 158 (2007).

REDSLOB, ROBERT, HISTOIRE DES GRANDS PRINCIPES DU DROIT DES GENS – DEPUIS L'ANTIQUITÉ JUSQU'À LA VEILLE DE LA GRANDE GUERRE (1923).

REINISCH, AUGUST, INTERNATIONAL ORGANIZATIONS BEFORE NATIONAL COURTS (2000).

REISMAN, MICHAEL, THE VIEW FROM THE NEW HAVEN SCHOOL OF INTERNATIONAL LAW, INTERNATIONAL LAW IN CONTEMPORARY PERSPECTIVE (1992).

RICH, BRUCE, MORTGAGING THE EARTH: THE WORLD BANK, ENVIRONMENTAL IMPOVERISHMENT, AND THE CRISIS OF DEVELOPMENT (1994).

ROBERTS, ANDREW, SALISBURY: VICTORIAN TITAN 629 (2000).

RUGGIE, JOHN G., JUST BUSINESS: MULTINATIONAL CORPORATIONS AND HUMAN RIGHTS (2013).

RUSSETT, BRUCE M., GRASPING THE DEMOCRATIC PEACE: PRINCIPLES FOR A POST-COLD-WAR WORLD (1993).

SANDLER, TODD, GLOBAL CHALLENGES: AN APPROACH TO ENVIRONMENTAL, POLITICAL, AND ECONOMIC PROBLEMS (1997).

SANDS, PHILIPPE, PRINCIPLES OF INTERNATIONAL ENVIRONMENTAL LAW: FRAMEWORKS, STANDARDS AND IMPLEMENTATION (1995).

SCHMITT, CARL, THE CONCEPT OF THE POLITICAL (1932).

SCHMITT, CARL, THE NOMOS OF THE EARTH IN THE INTERNATIONAL LAW OF JUS PUBLICUM EUROPAEUM (1950).

Schumpeter, Joseph, Capitalism, Socialism and Democracy (1942).

Sen, Amartya, Development as a Freedom (1999).

Seyerstad, Finn, Common Law of International Organizations (2008).

Shabtai, Rosenne, The Law and Practice of the International Court of Justice (3rd ed., 1985).

Shaw, Malcom N., International Law (7th edn, 2014).

Sheehan, Michael, The Balance of Power: History and Theory (2000).

Simmons, Beth A., Mobilizing for Human Rights: International Law and Domestic Politics (2009).

Sinclair, Ian, The Vienna Convention on the Law of the Treaties.

Skapska, Grazyna, From Civil Society to Europe: a Sociological Study on Constitutionalism after Communism (2011).

Taylor, Trevor, Utopianism in International Relations: British and American Perspectives (1985).

Temperley, Harold William V., The Foreign Policy of Canning 1822–1827 (1925).

Thomas, Daniel C., The Helsinki Effect: International Norms, Human Rights and the Demise of Communism (2001).

Tobin, Harold, The Termination of Multipartite Treaties (1993).

Toscano, Mario, The History of Treaties and International Politics (1966).

Triepel, Heinrich, International Law and National Law (1899).

Trubek, David, and Santos, Alvaro. The New Law and Economic Development : A Critical Appraisal (2006).

Tyler, Tom R., Why People Obey the Law (2006).

Uvin, Peter, Human Rights and Development (2004).

Vamvoukos, Athanassios, Termination of Treaties in International Law: The Doctrines of Rebus Sic Stantibus and Desuetude (1985).

Vile, M. J. C., Constitutionalism and the Separation of Powers (1967).

Villiger, Mark E., Commentary on the 1969 Vienna Convention on the Law of Treaties (2009).

Vreeland, James Raymond, The Imf and the Economic Development (2003).

Waltz, Kenneth N., Theory of International Politics (1979).

Welch, David A., Justice and the Genesis of War (1995).

Weston, Burns H., et al., International Law and World Order (2nd ed., 1990).

Wildhaber, Luzius, Treaty-Making Power and the Constitution: An International and Comparative Study (1971).

Winer, Anthony S., et al, International Law Legal Research (2013).

Wolfers, Arnold, Discord and Collaboration: Essays on International Politics (1962).

Wong, Joyce & Schuchard, Ryan. Adapting to Climate Change: A Guide for the Consumer Products Industry (2010).

YOUNG, ORAN R., INTERNATIONAL COOPERATION: BUILDING REGIMES FOR NATURAL RESOURCES AND THE ENVIRONMENT (1989).

ZARTMAN, WILLIAM & BERMAN, MAUREEN, THE PRACTICAL NEGOTIATOR (1982).

GIULIANA ZICCARDI CAPALDO, LA COMPETENZA A DENUNCIARE I TRATRATI INTERNAZIONALI 13 (1983).

ZOLLER, ELISABETH, PEACETIME UNILATERAL REMEDIES: AN ANALYSIS OF COUNTERMEASURES (1984).

II. Yearbooks

Allott, Phillip, *Language, Method and the Nature of International Law*, 45 BYIL (1971).

Buergenthal, Thomas, *The U.N. Human Rights Committee*, 5 MAX PLANCK UNYB (2001).

Feinberg, Nathan, *Unilateral Withdrawal from an International Organization*, 39 BYIL (1963).

Fitzmaurice, Gerald *Special Rapporteur on the Law of the Treaties, Second Report on the Law of the Treaties*, 2 UNYBILC 16 (1957).

Johnston, Douglas M., *Theory, Consent, and the Law of Treaties: A cross-Disciplinary Perspective*, 12 Aust. YBIL (1992).

Pellet, Alain, T*he Normative Dilemma: Will and Consent in International Law Making*, Aust. YBIL (1983).

Reinisch, August, *The EU and the Investor-State Dispute Settlement*, EYIEL (Marc Burgenger, et al. eds., 2017).

Sachariew, Kamen, *Promoting Compliance with International Envronmental Standards: Reflections on Monitoring and Reporting Mechanisms*, 2 YIEL (1992).

Tyagi, Yogesh, *The Denunciation of Human Rights Treaties*, 79 BYIL (2009).

Waldock, Humphrey, *Special Rapporteur on the Law of the Treaties, Second Report on the Law of the Treaties*, 2 UNYBILC 36 (1963).

Waldock, Humphrey, *Special Rapporteur on the Law of the Treaties, Sixth Report on the Law of the Treaties*, 2 UNYBILC 60 (1966).

Widdows, Kevin, *The Unilateral Denunciation of Treaties Containing No Denunciation Clause*, 53 BYIL (1982).

III. Chapters in Books

Alston, Philip, *The 'Not-a-Cat' Syndrome: Can the International Human Rights Regime Accomodate Non-State Actors?*, in NON-STATE ACTORS AND HUMAN RIGHTS 3 (Philip Alston ed., 2005).

Bhuta, Nehal, *Governmentalizing Sovereignty: Indexes of State Fragility and the Calculability of Political Order*, in Governance by Indicators: Global Power through Quantifications and Rankings 132 (Kevin Davis, et al. eds., 2012).

Bianchi, Andrea, *The Fight for Inclusion: Non-State Actors and International Law*, in From Bilateralism to Community Interest, Essays in Honour of Judge Bruno Simma 39 (Ulrich Fastenrath et al. eds., 2011).

Biermann, Frank, et al., *Studying the Influence of International Bureaucracies: A Conceptual Framework*, in Managers of Global Change, The Influence of International Environmental Bureaucracies 37 (Frank Biermann & Bernd Siebenhuner eds., 2009).

Bilder, Richard B., *Beyond Compliance: Helping Nations Cooperate*, in Commitment and Compliance – The Role of Non-Binding Norms in the International Legal System 65 (Dinah Shelton ed., 2003).

Boisson de Chazournes, Laurence, *Technical and Financial Assistance and Compliance: the Interplay*, in Ensuring Compliance with Multilateral Environmental Agreements 273 (Ulrich Beyerlin et al. eds., 2006).

Boyle, Alan, *Soft Law in International Law-Making*, in International Law 118 (Malcom D. Evans, 2nd ed., 2006).

Bradlow, Daniel & Hunter, David B., *The Future of International Law and International Financial Institutions*, in International Financial Intuitions and International Law 1 (Daniel Bradlow & David B. Hunter eds., 2010).

Bradlow, Daniel, I*nternational Law and the Operations of the International Financial Institutions*, in International Financial Intuitions and International Law 1 (Daniel Bradlow & David B. Hunter eds., 2010).

Cassell, Douglass, *Inter-American Human Rights Law, Soft and Hard*, in Commitment and Compliance – The Role of Non-Binding Norms in the International Legal System 393 (Dinah Shelton ed., 2003).

Chayes, Abram & Chayes, Antonia Handler, *Nonproliferation Regimes in the Aftermath of the Gulf War*, in After the Storm: Lessons from the Gulf War 49 (Joseph S. Nye & Roger K. Smith, 1992).

Chayes, Abram, et al., *Managing Compliance: A Comparative Perspective*, in Engaging Countries: Strengthening Compliance with International Environmental Accords, 39 (Edith Brown Weiss, Harold K. Jacobson eds., 2000).

Chinkin, Christine, *Normative Development in the International Legal System*, in Commitment and Compliance – The Role of Non-Binding Norms in the International Legal System 21 (Dinah Shelton ed., 2003).

Ciampi Annalisa, *Invalidity and Termination of Treaties and Rules of Procedures*, in The Law of Treaties Beyond the Vienna Convention 362 (Enzo Cannizzaro ed., 2011).

Delcourt, Barbara, *Theory of Compliance*, in MPEPIL (2013).

Di Leva, Charles, *International Environmental Law, the World Bank, and International Financial Institutions*, in International Financial Intuitions and International Law 343 (Daniel Bradlow & David B. Hunter eds., 2010).

Dorr, Olivier, *Article 18, Obligation Not to Defeat the Object and the Purpose of a Treaty Prior to Its Entry into Force, in* Vienna Convention on the Law of Treaties, A Commentary 219, 220 (Olivier Dorr & Kirsten Schmalenbach eds., 2012).

Falk, Richard. A., *The Relevance of Political Context to the Nature and Functioning of International Law: An Intermediate View*, in The Relevance of International Law 133 (Karl. W. Deutsch & Stanley Hoffman eds., 1968).

Fitzmaurice, Malgosia, *The Practical Working of the Law of Treaties*, in International Law 166 (Malcom D. Evans, 2nd ed., 2006).

Francioni, Francesco, *International 'Soft Law': A Contemporary Assessment*, in Fifty Years of the international Court of Justice, Essays in Honour of Sir Robert Jenning 168 (Vaughan Lowe and Malgosia Fitzmaurice Eds., 1996).

Francis, Laurel B., *Caribbean Community States and State Succession*, in Caribbean Perspectives on International Law and Organizations, 84 (Bertrand G. Ramcharan & Laurel B. Francis eds., 1989).

Franck, Thomas M., *Is the U.N. Charter a Constitution?*, in Negotiating for Peace 95 (Jochen Abr. Frowein et al., eds., 2003).

George, Erika R., *The Enterprise of Empire: Evolving Understandings of Corporate Identity and Responsibility*, in The Business Landscape and Human Rights Landscape: Moving Forward, Looking Back 19 (Jena Martin & Karen E. Bravo eds., 2005).

Ghebali, Victor-Yves, *The International Labour Organization: A Case Study on the Evolution of U.N. Specialised Agencies*, in International Organization and the Evolution of World Society 103 (Roberto Ago & Nicolas Valticos, eds., 1989).

Ginsburg, Tom, *Ancillary Powers of Constitutional Courts*, in Institutions and Public Law: Comparative Approaches 225 (Tom Ginsburg & Robert Kagan eds., 2005).

Grossman, Gene, M., Krueger, Alan B., *Environmental Impact of a North American Free Trade Agreement*, in Mexico-U.S. Free Trade Agreement 15 (Peter M. Garber ed., 1993).

Helfer, Laurence R., *Terminating Treaties*, in The Oxford Guide to Treaties 624 (Duncan B. Hollis ed., 2020).

Helfer, Laurence R., *Treaty Exit and Inter-Branch Conflict at the Interface of International and Domestic Law*, The Oxford Handbook of Comparative Foreign Relations Law (C.A. Bradley, ed., 2019).

Hoffmann, Stanley, *International Law and the Control of Force*, in The Relevance of International Law 133 (Karl W. Deutsch & Stanley Hoffman eds., 1968).

Holmes, Stephen, *Precommitment and the Paradox of Democracy*, in Constitutionalism and Democracy 195 (Jon Elster & Rune Slagstad eds., 1988).

Holsti, Kalevi J., *Governance without Government: Polyarchy in Nineteenth Century European International Politics*, in GOVERNANCE WITHOUT GOVERNMENT 30 (James M. Rosneau & Ernst-Otto Czempiel eds., 1992).

Hunter, David B., *International Law and Public Participation in Policy-Making at the International Financial Institutions*, in INTERNATIONAL FINANCIAL INTUITIONS AND INTERNATIONAL LAW 199 (Daniel Bradlow & David B. Hunter eds., 2010).

Jasanoff, Sheila, *Contingent Knowledge: Implications for Implementation and Compliance*, in ENGAGING COUNTRIES, STRENGTHENING COMPLIANCE WITH INTERNATIONAL ENVIRONMENTAL ACCORDS 63 (Harold Jacobson & Edith Brown Weiss eds., 1998).

Johnston, Douglas M., *The Environmental Law of the Sea: Historical Development*, in THE ENVIRONMENTAL LAW OF THE SEA 17 (Douglas M. Johnston ed., 1981).

Kauppila, Jenni, *Transnational Advocacy Networks in International Climate Policy, The Challenge of Raising the Voices of the Marginalised Effectively Without Compromising their Legitimacy*, in INTERNATIONAL CLIMATE CHANGE LAW AND POLICY: CULTURAL LEGITIMACY IN ADOPTION AND MITIGATION 138 (Thoko Kaime ed., 2014).

Koskenniemi, Martti, *After Globalization: Engaging the Backlash*, in GLOBALIZATION AND GOVERNANCE: INTERNATIONAL GOVERNANCE, EUROPEAN SOLUTIONS 453 (Robert Schutze ed., 2018).

Kuokkanen, Tuomas, *Putting Gentle Pressure on Parties: Recent Trends in the Practice of the Implementation Committee on the Convention on Long-Range Transboundary Air Pollution*, in NORDIC COSMOPOLITANISM – ESSAYS IN INTERNATIONAL LAW FOR MARTTI KOSKENNIEMI 315 (Jarna Petman & Jan Klabbers eds., 2003).

Lanchbery, John, *Long-Term Trends in Systems for Implementation Review in International Agreements of Fauna and Flora*, in THE IMPLEMENTATION AND EFFECTIVENESS OF INTERNATIONAL ENVIRONMENTAL COMMITMENTS: THEORY AND PRACTICE 73 (David G. Victor, et al. eds., 1998).

Lee, Roy S., *The Rome Statute and its Contributions to International Law*, in THE INTERNATIONAL CRIMINAL COURT AND THE MAKING OF THE ROME STATUTE 1 (Roy S. Lee ed., 1999).

Maclntyre, Alasdair, *The Indispensability of Political Theory*, in, THE NATURE OF POLITICAL THEORY 19 (David Miller & Larry Siedentop eds., 1983).

Martin, Lisa L., *Compliance or Effectiveness? Assessing the reach of (and Limits) of Treaty-Making*, THE OXFORD GUIDE TO TREATIES 82 (Duncan B. Hollis, ed., 2nd ed., 2020).

Martin, Lisa L., *The Rational State Choice of Multilateralism*, in MULTILATERALISM MATTERS: THE THEORY AND PRACTICE OF INSTITUTIONAL FORM 91 (John G. Ruggie ed., 1993).

McDougal, Myres S. & Lasswell, Harold D., *The Identification and Appraisal of Diverse Systems of Public Order*, in STUDIES IN WORLD PUBLIC ORDER 755 (Myres S. McDougal et al. eds., 1960).

McDougal, Myres S. & Reisman, Michael W., *International Law in Policy Oriented Perspective*, in The Structure and Process of International Law 103 (Ronald St. J. Macdonald, Douglas M. Johnston eds., 1983).

Meyer, Timothy, *Alternatives to Treaty-making – Informal Agreements*, The Oxford Guide to Treaties 59 (Duncan B. Hollis, ed., 2nd ed., 2020).

Mitchell, Ronald B., *Compliance Theory: An Overview*, in Improving Compliance with International Environmental Law 3 (Peter Roderick et al. eds.,1996).

Morelli, Antonio, *Commentary to Article 42 of the Energy Charter Treaty*, in Commentary on the Energy Charter Treaty (Raphael Leal-Arcas ed., 2018).

Morelli, Antonio, *Commentary to Article 47 of the Energy Charter Treaty*, in Commentary to the Energy Charter Treaty 484 (Rafael Leal Arcas ed., 2018).

Morelli, Antonio, *Paris Agreement: The Evolution of International Law Standards in the Post-Ontological Framework*, in Research Handbook on EU Energy Law and Policy 370 (Rafael Leal-Arcas R. & Jan Wouters eds., 2017).

Omorogbe, Yinka O., *Promoting Sustainable Development through the Use of Renewable Energy: The Role of the Law*, in Beyond the Carbon Economy: Energy Law in Transition 39 (Don Zillman, et al. eds., 2008).

Owada, Hisashi, *Pactum de Contrahendo, Pactum de Negtiando*, in MPEPIL (2008).

Payne, Anthony, *Westminister Adapted: The Political Order of the Commonwealth Caribbean*, in Democracy in the Caribbean: Political, Economic and Social Perpsectives 57 (Jorge Dominguez et al. eds., 1993).

Ponzano, Paolo, *The 'Spinelli Treaty' of February 1984: The Start of the Process of Constitutionalizing the EU*, in EU Federalism and Constitutionalism: The Legacy of Altiero Spinelli 3 (Andrew Glencross & Alexander H. Trechsel eds., 2010).

Prost, Mario, *Procedure to be Followed with Respect to Invalidity, Termination, Withdrawal from or Suspension of the Operation of a Treaty*, in The Vienna Convention on the Law of Treaties – A Commentary 1486 (Olivier Corten & Pierre Klein eds., 2011).

Ragazzi, Maurizio, *International Obligations Erga Omnes: Their Moral Foundation and Criteria of Identification in Light of Two Japanese Contributions*, in The Reality of International Law. Essays in Honour of Ian Brownlie 455 (Guy S. Goodwin-Gill & Stefan Talmon eds., 1999).

Raustiala, Kal, *NGOs in International Treaty-Making*, in The Oxford Guide to Treaties 150 (Duncan B. Hollis ed., 2012).

Reif, Linda C., *Environmental Policy: The Rio Summit Five Years Later*, in Canada Among Nations 1998: Leadership and Dialogue 269 (Fen Osler Hampson & Maureen Appel Molot eds., 1998).

Reincke, H. Wolfgang & Witte, Jan Martin, *Challenges to the International Legal System Interdependence, Globalization, and Sovereignty: The Role of Non-binding International Legal Accords*, in Commitment and Compliance – The Role of Non-Binding Norms in the International Legal System 75 (Dinah Shelton ed., 2003).

Ruggie, John G., *Epistemology, Ontology and the Study of International Regimes*, in CONSTRUCTING THE WORLD POLITY 85 (John G. Ruggie ed., 1998).

Russett, Bruce, *Politics and Alternative Security: Towards a More Democratic, Therefore More Peaceful World*, in ALTERNATIVE SECURITY: LIVING WITHOUT NUCLEAR DETERRENCE 107 (Burns H. Weston ed., 1990).

Ryngaert, Cedric, *State Responsibility and Non-State Actors*, in NON-STATE ACTORS DYNAMICS IN INTERNATIONAL LAW: FROM LAW-TAKERS TO LAW-MAKERS 163 (Math Noortmann & Cedric Ryngaert eds., 2010).

Schachter, Oscar, *International Legislation*, in 7 INTERNATIONAL ENCYCLOPEDIA OF THE SOCIAL SCIENCES [IESS] (1968).

Schuppert, Gunnar F., *The Changing Role of the State Reflected in the Growing Importance of Non-State Actors*, in GLOBAL GOVERNANCE AND THE ROLE OF NON-STATE ACTORS 371 (Gunnar F. Schuppert ed., 2006).

Shapiro, Martin M., *Law and Politics: The Problem of Boundaries*, in THE OXFORD HANDBOOK OF LAW AND POLITICS 767 (Keith E. Whittington, et al. eds., 2008).

Sikkink, Kathryn, *The Power of Principled Ideas: Human Rights Policies in the United States and Western Europe*, in IDEAS AND FOREIGN POLICY: BELIEFS, INSTITUTIONS AND POLITICAL CHANGE 149 (Judith Goldstein & Robert O. Keohane eds., 1993).

Siotis, Jean, *The Institutions of the League of Nations*, in THE LEAGUE OF NATIONS IN RETROSPECT: UN LIBRARY AND GRADUATE INSTITUTE OF INTERNATIONAL STUDIES SYMPOSIUM 19 (Walter De Gruyter ed., 1983).

Tzanakopoulos, Antonios, *Domestic Court as the 'Natural Judge' of International Law: A Change in Physiognomy*, in SELECT PROCEEDINGS OF THE EUROPEAN SOCIETY OF INTERNATIONAL LAW, INTERNATIONAL LAW 1989–2010, 155 (James Crawford & Sarah Nouwen eds., 2010).

Verdier, Pierre-Hugues & Versteeg, Mila, *Separation of Powers, Treaty-Making, and Treaty Withdrawal: A Global Survey*, in THE OXFORD HANDBOOK OF COMPARATIVE FOREIGN RELATIONS LAW (C.A. Bradley ed., 2019).

Von Bassewitz, Nadia, *International Climate Change Policy: Where do we Stand?*, in CLIMATE CHANGE: INTERNATIONAL LAW AND GLOBAL GOVERNANCE, VOLUME II: POLICY, DIPLOMACY AND GOVERNANCE IN A CHANGING ENVIRONMENT 101 (Oliver C. Ruppel, et al. eds., 2013).

Whittington, Keith E., et al. *Overview of Law and Politics, The Study of Law and Politics*, in THE OXFORD HANDBOOK OF POLITICAL SCIENCE 241 (Robert E. Godin ed., 2011).

Young, Oran R., Levy, Marc A., *The Effectiveness of International Environmental Regimes*, in THE EFFECTIVENESS OF INTERNATIONAL ENVIRONMENTAL REGIMES 1 (Oran Young ed., 1999).

Zaelke, Durwood, et al., *Domestic Enforcement Strategies*, in 1 MAKING LAW WORK: ENVIRONMENTAL COMPLIANCE AND SUSTAINABLE DEVELOPMENT 371 (Durwood Zaelke et al. eds., 2005).

IV. Articles

Abbott, Kenneth & Snidal, Duncan, *Hard and Soft Law in International Governance*, 54 Int'l Org. 3, 421 (2000).

Akehust, Michael, *Withdrawal from International Organizations*, 32 Current Legal Prob. 143 (1979).

Allott, Phillip, *The Concept of International Law*, 10 EJIL 31 (1999).

Alston, Philip, *The Populist Challenge to Human Rights*, 9 J. Hum. Rts. Practice 1 (2017).

Alvarez, Jose E., *Are Corporations 'Subjects' of International Law?*, Santa Clara J. Int'l L. 9, 1 (2011).

Alvarez, José E., *Hegemonic International Law Revisited*, 97 AJIL 881 (2003).

Antoine, Rose-Marie B., *Opting Out from the Optional Protocol – Is this Inhumane?*, 3 Caribbean L. Bull. 28 (1998).

Arend, Anthony C., *Do Legal Rules Matter? International Law and Politics*, 38 Va. J. Int'l. L. (1998).

Arp, Bjorn, *Denunciation Followed by Re-Accession with Reservations to a Treaty: A Critical Appraisal of Contemporary State Practice*, LXI Netherlands Int'l L. Rev. 141, 157 (2014).

Asada, Masahiko, *Arms Control Law in Crisis? A Study of the North Korean Nuclear Issue*, 9 J. Conflict & Sec. L. 331 (2004).

Ausbel, Jesse, H. & Victor, David G., *Verification of International Environmental Agreements*, 17 Ann. Rev. Energy & Env. 1, 20 (2003).

Backer, Larry Catá, *Private Actors and Public Governance Beyond the State: The Multinational Corporation, the Financial Stability Board, and the Global Governance Order*, 18 Ind. J. Global Legal Stud. (2011).

Barro, Robert J. & Gordon, David B., *Rules, Discretion and Reputation in a Model of Monetary Policy*, 12 J. Monetary Econ. 101 (1983).

Bassiouni, M. Cherif, *International Crimes: Jus Cogens and Obligatio Ega Omnes*, 59 Law & Contemp. Probs. 63, 67 (1997).

Bates, Ed, *Avoiding Legal Obligations Created by Human Rights Treaties*, 57 Int'l & Comp. L. Q. 751 (2008).

Baxter, Richard R., *International Law in "Her Infinite Variety,"* 29 Int'l & Comp. L. Q. 549 (1980).

Bittermann, Henry J., *Negotiations of the Articles of Agreement of the International Bank for Reconstruction and Developments*, 5 Int'l L., 59 (1971).

Blociszewski, Jacques, *L'Annexion de la Bosnie et de l'Herzegovine*, 17 Rev. Gén de Dr. Int. Pub. 417 (1910).

Bolton, John R. *Should We Take Global Governance Seriously?*, 1 Chi. J. Intl' L. 205, 212 (2000).

Bradley, Curtis A. & Goldsmith, Jack L., *Presidential Control Over International Law*, 131 HARV. L. REV. 1201 (2018).

Bradley, Curtis A., *Treaty Termination and Historical Gloss*, 92 TEX. L. REV. 773 (2014).

Bradlow, Daniel & Grossman, Claudio, *Limited Mandates and Intertwined Problems: A New Challenge for the World Bank and the IMF*, 17 HUM. RTS. Q. (1995).

Brewster, Rachel, *The Domestic Origins of International Agreements*, 44 VA. J. INT'L. L. 501 (2004).

Briggs, Herbert W., *Unilateral Denunciation of Treaties: The Vienna Convention and the International Court of Justice*, 68 AJIL 51 (1974).

Cardozo, Michael, *Sovereign Immunity: The Plaintiff Deserves a Day in Court*, 67 HARV. L. REV. 608 (1954).

Caron, David D., *The International Whaling Commission and the North Atlantic Marine Mammal Commission: The Institutional Risks of Coercion in Consensual Structures*, 89 AJIL 154 (1995).

Cassel, Douglas, *Does International Human Rights Law Make a Difference?*, 2 CHI. J. INT'L. L. 121 (2001).

Charney, Jonathan, *Universal International Law*, 87 AJIL 529 (1993).

Chasek, Pamela, *A Comparative Analysis of Multilateral Environmental Negotiations*, 6 GROUP DECISION & NEGOT. 437 (1997).

Chayes, Abram, *An Inquiry into the Workings of Arms Control Agreements*, 85 HARV. L. REV. 905 (1972).

Chimni, B. S., *A Just World Under Law: A View from the South*, 22 AM. U. INT'L L. REV. 199 (2007).

Chimni, B. S., *Cooption and Resistance: Two Faces of Global Administrative Law*, 37 N.Y.U. J. INT'L L. & POL. 799 (2005).

Chimni, B. S., *Third World Approaches to International Law: Manifesto*, 8 INT'L COMMUN. L. REV. 3 (2006).

Crawford, James, *The Current Political Discourse Concerning International Law*, 81 MOD. L. REV. 1 (2018).

Crump, Larry & Zartman, William, *Multilateral Negotiation and the Management of Complexity*, 8 INT'L NEGOT. 1 (2003).

Downie, Christian, *Prolonged International Environmental Negotiations: the Roles and Strategies of Non-State Actors in the EU*, 16 INT'L ENVTL. AGREEMENTS 5 (2016).

Dupuy, Pierre-Marie, *Soft Law and the International Law of the Environment*, 12 MICH. J. INT'L L. 420 (1991).

Durkee, Melissa J., *The Business of Treaties*, 63 UCLA L. REV. 264 (2016).

Evatt, Elizabeth, *Democratic People's Republic of Korea and the ICCPR: Denunciation as an Exercise of the Right of Self Defence?*, in 5 AUST. J. HUM. RTS. 215 (1998).

Fee, Elizabeth et al., *At the Roots of The World Health Organization's Challenges: Politics and Regionalization*, 106 AM. J. PUB. HEALTH 11 1912 (2016).

Galbraith, Jean, *Contemporary Practice of the United States Related to International Law*, 113 AJIL 813 (2019).

Galbraith, Jean, *From Treaties to International Commitments: The Changing Landscape of Foreign Relations Law*, 84 U. Chi. L. Rev. 1675 (2017).

Galbraith, Jean, *Rejoining Treaties*, 106 Va. L. Rev. 73 (2020).

Garner, James W. *The Doctrine of Rebus Sic Stantibus and the Termination of Treaties*, 21 AJIL 509 (1927).

Ginsburg, Tom, *Locking in Democracy: Constitutions, Commitment, and International Law*, in 38 N.Y.U. J. Int'l L. & Pol. 707 (2006).

Goldsmith, Jack, *Sovereignty, International Relations Theory, and International Law*, 52 Stan. L. Rev. 959 (2000).

Goldsmith, Jack, *The Contributions of the Obama Administration to the Practice and Theory of International Law*, 57 Harv. Int'l L.J. 11 (2016).

Goldwater, Barry M., *Treaty Termination is a Shared Power*, 65 A.B.A. J. 198 (1978).

Goodman, Ryan, *Human Rights Treaties, Invalid Reservations and State Consent*, 96 AJIL 3, 531 (2017).

Gragl, Paul & Fitzmaurice, Malgosia, *The Legal Character of Article 18 of the Vienna Convention on the Law of Treaties*, 68 Int'l & Comp. L. Q. 699 (2019).

Gross, Leo, *The Peace of Westphalia 1648–1948*, 42 AJIL 20 (1948).

Gruchalla-Wesierski, Tadeusz, *A Framework for Understanding "Soft Law"*, 30 McGill L.J. 37 (1984).

Guzman, Andrew T. & Meyer, Timothy L., *International Soft Law*, 2 J. Legal Analysis 171 (2010).

Guzman, Andrew T., *A Compliance-Based Theory of International Law*, 90 Cal. L. Rev. 1823 (2002).

Guzman, Andrew T., *The Cost of Credibility: Explaining Resistance to Interstate Dispute Resolution Mechanisms*, 31 J. Legal Stud. 303 (2002).

Hafner-Burton, Emily M., *Sticks and Stones: Naming and Shaming the Human Rights Enforcement Problem*, 62 Int'l Org. 689 (2008).

Hannum, Hurst, *The Status of the Universal Declaration of Human Rights in National and International Law*, 25 Ga. J. Int'l. & Comp. L. 287 (1996).

Helfer, Laurence R., *Exiting Treaties*, 91 Va. L. Rev. 1579 (2005).

Helfer, Laurence R., *Overlegalizing Human Rights: International Relations Theory and the Commonwealth Caribbean Backlash Against Human Rights Regimes*, 102 Colum. L. Rev. 1832 (2002).

Herbst, Jochen, *Observations on the Right to Withdrawal from the EU: Who Are the Masters of Treaties*, 6 German L.J. 1755 (2005).

Hershey, Amos S., *History of International Law Since the Peace of Westphalia* 6 AJIL 30 (1912).

Heymann, Philip B., *The Problem of Coordination: Bargaining and Rules*, 86 HARV. L. REV. 797 (1973).

Higgins, Rosalyn, *Conceptual Thinking About the Individual in International Law*, 4 BRIT. J. INT'L STUD. 1 (1978).

Hoffman, Stanley, *The Crisis of Liberal Internationalism*, 98 FOREIGN POL'Y 159 (1995).

Hollis, Duncan B. & Newcomer, Joshua J., *Political Commitments and the Constitution*, 49 VA. J. INT'L L. 507 (2009).

Hollis, Duncan B., *Why State Consent Still Matters*, 23 BERKELEY J. INT'L L. (2005).

Howse, Robert & Teitel, Ruti, *Beyond Compliance: Rethinking Why International Law Really Matters*, in 1 GLOBAL POL'Y, 127 (2010).

Hunter, David, *Civil Society Networks and the Development of Environmental Standards at International Financial Institutions*, 8 CHI. J. INT'L L. 2 (2008).

Hurd, Ian, *Legitimacy and Authority in International Politics*, 53 INT'L ORG. 379 (1999).

Jeswald W. Salacuse, *The Emerging Global Regime for Investment*, 51 HARV. INT'L L.J. 427 (2010).

Johnstone, Ian, *Treaty Interpretation: The Authority of Interpretive Communities*, 12 MICH. J. INT'L L. 371 (1991).

Joung, Donald A., *Contributions to International Law and World Order by the World Court's Adjudication of the Icelandic Fisheries Controversy*, 1 B.C. INT'L & COMP. L. REV. 175 (1977).

Kaprio, Leo A., *Forty Years of WHO in Europe: The Development of a Common Policy*, 40 WHO REGIONAL PUBLICATIONS 4 (1991).

Katz, Stephen R. *Issues Arising the Icelandic Fisheries Case*, 22 INT'L & COMP. L. Q. 83 (1973).

Kennedy, David, *The Move to Institutions*, 8 CARDOZO L. REV. 841 (1987).

Keohane, Robert O. & Martin, Lisa, *The Promise of Institutionalist Theory*, 20 INT'L SEC. 39 (1995).

Keohane, Robert O., et al., *Legalized Dispute Resolution: Interstate and Transnational*, 54 INT'L ORG. 456 (2000).

Keohane, Robert O., *International Relations and International Law: Two Optics*, 38 HARV. INT'L L.J. 487 (1997).

Keohane, Robert O., *The Demand for International Regimes*, 36 INT'L ORG. 325 (1982).

Kirgis, Frederic L., *Some Lingering Questions about Article 60 of the Vienna Convention on the Law of Treaties*, 22 CORNELL INT'L. L.J. 3, 549 (1989).

Klabbers, Jan, *The Relative Autonomy of International Law, or the Forgotten Politics of Interdisciplinarity*, 1 J. INT'L L. & INT'L REL. 35 (2005).

Klingenberg, Hans, *Elements of Nordic Practice 1998: Denmark*, 68 NORDIC J. INT'L L. 163 (1999).

Koh, Harold H., *Foreword: On American Exceptionalism*, 55 STAN L. REV. 1479 (2003).

Koh, Harold H., *Presidential Power to Terminate International Agreements*, 128 YALE L.J. F. 432 (2018).

Koh, Harold H., *Why Do Nations Obey International Law?*, 106 YALE L.J. 2599 (1997).

Koremenos, Barbara, et al., *The Rational Design of International Institutions*, 55 INT'L ORG. 761 (2001).

Koremenos, Barbara, *Loosening the Ties that Bind: A Learning Model of Agreement Flexibility*, 55 INT'L ORG. 289 (2001).

Koremenos, Barbara, Nau, Allison, *Exit, No Exit*, 81 DUKE J. COMP. & INT'L L. 81 (2010).

Koskenniemi, Martti, *Less is More: Legal Imagination in Context*, 31 LEIDEN J. INT'L L. 469 (2018).

Koskenniemi, Martti, *The Fate of Public International Law: Between Technique and Politics*, 70 MOD. L. REV. 1 (2007).

Koskenniemi, Martti, *The Politics of International Law – 20 Years Later*, 20 EJIL 7 (2009).

Koskenniemi, Martti, *The Politics of International Law*, 1 EJIL 4 (1990).

Kratochwill, Friederich, Ruggie, John G., *International Organization: A State of the Art on an Art of the State*, 40 INT'L ORG. 753 (1986).

Kwang-Sheng, Yang, *China Abrogating Unfair Treaties with Powers*, 25 CURRENT HIST. 697 (1927).

L'Heureux-Dubé, Claire, *The Importance of Dialogue: Globalization and the International Impact of the Rehnquist Court*, 34 TULSA L.J. 15 (1998).

Leal-Arcas, Rafael & Morelli, Antonio, *The Resilience of the Paris Agreement: Negotiating and Implementing the Climate Regime*, 31 GEO. ENVTL. L. REV. 1 (2018).

Leal-Arcas, Rafael, *Mega-Regionals and Sustainable Development: The Transatlantic Trade and Investment Partnership and the Trans-Pacific Partnership*, 6 RENEWABLE ENERGY L. & POL'Y REV. 4 (2015).

Levesque, Christian A., *The International Covenant on Civil and Political Rights: A Primer for Raising a Defense Against the Juvenile Death Penalty in Federal Courts*, 50 AM. U. L. REV. 756 (2001).

Lipson, Charles, *Why Are Some International Agreements Informal?*, 45 INT'L ORG. 495 (1991).

MacGibbon, I.C., *Estoppel in International Law*, 7 INT'L & COMP. L. Q. 468 (1958).

Malloy, Timothy F., *Regulation, Compliance and the Firm*, 76 TEMP. L. REV. 451 (2003).

Manner, George, *The Object Theory of the Individual in International Law*, 46 AJIL 428 (1952).

Martin, Antoine, *L'estoppel En Droit International Public*, in 9 INT'L J. L. LIBR. 130 (1981).

Martin, Lisa L., *Credibility, Costs, and Institutions: Cooperation on Economic Sanctions*, 45 WORLD POL. 3, 406 (1993).

McGinnis, John, Rappaport, Michael B., *Symmetric Entrenchment: A Constitutional and Normative Theory*, 89 VA. L. REV. 385 (2003).

McGory, Glenn, *Reservation or Virtue? Lessons from Trinidad and Tobago's Reservation to the First Optional Protocol*, 23 HUM. RTS. Q. 769 (2001).

McGregor, Richard, *Zhou's Cryptic Caution Lost in Translation*, FINANCIAL TIMES (Jun. 10, 2011).

McKenzie, Lachlan, *Overcoming Legacies of Foreign Policy (Dis)interests in the Negotiation of the European Union-Australia Free Trade Agreement*, in 72 AUSTL J. INT'L. AFF. 255 (2018).

McLachlan, Campbell, *The Assault on International Adjudication and the Limits of Withdrawal*, 68 INT'L & COMP. L. Q. 499 (2019).

Meernik, James, et al., *The Impact of Human Rights Organizations on Naming and Shaming Campaigns*, 56 J. CONFLICT RESOL. 233 (2012).

Mertus, Julie, *Considering Non-State Actors in the New Millennium: Toward Expanded Participation in Norm Generation and Norm Application*, 32 N.Y.U. J. INTL L. & POL. 537 (2000).

Meyer, Timothy, *Good Faith, Withdrawal, and the Judicialization of International Politics*, 2 QUESTIONS INT'L L. 3 (2014).

Mitchell, Gregory, *Taking Behavioralism Too Seriously? The Unwarranted Pessimism of the New Behavioral Analysis of Law*, 43 WM. & MARY L. REV. 1907 (2002).

Mitchell, Ronald B., *Sources of Transparency: Information Systems in International Regimes*, in 42 INT'L STUD. Q. 109 (1988).

Mitter, Rana ,*1911: The Unanchored Chinese Revolution*, 208 CHINA QUART. 1009 (2011).

Moravcsik, Andrew M., *Taking Preferences Seriously: A Liberal Theory of International Politics*, 51 INT'L ORG. 513 (1997).

Moravcsik, Andrew, *The Origins of Human Rights Regimes: Democratic Delegation in Postwar Europe*, 54 INT'L ORG 217 (2000).

Morgenthau, Hans J., *Positivism, Functionalism, and International Law*, 34 AJIL 260 (1940).

Moriarty, James J., *Congressional Claims for Treaty Termination Powers in the Age of the Diminished Presidency*, 14 CONN. J. INT'L L. 123 (1999).

Morosini, Fabio C., *Trade and climate change: Unveiling the principle of common but differentiated responsibilities from the WTO Agreements*, 42 G. WASH. INT'L L. REV. 713 (2010).

Murphy, Sean D., *Contemporary Practice of the United States Relating to International Law*, 97 AJIL 962 (2003).

Newcombe Morse, Howard, *The New Secession, A Study of the Legal Right of the United States to Withdraw from the United Nations*, 57 DICK. L. REV. 134 (1952).

Nolan, Justine, *Refining the Rules of the Game: The Corporate Responsibility to Respect Human Rights*, 7 UTRECHT J. INT'L & EUR. L. 30 (2014).

O'Rourke, Dara, *Outsourcing Regulation: Analyzing Non-Governmental Systems of Labor Standards and Monitoring*, 31 POL'Y STUD. J. 1 (2003).

Orbell, John M., et al., *Do Cooperators Exit More Readily tan Defectors?*, 78 AM. POL. SCI. REV. 147 (1984).

Pauwelyn, Joost & Hamilton, Rebecca, *Exit from International Tribunals*, 9 J. INT'L DISP. SETTLEMENT 679 (2018).

Payandeh, Mehrdad, *The Concept of International Law in the Jurisprudence of H.L.A. Hart*, 21 EJIL 4 (2009).

Perez, Antonio F., *Survival of Rights Under the Nuclear Non-Proliferation Treaty: Withdrawal and the Counting Right of International Atomic Energy Agency Safeguards*, 34 VA. J. INT'L L. 749 (1994).

Persson, Stefan, *Deadlocks in International Negotiations*, 29 COOPERATION & CONFLICT 211 (1994).

Petersen, Niels, *How Rational is International Law?*, 20 EJIL 1247 (2010).

Petsche, Markus, *Jus Cogens as a Vision of the International Legal Order*, 29 PENN ST. INT'L L. REV. 233, 238 (2010).

Posner, Eric A., *Law, Economics, and Inefficient Norms*, 144 U. PA. L. REV. 1697 (1996).

Posner, Eric A., *Liberal Internationalism and the Populist Backlash*, 49 ARIZ. ST. L.J. 759 (2017).

Prasad, M. S. V., Sandhya Sri, B., *Corporate Response to Climate Change: What do Stakeholders Expect*, 2 AUSTRALASIAN ACCOUNTING BUS. & FIN. J. 67 (2008).

Quigley, John, *The United States' Withdrawal from International Court of Justice Jurisdiction in Consular Cases: Reasons and Consequences*, 19 DUKE J. COMP. & INT'L L. 263 (2009).

Ramsey, Michael D., *Evading the Treaty Power?: The Constitutionality of Nonbinding Agreements*, 11 F.I.U. L. REV. 371 (2016).

Ratner, Steven R., *Does International Law Matter in Preventing Ethnic Conflict?*, 32 N.Y.U. J. INT'L L. & POL. 591 (2000).

Ratner, Steven R., *Precommitment Theory and International Law: Starting a Conversation*, 81 TEX. L. REV. 2055 (2003).

Ratner, Steven R. & Slaughter, Anne Marie, *Appraising the Methods of International Law: A Prospectus for Readers*, 93 AJIL 291 (1999).

Raustiala, Kal, *Compliance & Effectiveness in International Regulatory Cooperation*, 32 CASE W. RES. J. INT'L L. 387 (2000).

Raustiala, Kal, *Form & Substance in International Agreements*, 90 AJIL 581 (2005).

Rogoff, Martin A., *The International Legal Obligations of Signatories to an Unratified Treaty*, 32 ME. L. REV. 263 (1980).

Rosenne, Shabtai, *The Settlement of Treaty Disputes Under the Vienna Convention of 1969*, 31 HEIDELBERG J. INT'L L. 61 (1979).

Sand, Peter H., *Institution-Building to Assist Compliance with International Environmental Law: Perspectives*, 56 HEIDELBERG J. INT'L L. 3, 776 (1996).

Schachter, Oscar, *In Defense of International Rules on the Use of Force*, 53 U. CHI. L. REV. 69 (1986).

Schachter, Oscar, *The Decline of the Nation-State and its Implications for International Law*, 36 COLUM. J. TRANSNAT'L L. 7 (1997).

Schachter, Oscar, *The Twilight Existence of Nonbinding International Agreements*, 71 AJIL 296 (1977).

Schiffrin, Natalia, *Jamaica Withdraws the Right of Individual Petition under the International Covenant on Civil and Political Rights*, 92 AJIL 563 (1998).

Schroeder, Paul W., *Did the Vienna settlement rest on a balance of power?*, 97 AM. HIST. REV. 683 (1992).

Schwelb, Egon, *Withdrawal from the United Nations: The Indonesian Intermezzo*, 61 AJIL 661 (1967).

Scott, David C., *Presidential Power to Un-Sign Treaties*, 69 U. CHI. L. REV. 1447 (2002).

Shaffer, Gregory, *How Business Shapes Law: A Socio-Legal Framework*, 42 CONN. L. REV. 147 (2009).

Simma, Bruno, *Reflections on Article 60 of the Vienna Convention on the Law of Treaties and its Background in General International Law*, 20 ÖSTERREICHISCHE ZEITSCHRIFT FÜR ÖFFENTLICHES RECHT (AUSTRIAN JOURNAL OF PUBLIC AND INTERNATIONAL LAW – OZOR) 59 (1970).

Simmons, Beth A., *Capacity, Commitment, and Compliance: International Institutions and Territorial Disputes*, 46 J. CONFLICT RESOL. 829 (2002).

Simmons, Beth A., *International law and State Behavior: Commitment and Compliance in International Monetary Affairs*, 94 AM. POL. SCI. REV. 819 (2000).

Slaughter Burley, Anne-Marie, *International Law and International Relations Theory: A Dual Agenda*, 87 AJIL 205 (1993).

Slaughter Burley, Anne-Marie, *International Law in a World of Liberal States*, 6 EJIL 503 (1995).

Slaughter Burley, Anne-Marie, *Judicial Globalization*, 40 VA. J. INT'L L. 1103 (2000).

Snidal, Duncan, *Coordination versus Prisoners' Dilemma: Implications for International Cooperation and Regimes*, 79 AM. POL. SCI. REV. 923 (1985).

Spiro, Peter J., *Disaggregating U.S. Interests in International Law*, 67 LAW & CONTEMP. PROBS. 195 (2004).

Steinberg, Richard H., *In the Shadow of Law or Power? Consensus-Based Bargaining and Outcomes in the GATT/WTO*, 56 INT'L ORG. 339 (2002).

Steinberg, Richard H., *Judicial Lawmakig and WTO: Discursive, Constitutional and Political Constraints*, 98 AJIL 247 (2004).

Steohenson, Matthew C., *Court Of Public Opinion: Government Accountability And Judicial Independence*, 20 J. L. ECON. & ORG. 379 (2004).

Stephan, Paul B., *Privatizing International Law*, 97 VA. L. REV. 1573 (2011).

Stephan, Paul B., *The New International Law – Legitimacy, Accountability, Authority and Freedom in the New Global Order*, 70 U. Colo. L. Rev. 1555 (1999).

Sunstein, Cass R., *Behavioral Analysis of Law*, 64 U. Chi. L. Rev. 4, 1175–1195 (1997).

Sunstein, Cass R., *Behavioral Law and Economics: A Progress Report*, 1 Am. L. & Econ. Rev. 115 (1999).

Sykes, Alan O., *Protectionism as a "Safeguard": A Positive Analysis of the GATT "Escape Clause" with Normative Speculations*, 58 U. Chi. L. Rev. 255 (1991).

Tor, Avishalom, *The Methodology of the Behavioral Analysis of Law*, 4 Haifa L. Rev. 237 (2008).

Trimble, Phillip, *Globalization, International Institutions and the Erosion of National Sovereignty*, 95 Mich. L. Rev. 1944 (1997).

Weil, Prosper, *Toward Relative Normativity in Law?*, 77 AJIL 413 (1983).

Weiler, Hans N., *Withdrawing from Unesco: A Decision in Search of an Argument*, in 30 Comp. Educ. Rev. 32 (1986).

Weingast, Barry, *Constitutions as Governance Structures: The Political Foundations of Secure Markets*, 149 J. Inst. Theoretical Econ. 286 (1993).

Weingast, Barry, *The Political Foundations of Democracy and the Rule of Law*, 91 Am. Pol. Sci. Rev. 245 (1997).

Widdow, Kevin, *The Denunciation of International Labour Conventions*, 33 Int'l & Comp. L. Q. 1052 (1984).

William C. Bradford, *International Legal Compliance: An Annotated Bibliography*, 30 N.C.J. Int'l L. & Com. Reg. 379 (2004).

Willismson, Oliver, *Credible Commitments – Using Hostages to Support Exchange*, 73 Am. Econ. Rev. 519 (1983).

Winslow, Charles-Edward A., *International Health*, 41 Am. J. Pub. Health 12 1455, 1458 (1951).

Wolff, David, *Reasserting its Constitutional Role: Congress' Power to Independently Terminate a Treaty*, 46 U. S.F. L. Rev. 953 (2012).

Wood, Stepan, et al., *International Law and International Relations Theory: A New Generation of Interdisciplinary Scholarship*, 92 AJIL 367, 369 (1998).

Woolaver, Hannah, *From Joining to Leaving: Domestic Law's Role in the International Legal Validity of Treaty Withdrawal*, 30 EJIL 73 (2019).

Yoo, John C., *Rejoinder: Treaties ad Public Lawmaking: A Textual and Structural Defense of Non-Self-Execution*, 99 Colum. L. Rev. 2218 (1999).

Young, Oran R., *Hitting the Mark: Why are Some International Environmental Agreements More Successful than Others?*, 41 Environment 8 (1999).

Young, Oran R., *International Regimes: Toward a New Theory of Institutions*, 39 World Pol. 104 (1986).

Yu, Peter K., *Six Secret (and Now Open) Fears of ACTA*, 64 SMU L. Rev. 975 (2011).

V. Online Periodicals and News

Allott, Philip, *UK/EU Withdrawal Agreement: A Legal Speculation*, UK Constitutional Law Association (Nov. 7, 2018), available online at: [https://ukconstitutionallaw.org/2018/11/07/philip-allott-uk-eu-withdrawal-agreement-a-legal-speculation/].

Anderson, Scott R., *Walking Away from the World Court*, Lawfare (Oct. 5, 2018), available online at: [https://www.lawfareblog.com/walking-away-world-court].

Bartunek, Robert-Jan, *EU and Canada to Sign Trade Pact after Belgians Strike Key Deal*, Reuters (Oct. 29, 2016), available online at: [https://www.reuters.com/article/us-eu-canada-trade-id].

Benz, Eleanor *The Inter-American Court's Advisory Function Continues to Boom – A Few Comments on the Requests Currently Pending*, EJIL:Talk! (Nov. 25, 2019), available at: [https://www.ejiltalk.org/the-inter-american-courts-advisory-function-continues-to-boom-a-few-comments-on-the-requests-currently-pending].

Boese, Wade, *US Withdraws from ABM Treaty, Global Response Muted*, Arms Control Today (Jul. 1, 2002), available online at: [https://www.armscontrol.org/act/2002_07-08/abmjul_aug02].

Borger, Julian, *Bush Kills Global Warming Treaty*, in The Guardian (Mar 29, 2001), available online at: [https://www.theguardian.com/environment/2001/mar/29/globalwarming.usnews].

Borger, Julian, *US Says it Will Pull Out of INF Treaty if Russia does not Comply Within 60 Days*, The Guardian (Dec. 4, 2018), available online at: [https://www.theguardian.com/world/2018/dec/04/us-inf-russia-nuclear-treaty-deadline].

Bradley, Curtis A., *Exiting Congressional-Executive Agreements*, 67 Duke L.J. 1615 (2018).

Bradley, Curtis A. & Helfer, Laurence R., *Treaty Exit in the United States: Insights from the United Kingdom or South Africa?*, in 111 AJIL Unbound 428 (2017), available online at: [https://www.cambridge.org/core/journals/american-journal-of-international-law/article/treaty-exit-in-the-united-states-insights-from-the-united-kingdom-or-south-africa/a908b76aee6edeac15b1a427a1937004].

Bradlow, Daniel, *What Paris Climate Deal Can Teach us about Solving the World's Most Complex Problems*, The Conversation (Dec. 17, 2015), available online at: [https://theconversation.com/what-paris-climate-deal-can-teach-us-about-solving-the-worlds-most-complex-problems-52162].

Brilmayer, Lea, Yemane Tesfalidet, Isaias, *Treaty Denunciation and "Withdrawal" from Customary International Law: An Erroneous Analogy with Dangerous Consequences*, 120 Yale L.J. F. (2011), available online at: [https://www.yalelawjournal.org/forum/treaty-denunciation-and-qwithdrawalq-from-customary-international-law-an-erroneous-analogy-with-dangerous-consequences].

CDP, *Business and the Paris Agreement, Corporate Support for a Global Agreement on Climate Change*, CDP Policy Briefing (Oct. 11, 2015), available online at: [https://www.cdp.net/Documents/policy/corporate-support-global-agreement-on-climate-change.pdf].

CDP, *Global Climate Change Report 2015, At the Tipping Point*, CDP Report 4 (Oct. 2015), available online at: [https:// rackcdn.com/cms/reports/documents/000/000/578/original/CDP-global-climate-change-report-2015.pdf?1470050331].

Crunden, E.A., *EU will only make trade deals with nations that ratify Paris climate agreement*, Think Progress (Feb. 6, 2018), available online at: [https://thinkprogress.org/eu-paris-us-decd4aad9145/].

De La Baume, Maia, *Walloon Parliament Rejects CETA Deal*, POLITICO (Oct. 14, 2016), available online at: [https://www.politico.eu/article/walloon-parliament-rejects-ceta-deal/].

De Spiegeleire, Stephan et al., *The Raise of Populist Sovereignism*, The Hague Center for Strategic Studies (2017), available online at: [https://www.government.nl/documents/reports/2017/09/20/the-rise-of-populist-sovereignism-—-what-is-it-where-it-comes-from-and-what-is-means-for-international-security-and-defense].

Dupre, Mathilde, Lere, Samuel, *Trade and climate: How the EU can protect the Paris Agreement*, Euractiv (Feb. 28, 2018) available online at: [https://www.euractiv.com/section/climate-environment/opinion/trade-and-climate-how-the-eu-can-protect-the-paris-agreement/].

European Commission, *EU and Japan finalise Economic Partnership Agreement*, European Commission Press release (Dec. 8, 2017) available online at: [http://trade.ec.europa.eu/doclib/press/index.cfm?id=1767].

Ganan Almond, Roncevert, *U.S. Ratification of the Law of the Sea Convention*, The Diplomat (May 24, 2017), available online at: [https://thediplomat.com/2017/05/u-s-ratification-of-the-law-of-the-sea-convention/].

Getler, Michael, *UNESCO Withdrawal Weighed by Thatcher*, The Washington Post (Nov. 21, 1984), available online at: [https://www.washingtonpost.com/archive/politics/1984/11/21/unesco-withdrawal-weighed-by-thatcher/ba4bb65a-a6c0-4f9d-ad46-615f317e4e72/].

Gramer, Robbie, *Why Russia Just Withdrew from the ICC*, Foreign Policy (Nov. 16, 2016), available online at: [https://foreignpolicy.com/2016/11/16/why-russia-just-withdrew-from-icc-putin-treaty-ukraine-law/].

Hariri, Yuval Noah, *We Need a Post-Liberal Order Now*, The Economist (26 Sept. 2018), available online at: [https://www.economist.com/open-future/2018/09/26/we-need-a-post-liberal-order-now].

Hepler, Lauren, Grady, Barbara, *How Much do Companies Really Care about COP21?, Green Biz*, (Sept. 9, 2015), available online at: [https://www.greenbiz.com/article/how-much-do-companies-really-care-about-cop21].

Holland Steve, & Nichols, Michelle, *Trump Cutting U.S. Ties with World Health Organization over Virus*, Reuters (May 29, 2020), available online at: [https://www.reuters.com/article/us-health-coronavirus-trump-who/trump-cutting-u-s-ties-with-world-health-organization-over-virus].

Hunt, Alex & Wheeler, Brian, *Brexit: All you need to know about the UK leaving the EU*, BBC (Nov. 22, 2018), available online at: [https://www.bbc.com/news/uk-politics-32810887].

Hurd, Hilary & Chachko, Elena, *U.S. Withdrawal from INF Treaty: The Facts and the Law*, Lawfare (Oct. 25, 2018), available online at: [https://www.lawfareblog.com/us-withdrawal-inf-treaty-facts-and-law].

Igunza, Emmanuel, *African Union backs mass withdrawal from ICC*, BBC (Feb. 1, 2017), available online at: [https://www.bbc.com/news/world-africa-38826073].

International Bar Association, *Peru's Withdrawal from the Jurisdiction of the Inter-American Court*, IBA (Aug., 1999), available online at: [https://www.ibanet.org/human_rights_institute/about_the_hri/hri_activities/hri_media/hri_interventions/archive/000899_peru.aspx].

International Criminal Court (ICC), *Statement of the Prosecutor of the International Criminal Court, Fatou Bensouda, on opening Preliminary Examinations into the situations in the Philippines and in Venezuela* (Feb. 8, 2018), available online at: [https://www.icc-cpi.int/Pages/item.aspx?name=180208-otp-stat].

Keppler, Elise, *AU's 'ICC Withdrawal Strategy' Less than Meets the Eye, Opposition to Withdrawal by States*, Human Rights Watch News (Feb. 1, 2017), available online at [https://www.hrw.org/news/2017/02/01/aus-icc-withdrawal-strategy-less-meets-eye].

Kirgis, Frederic L., *North Korea's Withdrawal from the Nuclear Non-Proliferation Treaty*, 2 ASIL Insights 8 (Jan. 24, 2003), available online at: [https://www.asil.org/insights/volume/8/issue/2/north-koreas-withdrawal-nuclear-nonproliferation-treaty].

Kirgis, Frederic L., *President Bush's Determination Regarding Mexican Nationals and Consular Convention Rights*, 9 ASIL Insights 9 (Mar. 9, 2005), available online at: [https://www.asil.org/insights/volume/9/issue/9/president-bushs-determination-regarding-mexican-nationals-and-consular].

Koh, Harold H., & Gostin, Lawrence O., *How to Keep the United States in the WHO, Immediate Withdrawal Would Be a Global Health and a Legal Disaster*, Foreign Affairs (Jun. 5, 2020), available online at: [https://www.foreignaffairs.com/articles/world/2020-06-05/how-keep-united-states-who].

Koh, Harold H., *Triptych's End: A Better Framework to Evaluate 21st Century International Lawmaking*, 126 YALE L.J. F. 338 (2017).

Lewis, Joanna, *The U.S.-China Climate and Energy Relationship*, Center for Strategic & International Studies (CSIS), Parallel Perspectives on the Global Economic Order (Sept. 22, 2017), available online at: [https://www.csis.org/us-china-climate-and-energy-relationship].

Liptak, Kevin, Acosta, Jimmy, *Trump on Paris accord: 'We're getting out'*, CNN (Jun. 2, 2017), available online at: [http://www.cnn.com/2017/06/01/politics/trump-paris-climate-decision/index.html].

Lynch, Colum, *U.S. to Pull Out of UNESCO, Again*, Foreign Policy (Oct. 11, 2017), available online at: https://foreignpolicy.com/2017/10/11/u-s-to-pull-out-of-unesco-again/].

McCoy, Jennifer L., *Venezuela Withdraws from the Organization of American States after Being Cited for Violation of the Inter-American Democratic Charter*, Scholar Strategic Network (May 2017), available online at: [https://scholars.org/sites/scholars/files/ssn_basic_facts_mccoy_on_the_oas.pdf].

McKeever, Amy, *Here is What We'll Lose if the U.S. Cuts Ties with WHO*, National Geographic (Jul. 10, 2020), available online at: [https://www.nationalgeographic.com/science/2020/07/what-we-will-lose-if-united-states-cuts-ties-with-world-health-organization].

McNeil Jr., Donald G. & Jacobs, Andrew, *Trump says US is leaving WHO, but experts aren't so sure*, The New York Times (May 30, 2020), available online at: [https://www.nytimes.com/2020/05/29/health/virus-who.html].

Morra, Francesca, Parola, Lorenzo, *Any Consequences Stemming from Italy's Withdrawal from the Energy Charter Treaty* (May 15, 2015), available online at: [http://www.ispionline.it/it/energy-watch/any-consequences-stemming-italys-withdrawal-energy-charter-treaty-13323].

Nelson, Tracy, *Exiting the United Nations: Paths and Potential*, Yale Journal of International Law (Mar. 2, 2017) available online at: [http://www.yjil.yale.edu/exiting-the-united-nations-paths-and-potential/].

Nicolaides, Gia, *ANC Set on Withdrawing from the ICC*, Eye Witness News (Jul. 5, 2017), available online at: [https://ewn.co.za/2017/07/05/anc-dead-set-on-withdrawing-from-icc].

Phinnemore, David, *Could the UK rejoin the European Free Trade Association (EFTA) after Brexit?*, The Conversation (Jul. 19, 2017), available online at: [http://theconversation.com/could-the-uk-rejoin-the-european-free-trade-association-efta-after-brexit-81208].

Piccone, Ted, *U.S. Withdrawal from UN Human Rights Council is 'America Alone'*, Brookings (Jun. 20, 2018), available online at: [https://www.brookings.edu/blog/order-from-chaos/2018/06/20/u-s-withdrawal-from-u-n-human-rights-council-is-america-alone/].

Pillai, Priya, *The African Union, the International Criminal Court, and the International Court of Justice: At the Fault Lines of International Accountability*, 10 ASIL Insights 22 (Aug. 22, 2018), available online at: [https://www.asil.org/insights/volume/22/issue/10/african-union-international-criminal-court-and-international-court].

PWC, *CEO Pulse on Climate Change, Countdown to a Deal on Climate Change: What does this Mean for Business Success?*, PWC Global (Jul. 2015), available online at: [http://download.pwc.com/gx/ceo-pulse/climatechange/index.htm].

PWC, *Growth in Complicated Times, 19th Annual Global CEO Survey, (Jan. 2016)*, available online at: [http://www.pwc.com/gx/en/ceo-agenda/ceosurvey/2016.html].

Rauhala, Emily, Demirjian Karoun, et al., *Trump Administration sends letter withdrawing US from World Health Organization over coronavirus response,* The Washington Post (Jul. 7, 2020), available online at: [https://www.washingtonpost.com/world/trump-united-states-withdrawal-world-health-organization-coronavirus/2020/07/07/ae0a25e4-b550-11ea-9a1d-d3db1cbe07ce_story.html].

Reuss, Alejandro, *What's Behind the Withdrawals from the World Bank, IMF?*, NACLA (Sept. 4, 2007), available online at: [https://nacla.org/news/what's-behind-withdrawals-world-bank-imf].

Roberts, Timmon, *One Year Since Trump's Withdrawal from the Paris Climate Agreement*, Brookings (Jun. 1, 2018), available online at: [https://www.brookings.edu/blog/planetpolicy/2018/06/01/one-year-since-trumps-withdrawal-from-the-paris-climate-agreement/].

Rone, Julia, *Why Europeans May Not Want a US Trade Deal*, The Washington Post (Oct. 4, 2018), available online at [https://www.washingtonpost.com/news/monkey-cage/wp/2018/10/04/why-europeans-may-not-want-a-u-s-trade-deal/?noredirect=on&utm_term=.9b40134f2b7e].

Scharf, Michael P., *Results of the Rome Conference for an International Criminal Court*, 10 ASIL Insights 3 (Aug. 11, 1998), available online at: [https://www.asil.org/insights/volume/3/issue/10/results-rome-conference-international-criminal-court].

Sloat, Amanda, *What Next for Brexit: Britain Plays the Ultimate Game of 'Deal or No Deal'*, Brookings (Mar. 7, 2019), available online at: [https://www.brookings.edu/blog/order-from-chaos/2019/03/07/what-next-for-brexit-britain-plays-the-ultimate-game-of-deal-or-no-deal/].

The Guardian, *Canada Pulls Out of Kyoto Protocol*, The Guardian (Dec 13, 2011), available online at: [https://www.theguardian.com/environment/2011/dec/13/canada-pulls-out-kyoto-protocol].

The Guardian, *North Korea Withdraws from Nuclear Treaty,* The Guardian (Jan. 10, 2003), available online at: [https://www.theguardian.com/world/2003/jan/10/northkorea1].

The New York Times, *Clinton's Words: "The Right Action"*, The New York Times (Jan. 1, 2001), available online at: [https://www.nytimes.com/2001/01/01/world/clinton-s-words-the-right-action.html].

UN News, *Canada's Withdrawal from Kyoto Protocol Regrettable – UN Climate Official* (Dec 13, 2011), available online at: [https://news.un.org/en/story/2011/12/398142].

UNFCCC News, *Global Business Community Comes to Paris with Solutions for Taking on the Climate Challenge Across the Board*, Press Release (Dec. 8, 2015), available online at: [https://unfccc.int/news/lpaa-focus-on-business-global-business-community-comes-to-paris-with-solutions-for-taking-on-the-climate-challenge-across-the-board].

UNOHCHR News, *Climate Change: UN Expert Welcomes Historic Paris Agreement, but Calls Upon States to Scale up Efforts to Meet the 1.5 Celsius Degrees Target* (Apr. 21, 2016), available online at: [http://www.ohchr.org/EN/NewsEvents/Pages/DisplayNews.aspx?NewsID=19850&LangID=E].

UNOHCR News, *High Commissioner Bachelet calls on States to take strong action against inequalities* (Mar. 6, 2019), available online at: [https://www.ohchr.org/EN/NewsEvents/Pages/DisplayNews.aspx?NewsID=24265&LangID=E].

Valls, Raquel, *Withdrawal, expulsion and suspension of a member state of the Council of Europe*, CVCE (Jul. 8, 2016), available online at [https://www.cvce.eu/content/publication/2006/1/9/f9b31f98-f1a1-407c-97ad-7e92363117fd/publishable_en.pdf].

Wang, Zheng, *China and UNCLOS: An Inconvenient History*, the Diplomat (Jul. 11, 2016), available online at: [https://thediplomat.com/2016/07/china-and-unclos-an-inconvenient-history/].

Woolaver, Hannah, *Domestic and International Limitations on Treaty Withdrawal: Lessons from South Africa's Attempted Departure from the International Criminal Court*, in 111 AJIL UNBOUND 450 (2018), available online at: [https://www.cambridge.org/core/journals/american-journal-of-international-law/article/domestic-and-international-limitations-on-treaty-withdrawal-lessons-from-south-africas-attempted-departure-from-the-international-criminal-court/ca118db7a9bfb8afb079784b05259d7b].

World Economic Forum, *Open Letter from CEOs to World Leaders Urging Climate Action* (Nov. 23, 2015), available online at: [https://www.weforum.org/agenda/2015/11/open-letter-from-ceos-to-world-leaders-urging-climate-action/].

VI. Conference Proceedings

Crawford, James, *Holding International Organizations and their Members to Account*, FIFTH STEINKRAUS-COHEN INTERNATIONAL LAW LECTURE AT UNIVERSITY OF LONDON (Mar., 2007).

Dañino Zapata, Roberto, *Why Treaties Matter*, FIRST ANNUAL CONFERENCE, INTERPRETATION UNDER THE VIENNA CONVENTION ON THE LAW OF THE TREATIES – 25 YEARS ON (Jan., 2006)

Freeman, Bennett, *To What Extent can Voluntarism Provide Answers?*, Wilton Park Conference on Business and Human Rights: Advancing the Agenda (Oct., 2005).

Shihata, Ibrahim F.I., *The World Bank and Human Rights*, International Commission of Jurists Conference on Economics, Social and Cultural Rights (1998).

Von Bernstorff, Jochen, *Non-State Actors in law-making and in the shaping of policy, On the Legality and legitimacy of NGO participation in international law*, Study for the Preparation of the Kondrad-Adenauer-Foundation's Conference on International Law (Nov., 2007).

VII. Research Papers

Aldy, Joseph E. & Pizer, William A., *Comparability of Effort in International Climate Policy Architecture* (The Harvard Project on Climate Agreements Discussion Paper 3, 2014).

Berger, Axel, et al., *Towards "Greener" Trade? Tracking Environmental Provisions in the Preferential Trade Agreements of Emerging Countries* (German Development Institute Discussion Paper 2, 2017).

Congressional Research Service, *Treaties and Other International Agreements: The Role of the United States Senate* (Study Prepared for the Committee on Foreign Relations of the United States Senate, S. Prt. 106–71, 2001).

Leal-Arcas, Rafael, *Three Thoughts on Brexit* (Queen Mary University of London School of Law Legal Studies Research Paper 249, 2016), available online at: [https://papers.ssrn.com/sol3/papers.cfm?abstract_id=2875715].

Spiro, Peter J., *NGOs in International Environmental Lawmaking: Theoretical Models* (Temple University Legal Studies Research Paper 26, 2006), available online at: [https://papers.ssrn.com/sol3/papers.cfm?abstract_id=937992].

Index

www.ingramcontent.com/pod-product-compliance
Lightning Source LLC
Chambersburg PA
CBHW071324230926
51849CB00002B/314